Reader

Green Egg gives me a new perspective... I re the *Green Egg* because it has in it things I not find elsewhere. **—Robert A. Heinlein.**
Author of Stranger in a Strange Land

In March of 1968, the *Green Egg* appeared...it grew over 80 issues into a 60-page journal, becoming the most significant periodical in the Pagan movement during the 1970s.
—J. Gordon Melton
Encyclopedia of American Religions

It took a catalyst to create a sense of collectivity around the word *Pagan,* and in the United States the Church of All Worlds and its *Green Egg* filled this role. CAW helped a large number of distinct groups to realize they shared a common purpose, and this gave the phenomenon new significance. CAW and Tim Zell, by using terms like *Pagan* and *Neo-Pagan* in referring to the emerging collectivity of new earth religions, linked these groups, and *Green Egg* created a communications network among them. It is popular today to talk about 'synergy'—a combination that has a greater effect than the simple addition of its components—and that perhaps best describes the effect of *Green Egg*. It connected all the evolving and emerging Goddess and nature religions into one phenomenon: the Neo-Pagan movement.
—Margot Adler
Drawing Down the Moon

Green Egg established the identity of modern Paganism as a response to a planet in crisis, and its spiritual core lay in the concept of the Earth as a single, divine, living organism. The mission of Pagans, according to this concept, was to save 'her' by a transformation of the values of Western society. **—Ronald Hutton**
Triumph of the Moon:
A History of Modern Pagan Witchcraft

Green Egg is one of the leading voices of the Neo-Pagan movement in North America, a movement that is attracting increasing numbers of followers who are alarmed at the wholesale destruction of our planet and disappointed with the lack of nature reverence in the mainstream religions. Pagans and Neo-Pagans celebrate the Earth and all its mysteries and beauties. Like Native Americans and like their own pre-Christian European ancestors, they honor the spiritual forces inherent in the

for all those trying to develop a life-style that is both spiritual and natural, reverential and joyous.
—Ralph Metzner, Ph.D.
President of the Green Earth Foundation

It is always with a feeling of excitement that I await my next issue of the *Green Egg*. It provides a breath of fresh air in the too-often sanctimonious and occasionally stuffy atmosphere of the New Age. It offers an unusual framework for the open debate of lofty ideas, controversial proposals and little-known facts. It is designed to feed intellectual curiosity, but it is never pompous, even when it dares to report on those issues the official media would like the public to forget, or to ignore. **—Jacques Vallée**
Author of Forbidden Science

Many thanks for the latest issue of *Green Egg* which was at its usual high standard, full of thought-provoking and interesting material which confirms your status as one—if not *the*—best Pagan magazine in the universe. May GE live long and prosper! **—Mike Howard**
Editor, *The Cauldron*, Cardigan, Wales

I congratulate you on 100 issues of controversy, taking chances, being courageously concerned with presenting all sides, and for pushing the envelope in excellence, Pagan-style...You can be very proud of yourselves.
—Lunaea Weatherstone
Editor, *Sagewoman*, Santa Cruz, CA

The Church of All Worlds' *Green Egg* remains the great Pagan publication: besides unearthing old gods and birthing new ones (call on Squat the next time you need a parking place), the *Green Egg* Reader's Forum is the best print intro to the fractious, funny, sexy texture of Pagan community. **—Erik Davis**
Village Voice Literary Supplement, Nov. 1993

The *Green Egg* has become one of the staples of Pagan life in the United States, and rightly so in my opinion. For many years it has been a melting pot for Pagan opinion and experience; a means for elders to share and beginners to learn. Paganism without the *Green Egg* would be unthinkable! **—Ray Buckland**
Author of Buckland's
Complete Book of Witchcraft

Green Egg Omelette
Copyright © 2009 by Oberon Zell-Ravenheart

BOOK TITLE: GREEN EGG OMELETTE
EDITED BY KIRSTEN DALLEY AND OBERON ZELL-RAVENHEART
TYPESET BY OBERON ZELL-RAVENHEART
Cover design by Lu Rossman/Digi Dog Design NY
Printed in the U.S.A. by Book-mart Press

To order this title, please call toll-free 1-800-CAREER-1 (NJ and Canada: 201-848-0310) to order using VISA or MasterCard, or for further information on books from Career Press.

The Career Press, Inc., 3 Tice Road, PO Box 687,
Franklin Lakes, NJ 07417
www.careerpress.com
www.newpagebooks.com

Library of Congress Cataloging-in-Publication Data
Available upon request.

Green Egg Omelette

An Anthology of Art and Articles from the Legendary Pagan Journal

Edited by Oberon Zell-Ravenheart
Forewords and Chapter Introductions
by Chas S. Clifton and Christopher Penczak

 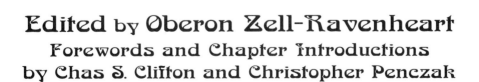

New Page Books
A division of The Career Press, Inc.
Franklin Lakes, NJ

Foreword by Christopher Penczak

LOVE OMELETTES! I really do. When on the road, touring the Pagan festivals and metaphysical shops, they become a staple for me. Though traditionally a breakfast food, I've had them at all hours of the day. They are a good road food, found fresh at diners and cafes wherever I go. Omelettes can be good for you, with a balance of proteins and vegetables. They can be a surprise, with hidden ingredients you didn't expect. And they can be made to order, with only the things you like cooked inside. You get to pick and choose from a wide range of foods to be a part of your dining experience. In short, they can be a fun way to satisfy your cravings.

Think of Oberon Zell-Ravenheart as your omelette chef on this Pagan path. While it can be fun to custom order, you can miss out on some great tastes, things you wouldn't venture to try unless it was prepared for you. When you listen to the advice of a well-seasoned expert, you get to try out many different flavors and combinations you didn't know existed. In *Green Egg Omelette,* Oberon has taken a wide range of flavors, found in the voices of some of most influential teachers and authors of the NeoPagan movement, and brought them together in one experience. Like an omelette, each retains its own individuality, but the sum of the parts creates a unique experience for the reader. In the context of this book, you have an experience of modern Paganism in one place and one time. Rather than hunt down individual articles like separate ingredients, you can enjoy them as one whole. Some will be very well-known to you, like an old favorite. It can be interesting to see where someone was in their path and teachings, to appreciate where they are now. Others will be a brand new surprise. You might fall in love with them too, or find they are not your taste. If you like them, you could hunt down other aspects of that author's work, and find a hidden history to our community previously unknown to you. If they are not to your liking, you at least widened your palette and experienced something new and different. Your discerning taste will be better for it, because sometimes we don't know what we like until we try a few things we don't like. And even still, years later, we might go back and find a new appreciation for something we tried in the past.

Though it might sounds strange, or even silly, omelettes by their very nature, embody one of the great mysteries. *Green Egg Omelette* also embodies the mystery, albeit in a lesser form. Whenever two seemingly separate and opposed experiences are brought together and both are seen as true, a gateway to the mysteries opens. In the greater mysteries we face the paradox of all being separate and individual, but all being part of the same spirit, the same web of life. How can we be both separate and one? Therein lies the mystery. The omelette shows the separate ingredients, yet they are all one in the omelette. I'm not saying contemplation upon eating an omelette will make you any wiser, but a compilation such as *Green Egg Omelette,* and years of reading *Green Egg* magazine opens you up to a mystery in the Pagan community. How can we all have such diverging and separate opinions, yet all be in one spiritual movement? How can we all have such different experiences and views on the divine, life and the manner in which to practice, yet we are all bound together by a shared sense of spiritual purpose, even when we cannot articulate the connection very well? How can we so often be fractious and divided, yet come together when needed for the greater good? I don't know how, yet there the mystery is found.

Green Egg demonstrates the wide variety of opinions and paths, yet at the time we all found voices in its pages. It began before I was even born, and existed for many years before I knew what it meant to be a Pagan. Yet it was still there waiting for me when I tip-toed out into the Pagan community and nurtured me for quite a while, exposing me to different ideas, traditions and politics, often conflicting, or at least challenging, assumptions made by more mainstream writers and teachers. It forced me to reflect and think on what I really believed and practiced, rather than parrot back anyone else's answers.

Through *Green Egg*'s articles and letters I was first introduced to Leo Martello, someone I consider somewhat a spiritual, if not genetic ancestor due to some shared spiritual and ethnic heritage. I'm indebted to the magazine for opening my awareness to other notables in our community, like Gwydion Pendderwen, Ed Fitch and Chas Clifton. As I look back at these pages considered for the compilation, I'm reintroduced to favorite authors and teachers, like Anodea Judith, Robert Anton Wilson and Fred Lamond, with fresh eyes.

And of course it brought my attention to Tim "Otter" turned Oberon Zell-Ravenheart, the Church of All Worlds, and Robert A. Heinlein's *Stranger in a Strange Land*. Through his work, I explored the mysteries of "Thou Art God/Goddess" and "May you never hunger/ thirst." There are really too many voices to name that have influenced me from the pages of *Green Egg*. In fact, I'm indebted to *Green Egg* for another reason. *Green Egg* was the first national forum where I had a chance to be heard many years ago. It brought established elders together with fresh new voices and gave us all exposure to an ever-widening community. It wasn't too long after that publication that my own work developed from a local New England teacher and minister to an author with a wider role in our community.

For many years, Oberon was one of the few voices in the wilderness of the Pagan path, blazing new trails and showcasing other trail-blazers. For those of us in the next generation who reap the benefits of all the hard work of our elders, we need to know where we have been, to truly know where we can go. *Green Egg Omelette* offers a spectacular insight into the hearts and minds of those who have gone before and continue to guide and lead. If we ever hope to fill those shoes, we need to know the path. I hope you will take a bite with me and explore the flavors of the past, perhaps for the first time, so we can all contribute to our future.

Blessed Be, Christopher Penczak

Acknowledgments

First, I would like to thank Julie Epona O'Ryan, for arranging for Chas Clifton and me to get together with Michael and Laurie of New Page at the International New Age Trade Show in Denver last year, where we discussed the idea of this anthology. Julie also did the final proofing and provided secretarial support.

I thank Chas for his enthusiasm, and for writing the Introduction, as well as introducing each chapter. He also helped a great deal in making the painful choices of what pieces to leave out of this first compilation.

Skip Ellison provided scans of several hundred of his favorite items from his own collection of GE back issues, and this was our starting point for what to include here.

I would like to extend particular appreciation to each of the succession of *Green Egg* editors other than me who made the magazine what it was—and is. In order, these have been Tom Williams, Diane Darling, Maerian Morris, and now Ariel Monserrat. Each of them has written a piece here about their experience at the helm.

And finally, I wish to thank all of the many contributors to *Green Egg* over the past 40 years—only a handful of whom could be represented in this first volume. These are the best writers, artists, and poets of the worldwide Pagan Renaissance since its earliest glimmerings, and I look forward to being able to present more of their wondrous work in future *Green Egg* compilations.

Every effort has been made to acknowledge correctly and contact the source and/ or copyright holder of each selection in this anthology, and we apologize for any unintentional errors or omissions, which will be corrected in future editions of this book.

—Bright Blessings, Oberon 6/08

Table of Contents

Table of Contents

Table of Contents

Introduction by Chas S. Clifton

N THE EARLY 1970S, HANS HOLZER (B. 1920), A PROLIFIC NEW YORK–BASED AUTHOR of books on parapsychology, ghost-hunting, and reincarnation, turned his attention to the growing Pagan movement. He was already a friend of Sybil Leek, an English Witch who had moved to the United States in the early 1960s, and the two of them had collaborated on many ghost-hunting forays. Now he traveled across the United States visiting traditional Witches, creators of new Pagan movements, and ceremonial magicians, producing a book called *The New Pagans: An Inside Report of the Mystery Cults of Today*.[1] In order to flesh out his book, Holzer included Anton LaVey's Church of Satan and the Process Church of the Final Judgment, plus some lesser-known Satanists—they all fit under the heading of "mystery cults."

On page 123, Holzer mentions *Green Egg*, "mimeographed newsletter of the Church of All Worlds." He called it "part of the young movement towards pantheistic faith," describing *Green Egg* as "a catchall of neopagan thought, American Indian thinking, witchcraft, ecology, and the sort of thing that goes down well with an increasing number of young people." And then Holzer turned his attention towards a Chicago-based Pagan group to which he devoted 14 pages. That Chicago group has apparently disappeared—but *Green Egg* did not disappear.

From the late 1960s through its current digitized PDF-based version—and with a multiplicity of subtitles ("A Magazine of Goddess and Nature Religion," "A Journal of the Awakening Earth," "A Journal of the New Pagan Renaissance" were some of them)—*Green Egg* has been North America's leading source of Pagan vision and inspiration. Particularly in the 1970s and 1980s, before the spread of the Web, it also provided Pagans of all sorts with an essential resource for networking—and sometimes for squabbling with each other—in its "notorious Green Egg forum." As on online forums today, letter-writers offered information about themselves and their groups, produced indecipherable rants, shared their visions, and occasionally flamed each other in exchanges that lasted for months (since GE came out roughly every six weeks). For the great majority of actual or potential Pagans, who had no metaphysical bookstore or coffee shop to hang out in and make connections, *Green Egg*'s forum and ads provided the best way to find each other. (I know—I found my first coven by responding to a letter that the high priest had written for the forum.)

But since thirty-year-old arguments between leading figures in the Pagan movement might not be so interesting today, we have chosen not to reprint them. Instead, we have assembled a collection of *Green Egg* writing that is timeless. Although it was officially the voice of the Church of All Worlds, formed by Tim (now Oberon) Zell and Lance Christie in 1967, *Green Egg* inspired all kinds of Pagans. More than that, it formed a bridge between the European-based Pagan traditions that claimed to carry on elements of the past (such as Celtic Wicca, Druidism, and various reconstructionist groups) with homegrown American Pagan-isms such as Feraferia and the Church of All Worlds itself with their broader ecological visions.

That was the freshness of *Green Egg*. While some of the contributors with, for example, traditional Wiccan backgrounds, would argue over degree systems and what constituted a valid initiation, anyone reading the magazine might have felt the shared vision of humanity no longer alienated from Mother Earth but joyfully participating in Her creations—and destructions.

When you read this anthology, one thing that you will not see a lot of is "how-to" Pagan writing. There is no "use the amazing powers of Witchcraft" writing, although in the "Magick, Arts, & Crafts" chapter you will find Marion Zimmer Bradley, the noted fantasy writer, discussing how to fit a household altar into a busy household. *Green Egg* was about experience and moving forward.

I also credit *Green Egg* with helping us to think of our Pagan traditions as "nature religion." Wicca had arisen in England around 1950 as a reconstruction of "fertility religion" (which was how Margaret Murray, Gerald Gardner, and others conceived of Stone Age religion) but with more emphasis on the erotic element and a more abstract idea of fertility that included children of the mind and spirit was well as children of the body. English Wicca promoted the myth that it was a direct continuation of pre-Christian religion, which was not true except perhaps in a psychic sense. This Wicca, a small-group mystery religion, arrived in the United States in the 1950s through Gardner's books, such as *Witchcraft Today*, and in the early 1960s through the arrival of British Witches themselves.[2]

In the United States, however, Wicca encountered a type of "nature religion" that had been growing since the early nineteenth century. This nature religion considered America's forests and mountains to be the equivalent in splendor of Europe's castles and cathedrals—and to be even better, for the forests and mountains came directly from divinity and—if understood correctly—carried a divine message in their forms. Nature could be a source of spiritual value as much as could any religion's holy book—that idea was in some Americans' minds long before anyone spoke of "ecospirituality" or "Gaia." Some of the first homegrown American Pagan groups of the mid-twentieth century, such as Feraferia in Southern California and the New Reformed Orthodox Order of the Golden Dawn in the San Francisco Bay Area, carried on the trend of making temporary temples in wild lands outside the cities. When Oberon (Tim) Zell wrote "Theagenesis: The Birth of the Goddess" (Chapter 4), he was thinking within an old American tradition while re-visioning it within a Pagan framework—nature religion that really was *religion*. Other writers in this book grapple with how to refashion consciousness to live in a polytheistic reality where Earth was not just dead "matter" used by human beings until those human beings abandoned it for better, brighter lives in Heaven (or eternal torments in Hell).

Of course, the new Paganism was not just an American production: British writer Tony Kelly's essay "Pagan Musings" was enormously influential with its vision of hidden and marginalized Pagans regrouping to create a Pagan society. All of the authors in the "New Pagans" chapter responded to a new sense of Pagans as a hidden tribe whose members began to recognize each other. As Vicki Rhodes wrote in issue 69, "I who am an Earthborn child must have a place where I can meet others like myself. A place where we can share our respect for the Mother and ideas on how to live in Harmony with Her in a world so intent on destroying Her." Others began to seek traces of their Pagan ancestors and of ways of living in the world that had been devalued by both Abrahamic monotheisms (Judaism, Christianity, Islam) and materialist creeds such as Communism and runaway capitalism. Others sought to re-frame gender relations and to try alternative forms of bonding within a Pagan context.

The Neo-Paganism described in the earlier issues of *Green Egg* is not so "neo-" anymore. Slowly we are becoming part of the contemporary religious scene and our voices are—sometimes—being heard. As we go forward, let's re-visit some of the best Pagan dreams, humor, and entertainments of the past for inspiration on our journey.

---

1 Hans Holzer. *The New Pagans: An Inside Report on the Mystery Cults of Today*. Garden City, N.Y.: Doubleday, 1972.
2 This history and the development of American Paganism as "nature religion" is the subject of my book *Her Hidden Children: The Rise of Wicca and Paganism in America* (Lanham, Maryland: AltaMira Press, 2006).

Chas Clifton lives in the Wet Mountains of southern Colorado. He edits Llewellyn Publications *Witchcraft Today* series, which includes *The Modern Craft Movement* (1992), *Rites of Passage* (1993), and an upcoming anthology on Witchcraft and shamanism.

Green Egg: The 40-Year-Old Hippie

*by **Oberon Zell-Ravenheart**,*
GE Founder and
Publisher Emeritus

"1968" was the title and subject of a recent television documentary hosted by Tom Brokaw. The two-hour special highlighted many of the world-shaking events of that tumultuous year, including:

- The New Year's Tet Offensive, beginning the bloodiest year of the Vietnam war, with 16,500 US soldiers killed;
- Huge nationwide anti-war protests, urban riots, and student uprisings—brutally suppressed by police;
- Sex, drugs, rock'n'roll, love-ins, the Grateful Dead, the Free Clinic—all in Haight/Ashbury, San Francisco;
- Ken Kesey's Merry Pranksters, and the 2nd season of the Smothers Brothers Comedy Hour;
- LBJ declines the nomination for a second term as President; Eugene McCarthy becomes Democratic front-runner;
- *Hair* debuts on Broadway, and *2001: A Space Odyssey, Planet of the Apes*, and *Rosemary's Baby* appear in theaters;
- Martin Luther King and Robert Kennedy are assassinated; widespread rioting follows;
- The Democratic National Convention in Chicago nominates Hubert Humphrey, amid savage "police riot" against protesters, while the whole world watches on TV;
- "Women's Liberation" movement debuts with theatrical protest against Miss America Pageant;
- Russian tanks crush populist revolt in Czechoslovakia;
- Richard Nixon is elected President by a 1% margin;
- And finally, at Christmas, Apollo 8 circles the Moon, returning the first photos of the Earth from space.

But one event of significance in that year was overlooked in that documentary…

Tim Zell 1968

In March of 1968, the *Green Egg* appeared…it grew over 80 issues into a 60-page journal, becoming the most significant periodical in the Pagan movement during the 1970s. —J. Gordon Melton, *Encyclopedia of American Religions, 1979*

40 years ago, on March 4, 1968, the six-year-old Church of All Worlds (CAW) received its official charter from the state of Missouri as a non-profit religious corporation. That same month, we rented a huge four-story Victorian mansion on Gaslight Square in St. Louis for our temple, and published the first issue of *Green Egg*. It was only a single page, dittoed in green ink (on our very own ditto machine!), and contained a brief introduction to the CAW and a calendar of upcoming events, including our first Ostara (Spring Equinox) festival (see next page). This was the year following the Summer of Love, and my son, Bryan, was 4½ years old.

Green Egg was originally conceived as one of three CAW membership newsletters—the one for the outer, or first "Ring," comprising Circles 1-3 of the Church's nine circles of membership. The 2nd Ring newsletter (for more involved members of Circles 4-6) was called *The Scarlet Flame*, of which only half a dozen or so were actually published in those early years. The 3rd Ring newsletter, *Violet Void*, was designed for the Priesthood, but only

VOL. 1 GREEN EGG No. 1
FIRST PAGAN CHURCH OF ALL WORLDS

The Church of All Worlds is what is called a modern "Pagan" religion. By this is meant that it is basically a life-affirming religion without supernatural ememts, such as the Dionysians, the Epicurians, the Stoics, the Druids, the Transcendentalists and the Existentialists. The Church regards metaphysical questions as irrelevant, and leaves them up to the individual to ask as well as to answer. The theological position of the Church of All Worlds takes the step beyond Humanism (which states that God is Mankind) by affirming that man indi- vidually is God — but only to himself, as every other individual is also.

We teach that man is himself ultimately free, ultimately responsible — for his life, his actions, and his salvation (which is defined however he wishes). We reject utterly the concept of original sin and inherent human evil. The three basic commandments of the Church of All Worlds are: Know yourself; Believe in yourself; Be true to yourself. These are set forth as a guide towards becoming more fully human and self-actualizing, which is regarded as necessary before one can hope to function fully with his brothers. In this context, it is accepted that hypocrisy is the only sin, and that the Golden Rule is the basic ethical imperative. Again, the metaphysical questions, such as that of life after death, the purpose of the universe, and the possibility of a guiding intelligence behind natural phenomena, are not regarded as relevent to the Church of the human commu- nity, and the individual, if he so chooses, may treat them howsoever he wishes. Consequently, on those issues, Pagans have a large variety of opinions which are still, however, accepted as only opinions.

Pagans believe that each individual must work out his or her own faith by which to live. Consequently, we are a "free" church with no creeds. The priest or speaker is granted complete freedom of the lecturn, and this freedon also extends to the listeners. The only guides for Pagans in their faith are reason, conscience and experience. We congregate for stimulation, friendship, service and self-expression.

Welcome to the First Pagan Church of All Worlds! Our meetings are cur- rently being held on Thursday nights at our Agora lounge above The Exit, at the corner of Westminster and Boyle in St. Louis. Almost anything is likely to hap- pen, from a lecture and discussion to a hootenanny and folk dancing. Come see!

Advancement in the Church of All Worlds through increasing understanding and privileges is accomplished by means of a series of educational and develop- mental activities. To qualify eventually for a red card, you are expected to accomplish the following:
1. Read and report (1-page written or oral) on The New Genesis by Berenda.
2. Read and report on The Prophet by Gibran.
3. Attend one lecture on Paganism by a high priest.
4. Read and report on Stranger in a Strange Land by Heinlein.
5. Attend second lecture on Paganism.
6. Read and report on Anthem by Rand.
7. Read and report on Gulf by Heinlein (from Assignment in Eternity).
8. Attend third lecture on Paganism.
9. Take Edwards Personal Preference Schedule (EPPS).
10. Give dissemination drill on Paganism or the Church of All Worlds.

March 20, 1968   Thou art God, Irrev. Tim Zell
                                                  High Priest, CAW

one issue was ever produced. These were all printed in colored ditto ink, these being the only colors available other than black (which was really a rather dismal grey), and the colors were also linked to the three degrees of initiation in Wiccan and other magickal traditions.

At that time, the Church of All Worlds was intimately involved and allied with Feraferia ("Wild Festival") of California, the only other group we had found willing to embrace the self-designation "Pagan," which I and the CAW had adopted just six months previously and were busily promoting. Feraferia's brilliant and artistic founding genius, Fred Adams, had introduced us to the "Druidic Tree Calendar" as delineated in Robert Graves' *The White Goddess*. Thus I published our early issues of *Green Egg* on that 13-month annual cycle.

With Fred, we founded the Council of Themis, the first Neo-Pagan ecumenical alliance, bringing in the Egyptian Church of the Eternal Source and our first Wiccan group, the Coven of the Cat—soon followed by about a dozen others. After a few promising years, the Council disintegrated, but some of the surviving groups went on to found, in 1972, the Council of Earth Religions.

Over the next few years, the little newsletter grew. With issue 23 I added a few pages of letters; then articles of philosophy; then writeups on other groups, artwork, prayers, poetry, newsclippings, short stories, cartoons and comic strips… I called the lettercol "The Forum," and it soon expanded to occupy a third of the magazine, becoming by far its most popular (if often contentious) feature. I also traded in our little ditto machine for a mimeograph and an electric stencil cutter acquired from a friend who'd been using it to publish a science-fiction fanzine.

Julie

At that time (early 1970), a significant lover named Julie Carter came into my life, and over the next three years the two of us became a formidable partnership in the Church and the magazine. Julie contributed lovely artwork and insightful articles, and often turned the crank on the press. She was with me upon the occasion of my epiphanic

"TheaGenesis" vision, Sept. 6, 1970—tl entire planetary biosphere comprises ι body of a single vast living organism universally identified as "Mother Earth;" a concept later popularized by British scientist James Lovelock as "The Gaia Hypothesis."

In 1971 I finally initiated correspondence with Robert Heinlein, and his warm and lengthy letters back have been excerpted in both *Green Egg* (#82, 85, 89) and his posthumous *Grumbles From the Grave*. He wrote that "I have enjoyed reading the *Green Egg* and have been stimulated by it." In another letter, he said: "*Green Egg* gives me a new perspective... I read the *Green Egg* because it has in it things I do not find elsewhere."

With Vol. IV #40 (7/1/71), I began writing and publishing an extended series of articles on the new Earth-based (later called "Gaean") thealogy I was developing as a result of my TheaGenesis vision the previous Fall. These papers had quite an impact on the emerging Pagan community, and some of them were widely reprinted.

Tim Zell propagated his ideas through the late 1960s and early 1970s in the Church's newsletter, which grew into the periodical, *Green Egg*. It established the identity of modern Paganism as a response to a planet in crisis, and its spiritual core lay in the concept of the Earth as a single, divine, living organism. The mission of Pagans, according to this concept, was to save 'her' by a transforma-

Green Egg collating party, 1974

f Western society.

Triumph of the Moon,
Press, 2000; pp. 351-52

...e added a front cover and
...thing together into a real
magazine of 34 pages. With Vol. V, #46 (Ostara 1972) we dropped back to 8 issues a year, coming out in conjunction with the eight Sabbats of the Wheel of the Year. In July of that year, CAW was granted 501(c)(3) federal tax exemption as a non-profit religious organization, becoming the first of the new Pagan religions to become officially recognized at the Federal level in the US.

With issue #51, we introduced an off-set-printed wraparound cover, with 48 pages inside. Shortly thereafter we bought a Rex Rotary desktop offset press and aluminum platemaker. Because 8½"x14" was the largest paper we could put through our little printer, we went to a 7"x8½" format as of Vol. VI, #53 (Ostara 1973). A year later we traded in our little press for a big Multilith, but the small magazine format remained the same through Vol. IX, #80 (Yule 1976); the final issue produced in that era, with 60 pages. During that period, the people running the press were Morning Glory, Steve Egbert, Ed Short, and CAW High Priest Don Wildgrube.

The primary mission of the *Green Egg,* as I saw it, was not merely to be a vehicle for the dissemination of CAW's teachings, but to catalyze, foment, and foster the emergence of a diverse worldwide Neo-Pagan movement and community. To this end, we were remarkably successful, attracting the best writers, thinkers, and artists of the new Pagan Renaissance. One of our most popular regular contributors was my water-brother Robert Anton Wilson, long before he wrote his amazing *Illuminatus* trilogy.

It took a catalyst to create a sense of collectivity around the word *Pagan,* and in the

United States the Church of All Worlds and its *Green Egg* filled this role. It was Tim Zell who picked up the term.... For this reason alone the Church of All Worlds deserves a large place in this story.... CAW helped a large number of distinct groups to realize they shared a common purpose, and this gave the phenomenon new significance. Until then, each group had existed on its own, coming into contact with others only at rare events like the Renaissance fairs in California or science fiction conventions. CAW and Tim Zell, by using terms like *Pagan* and *Neo-Pagan* in referring to the emerging collectivity of new earth religions, linked these groups, and *Green Egg* created a communications network among them.

—Margot Adler, *Drawing Down the Moon,*
Viking Press; 1979, p. 277

Morning Glory on Rex Rotary Press,

As the magazine became a major production, we started holding collating parties at our home to put each issue together. In October of 1975, Margot Adler, traveling around the country gathering material for her landmark book on the Pagan movement, showed up at one of these, and described the experience thus:

Eight or nine people sat around a long low table that was covered with stacks of freshly-printed pages.... The sound of friendly chatter mingled with the rustling of pages, the steady firing of a stapling machine, and the occasional crunching of popcorn, which was being passed around in a large bowl.... Only one person in the room was wearing any clothes, a fact that didn't seem particularly noticeable after a few minutes.... Everyone—dressed or undressed—was engaged in the business of the day, which was sorting, collating, stapling, and mailing the 74th issue of *Green Egg.* This peculiar journal had become one of the most important sources of information on Neo-Paganism, and played a key role in facilitating communication among Neo-Pagan groups.

—Margot Adler, *DDTM,* pp. 265–6

Morning Glory

Otter Zell
1984

I was sole editor and typist until issue #60 (Oimelc, 1974), when my newly discovered soulmate, Morning Glory, joined me as Ass't Editor and printer. By #62, she was Co-Editor, and so it remained until #73 (Mabon 1975), when Tom Williams became Features Editor, and Morning Glory and I dropped back to typesetting and editing the Forum, preparatory to our leaving St. Louis for the West Coast. By #76 (Oimelc 1976), we were gone, and Tom was completely in charge. He put out four issues before deciding to head west himself, "following," he said, "in his Primate's knuckleprints." Tom left the magazine in the hands of Don Wildgrube, who managed to put out one more issue at Yule of '76. But with many of the old Nest leaving for Califia, the energy and creativity that had sustained the magazine over the past decade were no longer there, and further publication was abandoned. The legendary *Green Egg* vanished into oblivion. Margot says of this period:

> By 1978…CAW's role as catalyst for the Neo-Pagan movement had ended, at least temporarily, with the death of *Green Egg*. How important *Green Egg* was to the Neo-Pagan community is a matter of controversy. There are many who welcomed its death with a sigh of relief. But others, including myself, believed that it was a key to the movement's vitality and that its death in 1976 was a blow from which the movement is only now recovering…. It is popular today to talk about "synergy"—a combination that has a greater effect than the simple addition of its components—and that perhaps best describes the effect of *Green Egg*. It connected all the evolving and emerging Goddess and nature religions into one phenomenon: the Neo-Pagan movement.
>
> —Margot Adler, *Drawing Down the Moon,* pp. 294-5

Meanwhile, Morning Glory and I spent the next decade having amazing adventures. We traveled around the West in an old School bus I refitted as mobile living quarters—with a 10-ft. Burmese python, a 6-ft. boa constrictor, a possum, a kitty, two tarantulas, and a colony of rats (snake food). Spending a year in Eugene, Oregon, we campaigned to ban whaling, save dolphins from tuna nets, and keep sodium fluoride (rat poison) out of the city water. We taught college classes, and trained Witches. We joined the Oregon Country Faire. We spent eight years homesteading in a 5,600-acre back-to-the-land Hippie community in the Misty Mountains of Mendocino County, NorCalifia. We planted thousands of trees on logged-over lands. My son Bryan, now 18, came to live with us. We raised living Unicorns, which we exhibited at Renaissance Faires throughout North America, before landing a four-year exhibition contract with the Ringling Bros./Barnum & Bailey Circus.

And in 1984, we added a third partner to our lives—a stunning and brilliant redhead named Diane Darling, with a great kid named Zack. Together we mounted a diving expedition to New Guinea in quest of Mermaids (found 'em, too!). We all moved off the land, and settled in an old resort on the Rushing River, which became known as "The Old Same Place." We opened a magickal store in the nearby town of Ukiah, which we called "Between the Worlds." We founded the Ukiah Hometown Festival, and for years MG and I led the parade down Main Street, in full Ren Faire regalia as a Wizard and Enchantress—with a Unicorn! We helped create huge public celebrations for the 20th anniversaries of Earth Day and the Summer of Love, at which we ceremonially passed the torch to the next generation. Our lives were filled with wonder and magick.

"It was 20 years ago today..."

Beginning in the mid-80s, with a whole new circle of friends and Waterkin, (including Anodea Judith, Tom Donohue, Marylyn Motherbear, D.J. Hamouris, and many others) and some old ones from St. Louis (Tom Williams, Charlie Leach, Orion Stormcrow, Michael Hurley), we revived the long-dormant Church of All Worlds and rebuilt it into an international Pagan Church—even becoming the first non-Anglican church to be fully-recognized in Australia!

Oberon Zell - 1994

And finally, 20 years to the day after the original founding of *Green Egg,* we decided it was time to bring it back. Episcopal Priest Sidney Lanier donated $300, with which we sent out a mailing announcing the return of GE, and soliciting advance ads and subscriptions. Enough money came pouring in to print a first issue.

Diane, Morning Glory, a talented Hippie printer named Verge Belanger, and I pulled out all the stops, and on Beltane (May Day) of 1988, Vol. XXI, #81 of *Green Egg: The Next Generation* burst upon the Pagan scene emblazoned with a gorgeous full-color split-fountain image of a rising Phoenix on its cover. Sadly, Robert Heinlein died on May 8, before we could send him a copy.

With Diane Darling as "Domineditrix" and me as Publisher and designer, *Green Egg* soon resumed its former place as the vanguard journal of the Neo-Pagan resurgence. Over the next decade, this now-legendary magazine went on to garner numerous awards, including the Wiccan-Pagan Press Alliance (WPPA) Silver Award for "Most Professionally Formatted Pagan Publication;" the Dragonfest Awards for "Most Attractive Format" and "Best Graphics;" and three times, the WPPA Gold Award for "Readers' Choice."

Morning Glory's article, "Bouquet of Lovers," wherein she first coined the terms *polyamory* and *polyamorous,* was published in *Green Egg* 89 (Beltane 1990). With this terminology to describe it, another entire movement was catalyzed.

Since we had *Green Egg,* people kept asking us "What about ham?" So we initiated a kid's supplement, with Diane's son Zack as editor, and called it *HAM (How About Magic?).* The first issue was Mabon, 1989, and other kid editors took their turns over the years. In 1992 *HAM* won the Dragonfest Award for "Best Fiction."

In October of '93, we finally moved the *Green Egg* offices out of the spare rooms in our homes, and rented a real office building, which became the Administrative Office of the Church as well. Two years later, we moved everything into a large storefront in downtown Ukiah, where we also provided walk-in copy services to the public.

Personalities

The staff of *Green Egg* expanded to include a number of talented and dedicated people. In addition to Diane and me, Morning Glory served as Poetry Editor for issues #81-96. Daniel Blair Stewart became our official Staff Artist with #90, and remained throughout all following issues. Aeona Silversong was our Ad Mgr. for #95-126, followed by LaSara Firefox (#127-130) and Carolyn Whitehorn (#131-136). Mongo Bearwolf took over design and layout from me for #102-108, to be succeeded by Cinnamon Sky (#109-112), and finally Jeanne Koelle (#113-136). Orion Stormcrow came onboard as our accountant and Business Mgr. (#106-114), followed by Apple, Melian, James Assad, and finally, Jeanne Koelle. Orion also served as Forum Editor (#113-123), succeeded by Ian Lurking Bear (#124-136). Orion became Assoc. Publisher with #115.

But with all this success, and so many people involved, there soon arose conflict, contention, and power struggles. In July of 1994, Diane left *Green Egg* to be succeeded as Editrix by Maerian Morris, newly wed to Orion Stormcrow (with MG and I officiating). A brilliant editor, Diane went on to edit *Green Man*, and later *PanGaia*.

At the CAW Board of Directors meeting held on Sept. 13 of 1996, as the culmination of an intense and bitter dispute as to who had ultimate editorial authority over the publication, control of the *Green Egg* was wrested away from me, and the position of Publisher was handed over to Orion (the newly-elected President of the Board). I was given the honorary title of "Publisher Emeritus," with no more say in the content, vision or direction of the magazine I had created.

Although devastated by what I felt to be profound betrayals, I continued to write for the magazine, as I believed it to be an essential service to the greater Pagan community, and I didn't want to see it disappear again.

Orion quit after seven issues (#117-123) and Jeanne took over as Publisher with #124, continuing until the end.

But a few years later, after the 136th issue at the turn of the Millennium, the CAW Board of Directors dissolved the magazine altogether, and once again, Pagandom's most legendary publication seemed destined to become but a footnote in history. I arranged with Anne Niven for *PanGaia* magazine to pick up GE's subscribers, so as to at least soften the blow, and I turned my attention to creating sculpture designs of gods and goddesses for our Ravenheart family business, Mythic Images. Of these, the centerpiece is "The Millennial Gaia"—a three-dimensional representation of my 1970 "TheaGenesis" vision (see p. 91).

In 2002, I signed up with New Page Books to write a *Grimoire for the Apprentice Wizard*. To do so, I gathered together a number of sages and mages, elders and leaders in the worldwide magickal community into the Grey Council, which served as an advisory council to ensure that this book would contain the most authentic wisdom and teachings we could collectively offer to the next generation. Hitting the stands at Oimelc, 2004, the *Grimoire* was an instant success, inspiring the subsequent creation of the Grey School of Wizardry, and inaugurating my new career as an author.

The Phoenix rises—again!

Meanwhile, in September of 2004, the Church of All Worlds was formally "dissolved" by its Ohio-based Board of Directors. The following Spring, however, we discovered that CAW's California corporate status was still intact, as was our Federal 501(c)(3). And so a number of dedicated members, old and new, began what we call "the Third Phoenix Resurrection of the CAW," rebuilding our beloved Church from the ashes, incorporating all the lessons learned from decades of successes and failures.

Well, it wasn't long before the revival of *Green Egg* came up. In the final phases of its previous incarnation, prior to its demise, I had advocated taking it online, as this seemed to me the wave of the future. And in early 2007, my dear friends Ariel Monserrat and Tom Donohue proposed doing just that—with my sanction and support. I was happy to give my blessings, and just as 20 years ago, this third incarnation of *Green Egg* once again featured a rising Phoenix on the cover of its inaugural issue, at Ostara of 2007! With Ariel and Tom now at the helm, and several old staff members (such as Ian Lurking Bear) back onboard, *Green Egg* has resumed its pioneering voyage of exploration at the forefront of the worldwide Pagan Renaissance. Its continuing mission—"to boldly go where no Pagan publication has gone before."

As acknowledged in every history of modern Paganism, the articles, poetry, art, and letters published in *Green Egg* over four decades informed, inspired, and shaped the emerging Pagan community into the fastest-growing religious movement in the English-speaking world. This first anthology of favorite writings from those legendary issues opens a window into the birth, infancy, and adolescence of a transformative cultural revolution that is now, in the 21st century, entering its maturity. Experience the magick, the mystery, the humor and history as it first appeared—in the pages of the *Green Egg*!

Keeping the Flame Alive
The Preservation and Transition of Green Egg

by **Tom Williams**,
GE Editor 1975-'76

It was 1975 and *Green Egg* had grown from a mimeographed sheet to a regular publication with a bulk mailing permit and a growing following of subscribers. It was a major Pagan journal put together with the editorial dedication of Oberon (then Tim) Zell and regular mailing parties held in the Zell household. These consisted of naked people sitting around collating pages, eating popcorn, folding, stapling and affixing mailing labels in zip-sorted order and putting them into what then looked like ponderous mailing bags to be schlepped to the post office for distribution to the world. We had actually acquired our own printing press—a Multilith offset press that was housed at a variety of locations and used to produce *Green Egg* and various other materials that CAW wished to send out into the world.

It was also a time of change. Oberon and Morning Glory were yielding to the call of the West and carefully planning a transition to the West Coast—initially to Oregon. At that time, they sold their house and were working on transforming a used red school bus into a living and driving fantasy dubbed the "Scarlet Succubus." During this transition time they found their way into my living room along with all the wonder, chaos and fantasy that seemed to follow them in their daily existence. And they brought the *Green Egg* with them.

It was therefore inevitable that I would eventually segue into the heir to the editorial duties as they moved ever closer to the drive west. Once they had vacated their house, which was being rented pending sale, we moved all the *Green Egg* materials to my house—including several palettes of back issues complete with their complement of resident cockroaches. There ensued a battle royal with the invasive insects that was eventually won by the judicious application of boric acid to all the baseboards of the house.

We brought in a drafting table, file cabinets and archives and continued the production of *Green Egg* from my house in St. Louis without missing a beat. Gradually, we weaned me from apprenticeship to full editorhood before Oberon and Morning Glory climbed aboard "Scarlet" and took off for the Western realms leaving us in a void and me with a determination to get out of St. Louis as well and soon to head West myself.

Still, during 1976, I soldiered on as editor of *Green Egg,* which turned out to be a vastly rewarding experience. I forged many relationships with members of the national Pagan community, got involved in heavy and silly controversies and was able to exercise creativity and put my own modest stamp on the character of the publication.

Green Egg grew and prospered during this year, but much of the wonder and charm of the CAW experience had left with the Primate and his mate.

Still, the production of the publication proceeded on schedule with amazing contributions from the Pagan community and the ever-lively give and take of the already famous Forum, the letters section. I still remember the Yule issue of 1976 with all the compliments we got for the cover design. I also remember getting reamed by some readers in rather more conservative milieus for some of the more, er, shall we say, risqué cover art that we sent out.

The famous mailing parties had moved

to my living room and all in all, the transition had been smooth, the magazine was published regularly and kept on budget—if not wildly profitable, at least it was paying for itself and we could sustain it financially.

For all of you youngsters out there, please imagine that all this was done without any form of computer or digital storage or laser printer at all—nada. We set type on an IBM Selectric typewriter and layout was done by cutting strips of typed text and illustrations and affixing them to a page with wax. From these, offset plates were made photographically for the press. It was painstaking work and any revisions had to be retyped and re-laid out. I guess you could say it was a labor of love...or obsession. I acknowledge the efforts of those who volunteered to do the typing, ran copy over to my house and basically kept the effort alive. It was not easy.

Still, we got great submissions from all over the Pagan community and the sense of being in the center of what was happening was immense.

But the siren call of the Western Lands would not be stilled and there was a fading trail of my Primate's knuckle prints that led from my doorstep out into those lands. So I got myself a miniature version of Scarlet—a red VW bus with a shark's jaw on the spare tire in front—and fixed it up with a fridge, a bed and storage and prepared to make my own exodus. The question now was—What was to become of *Green Egg*?

By the early summer of 1977, it was time for another transition, but this one was not very auspicious. The people left in St. Louis, although good-hearted and enthusiastic, were not experienced and steeped in the philosophy of CAW nor did they have the needed connections to the wider Pagan community. I had at least been a CAW Priest for eight years prior to this. Still, I was heading West and we had to try to keep up continuity.

As I prepared for my exodus, I transferred the files, equipment and materials to those who had volunteered to take over. And one day, I loaded up my van with my most important worldly possessions and started driving West. *Green Egg* had one last issue after my departure and when we finally saw it, we agreed that it was probably just as well that there would not soon be a further one. *Green Egg* was to go into dormancy for a period of time.

It was time to wait and let a new incarnation of *Green Egg* arise at the proper time. We had kept the spark alive, but it would be another time until it was fanned once more into a bright and living light.

Domineditrix

by *Diane Darling*, GE Editrix 1988-'94

Oh, those were the days. Living at the Old Same Place on the Russian River in a little Pagan/hippie enclave, surrounded by water, highway and rednecks. With an owl in the living room, a unicorn in the back yard and magic in the air, we were happy in our loves, our work, our environment. Church of All Worlds was revived and ticking over nicely, bringing a tide of interesting people and ideas into our lives and everything seemed possible.

Then one day in 1987, Otter brought home a computer. Of course, we'd all seen computers before, at the publishing office where Otter worked. But the idea of actually having one in his house seemed like a typically strange and silly idea, until he proposed that we also revive *Green Egg*.

Ah, *Green Egg*. It didn't mean much to me, having missed all the early days of the founding of the Church of All Worlds and publication of the first 80 issues of *Green Egg*. Otter had showed me a few copies in the course of the years we'd been together, but I was underimpressed, you might say.

I already had a full life, with a growing son, a job I loved, friends, lovers, CAW events, my Buddhist practice and sangha, ceramic art, songwriting and performing, a burgeoning menagerie and garden. But I reckoned I could work some typesetting, editing,

and proofing somewhere in there, and Otter would do the rest, whatever that was.

Not a year later there was a computer in my house, too, a little Mac SE, as I recall, with a black and white screen about as big as a paperback book. It served me very well for the simple writing and editing that was my job. Soon, however, the spare room in my cabin began morphing into an office, with file cabinets, shelves groaning with books waiting for review, a desk for using crude writing instruments, and a carrel for the Mac and its friends and successors. Otter, Morning Glory and I collaborated closely on the first several issues, then, over the years, the many components of generating a magazine shifted between Otter and me, each doing what we loved and what we were capable of. Much later we were able to recruit other people to take on advertising and design, and towards the end of my tenure at GE, we had a little paid staff and were even paying some contributors.

That's how we did *Green Egg*, but why did we do it? What were we thinking?

I thought we were saving the world by reviving human consciousness of the sacred living Earth and of our true ancestral roots. We spread word of the beauty of the spirituality of our ancestors that NeoPagans worldwide were developing into a very modern faith. By displaying and discussing our own, then-radical lifestyle experiments, we hoped to turn the wheel of social evolution for the benefit of our Mother.

I saw *Green Egg* as a portal for ideas and myself as a midwife, drawing forth the genius of our Pagan community and displaying it for all to contemplate. We took on some great issues: sex, drugs, cosmology, ecology and activism, polyamory, mythic beasts, ancestral art, fantasy, music. And that was just the first issue (#81, Beltane 1988)! Though these topics remained favorites, subsequent issues discussed even more interesting subjects and included articles, interviews, poetry and fiction by many people who were then or went on to become leaders in their fields.

It was certainly exhilarating being on the bridge of such a powerful publication and we had pretty much complete freedom, recognizing no box out of which to think. OZ, MG and I conferred on all the early issues and we wrote, edited and published miles of copy, much of which has, in the long view, shaped the course of Pagan thought and activity.

As our readership grew, so did the burden of the more mundane aspects of running a magazine. I took on the business end of things, in addition to editing and writing and communicating with writers and artists and later managing our small staff. I did this not from any love for the nuts and bolts of business, but only because I was the one among us with a head for it and it had to be done.

Though it helped after several years when we could pay ourselves a little something, and then a little more, I was burning out. The triadic relationship among OZ, MG and me suffered terribly under the strain of running the magazine and the Church and living lives that were to say the least very unusual, and sadly our bonds frayed and broke. We parted our handfasting honorably, but the grim madness at the *Green Egg* office burned hotter and in 1994 I left with a shattered heart.

Green Egg was an important vehicle for the journey of NeoPaganism in general and many individual Pagans in particular. I am proud of every issue in which I had a hand. We were surfing the bleeding edge of cultural shift and, though there were sacrifices and casualties, the collective influence of Pagan thought and passion can today be felt in the field of human consciousness. May our efforts then and now suffice to save our biome, and may we love and celebrate the magic in our lives.

The 5ᵗʰ Element

by *Maerian Morris, GE Editor 1994-2000*

Many of us in the Pagan Communi-
ty have held magickal tools in our hands. We
sweep 'round the Grove with a Sword stream-
ing a crackling blue plasma. At the bonfire,
we hold aloft a Wand tipped with a shining
clear crystal, and refracted firelight glistens
upon a Circle of Love and Trust. We smile
into a lover's eyes over a carefully cradled
Cup as a sparkling dagger dips downwards.
We kneel in the North to lift a hand-crafted
clay Plate laden with sweet grain cakes and
gladly pass it sunwise.

In the Summer of 1994, I was handed
such a Tool. A fragile *Green Egg* dropped
rather dramatically into my hands. I stepped
up to catch it and regarded it with surprise. I
am not sure that I knew quite what it was. I
know I didn't know what it would ask of me,
or what it would give me in return.

The *Green Egg* encompasses all the Sa-
cred Tools I mentioned here. Over the years
it has been a stunning Tool of communica-
tion—an elucidator of Pagan ideas through
its articles and features, a voice for the
Church of All Worlds through its Nesting
Notes and editorials, a facilitator for commu-
nity dialog though its Forum. The *Green Egg*
is also a creature of inspiration—its poetry
and the art that has graced its covers and
pages over the years have offered our com-
munity the chance to share our creative pas-
sion with one another. And the *Green Egg* is
a Grail. It has been a wellspring of emotional
explorations of alternative paths to Love, and
a font of expressive heartfelt blessings that
have showered over our far-flung readership
and brought us more closely together. Equal-
ly, and magickally, our shared *Green Egg* has
been a Tool of and for the Earth. It has nour-
ished us with much needed basic approach-
es to Nature, grounded us in a variety of rit-
uals and traditions, and it has acted
as a springboard in defense of its
namesake—that rotating and revolv-
ing *Green Egg* we all treasure, honor
and seek to protect.

As *Green Egg*'s editor I often
felt I was wielding this magickal tool for
the Earth and in service to you all. It was a
humbling and gratifying and amazing expe-
rience. Personally, the *Green Egg* gave me
an opportunity to share with you not just
whatever gifts of Word-crafting I might have
possessed, but also a chance to offer a
glimpse into my own personal adventures.
Synchronicity is a powerful and delightful
(and fun) indicator of magickal energies. I
continually found myself delighted to dis-
cover a synchronic thread tying my personal
experiences to the themes we were exploring
in the pages of *Green Egg*. It was delightful
to take my editorials in the direction of per-
sonal rants and storytelling, and to write what
amounted to a love letter to those I perceived
as the family of the *Green Egg* readership.
Through those rants, stories and love letters
I hope we all managed to more personally
explore and celebrate the many eclectic and
ancient energies that contribute to the Pagan
communities that have made up our reader-
ship over the years.

I was given the gift of editing the CAW's
publication while simultaneously walking a
Labyrinth that led me inwards to the discov-
ery of what it means to be a Priestess of Gaia.
This was in a time when our community and
the Earth were clearly descending into dire
need. Over the years in which I edited *Green
Egg* we expanded from a quarterly publica-
tion to a bimonthly. We also shifted from a
somewhat random approach to a thematic ex-
ploration of our subject matter. This allowed
us to more deeply look into those aspects
which were facing our maturing Pagan com-
munity. These aspects included such topics
as the raising of Pagan children, aging in our
community, and law. This approach also gave
us a chance to dive more deeply into the var-
ious threads that weave into our amazing

cultural web. We explored such themes as TechnoPaganism, Faeries, Druidry, and contributions from the African Diaspora. We expanded upon the inter-faith dialog to more thoroughly delve into mythic contributions from Hinduism, Buddhism, and Judaism. We even danced into the ecstatic community surrounding the Grateful Dead.

While we explored the issues facing our larger communities and readership, we also entered a transformative and painful time for the Church of All Worlds. I learned more than I ever expected about service and gratitude. It was, at times, amazingly difficult to navigate those years. Editing a bimonthly publication such as *Green Egg,* while simultaneously raising four children and communicating with a fractious and dynamic Pagan Community and Clergy (as both bodies were just diving into the age of the internet) was more than a full time job. All of the employees of *Green Egg* worked exceptionally long hours and the publication was often then faced with a painful choice—pay the steeply rising costs of paper and printing or distribute the employees' paychecks. The printer often won over our strident protest and dismay, and the personal cost to our families was surprisingly high. But what an honor and a joy it was to approach the flood of contributions that came to *Green Egg* every day! What a delight to ramble through the amazing art and contributions of such artists and writers as Paul Rucker, Anodea Judith, Ralph Metzner, and Dragon Singing! What an incredible experience to craft one's personal adventures into tales that were destined for the hands and hearts of the Pagan Community!

From the Dionysian revels of the Grateful Dead to the contemplative voice of the Dalai Lama speaking on Buddheo-Paganism, my editing years were lit with amazing opportunities to wield those four great magickal tools the *Green Egg* encompasses. While I faced the most difficult and painful years of my life, this too was a gift: from the Sword I learned to draw clean boundaries, from the Wand I discovered how to allow my passions to flame forth, from the Cup I drank deep of both sadness and joy, and from that great plate of sustenance I found the whole World supported me upon my next journey. I wish such bounty for all who have loved and read *Green Egg* over the years, and to my "descendent," the current editor of *Green Egg*, I most lovingly "bequeath" my take on the wielding of this Magickal Tool. May You Never Thirst, Thou Art God/dess.

Bringing Us All Together

by Ariel Monserrat, GE Editor 2007-

I first came into contact with *Green Egg* back in 1996. I was in Barnes & Noble, looking over the magazine rack. I noticed an unusual-looking magazine with a headline that read "Sex and Spirituality." Now here was a subject I had been struggling with for some time. I had been raised in a Christian home—with the Christian idea of sex being separate from spirituality—and it wasn't working for me. I was looking for a way to integrate the two, so that sex could be part of a spiritual path. And here, amazingly, was an article about it! I quickly scooped up what turned out to be the last copy, hurried home and read the entire magazine front to cover.

I was astounded, at the very least, by the innovative nature of the articles. Clearly, here was a magazine whose writers thought outside the box! I was both hooked and intrigued. From then on, I read every *Green Egg* issue I could get my hands on. Little did I know how important *Green Egg* would become to me!

In that issue, was an ad for a Pagan festival called Ancient Ways in Northern California. I knew I had to attend, so I went off to the gathering and that is how I was introduced to Paganism. I wonder how many people came to Paganism because of *Green Egg*.

In 2000, *Green Egg* ceased publishing and I was very disappointed. *Green Egg* had been a sort of gathering place for intelligent and innovative Pagan viewpoints. Back before the internet, there was no way for Pagans to find each other, except through some sort of classified ads or postings at a Pagan store, *if* you could find one in your area. *Green Egg* became an important web that brought us all together.

By the year 2000, we of course had the internet and networking took on a whole new face. Now it was easy to connect with other Pagans, be they individuals or groups. By this time, there were also a number of other Pagan magazines. Still, *Green Egg* was somehow different from the others and offered something unique—innovative ideas.

In the seven years that *Green Egg* was shut down, I sorely missed it, as did many other people. I kept hoping someone would revive it. I ran into many Pagans who missed *Green Egg*. During those seven years, my life took on a whole new direction. I married, retired and moved to Tennessee with my husband. We fell in love with the beautiful green summers of Tennessee.

The winters, however, are a different story. There is not one blade of grass, leaf, or anything else that is green. The trees are naked, brown and gray, as is the rest of the landscape. It can get down to 3 degrees Fahrenheit and when the wind blows strongly, it feels like someone opened the door to the North Pole. Winter here lasts for four solid months and can get monotonous due to the lack of outside activities, as it's just too cold.

It was during one of these long winters, on a cold night in January of last year, that my husband, Tom, and I were sitting in front of the fireplace, chatting about the day's events. I was restless with cabin fever, impatiently waiting for spring and looking for something to do. I remembered *Green Egg* for some reason, and wished I had a *Green Egg* issue to read during this bleak time of year. It was then that the idea came to me. Hey, Tom and I are retired, why couldn't *we* revive *Green Egg* and manage it? We had the time, resources, motivation and ability, as we both are writers. I knew immediately that this was something I had to do. So Tom and I wrote up a business proposal for *Green Egg*, submitted it to Oberon, who approved it, and we were on our way.

I have always felt that Oberon entrusting *Green Egg* to us has been a great honor. It is a sacred charge, one that I treasure very deeply. Managing *Green Egg* has been an exciting endeavor for me. I love getting e-mail from people I don't know who are researching Paganism and ask for help; getting e-mail that praises *Green Egg*; reading and editing articles; and a million other things that the job of Managing Editor and Publisher of *Green Egg* entails.

I would like to leave you, dear reader, with two thoughts: Years ago, at a Pagan gathering, I was talking to someone about some of Oberon's amazing work in the Pagan community. My companion turned to me and said, "Oberon is the one who brought us all together; and for that, I will always appreciate him." Indeed, *Green Egg* brought many of us together and helped to form the early Pagan community. Besides word-of-mouth, *Green Egg* may well have been the major thing that brought us together, before the days of the internet.

The second thought is this: Back in 2000, I went to my friend, Starwhite, troubled and in need of directions from an elder witch. I'll never forget her saying to me, "I love Oberon for the beautiful things he has created."

Indeed, Oberon has created many beautiful things. I think *Green Egg* is one of his most beautiful creations and I am both proud and honored to be a part of its history.

Chapter 1.
New Pagans
Introduction
*by **Chas S. Clifton***

EFORE THE 1970S, EVERYONE KNEW WHAT A "PAGAN" WAS. That was someone who ate, drank, and made merry, never giving a thought to what happened after death when they would face the awful judgment of God—and, boy, would they be surprised to learn about Hell. But in 2003, New York University Press would publish Michael York's *Pagan Theology: Paganism as a World Religion* as a serious theological book. Quite a bit had changed in thirty years! Paganism—or various Paganisms—was increasingly seen as designating a collection of new religions, new forms of old religion, and (among the most liberal-minded) could be applied to older "animistic" or "tribal" religions that had persisted through the centuries. *Green Egg* was a big reason for this shift in thinking, because it brought Pagans of all sorts together, rather than serving only one Wiccan tradition, Druid order, or whatever.

"Neo-Paganism" sought new ways of thinking about religion.[1] It was no longer a case of monotheistic believers versus atheists. As Isaac Bonewits writes in his "Aquarian Manifesto" (he briefly used "Aquarian" almost synonymously with "Neo-Pagan"), "Aquarians— NeoPagan, NeoChristian, Agnostic or of any Faith—are by definition tolerant of ALL Pro-Life Beliefs and Organizations. They do not proclaim the existence of any One-True-Right-And-Only-Way; but rather that every Sentient Being must find her or his own Path."[2] The contrast with the Abrahamic religions could not be stronger.

Tony Kelly, a British Pagan writer, produced an essay called "Pagan Musings," which was widely reprinted in the Pagan press. It makes the point that our religious innovation and creation started with sheer wonder at the cosmos: "We have walked in the magic forest, bewitched in the old Green Thinks; we have seen the cauldron and the one become many and the many in the one; we know the Silver Maid of the moon-light and the sounds of the cloven feet. We have heard the pipes on the twilight ferns, and we've seen the spells of the Enchantress, and Time be stilled." Not just wonder, but also sadness permeates this piece, a sadness of shrines neglected, old gods and ways forgotten, joy trampled under repression. And so he promises that days of Pagan wonder can be reclaimed.

As the new American Pagans found each other through Forum letters and advertisements in *Green Egg*, members of different groups began to see what they had in common as Pagans. The statement "Common Themes of Neo-Pagan Religious Orientation" was a beginning in the process that would produce Professor York's book thirty years later. It includes declarations of ecological wholeness, of an integration of Eros and religion, and an affirmation of the multiplicity of divine forms. This declaration, in effect, makes the point that divinity can appear within the material world, the "tangible [and] sentient," as York would later write. And it calls for religious freedom to be extended to Pagans too, foreshadowing a struggle for recognition that continues to this day.

---

[1] It is another sign of contemporary Paganisms' rapid growth and acceptance that many Pagans have dropped the "Neo-" prefix. As Graham Harvey, an English Druid and religious-studies professor has said, after fifty years we are not so "neo-" anymore.

[2] "Pro-life" in this instance is not the same as "anti-abortion."

The Neo-Pagan Alternative

by *Erinna Northwind, Church of All Worlds*

AYDAY, 1971. MANKIND SEEMS to be locked into a course of Terracide; the murder of the planet upon which he lives. The process involves, among other things:

1. A combination of willful apathy and real helplessness; lack of control over his institutions. Man cannot focus his attention on the problem or get excited about it. Apathy prevents him from acting individually and from organizing to do what he cannot do individually.

2. Inability to distinguish real values from symbols. Not only real enjoyment and happiness, but health and safety are sacrificed in favor of acquiring symbolic wealth and social status.

3. Profit-motivated proliferation of the use of materials and processes not fully understood, with no assurance of the harmlessness of the given use.

It is well-known that both overcrowding (lack of private space) and sex-repression produce fatigue and depression in the individual, among other ills. Both require the victim to develop a rigid, insensitive outer "shell" as a defense.

He can "shut out the world" by (going into his shell.) A person whose "shell" is sufficiently thick may actually experience reduced sensitivity in his skin, and may interpret pleasurable and painful stimuli conversely.

This shell enables him to shut out painful (or pleasurable—therefore painful) contacts, but it also shuts him in. His perception of reality outside himself is distorted. He cannot experience events normally. He may feel like a spectator in his own experiences.

Denied authentic experiences, he lives in an inner world of abstractions and symbols. His thinking becomes inhuman, machine-like. His aims and actions, while preserving a lunatic logic of their own, become irrational in relation to any normal interpretation of reality; inhumane, and rigidly patterned. He cannot himself test abstractions against reality to determine their relative validity. Hence there are hardly any limits to how far his fantasies can go. He is left suggestible to any appeal that does not attack his basic fears or excite his defense mechanisms.

Thus he can be brainwashed to accept premises any sensible person would dismiss as nonsense, such as: that it is immoral to steal a loaf of bread from a supermarket, virtuous to let one's family starve for want of it, commendably "good business" to misrepresent the weight and the contents of the bread one offers for sale, and one's civic duty to punish the bread-thief. Or, that we are condemned to eternal torment for the sin of coming into existence; that the God who condemns us is all-powerful, yet at the same time is unable to save mankind from hell except by submitting his only son to unspeakable tortures; that we please this God by suffering and self-mutilation, yet must regard him as a loving father. As Tom Paine put it while still a child, any human father that behaved that way would be hanged.

That society in the mass is afflicted with these malaises can be seen in the artificial lifestyle that is accepted as standard. People today live so far removed from direct contact with natural realities that they have only the dimmest ideas of how or where their food is produced, far less any idea of what the surface of their planet is like in the wild state. Many see the sky only through a veil of dirty air.

These causes of human impotence, seemingly a tangle of many strands, are merely different aspects of a single phenomenon: defiance of the elastic and gentle laws (but laws nonetheless, with definite penalties for violation) of Nature.

Man defies Nature by exceeding wise limits on his own numbers, and reproduces the behavior of overcrowded laboratory rats: he turns to sexual perversions (of which chastity is the most bizarre), he fouls his own nest, he kills his Children. He defies Nature by rejecting reality in favor of symbols; by exploiting Nature's mysterious powers without first understanding them, in the arrogant belief that there is nothing he does not know. The most primitive creatures that could be called human knew better than that.

The Church of All Worlds attempts to get at and correct the root causes of Terracide before the crime can be fully accomplished. The tools used include:

1. RELIGION. This is merely saying that there are processes we don't understand yet, and therefore we must not exploit them carelessly. But neither can we afford to ignore their existence, because by doing so we may run afoul of them. Since we do not understand them fully, and perceive them only intuitively, we can best talk about them metaphorically, in the language of myth. There are certain things we must do that bring no immediate concrete gain, yet we must do them for an object "bigger than our individual selves:" the saving of the planet. It is a religious act to use bio-degradable, phosphate-free detergent, which may be more expensive than the polluting kind. By acknowledging the religious nature of these concerns, Neo-Pagans are fighting apathy with a very powerful, very old force: the instinct to worship, which can be, and is in the *case* of the Church of All Worlds, superstition-free. Certainly a CAW Neo-Pagan is freer from superstition than the "hard-headed businessman," who values figures on paper above a life richly lived.

2. RETURN TO NATURE. By getting his fingers in the Earth the typical alienated man of today may experience healing of his riven self. Living close to Nature and working in cooperation with Her to produce his necessities and pleasures, daily experiencing the flavors of raw life, must work to reacquaint man with his own nature.

The natural environment is capable of pouring into us masses of subtle information about our own nature and identity and about the universe and our place in it, if we will only approach and be receptive. CAW works to preserve and restore natural wilderness, and to provide opportunities for people to experience contact with Nature and participate in producing their own food, by health-giving organic methods.

Members of the Church of All Worlds are asked to search for the difference between healthy natural desire and neurotic compulsion, and be guided by the former. Thus we serve Nature manifested in ourselves. We are encouraged to turn to Nature as a source of spiritual refreshment and bodily health, so that we can be of more use to ourselves and to our human family.

3. SMALL-VILLAGE LIFE. The Church of All Worlds is working towards establishing new communities to bring institutions down to manageable size. We wish to rely increasingly on the use of village-scale institutions of our own making, which are controllable, and work out solutions to them using our own cognitive apparatus and intelligence. This is in sharp contrast to the method in use today.

People are accustomed to having their personal problems, values, goals and methods selected and defined for them and imprinted on their passive brains by means of the hypnotic tube.

CAW's motto, "Thou art God/dess," is particularly relevant when we realize that most of humanity's problems come from thinking that someone or something *else* is God: money, the great father in Washington, the Church, our parents, General Motors; whatever we allow to make our decisions for us. When a man shares Godhood with all Nature he has the freedom and responsibility to act in his own behalf. He and no other is the architect of his own life. He and no other is responsible for his own decisions.

The Church of All Worlds is Paganism grown up. Where the ancient Pagans bowed before awesome Nature in their own helplessness, Neo-Pagans make peace with Her in the strength of our terrible technological arsenal. In maturity we know our power to preserve or destroy, and we also know on what we depend for life, and what it is we must be careful not to destroy but to preserve.

GE Vol. IV, No. 39 (5/30/71) 3–4

Reprinted, GE Vol. VIII, No. 70 (Beltane 1975)

The Rising Tide of Pagan Tradition

by *W. Holman Keith*
(author of *Divinity as the Eternal Feminine*)

 NUMBER OF TRENDS ARE EMERGing at this dawn of the Aquarian Age: the ascendancy of woman, the emancipation of sex, the shaking of the foundations of our secular and spiritual institutions. We are at the crossroads, and a choice of path must be made. Science, technology and collectivism are the prospects of the future—all of which tend to robotize man. Or, regression because of human failure and folly on a wide scale to the ancient rule of violence and force. If a great religion is to counter both of these possibilities it will be a religion in which man's deepest sensibilities are re-awakened as to the divinity of Nature, sex, the human person, as to the sacredness of life as of both time and eternity, aid as ideally and rightly itself the worship of the Divine. Of all the new religious developments of our time this presents the livest and profoundest issue.

In the days of the Apostle Paul, Diana of Ephesus and Her craftsmen who lived from the trade of Her cultus caused the Apostle some uneasy moments and no small opposition. The days of the great Temple at Ephesus were numbered, and Demetrius and his silversmiths were identified not with a lost cause—not in the larger perspective of history—but with their own utterly inadequate and unworthy version of the Goddess truth, in which commercialism predominated. This timeless truth was not timely at this stage. Christianity was to prevail, as both the destroyer and yet incorporator of Paganism. The Temple at Ephesus (one of the Seven Wonders of the ancient world) and the Temple at Jerusalem were both to pass off the scene.

But the truth of Nature, sex and femininity as divine manifestations of Supreme Being—to which the Temple of the Seven Wonders bore witness, however unworthily, as did an earlier temple at Jerusalem in its sexual rites—this truth is more durable and beautiful than those great worship centers of antiquity which were destroyed. This truth cannot be destroyed. Its recovery and full realization ethically will not mean a return of the decadence of Greece and Rome, reflected in their depraved debauchery, from which the asceticism of primitive Christianity was a rebound. This latter may have been the only possible and right response at the time, for all the right-thinking and well-intentioned, Christian or otherwise. But not to mention the ascetic excesses that developed in the early Christian Church, that were often unwittingly a kind of sensuality in reverse and a perversion, such austerity could not rehabilitate the flesh and its pleasure into any kind of nobility. Such precisely is the ethics and esthetics of the Goddess faith. Spirit must elevate and ennoble all the fullness of sense, in the name, spirit, and worship of the Divine. This is the only alternative, by the highest idealism and in the long run, to the debased sensuality that drags the spirit down into a loss of its integrity.

The ancient fertility faith and Goddess worship persisted well into historic times, even after the patriarchal social revolution, in such cult mysteries as those of Ishtar and Tammuz, Aphrodite and Adonis, Cybele and Attis, and in such great worship centers as those at Cyprus, Cyrene and Ephesus. The worship of Goddesses as subordinate to the All-Father (Zeus or Jupiter) persisted of course until the fall of Greco-Roman polytheism, brought about by the triumph of Christianity. This triumph must be re-assessed, in the name of an older and a newer truth.

The Goddess Venus, for all the Romans, including Emperor Augustus, the most proper Roman of them all, was the exemplar, guarantor, guardian of the effulgence of life, in Nature, in history, in human affairs and high adventure. For the Pagans the grandeur of Rome was inseparable from the glory of Venus, Venus Genetrix. The neo-Dianic religion—Aphrodisian, Feraferian, Wiccan—in claiming an indispensible truth and message for our time and crisis, is seeking to awaken the modern mind to a glory of the Divine that is lost to our orthodox religious thought. The complete routing of the Goddess truth in the three great monotheism except for certain disguised and minor survivals, principally in Christianity, made its eventual and triumphant return all the more inevitable. And the living Goddess will mean more in this day of desperate coming to grips with life and reality than in pre-Christian Paganism.

GOD IS DEAD! LONG LIVE THE GODDESS!

GE Vol. IV, No. 41 (Lughnasadh 1971) 6

The Very Model of a Modern Esotericist

*by **Bill Beattie,** from* Shadowplay
(with minor tweaking by Otter G'Zell)
Sung to the tune of "I Am the Very Model of a Modern Major General"
by Gilbert & Sullivan (from *Pirates of Penzance*)

I am the very model of a modern esotericist,
A seasoned astral traveler and an edifying exorcist,
A sparkling star astrologer, a dead adroit necromancer.
A dab hand as a palmist and a card as a Tarotmancer.
I've folk tradition lineage—both Celtic and Germanical;
I've channeled Robert Heinlein and I've busted cults Satanical;
Elusively mysterious in Eleusinian Mysteries,
I've proven eighty-three per cent of Velikovsky's histories.
My patent aphrodisiacs would make a satyr hornier;
I've manufactured unicorns in northern California.
In short, in matters magical I'm manic as a terrorist;
I am the very model of a modern esotericist!

I am the very model of a modern esotericist.
My mystic methodology's inherently empiricist;
I've tread the Cretan labyrinth on pathways that I travel on;
I won't deny the rumors that I ghostwrote Mists of Avalon.
A truly great Great Riter and a master of tantrickery,
I'm up the Shining Pathways 'til the Guardians are sick of me.
I dazzle Neo-Pagans as I breakdance round the Wicca ring
And, miracle of miracles, I even stop them bickering!
I've raised the ghost of Crowley in a Gnostic Mass invoking in
Sumerian, Bavarian, Etruscan and Enochian.
I'd sing another chorus, but I have to see my therapist;
I am the very model of a modern esotericist!

GE Vol. XXIV, No. 95 (Yule 1992) 2

Biotheology:
The Neo-Pagan Mission

by *Tim Zell*, *Primate, Church of All Worlds*

AUTHOR'S NOTE: This article was originally written in mid-1971, about nine months following a profound Vision I had on September 6, 1970, of our entire Earth as a single great living organism— a revelation I articulated the next weekend as a sermon to the congregation of the Church of All Worlds, titled "TheaGenesis: The Birth of the Goddess." I finally published it as an article in Green Egg *#40—Litha, 1971. I followed it with an ongoing series in each issue over the next few years, expanding upon the implications of this paradigm; this piece was the first of those sequel articles. For this and my other writings of the time, I coined the term* Terrebios—later *Terrabia (f.) —Latin for "Earthlife." This was in accord with the convention of scientific nomenclature in which Greek names are used for extinct creatures, and Latin for living ones. However, when, a year later, British atmospheric biochemist James Lovelock published his first essay—a letter to the editor—on the Earth as a living organism ("Gaia as Seen Through the Atmosphere," Atmospheric Environment, 1972), in which he used a variant of the ancient Greek name* Ge, *as proposed by novelist William Golding, I replaced Terrebia with Gaea or Gaia in my own subsequent writings and reprints. These writings were widely reprinted in other Pagan periodicals of the time, having, according to Margot Adler, a profound and transformative impact of imparting a passionate sense of mission and purpose to the emerging Neo-Pagan movement. –OZ, 4/17/08*

 E NOW KNOW THAT OUR PLANet, Mother Earth, is inhabited not by myriad separate and distinct organisms, each going its own way independent of all the others, but rather that the aggregate total of all the livings beings of Earth comprises the vast body of a single organism—the planetary Biosphere itself. Literally, we are all One. Further, we now realize that the being we have intuitively referred to as Mother Earth, The Goddess, Mother Nature, The Lady, is not merely a mythical projection of our own limited visions, but an actual living entity, *Terrabia,* the very biosphere of Earth, in whose body we are mere cells. Forced by this discovery to re-examine our. religious language and conceptualizations, we have arrived at the following definition of Divinity (which, incidentally, includes within it the essential nature of the Divine as expressed by all other religions): "Divinity is the highest level of aware consciousness accessible to each living being, manifesting itself in the self-actualization of that being." Thus the living Biosphere *is* Goddess in Her evolving self-actualization. As in the corporate body of the great planetary organism we are all One, so are we all God! (More correctly, we are all Goddess, since Mother Earth is of feminine gender.) This concept has been recognized, though not heretofore fully understood, in the basic aphorism of Neo-Pagan religion; the phrase. "Thou art God."

For generations untold people have looked in vain outside themselves for their Divinity—seeing an image reflected in the macrocosmic mirror, they recognized not their own selves, believing the image was in itself reality. In a sense, all religions are true, as they all describe that image mere or less accurately, but all before have failed to recognize that what they experienced was not without, but within; not transcendent, but immanent. Thus we see that the Humanists are right: God *is* Mankind. Also correct are the Pantheists in their recognition that God is all Nature. Even the Christians touch upon the truth when they realize that God is "revealed in the forests, the glens, the meadows...." The "religious experience" of mystics, which seems to show them "the naked face of God," is actually an experience of coming into complete attunement with this highest level of aware consciousness, often verbalized as a vision of "The Clear White Light."

Unfortunately, this experience of meeting ourselves face-to-face is all too rare, and generally interpreted with little comprehension and less insight. It can be brought about by intense meditation, fasting, sexual or religious ecstasy, or by various hallucinogenic chemicals. In all cases, the experience itself appears to be identical: an experience of total beingness, of ecstatic revelation. When it reaches the level of whole-species identification, it is known as *Gemeinschaftsgefühl:* "The Oceanic Experience," as described by Abraham Maslow, who says that the ability to have such experiences is one of the qualities of self-actualizing people. To anyone having such an experience, the phrase "Thou art God" becomes not merely an interesting philosophical speculation, but an amusingly obvious statement of an *a priori* fact of existence. It is equivalent to stating "Thou art That," or "I am alive!"

"Thou art God!" This bold proclamation of immanent Divinity is the cornerstone of the entire Neo-Pagan philosophy. Everything else is derivation. (Spoken while standing on one foot...) Heinlein says "all that groks is God." The key concept here is included in the word *grok*. It is commonly understood to mean a kind of total empathic understanding, in which identity of subject and object merge into One. To say "all that groks is God," however, and to be able to say "thou art God" to a grasshopper, entails either stretching this definition, or including it in a larger concept. Let us submit that such an all-embracing concept of grokkingness might be that of self-actualization: becoming what one potentially is (evolution). To say that a being *groks,* then, would be to say that it is being fully itself. To grok something would thus be to relate to it with ones full potential.

Thus, all plants and wild animals, all biomic organs, Terrabios, and the universe itself, grok. Self. Oneness. Identity. Purpose. Place. Only man and some of his domesticates do not, as a matter of course, grok. Only we do not instinctively know who we are and act accordingly. (We must recognize, however, that this root of virtually all human suffering is also the root of virtually all human greatness. Without the possibility of failure, success is meaningless.) So man has little species awareness, and kills his fellow man. So he has little life awareness, and

exterminates other species. So he has little environmental awareness, and desecrates his planet. And of course, man has too little self-awareness, and destroys his own being with his fears, anxieties, hates, doubts, and purposelessness, which he institutes into his religions, so shaping his societies.

For too long has man searched for his Divinity—always in the wrong places; without himself, rather than within. Prophets have glimpsed the truth, and have tried to point the way: "You are God(s) (Elohim)" (Psalm 82:6, John 10:34). Yet man has insisted on searching above, beyond, in stone, cloud, ether, whirlwind, pillar of fire or cathedral. And behold, nobody out there answered him. Not finding God where man looked, man concluded that God was dead, or never was at all.

And yet always there were some who did look inward, and knew. They found Divinity within themselves, and turning outward, saw this same Divinity manifest in each living creature, and in trees, seasons, sex, nature—Life itself. They celebrated Life, and their joy was an affront to the deadened sensitivities of the death-dancers, the Puritans, the monotheistic followers of the fanatic priests of anti-Life. And the celebrants of Life and Nature, the lovers of the great trees, the naked dancers of moonlit groves, were called *Pagans*—country people—and they were hunted out and put to death.

Monotheism is a synonym for genocide. The ancient Hebrews, waged war on the uncircumcised; the Moslems killed the Christians, Hindus and Jews; and the Christians—most efficient mass murderers of all—have decimated the ranks of American Indians, Jews, Africans, Islanders, Asians, and each other. "The only good Indian is a dead Indian." "The only good Gook is a dead Gook." And by their witch hunts, inquisitions, and stake they virtually exterminated our Paleo-Pagan predecessors.

But we are a Phoenix. In the midst of the most monolithic monotheistic state ever erected, Neo-Pagans are arising, coming together. We have rejected the sterility of transcendent Deity, and have found Divinity where it was all along: within each of us. Thou art God! Goddess bless us, everyone!

What, then, is the particular function of Neo-Paganism in the vast organism of Terrabios? As the only cells of the Noosphere yet to recognize the unity of our entire Biosphere, we are inevitably in the vanguard of the advancing consciousness that will ultimately result in the awakening of the great planetary Mind. Yet at this moment, in the hour before Dawn, we find Terraba—our Earthly Biosphere, our Great Mother Earth Goddess—is already dying from cancer of the brain. And what is worse, we find that this cancer is we ourselves—Mankind. "We have met the enemy and he is us" (Pogo). What can we do? Well, first we must cure the cancer. Of course, it is highly possible that the cancer may cure itself through radiation therapy—a global nuclear holocaust—but at what price to the Earth? Some have said that the Earth would probably be better off without man, but decapitation is a rather drastic cure for a brain tumor.

No, it is plain that the solution depends on Mankind awakening to a sense of his function and responsibility as a vital organ in the larger body of the planetary biosphere. It is an essential duty of all aware, intelligent people—and Neo-Pagans especially—to get behind every peace, ecological, and population-oriented movement we can find with all the support we can muster; to work for increased awareness and sensitivity of all to our present crisis; to initiate and encourage massive responses, creative and constructive, all levels. If we succeed, a glorious new stage in planetary evolution awaits us. If we fail, we lose all. For if Terrebia dies, we die with Her.

How can we shine this light into eyes blinded by generations of living in darkness? By telling about it, of course, but most of all, BY LIVING IT! *We* must each live our own lives as conscious Gods: aware, courageous and resolute. *We* must show by living examples what Man can be—and help others to follow in our footsteps. *We* must ourselves continue learning—growing and grokking—and become as guides and torchbearers to others who seek our path. *We* must establish alternate societies and communities, in which humans live in eco-psychic harmony with themselves, each other, and all life of their biome, demonstrating on a small scale the larger role of mankind upon the planet.

We must spread this message by any and all means possible, until it appears to all people everywhere as clear and as obvious as sunshine, and we must learn and teach others how and what must be done. If nothing else (and it is a great deal else!), it is a matter of survival. It is estimated by ecologists, that, at our present rate of population growth and environmental desecration, our Earth (and, just incidentally, Mankind) has less than thirty years of life. WE MUST SUCCEED! Or die trying....

GE Vol. IV, No. 41 (Lugnhasadh 1971) 67-8

Sabbat Songs

I hear the spirits beckon call
In quiet, wind-borne whisperings;
And Mother Earth has given birth
To dark, enchanting mysteries.

Come and sing the night with me;
In Sabbat songs our lives commune.
And we will love with heart and mind,
And dance with Sun and Moon.

See the fires upon the hill
Whose flames proclaim the Sabbat ground,
And hear the drums that bid us come
With pulsing, vibrant sound.

Below the castle towers we'll run,
While kings and Christians sleep,
And sing the ancient Sabbat songs
As through the flames we leap.

Those vernal flames will warm our blood,
And autumn winds will chill our souls.
You will wear your crescent crown,
And I my crown of gold.

—*Samm Dickens, CAW*

GE Vol. VIII, No. 75 (Yule 1975) 10

Common Themes of Neo-Pagan Religious Orientation

Abstracted from meetings of the ecumenical Council of Themis
Califia South Members, Summer 1970

Polytheism

Polytheism begins with the Female and Male principles, the Goddess and God, or Divine Lovers, from Whose love all creation is derived. The multiplicity of Goddess and God individualities are aspects of the infinite variety of creation stemming from Goddess and God. Slightly revising a saying, it may be asserted that the omnipotence of Divinity is merely another word for Its polytheistic unity. We find agreement with *Star Trek*'s "Vulcan Edict" that "the glory of creation is in its infinite diversity; and in the myriad ways in which our differences combine to create beauty and meaning."

Freedom of Worship

Through religious practice we, as individuals, strive to intensify and expand our experience of Divinity and our sense of dynamically harmonious relation with Great Nature.

Worship, as an essential part of religious practice, is both a venerating of and a communing with Divinity. Because people are unique individuals, we differ in our images, conceptions, and experience of Divinity and in our ways of worshipping this Divinity.

Therefore, freedom of worship is an indispensable condition of our development and fulfillment as human beings, so long as our worship is not seriously hurtful to others.

Full support may be asserted for Article 18 of the Universal Declaration of Human Rights: "Everyone has the right to freedom of thought, conscience and religion; this right includes freedom to change his religion or belief, and freedom, either alone or in community with others and in public or in private, to manifest his religion or belief in teaching, practice, worship and observation."

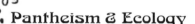

Art by Fred Adams

Pantheism & Ecology

Nature is Divinity made manifest, the perennial Love Feast of the Divine Lovers, Goddess and God, made manifest. It is creativity, continuity, balance, beauty and truth of Life.

Everything we encounter in the biosphere is a part of Nature, and ecology reveals the pattern of that is-ness, the natural relationships among all these things and the organic unity of all of them as a biospheric whole. Thus ecology shows the pattern of humanity's proper and creative involvement with Nature—that Nature which encompasses our own life and on proper relation to which our life and development depend.

Of all humanity's secular studies, ecology comes closest to bringing us to the threshold of religious relationship to our world. Ecology not only confirms the wonders of form and function that other secular studies have revealed, but it brings these into organic union with each other as one dynamic, living Whole; and it points out the conditions for the well-being of both this overall Unity and the parts that compose it.

An intensive realization of these conditions, and of one's own immediate role in their sustainment and development, brings one to the threshold of religious awe. To worship Nature, therefore, is to venerate and commune with Divinity as the dynamically organic perfection of the Whole.

Eroticism

The word is derived from *Eros,* the Greek God of Love. Love is the essence of Divinity, and is the "creative action of the universe." Eroticism in its religious reference venerates love play and the sexual act as divine, as creative physical expression of our union with Nature as we reconcile sexual opposites. Hence, love play and sex are natural and beautiful whenever shared in mutual consent.

Sexual freedom in this comprehensive sense is a primary doctrine of most Pagan religions. It is the freedom to express love sensually, to be physically natural, to be atone with Nature in the affectional functioning of the physical being, and to be free from guilt conditioned by repressive, anti-natural life styles. To deny or denigrate sexuality in humanity is to deny or denigrate Nature, and, therefore, Divinity.

Peacefulness & Self-Defense

If humans are creative beings, we have freedom of choice within the limits of our nature, conditioning, and vision. We can and must say both Yes and No. It is at our peril that we impair our capacity both for vigorous promotion of creative enterprise and for vigorous defense of such past achievement as continues to be of creative value.

We try to create and practice a style of living in which violence and the occasion for it are progressively reduced through both our own inner growth and our way of dealing with the outer affairs and conditions of our lives. In this sense we are wagers of peace and harmony within a context of delight in creative and sensuous living.

Since individual persons are unique in their experience and destiny, however, we expect to find considerable variation in the degree to which violence and the initiation of coercion, against both humanity and non-human nature, are condoned and practiced. We as Pagans deplore and censure all wanton violence and destruction, all exploitation, all murder, and all habitual coercion, including habitually punitive attitudes and practices. To Gods and men these are abominations.

Defense of home and loved ones against immediate threat of death or severe suffering is a natural reflex. When finesse fails to deflect or thwart such aggression, violence would seem to be the only recourse; save when all of those threatened can choose death as an immediately significant act in the pattern of overall harmony and freedom.

Life & After-Life:

The actualization of a person as a whole is dynamic, a continuing evolution, a vigorous and whole-hearted living in *this* life in *this* time-and-space world. Such view does not negate growth of specialization in life style or personal inclination, but it does negate the idea that this life in this world should be submitted as a matter of policy to restraint and chastisement, especially in its sensuous aspects, for the supposed benefit of a future, after-death life or condition.

Many Pagans, however, assert belief in reincarnation as a periodic flowering of the soul in sensuous flesh, in an objective body among objective surroundings. They further assert, therefore, that the quality and direction of our activity as moral beings is by no means without definite implication for the conditions of a soul's life between bodily death and rebirth.

Sacred Myths:

The sacred myths have an efficacy so subtle, comprehensive, and powerful as to preclude duplication in any other form than that of the myth itself. They are a tapestry of truths, but are not to be interpreted as reports of historical events. They are a dimension of theological reality and at the same time a subtle essence, like that of an herb, affecting the whole being of those who take them in, and especially that part of our being beyond the threshold of workaday awareness. They are a wondrous and inspired form of religious art.

Pagan Musings

*by **Tony Kelly**, Pagan Movement, Wales*

 E'RE OF THE OLD RELIGION, sired of Time, and born of our beloved Earth Mother. For too long the people have trodden a stony path that goes only onward beneath a sky that goes only upwards. The Horned God plays in a lonely glade for the people are scattered in this barren age and the winds carry his plaintive notes over deserted heaths and reedy moors and into the lonely grasses. Who knows now the ancient tongue of the Moon? And who speaks still with the Goddess? The magic of the land of Lirien and the old Pagan gods have withered in the dragon's breath; the old ways of magic have slipped into the well of the past, and only the rocks now remember what the moon told us long ago, and what we learned from the trees, and the voices of grasses and the scents of flowers.

We're Pagans and we worship the Pagan gods, and among the people there are Witches yet who speak with the moon and dance with the Horned One. But a Witch is a rare Pagan in these days, deep and inscrutable, recognisable only by her own kind, by the light in her eyes and the love in her breast, by the magic in her hands and the lilt of her tongue and by her knowledge of the real. But the Wiccan way is one way. There are many; there are Pagans the world over who worship the Earth Mother and the Sky Father, the Rain God and the Rainbow Goddess, the Dark One and the Hag on the mountain, the Moon Goddess and the Little People in the mists on the other side of the veil. A Pagan is one who worships the goddesses and gods of nature, whether by observation or by study, whether by love or admiration, or whether in their sacred rites with the Moon, or the great festivals of the Sun.

Many suns ago, as the pale dawn of reason crept across the Pagan sky, man grew out of believing in the gods. He has yet to grow out of disbelieving in them. He who splits the Goddess on an existence-nonexistence dichotomy will earn himself only paradoxes, for the gods are not so divided and nor the magic lands of the Brother of Time. Does a mind exist? Ask Her and She will tell you yes, but seek Her out, and She'll elude you. She is in every place, and in no place, and you'll see Her works in all places, but Herself in none. Existence was the second-born from the Mother's womb and contains neither the first-born, nor the unborn. Show us your mind, and we'll show you the gods! No matter that you can't for we can't show you the gods. But come with us and the Goddess Herself will be our love and the God will call the tune. But a brass penny for your reason!, for logic is a closed ring, and the child doesn't validate the Mother, nor the dream the dreamer. And what matter the wars of opposites to she who has fallen in love with a whirlwind or to the lover of the arching rainbow.

But tell us of your Goddess as you love Her, and the gods that guide your works, and we'll listen with wonder, for to do less would be arrogant. But we'll do more, for the heart of man is aching for memories only half forgotten, and the Old Ones only half unseen. We'll write the old myths as they were always written and we'll read them on the rocks and in the caves and in the deep of the greenwood's shade, and we'll hear them in the rippling mountain streams and in the rustling of the leaves, and we'll see them in the storm clouds, and in the evening mists. We've no wish to create a new religion for our religion is as old as the hills and older, and we've no wish to bring differences together. Differences are like different flowers in a meadow, and we are all one in the Mother.

What need is there for a Pagan movement since our religion has no teachings and we hear it in the wind and feel it in the stones and the Moon will dance with us as She will? There is a need. For long the Divider has been among our people and the tribes of man are no more. The sons of the Sky Father have all but conquered Nature, but they have poisoned Her breast and the Mother is sad for the butterflies are dying and the night draws on. A curse on the conquerors! But not of us, for they curse themselves for they are Nature too. They have stolen our magic and sold it to the mindbenders and the mindbenders tramp a maze that has no outlet for they fear to go down into the dark waters, and they fear the real for the One who guards the path.

Where are the Pagan shrines? And where do the people gather? Where is the magic made? And where are the Goddess and the Old Ones? Our shrines are in the fields and on the mountains, in the stars and in the wind, deep in the greenwood and on the algal rocks where two streams meet. But the shrines are deserted, and if we gathered in the arms of the Moon for our ancient rites to be with our gods as we were of old, we would be stopped by the dead who now rule the Mother's land and claim rights of ownership on the Mother's breast, and make laws of division and frustration for us. We can no longer gather with our gods in a public place and the old rites of communion have been driven from the towns and cities ever deeper into the heath where barely a handful of heathens have remained to guard the old secrets and enact the old rites. There is magic in the heath far from the cold grey society, and there are islands of magic hidden in the entrails of the metropoles behind closed doors, but the people are few, and the barriers between us are formidable. The Old Religion has become a dark way, obscure, and hidden in the protective bosom of the night. Thin fingers turn the pages of a book of shadows while the Sunshine seeks in vain His worshippers in His leafy glades.

Here, then, is the basic reason for a Pagan Movement: we must create a Pagan society wherein everyone shall be free to worship the goddesses and gods of Nature, and the relationship between a worshipper and her gods shall be sacred and inviolable, provided only that in her love of her own gods, she doesn't curse the names of the gods of others.

It's not yet our business to press the lawmakers with undivided endeavor to unmake the laws of repression and, with the Mother's love, it may never become our business for the stifling tides of dogmatism are at last already in ebb. Our first work, and our greatest wish, is to come together, to be with each other in our tribes for we haven't yet grown from the Mother's breast to the stature of the gods. We're of the Earth, and sibs to all the children of wild Nature, born long ago in the warm mud of the ocean floor; we were together then, and we were together in the rain forests long before that dark day when, beguiled by the pride of the Sky Father, and forgetful of the Mother's love, we killed Her earlier-born children and impoverished the old genetic pool. The Red Child lives yet in America; the Black Child has not forsaken the gods; the old Australians are still with their nature gods; the Old Ones still live deep in the heart of Mother India, and the White Child has still a foot on the old Wiccan way, but Neanderthaler is no more and her magic faded as the Lli and the Arehan burst their banks and the ocean flowed in to divide the Isle of Erin from the land of the White Goddess.

Man looked with one eye on a two-faced god when he reached for the heavens and scorned the Earth which alone is our life and our provider and the bosom to which we have ever returned since the dawn of Time. He who looks only to reason to plumb the unfathomable is a fool, for logic is an echo already implicit in the question, and it has no voice of its own; but he is no greater fool than he who scorns logic or derides its impotence from afar, but fears to engage in fair combat when he stands on his opponent's threshold. Don't turn your back on Reason, for his thrust is deadly; but confound him and he'll yield for his code of combat is honourable. So here is more of the work of the Pagan Movement. Our lore has become encrusted over the ages with occult trivia and the empty vapourings of the lost. The occult arts are in a state of extreme decadence; astrology is in a state of disrepute and fears to confront the statistician's sword; alien creeds oust our native arts and, being as little understood as our own forgotten arts, are just as futile for their unfamiliarity. Misunderstanding is rife. Disbelief is black on every horizon, and vampires abound on the blood of the credulous. Our work is to reject the trivial, the irrelevant and the erroneous, and to bring the lost-children of the Earth Mother again into the court of the Sky Father where reason alone will avail. Belief is the deceit of the credulous; it has no place in the heart of a Pagan.

But while we are sad for those who are bemused by Reason, we are deadened by those who see no further than his syllogisms as he turns the eternal wheel of the Great Tautology. We were not fashioned in the mathematician's computations, and we were old when the first alchymist was a child. We have walked in the magic forest, bewitched in the old Green Thinks; we have seen the cauldron and the one become many and the many in the one; we know the Silver Maid of the moonlight and the sounds of the cloven feet. We have heard the pipes on the twilight ferns, and we've seen the spells of the Enchantress, and Time be stilled. We've been into eternal darkness where the Night Mare rides and rode her to the edge of the abyss, and beyond, and we know the dark face of the rising Sun. Spin a spell of words and make a magic knot; spin it on the magic loom and spin it with the gods. Say it in the old chant and say it to the Goddess, and in Her name. Say it to a dark well and breathe it on a stone. There are no signposts on the untrod way, but we'll make our rituals together and bring them as our gifts to the Goddess and Her God in the great rites. Here, then, is our work in the Pagan Movement; to make magic where the gods would wish it, and to come together in our ancient festivals of birth, and life, of death and of change in the old rhythm. We'll print the rituals that can be shared in the written word; we'll do all in our power to bring the people together, to teach those who would learn, and to learn from those who can teach. We will initiate groups, bring people to groups, and groups to other groups in our common devotion to the goddesses and gods of Nature. We will not storm the secrets of any coven, nor profane the tools, the magic, and still less, the gods of another.

We'll collect the myths of the ages, of our people and of the Pagans of other lands, and we'll study the books of the wise and we'll talk to the very young. And whatever the Pagan needs in her study, or her worship, then it is our concern, and the Movement's business to do everything possible to help each other in our worship of the gods we love.

We are committed with the lone Pagan on the seashore, with he who worships in the fastness of a mountain range or she who sings the old chant in a lost valley far from the metalled road. We are committed with the wanderer, and equally with the prisoner, disinherited from the Mother's milk in the darkness of the industrial wens. We are committed too with the coven, with the circular dance in the light of the full moon, with the great festivals of the sun, and with the gatherings of the people. We are committed to build our temples in the towns and in the wilderness, to buy the lands and the streams from the landowners and give them to the Goddess for Her children's use, and we'll replant the greenwood as it was of old for love of the dryad stillness, and for love of our children's children.

When the streams flow clear and the winds blow pure, and the sun never more rises unrenowned nor the moon ride in the skies unloved; when the stones tell of the Horned God and the greenwood grows deep to call back Her own ones, then our work will be ended and the Pagan Movement will return to the beloved womb of our Old Religion, to the Nature goddess and gods of Paganism.

(Selene Community, Cân y Lloer, Ffarmers, Llanwrda, Sir Gaerfyrddin, Cymru, Wales)

GE Vol. VI, No. 55 (Litha 1973) 5–7

We Are the Freemen

*by **Regis of Amithaine** (Paul Edwin Zimmer)*

E ARE THE FREEMEN; THE WILD People. Our Yoga is the Yoga of the Changing Time. Tribesmen and Forest-Folk, we shall feed ourselves from the breast of Nature, and wandering in the wild, we shall not note when the Cities go up in suicidal smoke, and the worship of the Machine is gone forever.

In our clothes and our actions we blend ourselves with the eternal men, and we shall plant our seeds in the fertile place, and stalk the deer through the silent forest, and chip our arrows from the sounding stone. Our Freedom is within ourselves. The Machine Men will say that we live in the Past, and not know that they themselves are past. And we shall ride to Tournament and contend with Elvish Knights, and drink from springs the Unicorn has blessed, and we shall find the Holy Grail.

We are close to Faery; our dress is the dress of the dwellers of Faery, and our minds hold the magic of the Timeless Land. And the Lord and the Lady shall come to us in the embrace of Love, and we shall be One, One in the freedom of our hearts. The great forest is eternal, the Beloved of Pan, and in its green depths our Nests shall be established, and our tribes shall grow and flourish as we rear our Free Children, dwellers on the Borders of Faery.

All Time Is Now. Remember the ways of your ancestors, and don your shining armour. Leave the Machine, and ride into the forest. Leave behind the bomb and the gun, and take up the lance and shield and sword. Learn to live in the Wilderness, and leave the womb of the Machine behind forever. Clothe yourself in garments of old, and ride on the Quest of the Timeless Land.

We shall dwell in the forest, and study ancient Magic, and wander with the Elves and the deer. Our tribes shall grow in the Great Forests, far from the machines and free from fear. We shall learn the Arts of the Ancient Men, and dwell in Timelessness. We shall drink deep of Enchanted Potions, and chant the glory of the Timeless Land. And over us the Machine shall have no power, for we are the Freemen.

GE Vol. VI, No. 56 (Lughnasadh 1973) 6

Hymn of the Moon-Child to Diana

*by **Samm Dickens (Bran th' Blessed)** CAW*

Diana came down to the pearly pool
Upon her silent swift-hooved steed;
Came to the pool in the purple night,
Came to bathe in the bouyant light
That kissed across the cool, crystal waters.
The woods watched;
The winds waited —
For the Goddess had come to Her Temple.

From the moonlit meadows
The green grasses sang a silent song.
From the frozen forests
The tall trees sang along...
A silent hymn of love,
A soundless song of praise.

No man knelt to pray nor sang that night.
No man sought to hear that hymn
Nor see that sight.
For all mankind lay sleeping,
Dreaming of killing and weeping,
Filled with hate and distrust.

The Goddess is gone, is taken to flight;
Into the dark forest has followed the night;
Into the dismal, dark forest has gone.
The pale, placid pool is left alone,
But for the trees and the grasses.

GE Vol. VII, No. 68 (Oimelc 1975) 15

An Aquarian Manifesto

by *P.E.I. Bonewits,* ArchDruid, ADF

 LL INTELLIGENT BEINGS HAVE THE right to worship who, what, where, when, why, and how they wish; provided that they do not violate the similar rights of others. All intelligent beings have as well the right (some would say, "duty") to develop their talents—mental, physical, psychic, and others—to the highest degree possible; subject as always to the equal rights of others. It is in this complex interplay of rights that the children of the Aquarian Age may be distinguished from their ancestors of previous ages.

According to astrological tradition, the term "Aquarian Age" implies a time in which there is increased concern with the ways in which each individual can live by his or her own lights, while guaranteeing the same freedom to all others. All those, therefore, who work for the greater evolution of consciousness and freedom may be justly called "Aquarians," regardless of the day or year of their actual birth.

Aquarians—Neopagan, Neochristian, Agnostic or of any other faith—are by definition tolerant of all life-affirming beliefs and organizations. They do not proclaim the existence of any "One-True-Right-And-Only-Way" but rather that every intelligent being must find her or his own path.

We will not, however, in the name of tolerance or any other ideal, allow ourselves to be persecuted or exterminated by anti-life individuals or organizations, whether secular or religious.

As Aquarians we do not, in our religious services, magical rituals, psychic activities, or in our private lives, engage in the commission or encouragement of felony crimes-with-victims (as defined by civil law and modern sociological research). We do not therefore engage in murder, rape, maiming, torture of animals, grand larceny, or other heinous crimes; and we will no longer quietly accept accusations that we do.

Neither do Aquarians use our talents—whether we call them "psychic," "magical," "spiritual," "paranormal," or something else—to achieve ends or through means that, if done physically, would constitute such felony crimes with victims. Accusations in this area will not go uncountered either.

We know full well that new witchburners seek to once again light the stakes of persecution with the fires of bigotry and hate. Equally well do we know that, despite our innumerable differences with one another, the time has come for us to stand together against the forces of fear and oppression. The very survival of ourselves, our children, and our planet depends upon the outcome of our present struggles.

Therefore: we will use whatever means exist to preserve, protect and defend our religious, civil, economic, and human rights, as well as our reputations, from all those who would slander, libel, defame, suppress, or otherwise persecute us for our beliefs. We will no longer allow self-righteous followers of anti-life beliefs to prevent us from the free exercise of our human and constitutional rights. We will no longer allow anyone with impunity to publicly accuse us of being "Satanists," "devil worshippers," "charlatans," "lunatics," or any other loaded terms of slander and libel designed to denigrate, defame, or prevent us from the peaceful and legal spreading of our beliefs. We will no longer hesitate to bring civil suits and/or criminal charges against our would-be inquisitors whenever possible, no matter how wealthy or powerful they may be.

Aquarians together—Witches and wizards; Pagans and psychics; priests and parapsychologists; mystics, mediums and magicians; astrologers, diviners, and occultists of both sexes and all races, many faiths and traditions, ages and nationalities—hereby agree upon our battle cry as we declare war upon those who would persecute us:

NEVER AGAIN THE BURNING!

GE Vol. VI, No. 58 (Samhain 1973) 5

Author's Note: This was first published in 1973 CE, *as part of the founding of the Aquarian Anti-Defamation League, Inc. (now defunct). What became the official A.A.D.L. logo, minus the name of the organization, can be seen here. I originally designed it to be easy to turn into a graffiti stencil, and based it on the logos being used by the Black Panthers and other radical movements. I've released it for use by any Aquarian organizations and individuals who agree with the words of the Manifesto above and are not frightened off by its, let us say, "forceful" symbolism.*

The phrases "pro-life" and "anti-life beliefs" made some folks assume that A.A.D.L. and I were part of what became known as the "pro-life" (i.e.

anti-abortion rights) movement, but such was never our intent. I've always been pro-choice, but there were members of A.A.D.L. on both sides of that particular controversy.

The phrase I coined at the end became part of the vocabulary of the North American Neopagan community, though some Wiccans added the word "Times" at the end, to refer to the "Burning Times," i.e., the Renaissance persecutions of alleged "witches."

On my website I've clarified the phrasing, punctuation, and capitalization a bit to make the text easier to understand, but it's essentially as it was 25 years ago. We've come far as a movement since then, but we still have a long way to go. —PEIB

Why I Am a Pagan

by **Vicki Rhodes** *(PTE Luta Winyan), CAW*

HEN THE SPIRIT SWELLS WITHIN me, I love to go walking slowly through the small wooded park close to my home; or perhaps go and sit in the flower garden in the midst of the roses and marigolds, and oftentimes when I sit in the wonder of the plush green around me and the vast blueness over my head, I ask myself, "Why am I a Pagan?"

When no answer comes immediately, I lie down in the grass and close my eyes, letting my ears be filled with the sweet sounds of birds chirping and my nose be filled with the perfumed breath of the flowers. After all, I didn't come out here to ask myself deep philosophical questions; I came out here to tune into Mother and do a little meditating.

Soon it's time to return to the world of illusion, so I gather together what's been given up to the world of the senses, and walk toward home. I leave the roses nodding in the wind but carry their impression in my heart. I pause before the door to my house and take a last longing look at the great sky before exchanging it for the dinginess of my living room.

My parents are watching Billy Graham on television while he warns of all the hellfire and brimstone awaiting all those who have lived a life of evil. Evil, he says, lives in the hearts and minds of those who have fallen

prey to their natural instincts. My mother looks at me and says, "That's what will happen to you for disbelieving in the omnipotent power of God!"

Rather than defend myself and start another theological argument, I just keep quiet and thank the Goddess that I'm not the only one, and that there are others like me who feel about the Earth as I do.

The words "subdue the Earth" pound in my head like a sledgehammer pounding on concrete, accompanied with images of things I've seen and felt: a strip-mined hill in Wyoming that had the face of a woman who was crying blood-red tears; the trash in the Missouri River; the unbearable silence of an almost empty woods at sunset.

At last the question has an answer. I who am an Earthborn child must have a place where I can meet others like myself. A place where we can share our respect for the Mother and ideas on how to live in Harmony with Her in a world so intent on destroying Her. That's why I'm a member of CAW, why I've stayed as long as I have, and why I will continue to stay.

Why am I a Pagan? I prefer to their dogma my walks in the park where the Goddess can be seen and felt. If this is Paganism, then until it's called something else, I am a Pagan.

GE Vol. VII, No. 69 (Ostara 1975) 7

Older? Yes. Wiser? We Hope. But Still Hopeful.

Impressions of 30 years of Neo-Pagandom

by *Tom Williams*, CAW

"Tom Williams once told me that CAW's goal was to change the world. 'After all,' he said laughing, 'why be petty?' Another time he said that the goal of Neo-Paganism was to learn to 'see ourselves as a total entity—rational and irrational at once, within a total environment *and with a* total identification with all life.'" —Margot Adler, Drawing Down the Moon

HE ABOVE QUOTATION WAS MADE around 1975 or 1976 when Margot was conducting interviews for her book—over twenty years ago. In all, those of us who were around near the beginnings of the Neo-Pagan movement have had some thirty years to try to change the world or at least to examine our efforts in trying to do so. The past thirty years have been a period of maturation and aging. Maturation is the collection of experience and—more rarely—wisdom. Aging involves the expenditure of a finite store of time and energy. After a certain time, maturity will force you to assess your aging.

Maturing involves a process of socialization where—in crass terms—the starry-eyed idealist runs into cold reality. At that point you can either give up or develop strategy. That is to say, you learn in order to go forward. We have certainly found that the world has not changed simply because we thought it was a good idea. But neither have we given up. And the world has changed—albeit not always in ways we would have liked.

Now, we are looking at the rising of the Next Generation, of children born and raised as Neo-Pagans. Like it or not, those of us entering our fifties and some staring the sixties straight in the eyes will inevitably reflect on "what a long strange trip it's been," and the value of the time and energy we have expended in our lives. A great deal of that assessment will depend on what our expectations were. If our sole intent was to remold the world in our image or as one brash youth (named Williams) once put it, to see the last 2,000 years referred to as the "Christian interlude," we're likely to be bitterly disappointed.

Still, the world has changed and in that change there are elements that give rise to great hope as well as to great apprehension. The Neo-Pagan movement in the U.S. arose amid the clamor of the Vietnam war. For some, that war epitomized the life-denying patriarchal culture we had vowed to transform. Many, but not all, Pagans in the 60s were involved to some degree in opposing the war. The Vietnam war not only ended but it brought down a president once thought invincible. In 1989 the Cold War ended amid the shambles of Communism. But as many have pointed out, Communism was just a less-efficient, more oppressive aspect of the general industrial paradigm that has arisen from the biblical charge to have dominion over the Earth.

What, if anything, did we as Pagans have to do with these momentous events? I think we can certainly say that we were a part of the forces that brought them about. But the forces I speak of are so vast and complex that I'm tempted to ascribe such changes in world direction to the basic will of life to exist, a will that expresses itself in millions of ways—as hunger strikers, as demonstrators against all forms of injustice and cruelty, as recyclers, as Pagans doing rituals for peace, as prisoners of conscience being dragged to nameless dungeons and forgotten by all but a few loved ones; as native peoples struggling to retain ancestral lands; as protesters throwing themselves in front of logging trucks in the Pacific Northwest—as one lone young man standing down a tank in Tienanmen Square.

And we were there, too. We have done rituals, we have visioned, meditated, chanted, sung, invoked the Goddess and God, cast circles, done focused workings and harmonically converged. And something is happening. Something is awakening. Something deep and awesome within the life sphere of the planet is stirring and we think we may be in tune with what that is. Maturity, however, warns us against the hubris of thinking that we alone worked the magick that has brought it about.

To be even partially in empathy with this awakening or re-awakening conscious life force may be the greatest gift of all. To dance with it, with Her, to watch as an awareness of Her slowly permeates even the statements of politicians, appears in advertising and even issues from formerly tradition-bound pulpits, and to hope and pray that it is not too late, is, I believe, what maturity will grant to those who years ago set out to change the world.

Our challenges remain immense. The danger of destruction either by war or self-poisoning is not past and the outcome is by no means certain. I believe the biggest challenge in the near future lies in fundamentalism. Fundamentalism comes in many forms besides the Christian variety. There are the well-known Islamic and Hindu brands of fundamentalism. There is even a secular brand that shows up as clinging to old economic patterns (like the idea of endless material progress) that no longer work. I think we can be guardedly optimistic about even these dangers.

In the 1920s fascism arose partly as a reaction to the transformation from a basically agrarian to an industrial, money-based economy. Fascism contained heavy doses of nostalgia to cloak its brutality. By the same token, fundamentalism is a reaction to diversity. Diversity has been accelerated by the increased mobility of populations and by communications including the Internet. These things not only cause the mingling of ethnic groups. They also cause the spread of ideas. There is no plague worse for entrenched power than the spread of ideas. Today that spread cannot be stopped or even ultimately controlled.

The fundamentalist reaction will be and already is bloody. But I believe it is ultimately doomed. Diversity is our hope and ally. This is because somewhere within every sincerely held teaching, however buried by interpretation, distortion or political interest, there can be found affirmation. If people are exposed to enough different teachings they will begin to discover that common thread, the life-affirming little jewels buried under the dross deposited by dour-faced churchmen and mullahs.

—Jesse Wolf Hardin

It has been one of the missions of eclectic Neo-Paganism to mine many of the world's traditions (especially the wisdom of native peoples that may soon be lost forever) for these jewels and to make them accessible to others through honoring and understanding them. Many dedicated people have spent their lives pursuing obscure traditions and practices, assembling knowledge that eventually all leads back to Her in the many forms She appears to Her peoples. In many cases, these labors of love have been at the sacrifice of comfort and security and it's time we assessed that situation as well.

Since its birth in the early 60s, Neo-Paganism has not been noted for monetary opulence. On the one hand we can be proud that it hasn't produced any gurus with 14 Rolls Royces and flanked by guards with AK-47s. On the other hand, we haven't done very well at taking care of our people, especially those who forsook "straight" careers in their devotion to what they cared about. I can remember a time when the mere idea of supporting one's self, however frugally, by working full-time for a Pagan organization or publication was considered anathema. People were accused of living off the Pagan community for daring to suggest that they might earn some slim support in return for full-time work.

That has changed somewhat in the recent past and people are no longer chastised for eking out a meager existence. But by and large their economic situations remain marginal. The effectiveness and strength of Pagan organizations and publications has been directly hindered as a result. I attribute this ongoing and crippling situation to what I call "Pagan poverty chic." Pagan poverty chic, I think, stems from some corner of victim mentality that says it's noble to be destitute. This is the opposite of arrogantly flaunting one's wealth. Neither is noble. Overcoming, carrying on in spite of poverty is noble, but overcoming poverty means achieving some level of ease. Only with that level of comfort that doesn't worry about where the next meal or this month's rent is coming from is it possible to work effectively in the world (to change it) or to work effective magick.

In this area, Neo-Paganism does not receive high marks. Where other religious groups have started from scratch to acquire land, build churches and temples, pay clergy and lay employees standard wages, set up insurance and retirement funds for their members, and even found hospitals and retirement homes, what by comparison has this community accomplished? Even immigrant groups such as Cambodian, Vietnamese, Tibetan and other refugees have managed to establish religious and cultural presences in this country in the past thirty years by offering something of value to their own members and also by appealing to the greater society.

Now that some of the Neo-Pagan movement's founders and most dedicated workers have been able to secure some compensation for their labors, they find themselves in their fifties without much prospect of any retirement. Ah, we grasshoppers of those halcyon days didn't think about winter when the ants were storing up their provisions. But winter is coming and we live in a society that is heartless to those who have not looked after themselves or provided for their own. For all the talk of "family" among Pagans, not much has shown up in the form of IRAs or CDs to help those who have contributed their finite stores of time and energy, who have aged for this community. And can anyone say "health care"?

The words "family" and "community" are many-faceted and an excoriating critique of our material performance cannot deny the immensely positive interpersonal and tribal developments that have sprung out of the Neo-Pagan movement. We've all been treated to the laments of conservatives over the breakdown of "traditional family values." It's a truism to decry the evils of street violence, drugs, teen pregnancy, poverty-stricken abandoned single mothers and to attribute all this to the evil machinations of those who don't live in the old "leave-it-to-Beaver" patriarchal home with the working dad and the housewife mom. That paradigm has passed because of the enormous socio-economic upheavals of a changing world. What many in the Neo-Pagan movement have done is to offer alternative "family values" that can provide for some human happiness even if they don't fit the traditional mold.

Pagan family values offer a choice of life and love styles that range from monogamy to extended family to polyamorous relationships to gay and lesbian relationships to bisexuality, to alternative intentional communities. The variety is rich indeed. The common denominator, however, is that Pagan family values represent *choices—not* prescriptions—for individuals and groups with various affinities. They are aimed at letting people find their most effective ways of relating intimately and nurturing children. They are not tailored to the needs of an industrial Moloch.

Many Pagans have dared to live their choice of these family values, often at grave risk to themselves and to the very families they love. Nothing is more dangerous than people who perceive, however erroneously, that their own children are threatened by the lifestyles of others. Many states still have draconian laws poised to destroy the lives of people seeking a more human or humane way of manifesting family and love relationships. And this courage and commitment on the part of many Pagans who never dreamed of leading an organization or publishing so much as a leaflet. This is one intensely powerful way of changing the world.

Pagans do support one another, at least morally if not financially. And that is vital. Over the years, the community has built a network of groups, publications, some small businesses, and most importantly, a vast array of gatherings and festivals. This network of national, regional, and local gatherings is fast becoming a nation within a nation, a moveable feast of rituals, workshops, celebrations, and myriad interpersonal encounters. It is being reinforced by the growing importance of the Internet as a medium for contact—at least initial contact—among Pagans all over the world and, for that old bugaboo of fundamentalism, the interchange of ideas.

And here I think is where the richness of the Neo-Pagan experience really shines. It's not enough to change the world, because we can't change the world without changing ourselves—as above, so below; as within, so without. We create our own realities and influence the realities of others. The many circles of friends and lovers that expand and get closer over the years and that can now watch a new generation coming into its own are the best and most immediate reward. The deep personal experiences I'm sure most of us can reach back to and touch and those close relationships that have lasted over some thirty years give comfort to the idea of aging—a process I still prefer to compare to fine wine rather than to roses. These have been the gems at the heart of the whole experience. But you know, I'm now fifty years old and I still want to change the world.

GE Vol. XXIX, No. 115 (Sept.-Oct. 1996) 7–9

We Won't Wait Any Longer

by Gwydion Pendderwen
(for Bran and Moria)

We have trusted no man's promise,
We have kept to just ourselves;
We have suffered from the lies
In all the books upon your shelves.
And our patience and endurance
Through the Burning Times and now
Have given us the strength to keep our vow.

chorus: We won't wait any longer,
We are stronger than before.
We won't wait any longer,
We are stronger.

You have grazed away the heather
And have razed the sacred grove;
You have driven native peoples
From the places that they love.
Though your greed has been unbounded,
You have felt the pangs of shame
Every time you trod upon the Mother's name.

ch: We won't wait any longer. etc.

Though you thought you had destroyed
The memory of the Ancient Way,
Still the people light the bale fires
Every year on Solstice day.
And on Beltane Eve and Samhain
You can find us on the hill
Invoking once again the Triple Will.

ch: We won't wait any longer. etc.

Through the ages many races
Have arisen and have gone,
But dispersed among the nations
Of the world we linger on.
Now the time has come to take
The sacred Cauldron of Rebirth
And fulfill our ancient pledges to the Earth.

ch: We won't wait any longer. etc.

GE Vol. XXV, NO. 96 (Ostara 1992) 6

The Pagan Lindsay

by *Caroline Tully*

Outside of Australia, most people these days seem to know about Norman Lindsay only from the 1994 film Sirens. *However beautiful that film was, it was more of a showcase for nude shots of Elle McPherson than an informative look at one of Australia's most talented Neo-Pagan artists and personalities. —CT*

 ORMAN LINDSAY (1879-1969) WAS one of Australia's most controversial artists. Often accused of perverting the young, diabolism and pornography, Lindsay was really just somewhat ahead of his time in promoting a Greco-Australian Neo-Pagan aesthetic.

Lindsay was born in Creswick near Ballarat in Victoria to Methodist parents, and his grandfather had been a Methodist missionary in Fiji. The middle child of ten children, both Norman and his older brother Lionel became vehemently anti-Christian as they got older. A Graeco-Roman influence appears evident in Norman's teenage years and can be discerned in the old photographs of the Lindsay teenagers dressed in flimsy togas or rabbit skins performing made-up versions of classically inspired plays or posing theatrically for the camera decked in leafy wreaths and the household curtains.

Norman Lindsay (self-portrait, 1923)

Lindsay was a man of varied interests: Olympian mythology, Spiritualism, the lost continent of Atlantis, sexuality, women and nature all combined to form a unique and personal type of worldview which many would term "Pagan." Norman believed, like the Greeks, that the gods had come down from Olympus in ancient times and begotten children on the people of Earth. The blood of the Gods ran in the veins of this race of Olympians and revealed itself in those acts of creativity which set great painters, sculptors, poets, musicians and writers apart from and above the "unblest Earthmen."

Norman's Classical gods were wise, powerful and benevolent whereas he felt that the Christian god was a mischievous invention of latter-day myth-makers and responsible for endless human misery. When the Sydney printer and publisher Charles Shepard once suggested that Lindsay illustrate the Bible he replied "Oh no, no, no, couldn't think of it Charlie. It's a very dangerous book, had a very bad influence."

Lindsay believed that ascetic Christianity was the enemy of all the things he himself stood for and made his opinion evident in his painting *Pollice Verso*, which depicted a crucified male figure on a cross in front of a crowd of his typically buxom figures who are giving the Roman "thumbs down" sign. Criticised as "anti-Christian, anti-social and degenerate," Lindsay explained that the work did not represent Christianity, but asceticism, which he saw as anti-life.

The best representation of his philosophy, he felt, was "Woman as Creatress," explaining this idea thus: "When the first World War ended, my mind was in a turmoil of emotions generated by it and these had to find an outlet. I found it in a concept of life dramatised by antithetical forces: energy versus inertia, conflict between love and hate, light and darkness, creation and destruction. In this concept the one assurance of continuity was the re-creation of life which drives it on into the future, over all obstacles and through all infernos. For the central symbol of that conflict I chose the image of femininity."

When discussing the public's reaction to his work he explained, "We know that the puritanical hatred of life has only one taboo: the glorification of the sex-function. Degrade it, spit at it, make a joke of it, brutalise it, falsify it, evade it and mob morality will approve. But lyricise it, love it, bring to its creation in art a passionate intensity and the mob will crucify you, or try to." Lindsay despised what he called the "witch-burning furies of the mass mind" and responded to this kind of hypocritical attitude with his painting *Crucified Venus* which represents life and vitality crucified on the cross of denial and "wowserism."

Lindsay felt that ribaldry

"Crucified Venus" by Norman Lindsay (1925)

was a fact of life: "Among the Romans, save only for the cold and academic Virgil, there is not one poet or prose writer who does not use its freed imagery wherever a theme calls for it. All of them, Catullus, Horace, Ovid, Martial, Juvenal, Apuleius, Petronius, would have regarded a ban put on such a salient aspect of the spectacle of life as a rank absurdity, which it is. That ban arrived with the blight of Christianity, with its priestly hatred of the body and its obscene obsession with

sin which spread a dark miasma of joylessness over all experience which makes life worth living. Life became a penalty inflicted on man for being the thing he is, and which he was designed to be by the construction of his being. A writer who presents men and women as creatures truncated below the waist is exposed as one who goes about without his trousers saying, 'see, I have had my testicles removed'…. I am fanatic enough to believe that my thought is something the world needs."

Lindsay was spurred on in his pursuits by his personal "daemon." "I am not implying occultism in my use of that word 'daemonic.' Every mind which has given itself to self-expression in art is aware of a directing agency outside its conscious control which it has agreed to label 'inspiration.' The Greeks had no doubt about its being an Entity as distinct from the Ego. Poets are most aware of it." Art critic, Robert Hughes, feels that the prolific Norman Lindsay has some claim to be the most forceful personality in the arts that Australia had ever seen. Immensely energetic, his talents spanned painting, drawing, watercolour, etching, art criticism, polemics, philosophy, illustration, political cartooning, novels, poetry, and writing for children. He even made model ships and sculpted concrete fauns.

Norman Lindsay's name is synonymous with images of satyrs, maenads and wild-eyed,

"Venus in Arcady" by Norman Lindsay (1938)

lustful supernaturals congregating in an Australian landscape. An important inspirational figure for Australian Pagans, Lindsay is a "spiritual forefather" who was at the vanguard of the endeavor to acclimatise European Pagan deities to the Australian landscape—an ongoing project amongst many Australian Pagans today. A brave and opinionated fellow, Lindsay deserves to be revered as a champion of individuality and freedom of religion, as well as an enthusiastic Goddess worshipper. Pilgrimage to his shrine at Springwood in the Blue Mountains may result in fruitful possession by the Muse for the earnest seeker.

Bibliography:

Letters and Liars: Norman Lindsay and the Lindsay Family. Joanna Mendelssohn. (Angus & Robertson, 1996).

Norman Lindsay: Impulse to Draw. Lin Bloomfield. (Bay Books, 1984).

Norman Lindsay Etchings. Daniel Thoman. (Angus & Robertson, 1982).

Norman Lindsay: A Personal Memoir. Douglas Stewart. (Nelson, 1975).

Norman Lindsay Pen Drawings. Lionel Lindsay. (Ure Smith, 1974).

Norman Lindsay: The Embattled Olympian. John Hetherington. (Oxford University Press, 1973).

Portrait of Pagan. Jane Lindsay. (Angus & Robertson, 1973).

Norman Lindsay Watercolours. Godfrey Blunden. (Ure Smith, 1973).

Redheap. Norman Lindsay. (Angus & Robertson, 1930, 1972).

A Curate in Bohemia. Norman Lindsay. (Angus & Robertson, 1913, 1970).

Model Wife : My Life with Norman Lindsay. Rose Lindsay. (Ure Smith, 1967).

GE Vol. XXXII, No. 135 (Sept.-Oct. 2000) 24–27

Caroline Tully has been a Witch and Pagan since 1985. She is avidly interested in the many permutations of modern Paganism and has undergone initiation into several magickal systems including Witchcraft, the Church of All Worlds and the Ordo Templi Orientis. She is currently studying Classics and Archaeology at the University of Melbourne, Australia, with a focus on the Pagan religions on the ancient Mediterranean. A fervid article-writer, Caroline has been published in over 20 international Pagan publications including *The Cauldron, Green Egg* and *New-Witch,* and for six years was a feature writer and reviewer for Australia's *Witchcraft* magazine. She has also contributed chapters to *Practising the Witch's Craft* by Douglas Ezzy; *Pop! Goes the Witch* by Fiona Horne; and *Celebrating the Pagan Soul* by Laura Wildman. Caroline lives in Australia.

http://necropolisnow.blogspot.com

"Woman and Faun" by Norman Lindsay (1923)

Chapter 2.
New Witches, Greeks, & Druids
Introduction
by *Chas S. Clifton*

HE NEW NORTH AMERICAN PAGANISM HAD MULTIPLE POINTS OF ORIGIN. Some lay in a combination of personal encounter with the old gods reinforced by classical Greek literature, as was the case with Gleb Botkin's Church of Aphrodite, founded in 1939. W. Holman Keith, a member of the Church of Aphrodite (which died in the late 1960s with its founder) later became affiliated with another uniquely American group, Feraferia, which began in the mid-1950s. Keith is represented in the previous chapter with his essay, "The Rising Tide of Pagan Tradition." For writing by Feraferia founder Frederick Adams, see Chapter 4 for his essay, "The Divine Maiden."

Pagan Witchcraft "officially" reached North America in the early 1960s when Ray and Rosemary Buckland immigrated from the United Kingdom. While they were living on Long Island, they were the designated contact people in the United States for Gerald Gardner's Wiccan tradition. But Gardner's writings had appeared in bookstores and libraries here in the 1950s, and some people had already found them and begun to practice Wicca themselves, based on the books and on their own discoveries and experiences. The movement of American military personnel, particularly Air Force men, to and from bases in Britain also in some cases facilitated their contact with British Witches. Fred Lamond, who was in Gardner's coven before the latter's death in 1964, writes here of his own experience with Wicca's chief founder.

Ray Buckland's article "Which Witch is Which?" reflects both tensions between secretive Craft groups in the early 1970s and between them and some individuals who gained media attention for their public pronouncements about Witchcraft, what Buckland calls "Commercial Witches."[1] Reading between the lines, we can see that one of the people criticized was the British Witch Alex Sanders (1926-1988), who received a lot of media coverage in the United Kingdom; in the United States, he appeared to be targeting, among others, Louise Huebner, whose website still proclaims her as "The Official Witch of Lost Angeles," a title she gained in 1968.

Buckland later dropped some of his Gardnerian-tradition exclusivity, creating new forms of Witchcraft in which self-initiation was valid, for example. Gwen Thompson's "Wiccan-Pagan Potpourri" argues the case for secrecy, as it was seen at that time.

Although Wicca represents the largest segment of contemporary Paganism, here you will also find a vision of the future by Isaac Bonewits, a key figure in North American Druidism, which has a rather different history than the British variety; and an essay by Apollonious Sophistes, who rightly acknowledges the importance of ancient Greek Paganism in subsequent manifestations of Pagan religion in the West.

---

[1] See, for example, the Website of Louise Huebner, which after forty years still proclaims her to be "The Official Witch of Los Angeles,"*www.mentorhuebnerart.com/witchstuff/officialwitch.shtml.*

Which Witch Is Which?

by *Raymond Buckland, Ph.D.*

 NEWCOMER TO THE FIELD OF Witchcraft would be understandably perplexed at the various forms in which "The Craft" presently seems to manifest itself. Ten to fifteen years ago it was exciting enough to discover that Witchcraft was (a) a religion in its own right, rather than the perversion of another religion, and (b) still alive.

The man responsible—and with the necessary courage—for initially enlightening the general public was the late Gerald Gardner. He showed how one branch of Witchcraft had survived in Britain. That branch continues on both sides of the Atlantic today, labeled "Gardnerian" Witchcraft (as a tribute to Dr. Gardner's work the label is a good one, but descriptively is inaccurate).

Once Gardnerian Witchcraft had struggled up into a reasonably comfortable breathing position it was then joined by other forms of the Craft. British "Traditional" was one of the first of those to stand and be recognized. Druidic and Celtic witches were close behind.

With the publication, and later filming, of Ira Levin's book *Rosemary's Baby* a retrograde step was taken. Levin called his characters "witches" when, in fact, they were out-and-out Satanists. To those of the Craft who had spent so much time and energy in correcting such misconceptions it was a bitter blow. Pseudo "covens" sprang up left, right, and center. The general cry seemed to be "let's be Witches and form a coven!" Insofar as such groups attracted the "nuttier" element this was not a bad thing. But unfortunately, there were those who were true seekers; those who wanted, perhaps needed, the Craft. These were the ones harmed. To know, or just to feel instinctively, that the real thing exists; yet to meet nothing but cheap imitations is the worst possible torture.

"Commercial Witches" appeared. Miss Official Witch of Everytown; the Queen of All the Witches; King Witch...President Witch? Happily it was not too difficult to sort the sheep from the goats. By listening carefully to what such characters shouted it was soon obvious, to anyone of intelligence, who was really of the Old Religion and who was either self-deluded or an outright fraud.

At long last the Witches of the Americas are coming out into the open. Four or five years ago they were still keeping to themselves. So much so that when Susan Roberts (a cookbook author who has recently turned her eyes to Witchcraft) asked this writer of them, at that time I could tell her nothing. Therefore her later (unfortunately inaccurate) published comment was that I had come to the U.S. to establish a "British Empire of Witchcraft in the Colonies"! (Ludicrous when known that even at that time I was taking steps to become an American citizen!) But Miss Roberts' anti-British bias notwithstanding, her book *(Witches U.S.A.)* is good in that it is the first to really look at the Witchcraft native to the United States. This is a potpourri of traditions from all parts of Europe (naturally, due to the varied origins of the peoples themselves) but with new American-native ideas added and blended over the years. More such books would be welcome.

A form, or variation, of the Craft has come to light in Pennsylvania—traditionally the home of the hex. This variant is actually closer to Celtic Druidism than to anything Dutch or Amish, however. It is a branch of the Wicca that emphasizes the craft of augery.

Although these many and varied aspects of Witchcraft are initially confusing to the newcomer, to the majority of "established" Witches they are very exciting. In the past there has been more than a little distrust, suspicion (understandable), and outright antagonism (unnecessary) between the various factors. But now we seem to be approaching, rapidly, the point where it can be seen that all the above forms (excepting, of course, the pseudo-Satanic school) are *valid* forms; where it will benefit all to look at and try to understand the others. For example, if a Witch of one of the U.S. traditions has not previously heard the British term *skyclad* (meaning "naked"), rather than laughing hysterically and making adolescent remarks, far better for him to enquire *why* the term is used; *when* did it come into use, etc.

Covens—in Western Europe at least—are autonomous, so an overall leader or council is neither sought nor desired. Yet the idea of affiliation with such as the Council of Themis, or similar, would seem to have possibilities so far as the dissemination of information is concerned. It is to be hoped that such a group will help bring together the differences of the Craft. For the answer is not to *eradicate* the differences, but to *understand* them. Once they are understood within the Craft, how much easier it will be for the newcomer coming from outside the Craft.

GE Vol. V, No. 46 (Ostara 1972)

Raymond Buckland has had over fifty books published in the past forty years, with nearly two million copies in print and translated into seventeen foreign languages. He has served as Technical Director for movies, written screenplays, and lectured at colleges and universities across America. Raymond has been featured in newspapers and magazines, appeared on national television and radio talk shows and played character parts in movies. He has taught courses at colleges and universities and been a featured speaker at conferences and workshops. Recent books include *The Spirit Book*, *Buckland's Spirit Board*, *Buckland's Romani Tarot*, and *Torque of Kernow* (novel). *www.raybuckland.com*

Wiccan-Pagan Potpourri
by Lady Gwen Thompson (1928-1986), Welsh Tradition Wicca

 FUNDAMENTALIST CHRISTIAN RE-cently said to me: "Satan rules this planet!" I replied: "I know it." My answer was unnerving to the person making the statement due to the fact that Fundamentalists, along with numerous other Christian denominations, firmly believe that Witches and Pagans are "devil-worshippers." I did not elaborate upon the fact that we do not believe in a "devil" as such, but we *do* believe in a CONTROLLING FORCE that is anathema to our way of life as we would like to live it, and should be able to live it, upon this planet. Our ancient lore tells us that thousands of years ago there were two forces seeking control of the mode of life upon this planet: one group wishing to teach mankind the "facts of life" and the other to exploit mankind. There were many names applied to these beings: Gods, angels, Watchers, sons of God, etc. The leaders of these two opposing forces, for want of a better term or name, were referred to as The Lord of Light and The Lord of Darkness. There is no need to be specific about which of them wanted what. Oh yes, and lest we forget...their "hosts" (in modern terminology...armies).

The Christian Bible, garbled as it currently is, speaks of a battle in the "heavens"...well, we know there was one, although the Christians have their time-space continuum a bit mixed up...to the point where it is all done and over with, according to them. But, we know that as it was in the beginning so it will be in the end...giving us the Alpha and Omega of history. When Christians speak of "fallen angels" and "salvation," I merely reply: "Ummmm...of course." Then they are (gently?) felled with the statement: "If the Lord of *Light* lost the battle for control of Earth...who *won?*" They were taught that the Lord of Light was Lucifer, a very naughty angel who went against God and got *his*. Along with his followers, naturally it is clear that a large number of the followers of the Lord of Light were confined to Earth, bred with Earth people and produced what we now have as a breed of "different" beings, classified as people who "have the POWER" or "KNOWING ONES." Thus, we have an admixture upon this planet of Light and Darkness. The demarcation line becomes more obvious daily. Shall we call it "The Omega Caper"?

When it comes down to the nitty-gritty of hassles and bickering and the rest of the fertilizer...consider the fact that antagonistic elements of Darkness infiltrate for the express purpose of dimming the LIGHT. The sad tales of recorded history are replete with data on thousands of enlightened ones who brought forth progress upon the Earth as new inventions and new ways of thought in order to ADVANCE mankind. Were they not all ridiculed at one time or another? Was there not an element among mankind that continually sought to *prevent* progress? We have had our "Mighty Ones" who overcame the opposing and controlling forces to progress our people in spite of any obstacle...often at great personal sacrifice.

We are all well aware of the people who have been continually opposed to our space program...they give various and sundry reasons: "expensive" (so what?); "we need the money for the poor and needy;" or "we should not mess around with God's universe," etc. etc., blah, blah, blah. The numerous wars, inspired by Darkness, were also "expensive"...*very* expensive. The "poor and needy" wouldn't be about to get any of the lucre, and as for "God's universe"...it belongs to everyone to share equally. There is no need to be imprisoned upon the giant spaceship Earth if one wishes to go elsewhere. For those who are not already well aware of it... the battle is once more raging. This time, however, the thumb-screws are on the other pinkies.

Old Religionists who allow themselves to be photographed by the news media in the "altogether" (sky-clad), and often in positions that suggest obscene practices, are not doing the Old Religion any service whatsoever, but rather giving it a very black eye. Worship in such a case, if it *is* worship, should be sacred to the Goddess and God alone and not for the eyes of cowans to see and misinterpret. We live in a clothed society which is not all that ready to accept what *some* Witches or Pagans do. If we wish to get across the message that we are intelligent, dignified and worthy of respect ...just as much as the controlling religions of Earth...then we should not use back-door tactics, but utilize some of the Wisdom our forebears bestowed upon

us to give the proper impression of what and who we really are.

Many Witches ignore the age-old counseling of the Wise Ones as given in the Rede. Many different traditions have different redes. That is understandable, considering the time involved from Alpha to Omega. Our own particular Rede, however, has appeared within the past year in a perverted form. That is to say, the wording has been changed This is sad for those who are seeking the Light of the Old Religion, because it confuses them. The same thing was done to the ancient seals of Solomon, and thus we do not have his great wisdom as it was meant to be in the original form. Some would-be artists thought to "improve" upon the drawings of the seals, not realizing it was *not* artwork, but sacred symbolism...not to be tampered with. Thus, many wonder why the current seals so often bring them undesired results or no results at all.

We are not "into" Cabalistic magic, as such, but do not deny its relationship to our way of life. We have all received our lore from the same root source. As a Traditionalist, versed in lore taken from certain Witches of the British Isles, I can say that our own particular tradition consisted of the practices and beliefs of folk Witches and not those people who were generally wealthy enough to be formally educated. Country people were simple people and had simple rituals in practice and wording. Many never knew how to read or write, but they were not without their share of "nobles" who did know how. Many Old Religion dances and songs became the nursery rhymes and dances of children, following the centuries-old "Witch" trials. Thus, many legends and songs are almost child-like in their context...because this was the level of basic understanding of folk Witches at that time. Unable to openly express what they knew to be truth in actual "university" terms...they resorted to simple symbolism in ritual, legend, and drawings, and preserved their sacred heritage in the most comprehensive manner, and in a manner that would be ignored by their adversaries, for the most part. Our own particular form of the Wiccan Rede is that which was passed on to her heirs by Adriana Porter, who was well into her nineties when she crossed over into the Summerland in the year 1946. This Rede in its original form is as follows:

Rede of the Wiccae
(Being knowne as the Counsel of the Wise Ones)

1. Bide the Wiccan laws ye must
   in perfect love an perfect trust.
2. Live and let live–
   fairly take and fairly give.
3. Cast the Circle thrice about
   to keep all evil spirits out.
4. To bind the spell every time,
   let the spell be spake in rhyme.
5. Soft of eye and light of touch–
   speak little, listen much.
6. Deosil go by the waxing Moon–
   sing and dance the Wiccan rune.
7. Widdershins go when the Moon doth wane,
   and the Werewolf howls by the dread Wolfsbane.
8. When the Lady's Moon is new,
   kiss the hand to her times two.
9. When the Moon rides at her peak,
   then your heart's desire seek.
10. Heed the Northwind's mighty gale–
    lock the door and drop the sail.
11. When the wind comes from the South,
    love will kiss thee on the mouth.
12. When the wind blows from the East,
    expect the new and set the feast.
13. When the West wind blows o'er thee,
    departed spirits restless be.
14. Nine woods in the Cauldron go–
    burn them quick and burn them slow.
15. Elder be ye Lady's tree–
    burn it not or cursed ye'll be.
16. When the Wheel begins to turn–
    let the Beltane fires burn.
17. When the Wheel has turned a Yule,
    light the Log and let Pan rule.
18. Heed ye flower, bush an tree–
    by the Lady blessed be.
19. Where the rippling waters go,
    cast a stone and truth ye'll know.
20. When ye have need,
    hearken not to other's greed.
21. With the fool no season spend
    or be counted as his friend.
22. Merry meet an merry part–
    bright the cheeks and warm the heart
23. Mind the Threefold Law ye should–
    three times bad and three times good
24. When misfortune is enow,
    wear the blue star on thy brow.
25. True in love ever be
    unless thy lover's false to thee.
26. Eight words the Wiccan Rede fulfill–
    an it harm none, do what ye will.

The foregoing is explained fully to the initiated Witch. The contents of the Book of Shadows (our *public* name for it) must be orally taught as well as copied. All wording has its special meaning which the Wise can often quickly discern. Meditation is a most important adjunct to the learning of the Mysteries of the Old Religion. The number of Old Religionists currently abiding by the counsel of the Wise can be counted on the fingers of one hand and the thumb would be left over.

There is only one form of wisdom that time alone can bestow, and that is lessons learned from *experience*. Our children were taught to respect the old ones, even though they were often people of little formal education or very simple in their ways. They had lived long and had, therefore, experienced much of life and its ways. Their advice through *their own* lessons learned was considered invaluable, and thus they were held in deep respect for those things in which they had learned Wisdom. Children were not taught to strive for perfection, but for Wisdom. Perfection is a broad concept with different meanings for different people. It actually does not exist. The caution was: "Do not seek perfection in others unless you yourself can give it." Therefore...we have the counsel to "live and let live...."

When anyone refers to a particular Old Religion tradition as a "sect" it brings to mind bug spray. It is a poor term to apply to a sacred way of life, and the word "cult" is enough to set one's teeth on edge. Although Webster's now gives it a more dignified connotation, the general public and Webster do

not necessarily agree on all points of defini-
tion. There was originally just a single tradi-
tion of Witchcraft and many traditions with-
in Paganism due to country, customs, etc.
When certain priests of the early Christian
church became bored with their celibate life
they perverted their own religion by revers-
ing their rituals and brought forth Satanism.
Why they insisted upon calling themselves
Witches is anyone's guess, for the majority
of them still do it. Unless, perhaps, they are
so guilt-ridden about their practices and be-
liefs that they wish to place the blame else-
where. Genuine Witches and Pagans are not
running around cutting off the heads of black
chickens, nor are they offering up babies and
virgins to some obscure demon. We have too
much respect for life. It is almost useless to
try getting the truth across to those who do
not and will not understand our ways due to
a messed-up news media and the general
Christian-Judeo clamor for titillating read-
ing... such as evidenced in the book, *The
Devil on Lamas Night* by Susan Howatch,
whoever that is. It is a cross-continent ver-
sion of what the adversary imagines Witch-
craft to be or would like the reading public to
think it is. A quite exciting and well-written
book, to he sure. An accursed lie, however.
How unlike the beautiful writing of Mary
Stewart, author of the much read and be-
loved book, *The Crystal Cave,* and its se-
quel, *The Hollow Hills.* Mary Stewart is to
Susan Howatch what diamonds are to coal.

At this point I should like to quote from
a very learned patriarch of the Old
Religion...one whom we would refer to as a
"Wizen Elder" in our tradition. (Wizen be-
ing pronounced as "whizzen." It is derived
from the title Wizard...one highly skilled in
the arts of the Craft.) I feel he would not
mind my including his comments on book
authors at this point. They are simply stated:
"The Craft view is that a book is only a man
talking on paper and is no more accurate that
the spoken word by the same man. Any man
who talks for an extended length of time must
make a few mistakes. No book, therefore, not
even a college text, is 100% accurate. Also,
no man has all the facts about any particular

subject. There is always something more to
be told...something the author did not
know." I might only add that this applies to
female authors as well. "Speak little, listen
much."

Many in the Old Religion are now find-
ing it Wise to shun the limelight and keep
their activities secret from the public on all
levels. One might even say they are going
"underground." This includes many High
Priestesses and High Priests who are either
choosing to take their entire Covens "under-
ground" or to practice their religion quietly
by themselves. This is logical and sane at this
time in history. It does not mean a creeping
away into some hidden corner for fear of the
foe, but a carefully calculated plan to keep
the foe guessing. Considering the apparent
IQ level of many of our critics, the cerebral
exercise will do them good. Our forebears
did not go about thumping their chests and
proclaiming to the world at large "I am a
Witch!" simply because it was the "in" thing
or the current social "fad." They did not wish
to raise eyebrows or attract the adversary or
the ever-increasing horde of misfits. In dis-
cretion and Wisdom they preserved the old
truths...else we would not have them today.

Food for thought: I don't care what any-
one does just so long as they do not inter-
fere with Life, this planet, or me. Surprising
how limiting that can be. "As you sow...so
shall you reap" is not a Christian original...it
is the Threefold Law simply expressed in
farm language. Disharmony begets dishar-
mony and time travels in a CIRCLE, not a
straight line. The Serpent eating his own tail.
Perversions of ancient traditions often bring
ancient curses as well. The invisible becomes
manifest. Twin Earths exchanging bric-a-
brac. The insatiable guru-chasers; Book col-
lectors; Coven hoppers; name-droppers; and
ego-trippers. We've all had our share of them.
Monsters roam the planet in various guises.
People who seldom make *anyone* happy...
feigning Wisdom. Nobody can hear a whis-
per while they're talking. Wiccan-Pagan
teachings are not for everyone.

GE Vol. VII, No. 69 (Ostara 1975)

Pioneers of the Pagan Revival:
Gerald Brosseau Gardner
by "Robert" (Fred Lamond), CAW, Gardnerian Wicca

 HE MAN WHO MORE THAN ANY other initiated the Pagan and Witchcraft revival in the English-speaking world was born in 1884 to wealthy English parents. Like many born shamans, he was in poor health in his childhood and suffered from severe asthma throughout his life. His nurse persuaded his parents to let her travel with him to warmer climates in the winter, notably to the Far Eastern parts of the British Empire.

The close relationship with his nurse may have opened the channel with the Goddess within him, while his acquaintance with Malaya led him to become a rubber planter there in the 1920s and then Director of Customs, a post from which he retired in 1936 to return to England. While in Malaya, he published a book on the Malayan ceremonial knife—the *kris*—and was probably also initiated into some Malayan tribal cults.

He was certainly an esoteric seeker throughout his life. Free-Masonry was and is common among British businessmen and officials, but on his return to England he also joined the Golden Dawn and the OTO, though this is not mentioned in his official biography. Crowley would hardly have given him a charter to start his own OTO lodge when the two met in 1946 if Gardner had not already been an OTO member in good standing and shown himself to be a competent magician.

Gardner and Witchcraft

In the late 1930s, Gerald took up residence in Christchurch, Hampshire, on the edges of the New Forest. There he joined a Co-Mason lodge (a branch of Masonry that admits both men and women) that performed public rituals as the *New Rosicrucian Theatre*. He became intimate with a woman member, nicknamed "Dapho," who introduced him to the lodge's inner circle, the *New Forest Witches' Coven*. A few days before the outbreak of World War II, he was initiated into Witchcraft by the coven's High Priestess, Dorothy Clutterbuck, widow of an Indian Army major. He experienced the sense of "homecoming" familiar to initiate Witches, and felt this was what he had been looking for all his life.

In recent years, some would-be historians of the Pagan revival have cast doubt on the New Forest Coven's existence and claim that Gerald invented his brand of Witchcraft out of whole cloth. But both Doreen Valiente and two members of my coven met "Dapho," and Doreen Valiente also discovered Dorothy Clutterbuck's death certificate at Christchurch. A number of books have also recently appeared in France, describing French country Witchcraft and claiming links with a similar tradition in England: a spell casting and herbalist tradition practised mostly by solitaries.

Nor did Gerald invent the practice of meeting in covens. There are independent witnesses to the fact that the New Forest Coven existed before Gerald was initiated into it, and that it may have been one of the *Nine Covens* in whose formation the Essex farm laborer and cunning man George Pickingill (1816–1909) was instrumental in the 1890s.

A passionate hater of the Christian church, Pickingill had not kept his knowledge of sorcery as secret as was usual in family traditions, but was prepared to act as consultant to any group, including upper- and middle-class groups, interested in forming magical traditions that could supplant Christianity. If the Pickingill link is true, then that would be the link between Gardnerian Witchcraft and the family traditions that survived the Witchhunts of the Stuart and Cromwellian periods.

After the end of the New Forest Coven through the death or dispersal of its other members, Gerald did put together his *Book of Shadows* in an eclectic scissors-and-paste fashion from the most diverse literary and magical sources with the help of Doreen

Valiente, but that is what any Witch is supposed to do: the BoS being neither a Bible nor a Koran, but a personal record of rituals and spells that have worked in the past.

Ending Secrecy

Gerald's main contribution to the Pagan revival was to publicise Witchcraft after the repeal of the British Witchcraft Act in 1951: through the Witchcraft Museum on the Isle of Man that he bought from Cecil Williamson, through his books *Witchcraft Today* and *The Meaning of Witchcraft*, and through many press interviews. He did so in the teeth of opposition from all the family traditions, from other members of the New Forest Coven, and even from some of the initiates whom he had brought into the Craft, as Doreen Valiente recounts in her latest book, *The Rebirth of Witchcraft.*

Like all Witches, Gerald had taken an oath of secrecy at his initiation. But instead of interpreting it widely as not revealing the Craft's existence, he gave it the much narrower meaning of not revealing those things that could cause harm:

1. Initiates' names and addresses without their consent.
2. Spellcasting and herbal techniques, that can be dangerous in the hands of the untutored dabbler.
3. Discussion of spells outside the circle in which they were cast, so as not to dispel their power.

It is ironic that today it is the American Wiccan tradition that bears Gardner's name that is the most secretive of its rituals, even harmless celebratory seasonal rituals. Had it not been for Gerald's defiance of his Witch contemporaries, few of us if any would be practising Witchcraft today; even members of different traditions whose founders got the idea from Gerald's books.

An Easily Underestimated Man

Like Yoda in *The Empire Strikes Back,* Gerald made it easy to underestimate him. When I first met him in his London flat in the Fall of 1956, I found him a kind and very lovable old Edwardian gentleman, but totally lacking in charisma. At my initiation and in subsequent coven meetings, I was shocked at the mythological inconsistencies he had allowed to persist between the rituals he had borrowed from diverse sources, and concluded that he must be theologically illiterate. His obsession with flagellation also permeated his rituals in a manner embarrassing to those who did not share his tastes.

In his press interviews, he was also apt to embroider the truth. The young priestess who had initiated me had the face and figure of an Arthur Rackham elf: Gerald could not resist telling a reporter that she came from a hereditary Witch family, even though her background was in fact Armenian Jewish and she had only been initiated three years before me.

Within six months, I was thus faced with a far worse ordeal than the symbolic scourging I had received at my initiation: Was the supposed unbroken link to pre-persecution country Witchcraft equally phony? Had Gerald made the whole thing up?

I realised then that *it didn't matter!* At my initiation I had encountered the same eternal spiritual current of Love as in the arms of my first girlfriend, which had made me seek out a Goddess religion in the first place. Whatever its pedigree, Gardnerian witchcraft *worked* for me and expressed my religious feelings better than any other religious practice I had encountered. I also felt that to have invented such a powerful system Gerald would have had to be a far more competent magician than I was prepared to credit him at the time.

In my defence, I must add that I was not alone in underestimating Gerald. In the late 1950s, a Sufi Grand Master took a close interest in him and interviewed him for a biography, which was eventually published under the name of his friend Jack Bracelin *(Gerald Gardner, Witch)*. As the interviews progressed, the Sufi became more and more disillusioned with his subject. One day, taking tea at my house, he confided:

"Sometimes, when interviewing Gerald, I wished I was a reporter for a yellow scandal sheet. What marvellous material for an expose! And yet"—here he became thoughtful—"I have it on good authority" (I assume he meant the inner planes) "that this movement will be the religious cornerstone of the coming age. But rationally"—and he glanced despairingly at the sincere but woefully ignorant young people who surrounded him— "I can't see it!"

A Subtle Magus

It is only within the last year that I have realised that his lightweight image was an act that Gerald put on to force us to stand on our own feet. By forcing me (and doubtless most other initiates) to confront the question of the genuineness of the Craft so soon after my initiation, Gerald made me achieve in six months a degree of religious self-reliance that it would have taken me ten years to reach under the guidance of a truly charismatic and credible teacher like the aforementioned Sufi.

In the same spirit, Gerald never gave us any direct instruction in Witch religious concepts and spellcasting techniques. We learned spellcasting on the job in the circle, and picked up myths and concepts from the rituals themselves, notably the wonderfully moving *Charge of the Goddess*. During the informal conversations that followed rituals within the Circle, Gerald would tell us anecdotes about what happened in "Pre-Burning Times," and how Craft practice had been altered when it had to go underground.

That expression was, of course, a Geraldism. Since witches were never burned in

England but hung during the brief 120 years when they were persecuted there, the persecutions would never have been described in those words by a true family tradition Witch. But the anecdotes about a fictitious past were a mirror technique for implanting in our subconscious minds the ideas about what we ought to do in the future as the social and intellectual climate becomes more tolerant. Here are two examples:

Witchcraft as a Priesthood

"In Pre-Burning Times, Witches were the priests and healers of farming villages. The four seasonal *Great Sabbats*—Halloween, Candlemas, Beltaine and Lammas—were parties in which the whole village celebrated. It was everyone's singing, dancing and lovemaking that raised the energy that ensured fertility in animals and the year's crops.

"Only the Full Moon *Esbats* were restricted to initiated Witches, because that is when they performed potent healing and weather spells, which could only work if all the participants were fully attuned to each other and knew how to focus their minds.

"It is only the persecutions which have turned us into a 'priesthood without a congregation.'"

Jumbled Rituals

"Until quite recently, Witchcraft was a wholly oral tradition, in which initiates had to learn all rituals and spellcasting techniques by heart.

"When at last Witches were allowed to keep a written *Book of Shadows,* they had at first to write everything down in a jumbled manner, so that the spells wouldn't work if attempted by an untutored outsider who had found or stolen a Witch's BoS."

At the time, I took it for another of Gerald's attempts to weave an aura of spurious historical authenticity around the Craft, and thought no more about it. It is only five years ago, a full quarter century after that conversation, that it occurred to me that Gerald was telling us that the rituals he was handing to us in his BoS were also jumbled, to force us to think about what we were doing and not recite the rituals blindly.

The occasional mythological inconsistencies between rituals, the undigested Masonic rituals—with their references to "commanding angels and demons" in what is supposed to be a non-dualistic pantheist religion, the obsessional overemphasis on scourging are all presumably part of the same technique.

In fact, even in Gerald's day, the BoS rituals were recited just as they were written down without Gerald batting an eyelid. If we were too dumb to notice the wrong order, then let us perform them this way! But I wonder if he would have been amused or saddened if he had been told that today American Gardnerians dare not change a comma or a word in those parts of *The Book of Shadows* traceable to his day.

> *"Robert" (Fred Lamond in mundane life) has been a Pagan all his life, consciously since a mystical experience in the arms of his first girlfriend over 30 years ago, He was initiated into Gerald Gardner's first coven at Brigid 1957 and has remained a member since then. He is also a member of the Church of All Worlds.*
>
> *"Robert" is the author of* The Divine Struggle, *published by GE (1990). Fred Lamond earns his living as an independent, computer consultant and lecturer, giving industry-watching seminars to computer managers throughout Europe and North America. He now lives with his second wife in Austria.*

Vol. XXIII, No. 90 (Lughnasadh 1990) 14–15

Sabbats of That Old Time Religion

by *Roz Tognoli* ©1977

Ch: Gimme that old time religion
Gimme that old time religion
Gimme that old time religion
It's good enough for me!

Light and darkness stand together
Leafing birch and flow'ring heather
Brethren clad in fur and feather
Tell us Spring has come again!

Ch: Gimme that old time religion...

Hand in hand we leap the fire
To the meadows we retire
To fulfill Beltane desire
And give seed unto the land!

While the Solstice day is fleeting
Bull and stag again are meeting
For the honor of repeating
Vows that bind them to the Queen!!

Joy and fruitfulness abound
On Lughnasadh, the fertile ground
Reveals the gift of love that's found
When the Green God dies again!

For the Wintertide preparing
Harvest baskets we are bearing
Goddess bounty we are sharing
When the night and day are one!

As the waning year is ending
Young and old souls now are blending
Voices 'round the circle sending
Samhain joy across the worlds!

Through the endless night we shiver
Flames around the Yule log quiver
As we sing to praise the Giver
Of the Sun on Solstice morn!

Pagans gather in the clearing
For the end of Winter's nearing
And the Maiden is appearing
Bringing promises of Spring!

Meeting at the witching hour
By the bud and branch and flower
Folks are raising up the power
And that's where I want to be!

GE Vol. XXIX, No. 121 (Nov.-Dec. 1997) 13

Ḥellenic Ṇeo-Paganism

by *Apollonius Sophistes (Bruce MacLennan)*

"We Are All Greeks"

 ANY NEO-PAGANS WERE AWAK-ened to the old gods by an early encounter with Greek mythology, yet now they follow other traditions. A connection with the Earth is an essential part of both Neo- and Paleo-Paganism, and thus many Neo-Pagans look to their ethnic roots as a source of spirituality. At times, that ethnicity can be construed too narrowly. Some may reject a Hellenic[1] path simply because they're not of Greek descent.

Hellenic culture is a major component of the substratum of *all* European culture. It is worth recalling that by 327 BCE Alexander had carried Hellenic culture nearly to the Ganges and to the north of the Himalayas (and, of course, brought Eastern culture back to Greece, for his goal was a multi-ethnic society). The conquest of Greece by Rome was complete by 146 BCE, but in its defeat Greek culture conquered the Romans. It then spread with the Roman Empire, which by 44 BCE included the North African coast and extended north to the English channel; by 67 CE it included the south of England. Therefore the Hellenic tradition has been a part of the culture of Europe (and beyond) for at least 2000 years. To the extent that European culture has become Western culture, and Western culture has become world culture, the Hellenic tradition is ubiquitous. As someone quite rightly said, "We are all Greeks."

In particular, the Greek gods have never been far from the center of Western culture, and Greek mythology continues to be a major influence in literature, art and language.[2] For these reasons, I think it is accurate to say that the Greek gods *are* the gods of Western culture, wherever it exists in the world, and therefore that these gods are part of the ethnic background of everyone who feels Western in this sense, no matter what their race or geographic origin.[3] I'm not claiming the superiority of Hellenic or Western culture; my point is simply that the Greek pantheon is a natural choice for anyone at home in Western culture.

Practicalities of Hellenic Neo-Paganism

The Hellenic tradition has much to offer. While the gods can be known through many different pantheons, there are practical differences.

Since the Hellenic tradition stretches continuously from before Homer's time (say, 700 BCE), through the Christian era, to the present, there is a larger surviving body of literature, artifacts, history, art and religion from the Hellenic tradition than from any other Western Pagan tradition. This lore provides a solid basis for constructing a Hellenic Neo-Paganism.

The large corpus of surviving texts and the enormous body of scholarship makes reconstruction easier in the Hellenic tradition than in others, such as the Druid or Wiccan, which have been reconstructed from a less tangible evidence or oral tradition. Although these reconstructions may be very good, in the Hellenic tradition we have a better chance of understanding archaic thought, so that we can make informed decisions about what we accept or reject. With many of the other traditions it's nearly impossible to distinguish a practice tested for a hundred generations from one cooked up last week by someone who has just read *The Golden Bough* (or *The White Goddess*). The gods *are* living, and new traditions must be created, but it's also important to understand how They were worshipped in the old days.

The wealth of source material makes the Greek gods much more knowable as *personalities*. For me, the Germanic gods are still largely cardboard characters, and the Celtic gods are little more than a jumble of names. I realize that the understanding I do have of the Germanic gods has been formed as much by Wagner as by the Eddas, and it has been observed that Wagner's gods are really the Greek gods with German names! I think it's crucial to know the gods personally—intellectual understanding is not enough—and the way to Them is opened by a large corpus of myth, art, etc.

Of course, a practical disadvantage of the Hellenic path is that it's a comparatively small tradition in contemporary Neo-Paganism, so there are fewer organizations, periodicals, practical books and group activities. One reason why Hellenic Neo-Paganism is less popular may be that the very familiarity of the Greek gods robs them of the novelty of the Celtic, Wiccan, and other traditions.

How Patriarchal Is Hellenic Paganism?

The Hellenic religion is sometimes criticized for being patriarchal. While the society of Greek *mortals* was enormously patriarchal (the Romans were less so; the Etruscans less yet), Zeus's supreme position is really only nominal; He frequently gives in to other gods and goddesses. All the gods, or at least the twelve Olympians, are very nearly equal in power. Indeed Zeus got his job by means of Rhea's carefully laid plans, with the help of Gaia! In a sense He is Their instrument.[4]

In ancient times the immortal males and females had nearly equal power and respect. Observe also that the twelve Olympians are balanced in gender: Hera, Poseidon, Athena, Aphrodite, Apollo, Hermes, Zeus, Demeter, Hephaistos, Ares, Artemis, Hestia; six and six. As part of the transition to the Piscean age Hestia gave her position among The Twelve to Dionysos (a god of ambiguous gender), but Hestia was not demoted; She is the oldest Olympian, and still foremost in Their company.[5]

In terms of ritual, the Greeks and Romans respected the goddesses as much as the gods, and most of the public religious festivals were devoted to goddesses concerned with the cycles of nature and other "earthy" things. In addition, out of the 33 surviving "Homeric" Hymns, 17 are to gods, 15 to goddesses, and 1 to both (Apollo and the Muses)—approximately 50-50.

Are the Gods Immoral?

Sometimes the Greek gods are ridiculed for their immorality, but I think this betrays a misunderstanding of divinity. *The gods are not moral ideals.*

Nobody would suppose they would make themselves a better person by emulating Zeus, or even Athena or Apollo (let alone Hermes or Pan). (Indeed, aspiring to be like the gods is the most form of hubris, and invites Their wrath, as we see from many myths.) But this does not mean the gods are immoral. The gods have Their own morality, and it makes no more sense to apply Their moral norms to us, than it would to apply our moral norms to wolves. Gods, people and beasts are three different classes of beings, each with their appropriate morality (though there may be some overlap). For example, gods may engage in incest, perhaps to achieve some aim, such as begetting a new god with a specific character, and there is no reason to suppose that such incest would have any of the disastrous genetic and psychological consequences that it does for people. Gods are different, both genetically and psychologically, from people.

Therefore I think that the object of knowing the gods better is *not* to become more godlike, but to better comprehend Their will so that we don't oppose it, and if possible to enlist Their aid in our activities, both magical and mundane.

We worship the gods—we respect Them, acknowledge Them—because They are the *ineluctable powers of the universe,* neither good nor evil (because our moral categories are not appropriate for Them). For me the gods are the ultimate necessities of the universe, and hubris is a failure to abide by these necessities. As Philip Vellacott says, "The nature of a god is not to be man's friend, nor man's enemy, nor man's moral guide. It is the Hebrew and Christian tradition that presents God as embodying what ought to be, the ideal; the Greek god is the opposite of this, and stands for 'what is'—in human nature, in human society, and in the universe."[6]

Conflicts Among the Gods

If the Hellenic pantheon stand for "what is," what is revealed by the quarrels and deceptions of the gods? Naturally, we put these things into our own terms, but I think that the myths reflect actual conflicts between these ineluctable forces. Personally, I find the universe much more comprehensible when global and personal history is viewed as partially the consequence of interacting gods—sometimes working together, sometimes opposing one another, more often just going Their own ways, with the inevitable collisions.[7] (In other words: if *this* world is the orderly unfolding of the Master Plan of One God, then He or She must be schizophrenic!)

Recognizing the many gods and Their conflicting demands can lead to a healthier, happier, more balanced life. Consider the myth of the Judgment of Paris. He finds himself in a common enough situation: three goddesses demand

Paris's mistake was that he slighted the other two goddesses.

his attention. Poor Paris tries to avoid making the decision, but They will not let him off. In the traditional story he is offered kingship, heroism and love, but we may interpret the bribes as wealth, wisdom and love (still in our day, frequently, mutually exclusive choices). He gives the golden apple (inscribed "for the most attractive") to Aphrodite, and the result is disaster—the Trojan War. But his mistake was not that he gave the apple to the goddess of love, for She is a goddess nonetheless. Rather, Paris's mistake was that he slighted the other two goddesses. Had

he given the apple to Athena or Hera, the consequences would have been just as bad (although perhaps quite different in detail).

How could Paris have escaped this trilemma? That's difficult to say, but he should have tried to respect the sovereignty of all three goddesses. Perhaps he could have convinced Them to share the apple, each possessing it for a time, since at some times wisdom is most desirable, and at others power, and at yet others, love. Or he might have made propitiatory sacrifices to the losers. Perhaps it was simply a "no-win situation"—the Romans would say he was "between axe and altar."

It's characteristic of polytheism to confront such situations head on. There is no supposition that there must be a single Right Way, if only we could find it; polytheism acknowledges that sometimes there is no right answer. We must often make irrevocable decisions, honoring one god but dishonoring another, and we must pay the price to the offended gods, in spite of the fact that we couldn't avoid offending them. Luckily we often have options (analogous to dividing the apple) that were not available to Paris, which may mitigate the consequences. But I think polytheism forces us to acknowledge that sometimes there just isn't a Right Way.

How much more clearly we understand the world when we see that Hera, Aphrodite and Athena all have their demands! We don't fret over which is "God's Will" when we see that there are three goddesses, each with Her own will. If we decide that only one demand is the true "will of God," then we obey one goddess at the expense of disobeying the others—to our own sorrow! Although Paris may have been in a "no-win situation," he made the outcome worse by rejecting Hera and Athena. Unlike the Christian god, who proclaims His jealousy, the Olympian gods do not mind other gods being recognized. What They do mind is being rejected, and *that* They punish.[8]

Is it good or fair for gods to put mere mortals in such predicaments? No, but why suppose the gods are—by our standards—good or fair?

Belief in the Gods

Greek religion is very different from Christianity in that the gods don't care at all what you *believe,* so long as you worship Them. They demand *cultus* (from the same root as "cultivate")—tending the sacrificial fires, remembering Them—and one purpose of prayer and ritual is to nourish the gods and so rejuvenate them. The Greeks were quite explicit about this; a god could be hungry for the fragrance of the sacrificial fires. Then as now you can even be an atheist, so long as you recognize the gods and conform to Their will. Conversely, all the piety and faith in the world will not save you if you do not obey Their will. Greeks felt free to choose what they might believe, and so the Christian church fathers rightly called Hellenism the "father of all heresies" (from *hairesis,* choice).[9] Greek religion is a matter of *orthopraxy* (right doing) as opposed to *orthodoxy* (right saying).

The point is that the gods reward behavior in accord with Their will, and punish behavior not in accord, regardless of whether you believe in Them or not. Of course, if you believe in Them, you are more likely to know Their will and act accordingly, but there are no guarantees either way. An unbeliever may by chance do the right things; conversely a believer may misinterpret Their will, and act wrongly. However, wisdom and understanding is more likely to result in right action.

Notes

1. Because adherents of the old religion were called "Hellenes" (no matter what their nationality) in early Christian times, I will use this as an informal name for Neo-Pagans who follow a Greek or Roman tradition.
2. See Jean Seznec, *The Survival of the Pagan Gods* (Pantheon, 1953) and Edgar Wind, *Pagan Mysteries in the Renaissance* (Penguin, 1967).
3. David Miller, *The New Polytheism* (Harper & Row, 1974), pp. 11–12.
4. Kerenyi, *Gods of the Greeks,* pp. 9295.
5. *Larousse Encyc. Myth.* (Crescent, 1987), p. 136. The Twelve are listed in the zodiacal order given in Manilius (fl. 14 CE), *Astronomica,* 2.439–447 (i.e., Hera wards Aquarius, etc.). See also Seltman's *Twelve Olympians.*
6. Philip Vellacott, Intro. to Macy (1967) & Easton Press (1980) editions of his translations of Euripedes' *Medea, Hippolytus & The Bacchae,* pp. xii. See also Seltman, *Twelve Olympians.*
7. Otto, *Homeric Gods,* pp. 170–171.
8. Otto, pp. 170–171, 239–240.
9. Zielinski, *Religion of Anc. Greece,* pp. 6–7, 10–11. See also W. W. Hyde, *Greek Religion and its Survivals* (Cooper Square, 1963), pp. 8–10.

GE Vol. XXVIII, No. 109 (Summer 1995) 8–10

Dr. John Opsopaus (Apollonius) has practiced Magick and Divination since the 1960s and still presents workshops on Hellenic Magick and Neopaganism, Pythagorean Theurgy, Divination, and related topics. His fiction and nonfiction have been published in various Magickal and Neopagan magazines (over 30 publications). He designed the *Pythagorean Tarot* and wrote the comprehensive *Guide to the Pythagorean Tarot.* Opsopaus is a member of the Grey Council and is Dean of the Department of Ceremonial Magick of the Grey School of Wizardry. He is listed under "Who's Who in the Wiccan Community" in Gerina Dunwich's *Wicca Source Book.* *www.omphalos.org*

Hymn to Their Triple Will

*by **Maerian Morris***

to the tune of "Londonderry Air" (Danny Boy)

Evoe Kore
Ever will I love You
As sweet You dance
Upon the meadows green
Oh Lady Dear
Your song brings forth the flowers
Yet dearly do I love You
As Dark Hades' Queen
And I'll be there when Autumn
Tips the balance
And You go down for six months
Neath the ground
And I'll be true when Springtime
Comes to greet You
Evoe Kore,
Ever I'll love what I've found

Oh Lady of
The meadows green and golden
Dotted with blossoms
Tossing in the breeze
Why was I silent
When I saw You fallen
In Hades' grasp when innocent
You first were seized
Now I'll be there when Autumn
Tips the balance
And You go down for six months
'Neath the ground
And I'll be waiting for
You in the Springtime
For ever does my Lady
Ride the Wheel around

Persephone
Dark Queen of Hades' Kingdom
You hold Your sway
O'er mortals in Your place
Yet twice I've found You
Fair and in Your wisdom
I've come away alive
And renewed by Your grace
And I'll be here when Autumn
Tips the balance
And You descend to reign beside
Your King
And I'll be waiting at dawn

In the Circle
To greet You once again as You
Emerge in Spring

And Mother Demeter
I'll not deny You
As when I feared
And silence gripped my tongue
If You but call
And I anywhere hear You
I'll answer You and in Your honor
Sing this song.
And I'll be there when
Winter is upon us
And all the Land is dark and
Burnt by frost
I'll stand beside You 'til
You have Your Kore
No matter what the danger to me
Or the cost

Now I sing last
Of Grandmother Hecate
Of Black and Silver
Sickle, staff and bone
To You I'll come
To see what's next for learning
And in Your embrace sink
Once more into the stone.
For ever does the Wheel spin
Round the Seasons
The buds will burst and put forth
Grain and fall
The Maiden, Mother,
And the Crone Eternal
Hold forth their Triple Will upon
Us mortals all.

GE Vol. XXVIII, No. 109 (Summer 1995) inside front

Maerian Morris continues her wordsmithery, visual and marital arts, and arcane woo-woo in Califia's Bay Area. She has carried this work into the CyberWorld of Second Life as Maerian Dagger, the Faelf Elenarwen of Sidhevair. She resides there in her islands of Estrel, Ennyn and Minas Sidhevair.

The Future of Neopagan Druidism

by **Isaac Bonewits**, *Ar nDraíocht Féin*

RUIDRY (SECULAR) AND Druidism (religious) are, in this waning century of the Christian Interregnum, undergoing a true renaissance. ADF, Keltria, and the increasingly Neo-Pagan OBoD are growing rapidly as a new generation hears the call of the oaks and prepares for the next phase in the Gaian R/Evolution.

The Paleo-Pagan (ancient) Druids were the intellectual, artistic and spiritual leaders of the Celtic peoples, with their social caste counterparts the Godis, the Flamens, and the Brahmins in the other Indo-European cultures (and perhaps among the Yoruba). The true priests and priestesses of "the Old Religions" of our European (and West African?) ancestors; they were responsible for discovering, developing, and passing on the deepest wisdom and knowledge of their peoples from one generation to the next.

The archetype of the Druid as the trusted mentor and counselor has long been particularly powerful among Celts, and indeed among all who are familiar with the Arthurian mythos in English or French versions, for who is Merlin if not just such a Druid? While the Classical Greek and Latin references to Druids were split between positive "noble savage" and negative "bloodthirsty barbarian" stereotypes, what has been handed on through the centuries among the descendants of the French, British and Celtic peoples has been overwhelmingly positive.

The Meso-Pagan (mixed Pagan/Christian) Druid revivals built upon this positive image of Druids as counselors, sages, and teachers, while downplaying (or simply denying) the polytheistic aspects of authentic Paleo-Pagan Druidism. They invented silly tales of monotheistic, quasi-Masonic, protoChristian Druids and supposedly cryptoPagan "Culdees" (who were actually rather nasty early Christian fundamentalists), in order to deflect criticism and persecution from the repressive Christian forces then ruling the Western world.

Now the Neo-Pagan Druid movement, led by ADF's groundbreaking research, approach and practice, has planted the seeds for what is growing into a "forest MU of groves" stretching from ocean to ocean across North America. No longer needing to cater to the dominant paradigm, Druidism has again become a vibrant, Nature-centered, polytheistic and pluralistic public Pagan presence in the West, while leaving plenty of room for solitary mystics and philosophers, who may prefer to describe what they do as "Druidry."

In the late 70s I foresaw Neo-Paganism becoming a mainstream religious movement, with millions of members, and that this would be A Good Thing, both for the individuals involved and for the survival of the Earth Mother. Indeed, the Neo-Pagan community is growing at a geometric rate, both through word of mouth (and modem!) and with the help of the many do-it-yourself books now available, giving us an ever-greater impact on the mainstream culture as a whole.

I knew then that most of these new Neo-Pagans would want publicly accessible worship, teaching, counseling, and healing without having to become "clergy" themselves. These were services that most NeoPagan groups, whether calling themselves Druids or not, were simply unprepared to provide. So I began to share my vision of what Public Neo-Pagan Churches could he. I saw a movement of people and organizations dedicated to excellence in scholarship, liturgy, the arts, clergy training, and spiritual growth for all, whether clergy or laity. Since my personal spiritual calling has always been to the Druidic path, and since I was aware of resources that could ground Druidic spirituality in legitimate scholarly research about the Paleo-Pagan Druids, I called my vision one of "Neo-Pagan Druidism."

This vision eventually inspired the creation of Ar nDraíocht Féin: A Druid Fellowship, and attracted hundreds to join and work for its manifestation. We began with a great deal of publishing and organizational problems. I learned that it's hard to start an organization at the national level, without first creating local groups with experienced volunteers. Many people left us because of these problems, and some went on to start Neo-Pagan Druid groups of their own. Today, Neo-Pagan Druidism is a "movement," not just a single organization.

The vision was passed on by other public Neo-Pagan churches as well. For example, ADF, and CAW exchanged copies of our Grove/Nest Organizers' Handbooks and our Study Guides, each being inspired by the other. Various Neo- Pagan groups bought copies of these and other ADF (and CAW) publications, and modified the ideas to fit their local needs (often, unfortunately, lowering the standards in the process). Reliable estimates of the size of the Neo-Pagan community are rising to 200,000 to 500,000 people. This growing community has a growing need for competent clergy, clear goals, detailed doctrines and organizational sophistication.

Thirteen years ago, thinking mostly of Neo-Pagan Druids at the time, I said "Within thirty years we expect to see indoor temples and/or sacred groves throughout North America and Europe, staffed by full-time paid professional clergy. They'll provide the full range of needed services to the Neo-Pagan community, with no more 'corruption' than the Unitarians, the Buddhists, or the Taoists experience. We foresee globally televised Samhain rites at Stonehenge, and Beltane ceremonies attended by thousands in every major city. NeoPagan clergy will take part as equals in international religious conferences with clergy from other faiths. Our children will be able to wear Pagan religious emblems to school as easily as others now wear Jewish, Christian or Islamic ones.

"We see talented and well trained Neo-Pagan clergy leading thousands of people in effective magical and mundane actions to save endangered species, stop polluters, and preserve wilderness. We see our healers saving thousands of lives and our bards inspiring millions through music, video, concerts and dramas. We see Neo-Paganism as a mass movement, changing social, political, and environmental attitudes around the world and stopping the death-mongers in their tracks."

Halfway along that time span, the signs are obvious everywhere that I was, if anything, too conservative in my estimates. The number of covens, lodges, and other small home-worship focused, esoteric Pagan groups continues to explode alongside the groves, temples and other large-group-oriented, exoteric Pagan organizations. We are creating a complex and thriving spiritual ecosystem of interlinked traditions, worship techniques, and belief systems.

"WE CAN GO NOW. WE'RE NOT THE DRUIDS YOU'RE LOOKING FOR!"

Some will point to the recent upsurge in persecution and harassment, kidnappings and perjuries by fundamentalist Christians against Pagans and their families as evidence that our cauldron is half-empty and that we "should" retreat back into the shadows. I see our cauldron as half-full. Consider: Neo-Pagan clergy are already working with local interfaith councils across the U.S.A., and we were present in significant numbers at the Parliament of the World's Religions in 1993 CE. My son was able to stand with other pre-schoolers three years ago while the class sang Charlie Murphy's "Light Is Returning" in the Winter Holiday Concert; the teacher had specifically asked us for a Pagan holiday song to go along with the Christian, Jewish and secular ones!

There has been an explosion of books (granted, of a wide range of quality levels) about Wicca, Druidism, and Neo-Paganism in general, which are easily available in major chain bookstores, and which make it clear that the lies told about us are just that, lies.

The Religious Reich is correct about one thing, and one thing only. There is a culture war going on, between the neophobes and the neophiles, between the power hungry and the laid back, between those who are terrified of the global changes taking place and those who welcome them. It's easy to see our current attackers acting like dinosaurs, increasingly desperate to kill the mammals they sense will replace them. The very frenzy with which they seek to silence us proves that Neo-Paganism is becoming mainstream.

So what do I see as the future of Neo-Pagan Druidism? We'll be functioning, with our colleagues in the other Public Neo-Pagan Churches, as that mainstream's clergy, bards, healers, teachers, organizers, mediators, and activists. We'll be listening to the wisdom of the oaks and sharing it with future generations, just as the predecessors who inspire us did. We'll be deepening our connections to Gaia, the deities, the ancestors and the nature spirits, and helping others to deepen theirs as well.

Eventually, we'll go to the stars—after all, somebody has to provide chaplains for the Federation's starships!

Isaac Bonewits is the author of Real Magic, Authentic Thaumaturgy, *and most of* The Druid Chronicles (Evolved). *He is the founder and former ArchDruid of ADF, a bard (with two albums released,* Be Pagan Once Again *and* Avalon Is Rising), *a lecturer, and all-around trouble-maker. His Website is at* http://www.qed.net/ bonewits/ *and you can email him at* ibonewits@qed.net. *Currently, he is writing books on polytheology, liturgy, and the history of Druidism and Witchcraft.*

GE Vol. XXIX, No. 117 (Jan.-Feb. 1997) 4–6

Sometimes I Wonder

Words & music by **Gwydion Pendderwen**

Cat's in the kitchen and she's got a mouse,
And Fox has a squirrel up a tree;
Hawk's gone a-hunting and she caught a little grouse,
But none of them have left a bite for me.
What can you kill when you're high on a hill
And you never killed a critter in your life?
If I had me a gun I could have me some fun,
But all I got is this ol' pocket knife,

Now I wonder, how did I ever get myself in a place
Where I couldn't pick an apple off a tree?
Sometimes I blame it on the whole human race,
But sometimes I wonder if it's me, me, me,
Sometimes I wonder if it's me.

Truck wouldn't start, you know it's out of gas,
We all know that gasoline ain't free.
If I had me some cash or a high grade stash
I couldn't get the gas to come to me.
Now the tire's gone flat as a mortar-board hat
And there ain't another like it in the town,
So my torn back-pack's got my grocery sack
And I'm tryin' not let it get me down,

But I wonder, how did I ever get myself in a place
Where the gasoline and tires are never free?
Sometimes I blame it on the whole human race,
But sometimes I wonder if it's me, me, me,
Sometimes I wonder if it's me.

Roof isn't finished and it's pouring rain,
Now all of my clothes are soaking wet.
To live in this house, you know I'd have to be insane,
But I haven't caught a cold this winter yet!
Firewood's gone, used the last stick at dawn,
And there's mildew on everything I own;
Built my house in a mire, lost my tools in a fire
And I have to put a fence in all alone,

And I wonder, how did I ever get myself in a place
Where I couldn't get an ounce of sympathy?
Sometimes I blame it on the whole human race,
But sometimes I wonder if it's me, me, me,
Sometimes I wonder if it's me.

GE Vol. XXXII, No. 134 (May-June 2000) 4–6

Chapter 3.
Old Pagans
Introduction
by Chas S. Clifton

T O HAVE NEW PAGANS MEANS THERE MUST BE OLD PAGANS TOO, AND *GREEN EGG* writers over the years have looked back to pre-Christian eras. We have a long history of trying figure out "How did they do it back then?" It is no accident that the Pagan religious spectrum includes quite a few people who are called "reconstructionists," who use language, texts, archaeological sites, artifacts, and whatever else they can find to inform their present-day religious practice.

Secondly, it is refreshing and liberating to read historical accounts in which the Pagans were not the knuckle-dragging savages who needed to be "saved" (or else exterminated) by superior monotheistic cultures. (For a book-length experience, try Prudence Jones and Nigel Pennick's *A History of Pagan Europe*.) In this collection, for example, Michael York's article on Lithuanian Paganism stresses its connection with a larger Indo-European religious tradition, a thread also followed by Isaac Bonewits in "Gods of the West." Judy C. Murray's "Voodoo is Nigger Spelled Backwards" examines how racial attitudes prevented a clear look at transplanted West African polytheism, and Daniel Hanson's "History of the Druids" traces a line from the ancient Druids—who wrote nothing down themselves, so we must depend on writings by Romans who sometimes never met a Druid—to more recent attempts to resurrect and reconstruct Druidic spirituality. Michael Howard, who has explored the lost streets of Pagan Europe for many years, writes on dark goddesses of the North. Plus poetry by Diana Paxson and Gwendolyn Zak, a sniff around the Fairy mounds by Tom Kneitel, and essays by Tom Williams and Doug Plexico

I have included a piece of my own here, "Ostara at Anubis Caves," about the difficult question of whether certain ancient inscriptions on the Southern Plains were left by visitors from the Mediterranean basin who came before Columbus. The evidence can be startlingly convincing, but the idea of such visitors in Oklahoma and Colorado seems preposterous. Still, if they were here—and it's an enormous If—they were clearly polytheistic Pagans who marked the changes of the seasons through the stations of the Sun. If you like a mystery with no clear solution, try that one.

Some historians like to quote the English novelist L.P. Hartley, "The past is a foreign country: they do things differently there." There is a great deal about old Paganisms that we don't know. (What did a priest of Apollo do all day?) Ultimately, we cannot do more than look back briefly before we move on, for whatever we say or write about the past, we are saying or writing really about ourselves.

The Changing of the God

by *Tom Williams*, CAW

THERE ARE CERTAIN FEATURES IN the course of human cultural development which lead one to speculate anew on the much-hackneyed idea of a cyclic theory of history. And yet there are enough difference, signs of positive development, that the mind is drawn to consider the notion of progress in the process of human events. Any cyclic view of history postulates some unknown cause or force which somehow makes a culture grow old and weary so that it is ripe for renewal. But it is not my purpose to theorize on historical metaphysics; I have simply come across what I consider an interesting observation.

The world is coming to the conclusion of the Christian era and undergoing a transition into an era of Neo-Paganism which looks back to the old Pagan faith which preceded Christianity. A Pagan is tempted to view the period as "the Christian Interlude," and the question arises: What brought it on, what made possible such a period of animosity toward the Earth and life? We may never know the answer as to the cause, but it does seem that the Pagan peoples of northern Europe were overcome by a weariness or existential resignation about the time of Christianization which made them ripe for the other-worldly doctrines which Christianity preached.

The Norse world view was pervaded by the dark foreboding preceding Ragnarok, the end of all things, when the god and warrior, dwarf and the world-ash would be consumed by the all-engulfing fire. It was essentially a pre-Christian nihilism which could only be countered by one's stance in the face of inevitable doom. A heroic, even stoic posture facing death in battle was the key to Valhalla, but even Valhalla would be swept away in the fires of the End. Gone would be the gods and all great deeds. European man saw himself confronted by the black gaping maw of existence beyond which lay the void. The End would dissolve in chaos, as a verse of the *Voluspa-Saga* puts it: *"Skeggold skamold,*

skiltir kleptir. Windold, wargold, ado werold streypish." ("Axe-age, sword-age, shields are sundered. An age of wind, an age of wolves, before the world crumbles.")

For a long time it was possible to maintain the heroic posture; but any mind would eventually cry out for respite, be it even so illusory. It is exactly at this weakness that Christianity aimed its conversion efforts. An old German poem links the battle of Elias and Satan over the soul with the *Muspilli,* the terrible world conflagration. Elias is wounded and his blood drapes onto the ground igniting trees and mountains. The implication of course is that while the world passes away, the fate of the soul is decided by the battle between "eternal" forces. Even the warrior ethos was co-opted: an old Saxon poem, the *Heliand* depicts Christ as a clan leader and his disciples as loyal warriors and Peter cutting off the soldiers ear at Christ's arrest was ideally suited for such an interpretation.

Nietzsche once said that the peoples of Europe have to be made "sick enough" for Christianity. But perhaps that is too harsh a judgment. In the same work, *The AntiChrist,* he says that Christianity is a religion for "late men." Here, however, he is referring to the actual teaching of Christ which he sees as similar to the teachings of Buddha. It seems that "late men," people whose culture has run the gamut of optimism, aggressiveness and vitality are ready for a contemplative, peace-oriented faith, and such may have been the actual teachings of Jesus before they were perverted by the apostles.

Another compelling force which could forge a mentality of resignation and insecurity is the coming to the Earth-oriented Pagan faiths of a cosmology dominated by a male sky-god. The most apparent origin of such a deity seems to be the great cataclysms which Velikovsky talks about. A deity from the sky is unfathomable, capricious and destructive—just as a stray planet or comet is—while the Mother Goddess is a haven of security, reliable as the seasons, a provider of all nourishment and life. The reaction to the great fear generated by the passing of Venus and Mars was to try to appease this destructive force. Man could do nothing against it save prostrate himself, and thus the sky god's chief claim to worship was his power of destruction which could be visited with utter caprice.

A god whose chief power lay in destruction would naturally be associated with man's destructive powers, the chief of which is war. The oldest runic inscription we have is on the bronze helmet of Negau, dated before 200 BCE. There appears the word tEiWa, or *Teiwa,* the sky-god *Tice.* We find this as the Norse god *Tyr,* in Greek, *Zeus,* and Latin, *Deus.* After the cataclysms it may be assumed that all "normal" destructive forces of nature gained a new significance. Loki, associated with fire, is notoriously unpredictable, and thunderstorms are associated with the destructive power of the sky-god.

After the older Celtic and Pre-Celtic nature religions which were Goddess-oriented and matrifocal had been supplanted by a male god dominated Paganism, there followed a time of warlike adventurism with the migrations of the Goths and associated tribes and the exploits of the Norsemen being the chief feature of the end of this first Pagan era in Europe. The question that all of this leads to is: Where does one wind up by following a warlike, unpredictable male sky god? The answer seems to be: Nihilism and despair. For such a god is as chaotic as the external universe which engendered his belief. The human mind seeks reason and consistency in such a universe or god, and reason is constantly denied him. The only certainty is death and the end of all things.

Then along comes a religion that admits all these things, but has a new twist. Yes, God is inscrutable and wrathful but there is a way out, and the mind, weary and desperate, flings itself upon this straw in the storm. Let us make no mistake: Jehovah has most of the earmarks of your every day run-of-the-mill sky-god, but there is the escape clause of salvation. Of course, salvation is not for this life, so Ragnarok can come, the stars fall from Heaven and all will yet be well. The believer can learn to hate such a transient world as unimportant and post his hopes on an eternal world to come. For a while....

Early Christianity was a tremendously energetic religion and drew a gossamer veil over the abyss that men had seen. It created the unified universe of medieval Christendom which for a time stood rock-solid in faith, providing medieval man with a reliable orientation toward the albeit limited horizons of his universe. The practitioners of the Pagan faiths were forced to gather in darkling woods and glades and in secret hilltop places and yet a few kept the Old Ways alive through all the centuries of domination and persecution by righteous Mother Church.

I recount these known facts not to retell the history of religion but to try to examine the attitude of the practitioners towards life. After the shaken confidence of old Paganism, the Church attempted to restore certainty—first with consolation and later with the thumbscrew and the stake. For the main persecutions took place when the Church was establishing its rule (Charlemagne vs. the Saxons) and when it was losing its hold after the reformation (when most of the persecutions of witches and heretics took place). The assurance which the Church hoped to provide was shattered by the same thing that had unsettled the Old Pagans—external reality.

Many examples could be cited but the discoveries of Galileo show where things were headed. The realization that the moons of Jupiter revolve about the planet and must perforce pierce the crystal spheres of Aristotelian theory was more then just a blow to a cherished doctrine. The bloody things revolved about the planet whether the Pope wanted to look through the telescope or not and sooner or later people were going to see that fact. More devastating was the blow to certainty and assurance. If the moons of Jupiter do not conform to the crystal spheres of doctrines but float freely in empty space, what does that imply about the position and stability of the Earth? What about the freedom of man and the immutability of established authority? If planets can swing freely in space, if Popes can be fallible, cannot thrones be toppled, are we not all in a pretty fragile, precarious position? Where is Heaven if not beyond the crystal spheres which suddenly no longer exist? The world was once more cut loose from its moorings and man found himself adrift on an uncertain raft.

There were attempts to heal over this wound so brutally wrenched open by the perceiving eye. The romantic movement was the last such and was parodied in its later phase by people such as Heine who called it stage settings without convictions. The merciless incisive scorn of Nietzsche revealed the abyss once more to nihilists and existentialists and stripped away the curtain of false assurances. Christianity was faced with its crisis, with its look into the jaws of reality and has cringed. It has tried to cover its retreat with vague theories of Christian existentialism and mutterings of false hope, but the honest ones like Kierkegaard have refused this sacramental cup at the end. The attempts of Christianity to deny the caprice of the universe have failed because the universe is in fact capricious and does not conform to the demands of the human mind that it be rational and intelligible. It is the gap between the mind that demands reason and the universe which denies it that existentialists have called the absurd.

The absurd shocked the Old Pagans who were unprepared for it and somewhat understandably embraces Christianity. But the absurd thwarted Christianity which tried to deny it, and Christianity is crumbling because of that, and because of its denial of the real world along with the absurd. The real universe *is* absurd as far as the human perspective is concerned.

All this brings us to the Neo-Pagan transition in which we now find ourselves. It is clear that a whole host of Earth-oriented religions are rising up and harkening back to their early origins. The question I wish to consider here is: What is their world-view and attitude toward life? This is the point where my cyclic observation of religious listing is joined by the idea of progress and positive development. We see now unfolding before us a religion of the Earth, of immediate, pulsing life which does not sly away from the look into chaos. The attempts to cloak

the abyss have shattered, destroying many of those who cling to them.

For the New Pagan, the realization that the universe beyond is chaotic and unfeeling does not produce a miasma of despair. Just as the certainty of death increases the passion for this life, intensifies the immediate experience of here and now to a symphonic crescendo of joy, so does the view of our Earth as a tiny, fragile refuge of warmth and life in the midst of a cold and heartless universe increase our love and devotion to Her as the bountiful and providing Mother of our race. Science has taught us that there is no angry and vengeful god in the sky, but it does not comfort us with false assurance either. If Earth has been devastated by near misses with planetary bodies in the past, it could happen again for better or for worse. We must also remember that although we do not now understand the workings of the Cosmos and know that it can be a threat to us, there may come a stage in our consciousness when we will have as much appreciation and love for the workings of the universe as for our own planet.

That time is not yet and we can but look with awe at the cold vastness of space and view it as an unknown sea where there be monsters, but a sea that constantly challenges us to leave our warm green home and sail forth seeking those things man knows not yet of. Ours is the dichotomy of the womb and the open road, for at the same time we have been drawn to adore our Earth as never before. We see Her providence not only with our minds but we feel with our bodies the rhythm of Her seasons; the quickening sap makes the blood flow fresher and more freely. We are intimately a part of our Home with body and mind and though we may leave Her to journey forth, She is still with us and we are Her children and stewards. It is up to us to revere Her in the ways of the ancients who adored the Earth with a love they could feel and a knowledge they could intuit. We feel anew the pulse of the Earth, Her needs and urging, and we seek knowledge by all means we can, nor is technology to be rejected in and of itself. The Earth has spawned a seeking, inquiring race with an insatiable appetite for knowledge and experience. What is to be hoped for now is maturity and wisdom. Wisdom is the combination of knowledge with love and thus we Neo-Pagans must combine that knowledge which we possess and which we seek with our love and celebration of our green Mother planet, our one true home.

Though the children of Terra someday ride forth in ships powered by the very heart of the stars, may they always have this Earth to return to, Her sunny hills and cool valleys running with the unsullied water of life, cared for by their brothers and sisters, fellow children of a wakened planet.

GE Vol. V, No. 52 (Oimelc 1973) 11–13

Circles

Copyright © 1977 by **Gwendolyn L. Zak**
(additional verses as noted)
Reprinted by permission of the authors.
(to tune of *"Windmills"* by Alan Bell)

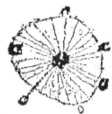

In days gone by, when the world was much
    younger,
We wondered at Spring, born of Winter's
    cold knife—
Wondered at the games of the Moon and
    the Sunlight;
We saw then the Lady and the Lord of all life!

chorus:
Around and around and around
Turns the good Earth;
All things must change as the seasons roll by—y!
We are the children of the Lord and the Lady,
Whose Mysteries we learn
From the Earth and the Sky!

In all lands the people were tied with the
    good Earth;
Plowing and sowing as the seasons declared—
Waiting to reap of the rich golden harvest;
Knowing Her love in the joys that they shared.

Through Flanders and Wales and the green
    hills of Ireland;
In the kingdoms of England and Scotland
    and Spain—
Circles grew up all along the wild coastlines;
We worked for the land with the sun and the rain!

Circles for healing and working the weather;
Circles for knowing the Moon and the Sun;
Circles for thanking the Lord and the Lady;
Circles for dancing the Dance never done!

(Barbara Weinberg):
In Egypt and Sumer, through Bharat and Mali,
As N'eilla and Bast and Inanna She came
Cities grew up near the jungles and deserts;
Her own know Her still by these ancient
    proud names.

On the water's far shore, some were called
    Anasazi;
Through tundra to desert and forest they came—
Leaving circles and spirals throughout
    Turtle Island;
Preserving the land in the Goddess's name.

(Ann Cass):
And we who reach for the stars in the heavens,
Lifting our eyes from the hedges and rows,
Still live in the love of the Lord and the Lady;
The greater the Circle, the more the love grows!

AUTHOR'S NOTE: Whatever people wish to do with the song is fine with me. I've always felt like it came through me and not from me, and, like the Craft, belongs to anyone it speaks to, to claim and personalize as they might feel appropriate. Thank you for your interest in, and enthusiasm for "Circles." It has been a joy to me to continuously find siblings and fellow travelers through this song. May we soon Merry Meet.
    In Love, Blessed Be,
    Gwen Zak, 1992

GE Vol. XXV, No. 97 (Summer 1992) inside front

The Cornish Faerie Faith

by *Tom Kneitel ("Phoenix")*
High Priest, Long Island Gardnerian Coven

HAT THE LITTLE PEOPLE LIVE IN the British Isles is no secret; English folklore abounds with tales of these creatures, although there seem to be specific areas (such as Wales, the Isle of Man, Ireland, etc.) which seem to be especially well-populated. Perhaps not as well known as a center of belief in the little folk is the area of Cornwall, at the southernmost tip of the British Isles.

Cornwall seems to have evolved in its own direction, apart from many other districts in England. There are many unusual and unique customs and festivals, and the Cornish people are a breed unto themselves. Even though Cornwall is a deeply religious area (it is said that there are more saints in Cornwall than there are in heaven), the Cornish people are well acquainted with folk magic, charms, superstitions, and odd legends—and, of course, the Faerie folk are a part of their daily life. These Faerie beliefs are interesting and in some respects rather different than elsewhere in England.

The Faeries of Cornwall may be divided into four classes: the *Small People,* the *Pixies* (pronounced Piskies or Pisgies), the *Spriggans,* and the *Knockers.* The first are harmless elfish little beings known all over England, whose revels on fine summer nights have often been described by favored individuals who have accidentally come upon them in the woods. As a rule, however, they wish to feel that they are invisible, and in Cornwall it is considered unlucky to call them by the name of *Faeries.*

When molested, Faeries can be spiteful and vexing and take great delight in thwarting people who meddle with them. When unmolested, they bring good fortune to the places they frequent. It is said that "they can't abear those whom they can't abide." There are tales of persons spirited away to the land of the Faeries, to become servants to the small people's children. However, the time is said to pass so pleasantly in that place that they have forgotten about their homes and relations. In fact, things go well until the human does some forbidden thing and incurs the wrath of the master. They are then punished by being put into a deep sleep, and upon awakening, find themselves on some moor near their own village. But homecoming is not too sweet, for their fate is to roam about aimlessly doing nothing more than hoping for return to the place from which they had been banished.

Most of those who are spirited away had come under the Faerie's power by eating or drinking something on the sly when they had surprised them at one of their midnight frolics, or possibly they had accepted a gift of fruit from the hands of a little being.

Faeries haunt the ancient monuments of Cornwall and guard their safety, being especially prone to bringing bad luck to any who would attempt to destroy such monuments.

These small people are thought to have been mentally retarded people who had committed no particular sins, but whom, when they died, were not accepted into heaven because of a lack of intellect. They are always thought, in one state or another, to have lived previously as humans.

While the small people go about in groups, the *Pixie* is a solitary being, at least in West Cornwall. In the eastern part of Cornwall the title "Pixie" seems to be applied indiscriminately to both tribes.

In the western section, the Pixie is a ragged little fellow, although quite merry ("to laugh like a Pixie" is a common Cornish simile), interesting himself in human affairs, threshing the farmer's corn at nights or doing other work, including pinching the maidservants when they do not complete their chores by bed-time, for the Pixies have little tolerance for those who are unclean.

Should the lucky possessor of one of these ambitious (and unpaid) Faerie servants (who do not object to taking food left for them) express thanks aloud, thus acknowledging that they are visible, or should the master attempt to reward the Pixie for his services by, perhaps, offering a new suit of clothes, the Pixie leaves the house, never to return. It is said that, upon leaving after being offered a bribe they might be heard to say something such as, "Pixie fine, Pixie gay, Pixie now will fly away!" Or, another parting shot reported is, "Pixie new coat, and Pixie new hood; Pixie now will do no more good!"

When in a mischievous mood, a Pixie is inclined to have some fun with a person found walking about at night, for they will (like Will of the Wisp) take them over hedges and ditches, sometimes round and round the same field, and then they are left to find their way home, which seems almost an impossibility even though they are not far from the path. The only remedy is to turn the stockings or pockets inside out which breaks the spell and permits reorientation. It is said, "Pixie led is often whiskey led."

In the past (and up to the early 19th Century), unbaptised children were said to turn, when they died, into pixies; gradually going through many transformations at each change, getting smaller until at last they become *meryons* (ants) and vanish. Another legend is that Pixies were Pagans of old, who, because they would not accept the new religion, were (for these sins) condemned to change first into Pixies; gradually getting smaller, and then, too, as ants, finally disappear. It is therefore unlucky to destroy an ants' nest in Cornwall, and a Witch in Cornwall has told me that a certain phase of the Moon she seeks out an ants' nest, into which she inserts her athame for the purpose of having it "magically recharged."

It was once a custom in Cornwall, when houses were built, to leave holes in the walls by which Pixies could enter; to stop them would drive away good luck. And in Cornwall, lead knobs, known as "Pixie's paws" or "Pixie feet" were once placed at intervals on the roofs of farmhouses to prevent the Pixies from dancing on them and turning the milk sour in the dairies. A prayer book might also he placed under a child's pillow as a charm to keep away Pixies who might steal the child

and leave a changeling in its place.

If Pixies are kind and helpful little beings, Spriggans or Sprites are spiteful creatures, never doing a favor for anyone. It is they who are the primary child stealers, placing their own ugly and peevish brats in place of human children. These changelings never thrive well under the foster-mother's care, the child never being satisfied when eating or drinking, or when being held. One way of attempting to soothe such a child is to bring it to the holy well at Puny (or St. Uny) near Cancred on the first three Wednesdays in May, dipping it until the child comes calm, or until the Spriggan comes to re-exchange the children. Another way of accomplishing the return of a child taken by the Spriggans is to put the changeling on the ashes pile and beat it well with a broom, then lay it naked under a church stile, leaving it there until nightfall when it is taken away and the natural child is returned.

Spriggans are said to guard the vast treasures that are supposed to be buried beneath the ground and in the cliff castles, and they are sure to punish any person rash enough to attempt to seek out such treasures. Those who have been foolish enough to dig for this treasure have recounted stories of having dug down for some depth when they have found themselves surrounded by hundreds of "ugly beings," who scare the treasure hunter to the point where the tools are soon abandoned and the diggings are "left in great haste." Such frights are said to have made people so ill that they have had to stay in bed for days. Should they ever summon sufficient strength to return to that spot, they will find the pit refilled, and no traces to show that the ground had ever been disturbed.

Knockers (pronounced knackers) are mine faeries, popularly supposed to be the souls of Jews who were sent by the Romans to work as slaves in the Cornish tin mines. In proof of this, they are said never to have been heard at work on Saturdays or other Jewish holy days, although they are compelled to sing carols at Christmastime. Small pieces of tin found in old smelting works are therefore known as "Jews' bowels."

These faeries haunt none but the richest tin mines, and many are reputed to have been discovered by their singing and knocking underground; and miners think that when they are heard it is a lucky omen and will reward them with a good ore lode.

Knockers, like Spriggans, are very ugly, and if you don't treat them in a friendly manner they can be extremely vindictive. They must never be spoken of disrespectfully, must never be told to keep quiet or to leave a place, and a small bit of food must be left for them by the miners who eat in the mine, in order to avoid their wrath.

Independently of these beings, the Cornish are also concerned with *Bucca,* the name of a local Cornish spirit that it was once thought necessary to appease. Fishermen left fish on the sands for Bucca, and in the harvest a piece of bread at lunch-time was thrown over the left shoulder, and a few drops of beer spilled on the ground as a libation to him, to insure good luck. Bucca, or bucca-boo, was, until most recently (and I have heard in some circles still is) the terror of children, who were often told when crying that if they didn't stop he would come and carry them off. It was also the name of a Cornish ghost, and is evidently the origin of the terms *bugaboo* and *bogeyman* which we use today. But today, in Cornwall, to call someone a "great bucca" simply implies that you think him a fool. There were two Buccas: *Bucca Gwidden,* the good spirit, and *Bucca Dhu,* a malevolent one.

GE Vol. VII, No 68 (Oimelc 1975) pp. 23–24

The Gods of the West
(to tune of "Men of the West")
by **P.E.I. Bonewits** *(Copyright © 1972)*

When you honor in song and in story
The Gods of the old Pagan men,
Whose blessings have covered with glory
Full many a mountain and glen,
Forget not the Gods of our fathers,
Who'll rally our bravest and best,
When Ireland is Christian and bleeding
And looks for revenge to the West.

(Chorus:)
So here's to the gods of our fathers,
Who'll rally our bravest and best
When Ireland is Christian and bleeding—
Hurrah! For the Gods of the West!

Oh the Sidhe hills with glory will shine then
On the eve of our bright Freedom Day,
When the Gods we've been wearily waiting
Come back from the Land of the Fey.
And over the land rise the Druids,
Awakening in every breast
A fire that will never be quenched, friends,
Among the true Gaels of the West.

Dublin will be ours ere the midnight,
And high over Bel-li-fast town,

Our Druid prayers then will be floating
Before the next sun has gone down!
We'll gather to speed the good work, our friends,
The Pagans from near and afar—
And Ireland will watch us expel ALL
The Clergy with feathers and tar.

And pledge us the Old Gods of Ireland,
Bold Connacht and all his brave crew,
Whose return, like the trumpet of battle,
Will bring hope to the Pagans anew.
As the Old Gods have brought to their feasthalls
From many a mountain and hill,
The Pagans who fell, so they're here, friends,
To lead us to victory still.

Though all the bright dreamings we cherished,
Went down 'neath the Churches and woe,
The Spirits of old still are with us,
Who *never* will bend to the foe!
And Connacht is ready whenever
The loud rolling tuck of the drum
Rings out to awaken the Pagans
And tell us our morning has come!!

GE Vol. VI, No. 59 (Yule 1973) 18

The Indo-European Heritage of Lithuanian Paganism

by *Michael York*

IN THE CURRENT DIALECTIC between traditional Paganism and American/British Neo-Paganism, the Old Religion of Lithuania plays an important role as Shamanistic/poly-theistic and folkloric spirituality continue to come to force. The ancient Lithuanian religion represents an authentic form of Paganism—similar to those which existed in the past and still do exist in parts of Asia and Africa and the Americas. Whereas Neo-Paganism is found chiefly in the new religious movements of Wicca and Goddess Spirituality and possesses close ties with Ceremonial Magic, Shamanistic polytheism unites Baltic religion with contemporary Druidism, the Sodalicium Romanum, and various forms of Asartu, Odinism and Vanirism. What these last all have in common is their Indo-European heritage.

Our earliest ancestors—who spoke a language from which Latin, Greek, Sanskrit, Gaelic, Lithuanian, Latvian and English, among others, all descended—had a world-view and a *view of the world* which, by to-day's religious standards, were incredibly beautiful. Over the course of history and the ravages of time. however, this world-picture came to be shattered, confused and largely lost. Today, an aspirant who attempts to re-cover this ancient spiritual outlook is like the person who tries to reassemble a gigantic jig-saw puzzle whose pieces are scattered around the world, many of which are irre-trievably lost and others are so disguised or distorted as to be beyond recognition. Nev-ertheless, together the ethnologist, the com-parative mythologist, the linguist and the archaeologist appear to be able to re-form the general outlines of our ancestral ideology. It must be stressed, however, that with so many lacunae and debatable positions pos-sible for so many of the remaining jigsaw pieces, any restructuring of the original world-picture is at best an *interpretation.*

The following presentation of the Proto-Indo-European religion upon which Baltic, Germanic, Celtic, Roman, Greek and Vedic mythologies are all derived is just that an interpretation or simply one way of looking at the pieces. Nevertheless, the following interpretation is one which the multitude of data and analysis appear to support. Since there is no space to furnish all the arguments, I shall present only the conclusions.

The Proto-Indo-European pantheon comprised seven basic figures or prototypes: Earth, Sky or Light, Thunder, Fire, Sun, Moon, and Dawn. In Lithuania, these dei-ties became known as Zemyna, Dievas, Perkunas, Gabija, Saute, Menulis, and Ausra. The proto-theogony begins with the Earth Mother, Zemyna, who produces a son (Die-vas) or a pair of twins (Dievas and Menulis). Dievas then becomes Zemyna's lover or hus-band and they produce the divine twins, the Dievo suneliai (Fire and Thunder/Lighten-ing) and a daughter (Dawn). Dievas next falls in love with his beautiful daughter and she gives birth to the Sun. In this proto-panthe-on, the Earth and Dawn are inevitably God-desses, while Heaven (Dievas) and Thunder (Perkunas) are male Gods. The remaining three deities are ambivalent—sometimes considered female, sometimes male. As a result, for the Batts and Germanic-speaking people, the sun is a Goddess, but for the Greeks, Romans and Vedics, the Sun is a God. Likewise the Batts, Slays, Germanics and Vedics consider the moon to be mascu-line; the Greeks and Romans take the moon as feminine.

Throughout this pantheon and the de-rivative mythologies we find several duali-ties—frequently expressed in the figures of the divine twins. The basic ideology may be summed up in the figures comprising the Earth and the Moon-God duality. In essence, the Indo-European world-view pictures hu-mans as Gods—in fact, humans are seen as the very twin of divinity. One of the religious

74

symbols for humanity is the moon as emblematic of the being who dies and is reborn. The moon is also the magical ambrosia, the food of the Gods. It is consumed and then replenishes itself so that it can be consumed again. But likewise, it is also the divine soma of which humanity—at least the shamans partake and then know their true divinity and place among the Gods. Most Indo-European ritual is a celebration of this twinship between humanity and the divine.

In a pantheistic understanding of our ancestors, all is God. The divine dynamic comprises a whole series of fluctuating dualities or polarities: light versus darkness, the material versus the spiritual, the positive versus the negative, the masculine versus the feminine. These polarities are constantly realigning. There is no fixed equation such as came to be made by Christianity and other transcendental religions in which the positive, masculine, spiritual and light were all identified and opposed permanently to the feminine, negative, material and dark. In the pantheistic understanding, the negative, dark and demonic nature of death is still very much divine and a necessary part of the great round of nature and the dynamic of regeneration. But whereas transcendentalism celebrates stasis, Paganism celebrates eternal evolution.

This pantheistic ancestral understanding presupposes, however, another duality. Consequently, apart from the divine duality, which is the full godhead, all of reality, there is that which is termed the divine-asurian dichotomy; that is, the all as opposed to the nothingness, the void or chaos of pre-existence. Another way to phrase this opposition is to consider it as one in which oblivion seeks to annul both the positive *and* the negative of all creation. This asuric nothingness endeavors

to reinstate the aboriginal void of oblivion, the complete annihilation of existence. To do this, it must incorporate within the plane of creation in order to work its subterfuge and efforts toward total cessation. In this way, it is often confused with the divine—especially the negative pole of the divine. For the ancients, apart from the utter blackness of night, the chief emblems or manifestations of the asurian were the volcano, the tempest, and the drought-producing rainless sky. Among the Indo-European godforms which the asurian assumed, we find Chaos, Uranus, Hephaistos, Varuna, Odin, and the Lithuanian Velnias. In time the deity-forms and the asura-forms tended to become conasurian in two related ways. Foremost, they worshipped the divine Gods as their ally and sacred alter ego in the struggle against the forces of oblivion. Secondly, they worshiped the asurian directly in a religious-magical attempt to transform it into the divine. Worship is literally 'the creation of worth.' Humanity, through religious expression, is the very maker of the divine; that which is of value.

In the recent past, Western Europeans and Americans, when faced with the spiritual bankruptcy of a secularized and overly technological society, have frequently traveled to India in search of their spiritual past. Now, with the liberation of the Eastern European countries and the liberalization of Lithuania and Latvia, I predict that in the future more Westerners will make the pilgrimage to the Baltic lands in search of their Indo-European roots and the living folkloric heritage which is to be found there—the most vital of all Europe. Much of the Pagan future—the real Pagan future—depends on the West's contact with her Baltic teachers and the ancient holy sanctuaries of her guardians' lands....

[Reprinted from *Romuva*, a journal of indigenous Baltic traditional religion and spirituality, #10, Winter 1992]

Vol. XXVI, No. 101 (Summer 1993) 15

Ostara at Anubis Caves

by Chas S. Clifton

HE DAY OF BEL IS GONE TO HELL," said Del Crandall, sipping coffee in the Copper Kitchen cafe in La Junta, Colorado.

It was hard to disagree. The morning of the spring equinox, March 20, 1993, had brought with it a completely overcast sky—the day looked a poor one for archaeoastronomy.

More coffee, the *Denver Post*, biscuits, gravy and green chile—by nine o'clock, a tiny patch of blue had appeared in the west. Weather on the High Plains often changes fast. We formed our caravan of four vehicles and headed south to await the equinox sunset at Anubis Caves.

The "trail boss" for our party of nine was Bill McGlone, a retired engineer, coauthor of *Ancient Celtic America*, and genial monomaniac on the topic of purported Old World rock inscriptions in the area. The last, of course, makes McGlone and his fellow epigraphers (scholars of ancient inscriptions) a nuisance to the American archaeology establishment.

McGlone's introduction to this particular heresy came from Barry Fell, oceanographer and marine biologist, retired Harvard University professor, and—in the archaeology establishment's eyes—total crackpot. Beginning in 1976 with *America B.C.*, Fell produced a string of books and papers detailing an elaborate scenario of pre-Viking transatlantic travel. A reader could come away believing Iberian Celts, Phoenicians , Egyptians, Hebrews and Bronze Age Scandinavians had whipped the ocean into froth with their oars before a curtain of silence fell in the early Christian Era.

In *America B.C.* Fell described and translated purported Old Irish inscriptions (a postulated early Q-Celtic tongue used in the Iberian peninsula before the general switch to Latin) written in Ogham characters on boulders and rock ledges in New England, West Virginia, Oklahoma, and Colorado, among other areas. Fell had studied Gaelic at the University of Edinburgh as well as becoming acquainted with known Ogham inscriptions in Ireland and the British Isles.

Fell's theories have received more support in Europe and North Africa than in North America, where our archaeologists denounce them as uninformed speculation. The Epigraphic Society, which he formed, suffered a split when some members, including McGlone and his co-author Phil Leonard, formed the Western Epigraphic Society (WES) upon concluding that Fell was too quick to draw sweeping conclusions from the available evidence. WES members continue to search out and record more possible inscriptions in Ogham and other scripts and a follow-up book to *Ancient Celtic America* is being readied for publication.

I had read and puzzled over Fell's books as they appeared; indeed, honeymooning in Ireland in 1978, my wife, Mary, and I made a point of visiting the collection of Ogham-inscribed stones at Ballintaggart, Co. Kerry, to see what authenticated Ogham looked like. After that, I had not given the subject more than casual thought until the early 1990s, when a couple we know suggested a joint trip to see Crack Cave and Picture Canyon.

Located on the Comanche National Grassland in southeastern Colorado and administered by the U.S. Forest Service, Picture Canyon is named for its collection of prehistoric rock art, human and animal figures incised by ancient natives. But it also holds Crack Cave, a narrow fissure in the sandstone with a number of the alleged Ogham writings and a series of marks cut in one wall. We went in November 1992, wrangling a key to the cave's protective grill from the ranger station staff in Springfield, Colorado, so that I could take inside photos of inscriptions and marks that are precisely illuminated by the equinox sunrise shining through the cave's east-facing entrance.

That visit led to more research and eventual personal contact with McGlone and his associates. The following March we anxiously watched the cloudy skies as we sped down a series of gravel roads toward the Oklahoma state line.

Of the eight major Pagan festivals, Ostara, the spring equinox, has always resonated the least with me. It seems compressed between the manifested inner fire of Candlemas/Oimelc and the more abundant energy of Beltane. In our climate, only a few hardy garden crops can be planted at Ostara since the last average frost date is still weeks away. And at our previous home I always associated this season with trying to find some dry but not too windy days when my neighbors and I could burn the dead grass and weeds in our common irrigation ditch, which then had to be dug and scraped of a season's worth of silt before the water was turned into it late in April. The equinox meant warm days alternating with blizzards; the first onset of hay fever from tree pollen; and a whole list of outdoor chores to be done. These combined to make Ostara for me a time of external anxiety rather than internal change.

Now, this trip had become a different way to mark the season, driving south across the ball of the Earth, 360 degrees of horizon visible, on a tawny grassland broken by an occasional field deep green with winter wheat. The day of Bel, the day of turning, was a day of driving, marked by occasional stops to admire rocks incised with deer, bighorn sheep, suns, and an entire vocabulary of unknown symbols covered by a brown patina ("desert varnish") that spoke of millennia. After many miles, the wide-open country began to break into mesas and shallow canyons. We had crossed an imperceptible divide from the Arkansas River drainage to the Cimarron.

Since the 1970s, three major and several minor groups of Ogham inscriptions have been found on a roughly north-south line between the two rivers. McGlone refers to this area as the "Ogham Corridor." Crack Cave is one of the three and the only one on public land. Another is called the "Sun Temple," and our destination was the third, Anubis Caves.

To these maverick epigraphers, one of the strongest arguments against the inscriptions being faked is that only when they were translated did anyone realize that the three sites were astronomically oriented. Another is that in this lightly populated area, the older ranchers remember the markings being there fifty years or more ago; they simply assumed that the Indians had made them. Thus it is unlikely that anyone rushed out with a chisel to make them so that they could be "discovered."

And, believe me, southeastern Colorado and western Oklahoma are not places where people were studying vanished alphabets and Old Irish a century ago. They were trying to raise cattle or wheat, and later they were coping with the droughts and Dust Bowl of the 1930s. Aside from a few archaeologists studying remains dating back to the Pleistocene, the locals usually consider "history" to have begun in the 1840s with the Santa Fe Trail.

Both Crack Cave and Anubis Caves contain inscriptions oriented to the equinoxes. In the former the rising sun and in the latter the setting sun cause shadows to move across a wall, precisely illuminating various ruler-like figures and diagrams.

At Crack Cave, a consonantal Ogham spells out "S-G-R-N," which Fell reads as *aois grian*, or "people of the sun." More important is

Fig. 1: The Anubis Caves are a series of small shelters in a low eroded cliff on private land in the Oklahoma Panhandle. (Photo-Chas Clifton)

another inscription translated to read "Sun strikes [here] day of Bel" together with a row of ray-like marks. Exactly half of the "rays" are illuminated by the equinox sunrise shining through the cave's narrow entrance. A day before or after and the illumination is off-center.

Anubis Cave 2 contains a more elaborate panel that includes a setting-sun disk with a smaller version "dangling" from it, a figure with a rayed solar head (interpreted as a solar deity), and a carving that looks very much like the jackal deity Anubis, complete with a flail, symbol of royal power. If the combination of an Egyptian deity with Celtic writing seems incongruous, McGlone and Leonard cite archaeological reports of Anubis altars from not only Spain and Gaul but Hungary, probably made in connection with the religion of Isis that spread throughout the Roman Empire.

At the Sun Temple (a site which I have not seen) other inscriptions are translated to read possibly "At Lugnasad (L-G-N-S) the summer Sun restores the gathering for sports" and "Season [for] reaping." An observer sitting with head against a faint ring chipped in the stone of the cliff wall near where an inscription may read "The ring along with the shoulder by means of Sun and hill," will see the Sun rise under a square notch in a projecting rock face.

When our road entered Oklahoma the surface changed from gravel to asphalt. Not long thereafter McGlone signaled a turn onto a dirt road, and I was looking at the very caves of which I had only seen drawings before.

I parked just inside a barbed-wire pasture gate. Mary and I decided to walk the last quarter mile. For one thing, the pasture was full of clumps of cholla cactus, but most of all, this was a pilgrimage of sorts for us, and it seemed right to approach the site on foot. Taking a shortcut, we arrived at the same time as the rest of our party.

But now the sky had refilled with broad bands of cloud—a front moving in from the west. The light was flat and grey—"portrait light," said the photographer from Boulder with a wry grin. A Say's phoebe perched at

Figure 2: *Epigrapher William McGlone discusses C-14 dating of lichens at Anubis Caves. Bison petroglyph by his shoulder is believed to have been made by prehistoric Indians. (Photo by Chas S. Clifton)*

the top of a leafless hackberry tree in front of the sandstone cliff containing the row of shallow caves. We all climbed in and out of the caves, photographing inscriptions, studying the modern (1870s and since) graffiti, watching the Sun's glow move behind the cloud towards the mesa top that formed the western horizon. In front of the caves, the valley floor was a flat silt deposit built up by centuries of flash floods eroding the dry land.

"Somebody ought to dig here," we joked. "Bel Town is out there, twenty feet down—the ruins of the smithy, the druid's house, the golden torts, the whole thing."

In truth, I was suffering a slight case of cognitive dissonance. Behind me were the inscriptions, old and patinated. Based on what I had seen in Ireland, they indeed looked like Ogham. In front of me were the hackberry trees and the mesa squatting across the valley, the Cimarron River drainage. It was easy to imagine the plains Apaches or the Comanches passing through, travelers on the Santa Fe Trail, buffalo hunters, cattle drives moving up from Texas.

Reaching further back, I could imagine, perhaps in a moister climate, the Folsom hunters seeking the long-gone giant bison of 11,000 years ago.

Those scenes are easier to imagine than what the inscriptions in the Ogham Corridor require one to suppose. First, seafarers must have left the Iberian peninsula and, following much the same path as Columbus, entered the Gulf of Mexico. (There is no dispute that ancient ships were adequate for the trip.) Then they must have found the Mississippi River. Next, they must have come up the Mississippi, paddling or poling against the current, to the mouth of the Arkansas. They then followed the Arkansas into present-day Oklahoma. Today, the river to that point is relatively large, its flow controlled by dams. But if the climate of perhaps 2,000 years ago were anything like today's, the Arkansas River in western Kansas and eastern Colorado or the Cimarron River in western Oklahoma would have been too shallow much of the year even for little boats. After a dry summer these rivers can diminish to a trickle. Travelers would have had to walk beside them.

In all, the land journey involved hundreds of miles, and at its end...a few hunters and gatherers, perhaps growing some crops in the flood plains of these intermittent rivers. For this some Celts crossed the ocean and observed the equinoxes? To trade for Indian corn and squash? The trip is no more than the shipwrecked Spanish explorer Alvar Núñez Cabeza de Vaca and his companions made in the sixteenth century, for example, but what was its motive?

An alternative hypothesis has the inscriptions cut by Indians who learned the alphabet and the language from Europeans, but, to me, that requires an equally complicated storyline.

McGlone and Leonard, working with some other archaeoastronomers, think one carving at the Sun Temple site depicts a conjunction of Saturn, Jupiter, and Venus in Gemini that occurred on 8 August 471 CE—almost on Lugnasad. Such precise dating makes the whole business even eerier.

I cannot completely reconcile the arid canyon, the mesa, the cactus, and the hack-berry trees with the inscriptions—not yet, at any rate. Yet the possibilities are powerful. After the known histories of European contact with the New World, the Ogham sites and other purportedly ancient inscriptions present almost an alternate

universe. We cannot say that Pagans would necessarily have been less brutal explorers than the *conquistadores* and the Puritans. After all, according to the sagas, the Norsemen attacked the inhabitants of "Vinland" and set off an escalating round of violence. By contrast, some Colorado inscriptions are translated to speak of trading, although what goods were traded is not known. And raiders, I think, would not be likely to make leisurely astronomical observations or to record a "gathering for sports."

Barry Fell translated an inscription from Anubis Cave 4 to read, "The Sun belongs to Bel. This cavern on the day of the equinox is consecrated for chanting of prayers to Bel." Our equinox sunset would occur at about 5:45 p.m.—early, since the mesa top was higher than the true horizon.

As the solar disk touched the mesa, the cloud bands opened and weak sunlight struck Cave 2's back wall. A rising wedge of shadow moved up across the figure called the Sun God until only his head was illuminated, a virtual mirror image of the sun disk above the mesa. As the rising shadow covered him, a "thumb" of shadow crossed the "Setting Sun" and stopped on the "Dangling Sun" that hangs off the end of it. Simultaneously, a wedge of light illuminated Anubis, "the jackal

Figure 3: The Anubis Caves carvings at the equinox sunset: the rising shadow has almost covered the "Sun God" and is halfway across the setting Sun disk. The carving interpreted as the Anubis figure is an Ogham inscription translated as "At sundown the shadow moves nearly to the jaw of the jackal of divinity" (Barry Fell). (Photo by Chas S. Clifton)

of the dusk." The Sun symbolically had left the heavens and entered the Underworld.

No chanting, but a 20th-century hymn of clicking camera shutters responded to the sacred interplay of light and shadow, and then the Sun was gone. We shouldered our camera bags and other gear. Somewhere down the canyon a coyote howled briefly.

I do not usually respond as deeply to the vernal equinox as to the cross-quarter days on either side of it. But this time, yes, I felt the turning of the year. I left Anubis Caves with a greater sense of mystery, a feeling of the present intersecting with multiple pasts and who knows what futures, on the pivot of the day of Bel.

> **Chas Clifton** lives in the Wet Mountains of southern Colorado He edits Llewellyn Publications' *Witchcraft Today* series, which includes *The Modern Craft Movement* (1992), *Rites of Passage* (1993), and an upcoming anthology on Witchcraft and shamanism.

Travel Information

Crack Cave, the only Ogham site on public land, is located in Picture Canyon, part of the Comanche National Grasslands. For maps and other information, write to: Comanche National Grasslands, US Forest Service, POB 127, Springfield, CO 81073. Telephone (719) 523-6591.

Springfield, CO, holds "equinox festivals" in March and September, including guided tours of Picture Canyon. For more information call the Springfield chamber of Commerce (719) 523-4061.

Further Reading

Feder, Kenneth, *Frauds, Myths, and Mysteries: Science and Pseudoscience in Archaeology.* Mayfield Publishing Co. 1990.

Fell, Barry, *America B.C.: Ancient Settlers in the New World*. New York Times Book Co. 1980.

Fell, Barry, *Bronze Age America.* Little, Brown 1982.

Frost, Frank J., "Voyages of the Imagination." *Archaeology* 46:2 (March/April 1993) 45–51.

Kelly, David H., "Proto-Tifinagh and Proto-Pgham in the Americas." *Review of Archaeology:* 11:1 (Spring 1990) 1–10.

McGlone, William R. & Phillip M. Leonard, *Ancient Celtic America.* Panorama West Books 1986.

Welcome

Open a way between the worlds,
Behold, the ravens fly;
Open a door into our hall,
Allfather now draws nigh!

His gifts to us are wit and will,
His wisdom sets us free;
A horn we raise in welcome to
The god of ecstasy!

Nine worlds there are upon the Tree,
Behold the ravens fly;
Who knows the secrets of them all?
The Wanderer draws nigh!

He knows the darkness and the light,
The heavens and the sea;
A horn we raise in welcome to
The god of ecstasy!

The Rider of the Tree draws near;
Behold the ravens fly;
The runes of power flare forth in might
For Galdor-father's nigh!

The patterns of our lives laid out
In sacred signs we see;
A horn we raise in welcome to
The god of ecstasy!

—Diana L. Paxson

The Dark Queens of Northern Europe

by Mike Howard, Editor, The Cauldron, London (art by Scott Fay)

HE HAG AND CRONE ASPECT IS the oldest form of the Goddess worshipped by our ancestors. In the Northern European religions of the Celtic, Germanic and Nordic peoples, the Dark Goddess is one of the divine triad of Maiden, Mother and Grandmother, the Triple Goddess. She is a deity of the underworld, death, transformation, sexuality, initiation and fate, Who weaves the Web of Wyrd and measures the lives of humankind. She is the Bitch Goddess with Her pack of hunting hounds. (The slang term "son of a bitch" originally referred to her male followers.)

In fairy tales, which are the old myths retold in a folk form, She is represented with Her spinning wheel as the faery godmother (literally "divine mother") Who offers the newborn baby gifts of long life and wealth. She is the wicked stepmother, with Her poisoned apple of immortality and Her mirror offering access to the otherworld. She is also the wise grandmother who initiates young women.

Her symbols are spindle or distaff, for weaving fate; the scissors or sickle for cutting the umbilical cord at birth; the silver cord at death and the throat of the Corn King; and the cauldron of inspiration and transformation. The sacred animals of the Dark Goddess are the sow, the cat, the vixen, the mare, the bat, the snake, the bear and the spider. Her birds are the owl, raven, crow, goose, crane and swan.

In Celtic mythology, the Hag Goddess has several forms depending upon the country of Celtia. In Wales She is the witch *Ceridwen*, also known as the White Sow, goddess of the underworld, earth and the grain. In Her sacred cauldron bubbles the mystical potion that inspires and transforms, as little Gwion found out when he tasted it and shapeshifted into the bard Taliesin. As Kathy Jones has said, "It is in Her cauldron that through time the Hag brews her alchemical

mixture of magical herbs, which give the ability to change shape, to travel between the words, to know the past, present and future." Ceridwen is the Supreme Goddess of initiation Who lives in the burial mound which is Her womb temple, offering entry into the Otherworld for both the living and the dead. Despite what Robert Bly says, it is the Goddess and the women who are Her human representatives who initiate men into the Mysteries.

In Scottish folklore the Hag Goddess is the *Cailleach* or Veiled Woman, the spirit of winter and darkness. She is handed the light wand of summer by Bridget or Brighde—another triple goddess—and at Her touch it is turned into the dark wand of wintertime. She sits on the summit of Her sacred Mountain, Ben Nevis, tapping the rocks with Her silver hammer until the Summer Goddess returns to reclaim the land from Her icy rule. The Cailleach is related to the warrior goddess *Skati*, and to *Skaldi*, goddess of hunting and winter, and *Skuld*, Who is one of the three *Norns* or Weird Sisters, the triple goddesses of fate and destiny in Norse mythology. The Cailleach also appears in Irish myth in the twin form of an old hag and a beautiful young woman. In the Irish context she is the Great Mother Goddess and the Goddess of the Land with Her human sacred kings. In one story She asks two brothers to kiss her. One does, briefly, but the other both kisses and embraces the Hag and is rewarded with the kingdom of Ireland, which is in Her power to give.

Another version of the Dark Goddess in ancient Ireland is the triple goddess known as the *Morrigan*, or Great Queen. She has strong links with Brighde and rules war and sexuality. Her sisters are *Badb* and *Macha*. Babd is the battle raven, Who can be either a hag or a young woman. Macha is the horse goddess of death and, like Kali in Hindu mythology, wears a necklace of human skulls.

Bob Stewart calls the Morrigan's divine type "the phantom queen of death, sexuality and conflict," ruling night and winter. He connects Her with *Andraste,* the hare goddess of the primeval forests of ancient Britain, Who was worshipped by Boudicca of the Iceni. In Irish myth the Morrigan makes love to Dagda, the Celtic allfather and fertility god, on Samhain Eve. This sacred marriage symbolizes the conjunction of the forces of life and death, darkness and light, which keeps the cosmos balanced and whole. The Morrigan survived in post-Christian folklore as the *banshee,* "woman of the Sidhe," or the Washer and the Ford, symbolizing the boundary between this world and the next. She is also the leader of the Wild Hunt. Popular belief surrounding the *Sid* or *Cruachain,* the faery cave in County Roscommon, says that at Samhain the Goddess rides out of this cave followed by a host of spirits of the ancestral dead.

The Morrigan is a warrior goddess Who flies over the battlefield disguised as a raven. In this role She has similarities with the Valkyries in Norse myth, Who are aspects of the death and battle goddess and also have a connection with the Norns. Originally the latter were probably a single deity called *Udr* or *Urtir,* the primal Earth Mother. As the three Norns, They are *Urd* (Fate), *Verdanti* (Being), and *Skuld* (Necessity) Urd looks back at the past; Verdanti gazes forward at the present; and Skuld sits covered in a veil, for She is the unknown future. The Norns, like all dark goddesses, are spinners and weavers. They spin the fate of humans on their spinning wheels and also guard the Web of Wyrd and the cosmic axis around which the heavens revolve. Like the Greek goddesses of fate, the Morai, one of the Wyrd Sisters spins the red thread of birth, another measures the white thread of life, and the third cuts the black thread of death. Also like the Morai, the Norns dwell in a cave, called the Hall of the Moon, by a sacred spring or pool on the cosmic tree Yggdrasil, which holds the nine worlds, or levels of reality, suspended in space. The Web of Wyrd not only controls fate and destiny and sustains creation, but the experienced shaman, witch or wizard can use it to travel between the worlds to the Otherworld, along the so-called spirit lines or spirit paths linking matter with spirit.

Two other goddesses in the Northern European tradition are also representative of the Dark Goddess: Freya and Hel. To the Norse and Germanic peoples, Freya, the Sow Goddess, was originally identified with Nerthus, the ancient Earth Goddess of the Bronze Age folk, Who was sometimes described as Freya's mother. Riding through the sky on Her Siberian tiger, She is the "mistress of enchantment," ruling magickal spells, trance states, shimmering (shapeshifting), prophecy, psychic vision and the sending of the *fetch,* or astral body, in spirit travel. She taught the runes to Odin and in Her shamanic role She is the teacher of the dark magickal system of sorcery known as the *seidr.* Freya's seer-priestesses are prototypes of the medieval witches. Freya has been depicted flying on a distaff or broomstick, an aspect of the traditional witch goddess.

Freya's handmaidens are the Disir or "divine grandmothers," acting as guardian spirits of the family and appearing in dreams to offer advice and warn of danger. They could also predict the death of members of the family and in this respect are similar to the Irish banshee and the faery godmothers of later folklore. Freya can claim half the souls of those slain in battle, leaving the other half for the Valkyries to collect and take to Valhalla on behalf of Odin.

Hel or Hela is the winged goddess queen of the underworld, situated in a hollow hill or womb-like cave. Her domain can only be reached by crossing a river of black water or a mist-shrouded sea. Odin plays the role of ferryman to the dead and the gates to Hel's queendom are guarded by a giant spectral hound. Hel is sometimes visualized with three faces–the Triple Goddess form again—or as a dual being, half rotting flesh and skull, half whole. Hel, or Holda, is the female leader of the Wild Hunt that rides through the winter sky collecting the souls of the dead. The Hunt is often preceded by an owl, the spirit of a nun called Ursula (a priestess of the bear goddess?), and by wild geese. Snow crystals float down from the wings of the geese. As the Wild Hunter, Hel is again associated with the spirit lines, ghost paths and death roads that in Northern European folk tradition lead the shaman and the souls of the dead to the underworld. In Norse mythology, the spirits of the dead travel down the Helwaeg, or Hel's Way, that leads from Middle Earth to the Dark Goddess' realm.

The Old Crone, Dark Hag, or Great Grandmother is an ancient and important archetypal image of Divinity. In Celtic myth and fairy tales, when the hero prince meets the old hag on the road and she asks for a kiss (or sometimes more!), if he obliges she turns into a beautiful princess. This story has a great truth about how we should acknowledge and work with both the bright and dark aspects of Divinity.

Michael Howard is a writer, magazine editor and publisher, and researcher. He has been involved in Witchcraft and the magical tradition for nearly forty-five years and has written over twenty books on these subjects. Since 1976 he has edited and published *The Cauldron,* the UK's leading magazine on traditional Witchcraft and Wicca. He was a member of the Order of the Morning Star in the sixties, was initiated into Gardnerian Wicca in 1969 and is currently a member of the traditional Witchcraft group known as the *Cultus Sabbati.* He lives in England.

GE Vol. XXVII, No. 106 (Autumn 1994) 8–9

The Way of Man and the Ways of Pan

The way of man
And the ways of Pan
Are basically the same.
But the advent of Jesus Christ
Caused another game.

The days of Pagans have returned,
The days before the Witches burned,
Before the Christians amok with rage
Caused a dark foreboding age.
The Age of Pisces, drab and dark,
The days of the Catholic spark
Which set the flame to many men,
In hopes that Pagans all would end.
Their cry was, "Thy will be done."
There was no freedom 'neath the Sun.

But now a new age has begun,
Where each man is his own "God's Son."
This age is for the freedom of man,
But some of us won't understand,
For some still carry another's cross,
And whine and cry and call him boss.
Sheep have no will of their own,
They won't believe what they are shown.
But some of us know we're unique,
And that the cross is weary and bleak.

I have no use for Bible-banging fools,
And Priests which use them as their tools.
All the Churches are full of lies,
They are used to deceive, and used to buy
The souls of men to keep them still,
To make them slaves by words of quill.

Begone ye madmen of deceit and shame,
I shall not bow in Jesus' name.
The Law today, "Do What Thou Wilt,"
And study more to fully understand,
It means "Our chosen will be done!"
No greater truth beneath the Sun!

—Doug Plexico

GE Vol. VI, No. 57 (Mabon 1973) p. 14

Voodoo is Nigger Spelled Backwards

by **Judy C. Murray**
Hillbilly Voodoo Witch
Whispering Willows Coven

 NEVER CEASE TO BE AMAZED AT the reactions of my colleagues and Craft kindred in the magickal community over the word "Voodoo." When I offered to teach a workshop on the subject during a Craft gathering, some feathers got ruffled. It was feared that since the word had such negative connotations, it might scare people away (that particular set of chickens no longer roosts with my flock). And when I was first applying to Covenant of the Goddess, I was questioned closely as to whether I used Christian iconography in my magick because of my Voodoo practice, since much American Voodoo uses Catholic images.

The ceramic icon that hangs on my wall is not the Virgin Mary; it is the lovely black Voodoo Goddess Erzuli, Goddess of Love and Beauty, the African-American Venus and my beloved patroness. The holy water and blessed salt I use in my wangas comes not from the local Catholic church, but from my Witch altar, with the traditional Book of Shadows blessings said over them ("I exorcise thee, oh creature of water....").

No offense to my Christian kin, but I am a Witch. As my kinfolk, the conjure women and root doctors of African-American Voodoo are Witches, and I worship as a Witch worships.

Furthermore, the root base for my coven's rites are Cherokee, not Judeo-Christian Qabalah. We were born in East Tennessee, not Rome or Jerusalem. We use the Cherokee totem animals instead of the archangels in our conjurings. The spirit of the Tsala-gi who lived here so long, and the blood of our African kin who were brutally lynched here, have given their magick to the ground and sunk our roots deeply. The Indians and the African-Americans, no less than the Europeans, are our forebears and the ancestors whom we honor in our rites.

Voodoo is a bad word to Americans in general and Craft people in particular. The word smacks of the non-acceptance and bias of the majority in the Bad Old Days. It has been applied to the Old Religion in an unfavorable manner, making it a dirty word like "devil worshipper" or "liberal Democrat." There has also been a flap in recent years over animal sacrifice among the Hispanic people in Florida who practice Santeria, the South American avatar of Voodoo. A lot of vegan "eggs are murder" Wiccans were quite upset over the slaughter of chickens and other sad-eyed farm animals as a part of native religion. (Interestingly enough, it was the Orthodox Jews, who also have to slaughter their meat animals using ritual, that supposedly were the original litigants in the case.)

Craft people in general have been working very hard at gaining public acceptance of late. Witches are actually welcomed into ministerial associations in Salem, the same town that once hung such people for even existing. We don't wish to see this good work undone. Any term that causes a knee-jerk echo of the old anti-Witch hysteria is carefully shunned for fear of sparking reprisals.

Everyone knows Voodoo is evil; Tarzan

movies tell us so.

Then of course, we Americans are desperate to hang on to the few hated-by-all minorities we have left. It just ain't cool to beat up niggers and faggots on Saturday night behind the Dairy Queen no more. It might get you fined for littering or something (unless you're a policeman in L.A.). Worse, Rush Limbaugh might laugh at us.

Most Americans have grown sick of this climate of political correctness. It took them a long time to swallow the concept of equality for women, Blacks, Hispanics, Jews, Catholics and Asians. And they keep changing their minds. They're still choking on gays, Moslems, Buddhists and Hindus; and they ain't about to let no Voodoo practicing Witches in the door. Just imagine the jokes on Jay Leno: ("So now Witches are wanting to be accepted as a real religion. What's next, the Vampire Anti-Defamation League and the pro-Werewolf Lobby, I mean, c'mon...")

Finally, not to tread on too many toes, but much of what many people call Wicca reminds me of watered-down cotton candy. This glowy-eyed Pollyanna attitude, the kind of Wicca that can be politically correct and palatable to the American public, often sacrifices essential parts of our religion in the process, Voodoo being one such part. Indeed, a number of so-called Wiccans are afraid of the very word Witch and disdain to use the term.

Voodoo is an extremely American faith; it is also an extremely accepting and adapting faith. It has had to be, given the plight of our Black kindred for the past few centuries. Just as it has worked well with Christianity and Native American faiths, so it works well with Celto-Saxon Wicca. Indeed, what is Voodoo if not African-American Paganism? It is interesting that Christianity or Islam are considered to be "true" African-American religions, and Voodoo is not. Why not? And this is true for African-Americans, too. Are Black people saying that a religion is valid only if it originated in the Middle East? Why aren't there Black people resurrecting the Egyptian mysteries or flocking to the Voodoo temples? Who knows? All I can say is: "It leaves more for me." Sorry, but there was

religion in Africa prior to 33 CE.

Interestingly enough, many African-Americans get somewhat perturbed at the thought of a White person practicing an African-derived religion. Why, they ask, do you even want to practice Voodoo? My answer: "Because it works."

As far as having any African ancestry, I don't know if I do. The human race evolved in Northern Africa, not to mention the debts our present society and our occultic religions owe to Africa as a whole and Egypt in particular; so all Terran humans have blood ties to Africa somewhere in their background.

Also, I have immediate ancestors who were either Confederate soldiers or slave owners. Perhaps it's a karmic thing. Few people know it, but many a White slave owner's children nursed on a Black woman's breast (read Alex Haley's *Roots* if you don't believe me). And, as all us good Witches know, mother's milk is heart-blood.

Let us not forget the tragic devastation to the Black people's lore and tradition. Lore and tradition are very important to us Celtic, Druid-derived Wiccans. By ancient rules of hospitality, since our immediate ancestors destroyed Black people's (and Red people's!) traditions, we must make them part of ours. It makes African Americans our kin, over and above the genetic ties we already possess. Their ancestors become ours, ours become theirs; their Gods are our Gods; we share the same parentage. My mother's Mother is Erzuli, who enflames me with love; my lord is Legba, the Voodoo Thoth-Anubis, the wily, crutch-walking trickster God who plays occasional software jokes on his little White daughter. That's all I need to know.

Why Voodoo? Because I have a knack for it. Because the Goddess Erzuli pierced my heart with a pink-green flame during one of my fledgling, amateurish childhood rituals. Because, like Wicca, it works.

Like the Celts, Voodoo people are very inclusive. The majority of Black Voodooists I meet simply regard me as sister Judy, not the honky devil come to rip them off. I get the same feelings from them that I get from any other tribal kindred; the same feeling that I often *don't* get around many self-proclaimed Wiccans.

Also being a religion with ties deep into the Stone Age, Voodoo dovetails perfectly with both Wicca and Native American shamanism. The three go together like sugar, milk and cocoa beans, making a whole greater than the parts. I guess you could say my religion is chocolate.

One dividing line between Wicca and Voodoo is the amount of noise generated during the ceremony. Many Wiccan covens, especially the Unitarian varieties, tend to be very staid, solemn and ceremonial in their practices (what we heathen hillbillies call "Episco-Wiccans"). Voodoo people tend to kick up quite a ruckus, especially when the Loa are riding.

Another unique feature of Voodoo is the veve, the symbol of the Loa we are invoking. The *ueve* (or vever) is a magickal design which we draw in cornmeal and/or other powders on the ground and then dance all over the top of, to raise the power we send out in our spellwork. We drop offerings of food, drink and other things onto the veve and then beat the drums and trample it into the ground while howling at the moon. The energies this raises are not to be believed!

And, not to upset yo' little White tummies none, but we do occasionally slaughter our chickens and turkeys. Some of our people hunt and fish on a regular basis, too; and, yes, it's done in a ceremonial way. To do it otherwise would be disrespectful of both the Gods and the chicken. I believe that if you're going to eat meat, you ought to look it in the eye at least once. Don't criticize me for pouring chicken blood into the ground as an offering for the Gods when you nibble on the Colonel's finger-licking carnage every Sunday. Compared to commercially-prepared meat, farm animals are slaughtered with less distress and by more humane methods. In case you didn't know it, meat from the store usually comes from an animal in great pain; i.e., chickens that were boiled alive then shocked to death on the rectum.

"And how were your chicken nuggets today, sir? Any fries with that?"

I won't lie to you for anything other than personal gain. I think that, while the work of public acceptance has been very important and mostly beneficial, there comes a point when we must choose between pleasing the Puritans and keeping our Craft. As anyone who meets me finds out, I am not only an unabashed Witch, but also an unabashed homo, and the very worst kind of homo, at that: the kind that wears dresses and does "the girl thing," without sacrificing "her" claim to manhood (I love Cloe Willena, my extended clitoris, a lot, thanks. Besides, who wants to wind up on Geraldo?)

In other words, I'm already socially unacceptable. If the Puritans get in an uproar over me, what else is new? Am I complaining? Sweet Hella's Icy Womb, no! I'm proud. Proud of my wo/manhood, proud of my vocation, proud of my rune-rattling, drum-pounding ancestors and their dark-skinned-heathen-Voodoo-Witchly ways.

It's not that I'm such a saint that I wouldn't succumb to the luxury of bigotry along with the rest of my fellow Americans and many of my fellow Wiccans, given the chance. It's simple that, given my religion, my sexuality, and my Voodoo heart, I really can't afford it.

Recommended Reading:

Gover, Robert, *Voodoo Contra*. Samuel Wieser, York Beach ME, 1985.

Haskins, Jim, *Voodoo and Hoodoo*. Original Publications, Bronx NY, 1988

Bertiaux, Michael, *The Voudon Gnostic Workbook*. Magickal Childe, New York, 1988

Rigaud, Milo, *Secrets of Voodoo*. Arco Publishing, NY, 1969

Deren, Maya, *Divine Horsemen: The Living Gods of Haiti*. McPherson, London, NY, 1953

Gonzalez-Wippler, Migene, *The Santeria Experience*. Llewellyn, St. Paul MN, 1992

I also heartily recommend the "New Orleans Voodoo Tarot" by Louis Martinie' and Sallie Ann Glassman: Destiny Books, Rochester VT, 1992. It's the same deck I use. The book is chock full of Voodoo lore and spells. The deck itself is gorgeous. Sallie is the same artist who did the Enochian deck.

Vol. XXVIX, No. 114 (July-Aug. 1996) 23–25

History of the Druids

by *Daniel Hansen Msc.D.*

DISCUSSING THE HISTORY OF THE Druids is a challenge. First, we have to decide who we are talking about when we use the name "Druid." Are we referring to the ancient Celtic priesthood of two millennia ago or the Masonic-type British Druids of two centuries ago? Or are we talking about the current crop of Nature-Worshipers? To clear up this confusion, I will refer to the ancient Druids as the Paleo-Druids, The Masonic-type Druids as the Meso-Druids, and the modern Druids as the NeoDruids. These divisions have been borrowed from the book *Real Magic,* and are Bonewits' terms, which were borrowed in turn from Robin Goodfellow and Tim Zell.

So, who are, or were, the Druids? To answer this, it's necessary to examine the history of each of these periods in the development of the Druids.

The Paleo-Druids

Despite all that is written about the Paleo-Druids, we really know very little about them. No one is sure when or where the Paleo-Druids originated or what they taught and believed. All we really do know has comes down to us from roughly thirty references made about them. These come from Classical Greek and Roman historians dating back from the fifth century BCE to the fifth century CE. There is a belief that the Druids were a pre-Celtic priesthood which was absorbed into the Celtic cultures of Britain, Ireland, and Gaul (France). The truth is we just don't know. In 55 BCE Julius Caesar speaks of them in some detail, but most modern scholars generally hold that by the time of Caesar the Druids were in a state of decline. The last contemporary reference to the Paleo-Druids occurred in 5th century CE Ireland and Scotland by early Christian missionaries who claim victory over the Druids and heathenism in general. It seems that virtually all of the information we have on Paleo-Druids comes from their enemies, the Greeks, Romans, and Christian missionaries

to Ireland and Scotland. The Druids themselves didn't commit any of their knowledge or lore to writing. They practiced an oral tradition, verbally passing their wisdom from one generation to the next. When a Druid died without passing his information on to a disciple or apprentice, his knowledge was lost forever.

Caesar tells us that it took up to twenty years to train a Druid. According to Irish tradition, it holds that it takes twelve years to train a Bard or *Filidh* (a sub-class of Druid). When, keeping this long training in mind, we look at the destruction of the Druidry center at Mona on the Isle of Anglesey off the coast of Wales, (where the Roman soldiers slaughtered the Druid defenders, cut down their oak grove, and, to ensure their inability to return, built a garrison on the site) we realize why this must have been such a serious blow to the Druids. It is believed that the few survivors fled to Manx, Scotland, and Ireland. In Ireland and Scotland, there were reports of Druids up into the fifth century CE when they opposed the advance of Christianity under St. Patrick and St. Colm Cille. Shortly after that, the records would indicate that the Druids disappeared completely.

The origin of the word Druid, is also somewhat obscure. "Druid" may have been derived from the Greek word *Drus* which means "an oak." Druids have been associated with the oak ever since this etymology was proposed. In Ireland, the Druids were called *Draoi* which means "sorcerer" or "associated with magic." In Wales, the Druids were known as Derwydd, "body of the oak." It has been speculated that the Irish Draoi and Welsh Derwydd were not actually Druids at all, however the argument is problematic because they are now generally associated with the ancient form of Druidism. From the Celtic language in general, the name Druid is believed to be derived from Deru, an oak and *Hud,* enchantment, and put together they make Dru-hud, "highly knowing." What we do know of the Paleo-

Druids is that they belonged to the final phase of the La Tene culture of the late Iron Age.

Druids were part of the Celtic hierarchy who were exempt from tribal obligations of war and taxation. From the ancient sources it has been speculated that the Druids were the scholars, judges, and philosophers of the ancient Celts as well as being their priests. Within their ranks they were divided into three subclasses: ovates (Vates in Gaul, Faiths in Ireland, and Ovydd in Wales) were the seers and doctors of Druidism; the Bards (Filidh in Ireland and Bardd in Wales) were the poets; and the Druids (Draoi in Ireland and Derwydd in Wales), who came from the noble class, were the repository of tribal lore, wisdom, and customary laws of the Celts. It is believed that the Druids had to advance through both the ovate and Bard castes before becoming members of the Druid caste. The corpus of the Paleo-Druid's knowledge is scrappy at best due to their lack of written records, but from what was written about them and folklore survivals it is possible to piece together many aspects and functions of the Paleo-Druids.

We know that they preached that the human soul was immortal and they had a simple philosophy: "The Gods must be worshipped (spiritual level), no evil done (mental level), and manly behavior maintained (physical level)" (Diogenes Laertius). Or put another way: worship the Gods, do no evil, and practice bravery. It took twenty years to train a Druid or twelve years for a Bard because they had a great body of knowledge which had to be memorized, usually in verse. They were the law-givers, had knowledge of astronomy and a lunar/solar calendar, used divination, and had prophetic powers. The Paleo-Druids knew the divine will of the gods and they presided over all animal and human sacrifice to ensure all forms of the ritual were done correctly to appease the gods. As near as we can tell, Druids worshipped in woodland sanctuaries or oak groves called Nemetons which had wooden images or were draped with embroidered tapestry. We know that the Druids did not build Stonehenge, nor did they erect any of the great stone circles found throughout the British Isles

and France. This does not mean that they didn't use these circles, although there is no evidence that they did, either.

The Paleo-Druids were viewed as a political threat to the Roman Empire. The Romans passed laws making Druidism illegal inside Roman territory. Later, the early Christian missionaries met stiff resistance from the Druids in Ireland, Wales and Scotland, but with a near endless supply of Christian soldiers, by the end of the 5th century CE, Druidism as a religion ceased to be. Druid lore continued under the protection of the Filidh/Bard or Poet class until the 17th century when it was finally silenced by English law. The Celtic Church, known as the Culdee, has been called a unique blend of Druidism with Christianity. One theory is that the original Culdee were in reality the last remnants of the Druids who opted to "convert" to Christianity. The early Celtic Church was not in line with the Roman Catholic Church until the 13th century when it was suppressed, ending the last remnants of the Paleo-Druids.

The Meso-Druids

The concept of Druidism wouldn't die out, and after more than a thousand years had passed, the Druids were revived. The revival began in England about the time of the end of the Neo-Classical period and during the beginning of their Romantic period in the wake of the European Renaissance. During this period, the concept of the "noble savage" became popular. To use Stuart Piggot's expression, it was at this time that the Druids-as-fact were set aside in favor of the Druids-as-wished-for.

The Meso-Druids first became active in 1694 with the revival of Mount Haemus grove in Snowdonia, Wales, by the antiquarian John Aubrey. The philosopher John Toland, inspired by Aubrey, became a member and, in 1717 at Primrose Hill, he brought together representatives from the existing Bardic circle from all over the British Isles. Together, they formed the first Meso-Druidic group called Uileach Druidh Braitreachas or the Universal Druid Bond (UDB). Toland served as the first Chosen Chief (Arch Druid, but they never actually used that title) until his death in 1722. He was succeeded by several notables to include the Rev. Dr. William Stuckley. Stuckley was a cleric and an antiquarian who was convinced that the Paleo-Druids built Stonehenge and that they were pre-Christian Christians. He wasn't alone in these opinions. Stuckley was followed by Edward Hatten, David Samwell, and the poet William Blake as Chosen Chief of the UDB.

For the most part these Meso-Druids did not view themselves as a religious movement at all, in fact most were good Christians with close ties to the Masonic Lodges. As a result, their organizational structure was heavily influenced by Free Masonry. Meso-Druids were primarily an esoteric organization which attracted Hermeticists, Rosicrucians, Cabbalists, and other occultists. All of these influences distorted the nature of the Druidic revival. Some of these early Druidic lodges could easily be described as a "friend's society" and were concerned with various charities. While it is clear that they were Druidic in name only and little else, it is important to note that a considerable amount of information on the Druids and Druidism was published during this time.

As can be imagined with these conflicting influences there were a great many schisms. At one point there were over thirty different Druid Lodges and orders. Some emphasized the esoteric side while others were more interested in charity work. Shortly after World War I, most of these Druid orders simply disappeared. The only extant groups which can trace their origin to the original UDB are the Ancient order of Druids (AoD), and the order of Bards, ovates, and Druids (OBoD). Most of the Meso-Druid groups viewed the Paleo-Druids as Nature's sages and philosophers and tried to reconcile Druidism with Christianity and some even went so far as to identify the Celts as one of the lost tribes of Israel. Paleo-Druids were said to have attributes similar to Western esoteric magical traditions. These included dancing clockwise, being a sacred caste, burning their dead, having animal cults, and some sort of wisdom teaching.

About the same time in Wales, the Meso-

Druid revival took a different direction under the influence of Lewis Morris, Ieuan Fardd (Rev. Even Evens), and more importantly by the controversial figure of Iolo Morganwg (Edward Williams). This Welsh Druidic revival concentrated on the old Welsh Bardic traditions. It was Iolo who had the most profound effect on the development of the Welsh Meso-Druids, he held that the Taliesin myth contained the complete complex systems of Druidism which was the Celtic equivalent of the Caballa. Iolo went so far as to write a work called the Barddas and pass it off as authentic deep Druidic lore. In his reconstruction of Druidism he created what he called the Sign of Awen or the Three Rays (/|\) which were supposed to represent Universal Majesty, Verity, and Love Infinite. His most lasting contribution to the Welsh Meso-Druid revival was the Eisteddod, still in existence today. This is a Welsh word that means "session." It became the traditional assembly of Welsh Bards and musicians where competitions were held and a "chair" was awarded to the Chief Bard. The modern festivals are held annually and they alternate between the North and South of Wales. Eisteddod festivals consist of competitions in poetry, literature, and the arts and crafts, and are intended to preserve and promote the Welsh language, culture, and nationalism.

Initially, the Welsh Meso-Druids were viewed as a political threat and British spies kept a close eye on the pro-Welsh activities of these Druids. Now the Eisteddod is a very prominent element spreading and strengthening the ties between the modern versions of the Welsh and British Meso-Druid groups.

Over the years and up to World War I, Meso-Druid lodges branched off a number of times, but shortly thereafter, most of the Meso-Druid lodges faded away. The Ancient Druid Order and the Order of Bards, Ovates, and Druids remain. It should be noted that while there are many local traditions and a typically Celtic resistance to change, some current Meso- Druid groups are beginning to blend with or embrace the Neo-Druid movement.

GE Vol. XXVIX, No. 117 (Jan.-Feb. 1997) 12–16

Chapter 4.
The Gods of Nature;
The Nature of Gods

Introduction

by *Chas S. Clifton*

 N THIS CHAPTER (AND IN CHAPTER 5) WE MOVE TOWARD THE IDEA OF PAGANISM AS "nature religion." The term nature religion has a special resonance in America, where since the early 19th century it was common for patriotic writers to match this continent's mountains and forests favorably with Europe's castles and cathedrals. America's were better, of course, because they were divinely corrupted, instead of being the egotistical projects of kings and popes! In addition, the 19th century produced a revolution against conventional medicine (as it then was)—"natural healing"—and the beginnings of the "natural" food movement. In addition, those forests and mountains that previously were seen as fit only for outlaws and savages now became places of divine power and poetic inspiration. We have the Romantic movement in art and music to thank for that change in outlook, as well as a line of mystics going back to the influential 18th-century Swedish mystic writer Emmanuel Swedenborg. (For more explication, see Catherine Albanese's short but thoughtful book *Nature Religion in America.*)

Into this swirl of attitudes came the new Pagan movement, where Feraferia's Fred Adams could imagine Pagans both swarming bulldozer operators with "tickles, kisses, and caramel-coated obscenities" while fighting environmental destruction in the courts. Imported Wicca rapidly morphed into "nature religion" when it hit these shores, a story I tried to untangle in my book *Her Hidden Children*. For many new Pagans, there was a simple equation: the planet and the Goddess were one. Tim (as he was called then) Zell pushed this idea the farthest in his 1970 essay "TheaGenesis": All living beings were part of one super-organism, and when the planet achieves consciousness, it will be a super-divinity. Other *Green Egg* writers took somewhat different tacks—that the "creator" and the "creation" were one (Matt Clark—who received a complimentary letter from Robert Heinlein for this) or that even if and when humans left Earth to explore beyond her orbit, "She is still with us and we are Her children and stewards. It is up to us to revere Her in the ways of the ancients who adored the Earth with a love they could feel and a knowledge they could intuit" (Tom Williams).

Grant Potts, one of the new generation of Pagan academics, suggests that all tellings and theologizing of Pagan gnosis need to be treated as "mythic acts of narrative," founded in our community, but not as dogmas that must be mindlessly adhered to. Thus we can look at the visions in this chapter not as something to be memorized and regurgitated but as sacred stories that guide us in relation to the planet, to deity, and to each other.

TheaGenesis:
The Birth of the Goddess
by Tim Zell (Oberon), CAW 8

AUTHOR'S NOTE: This essay was composed during the week following a profound Vision I had on September 6, 1970, of our entire Earth as a single great living organism—a revelation I articulated the next weekend as a sermon to the congregation of the Church of All Worlds, titled "TheaGenesis: The Birth of the Goddess." I finally published it in Green Egg *#40—Litha, 1971—and followed it with an ongoing series over the next few years, expanding upon the implications of this paradigm. For these earliest writings, I coined the term* Terrebios—*later* Terrabia (f.) —*Latin for "Earthlife." This was in accord with the convention of scientific nomenclature in which Greek names are used for extinct creatures, and Latin for living ones. However, when, two years later, British atmospheric biochemist James Lovelock published his first essay—a letter to the editor—on the Earth as a living organism (*"Gaia as Seen Through the Atmosphere,"* Atmospheric Environment, 1972), in which he used a variant of the ancient Greek name* Ge, *as proposed by novelist William Golding, I replaced Terrebia with Gaea or Gaia in my own subsequent writings. These were widely reprinted in other Pagan periodicals of the time, having, according to Margot Adler, a profound and transformative impact of imparting a passionate sense of mission and purpose to the emerging Neo-Pagan movement. Over the succeeding decades, I have expanded and modified this article in subsequent reprints, incorporating new information and new insights. For example, we now have a completely different understanding of what killed off the dinosaurs, rendering the below speculation moot. And I later expanded my view of the function of humanity within the biosphere to include that of reproductive system via space colonization. I plan to update and expand upon this thesis in a future book to be titled* GaeaGenesis: Conception and Birth of the Living Earth. —OZ, 4/20/08

ONCEPTUALIZATIONS OF DIVINITY vary from religion to religion, with adherents of each faith misunderstanding, often grotesquely, the nature of the Divine as understood by the members of other faiths. Thus conservatives of a given religious system often tend to feel that all other religions are "false" but their own, while liberals will go to the opposite extreme and contend that all religions essentially worship the same Deity, under different guises and customs. Both of these points of view grossly misrepresent the fundamental distinctions among the various religions, and try to adapt alien world-views to fit into their own frameworks of experience.

It may be said that all religions are "true," as indeed are all sincerely held opinions, in the sense that personal reality is necessarily subjective. In other words, what you believe to be true, *is* true, by definition. A Voudou death-course is as real to its victim, and *as*

effective, as being "saved" is to a Christian fundamentalist, or the kosher laws are to an Orthodox Jew. A flat Earth, with the stars and planets revolving around it, was as real to the medieval mind as our pent globe and solar system are to us. Hysteric paralysis and blindness are as real to the sufferer as their organic counterparts. The snakes and bugs of alcoholic and narcotic deliria are real to the addict, and so is the fearful world of the paranoiac. From the standpoint of human consciousness, there is no other reality than that which we experience, and whatever we experience is therefore reality—therefore "true." We can only distinguish the experiences of the objective world from those which lie entirely within our own minds when we compare notes with other people and arrive thereby at a consensus of reality. This consensus, however, is also subjective within the entire community, and is also liable not to be synonymous with objective reality (as in the case of the Geocentric cosmos). The question then arises, "How can we know objective reality?" and the answer, of course, is that we can't; not totally. However, we can arrive at very close approximations of objective reality by careful applications of the scientific method combined with creative insight, and by refusing to fill in the gaps in our knowledge with blind "leaps of faith."

Thus religions may be considered more or less objectively true (while recognizing that they are *all* subjectively true) by evaluating how much they depend on blind faith and belief over scientific understanding (and recognizing that we only speak of belief in the absence of knowledge; no one would say "I believe two plus two equals four."); how much they depend on tradition and authority over intellectual curiosity and honesty; how much (or how little) they are able to accommodate new discoveries in science; and how much (or how little) these discoveries substantiate their theories and world-views. These are the criteria for objective validation of religious viewpoints. No subjective validation is needed (or even possible).

The Paleo-Pagans, diversified though they were, held among them certain common viewpoints, Among these were: veneration of an Earth-Mother Goddess; animism and pantheism; identification with a sacred region; seasonal celebration; love, respect, awe and veneration for Nature and Her mysteries; sensuality and sexuality in worship; magic and myth; and a sense of Man being a microcosm corresponding to the macrocosm of all Nature. These insights, however, were largely intuitive, as science had not yet progressed to the point of being able to provide objective validation for what must have seemed, to outsiders, to be mere superstition, Twentieth-century Neo-Paganism, however, has applied itself and the science of its era to that validation, and has discovered astounding implications:

A single cell develops physically into human being by a process of continuous division and subdivision into the myriads of cells eventually required to make up an, adult body, groups of cells specializing to become the various organs and tissues needed for full functioning of the organism. Now, when a cell reproduces, the parent cell does not remain intact, but actually *becomes* the two new daughter cells. Since the same protoplasm is present in the daughter cells as was in the parent, the two daughter cells still comprise but a single organism; one living being. The original cell ceases to exist in that form, but its *life* goes on in the continuous evolution of the growing organism. Thus, the billions of cells of the adult human body continue to comprise a single living organism, even though different cells may be highly specialized, and some may even be mobile enough to travel independently around in the collective body.

No matter how complex the final form of the adult organism, no matter how diversified its component cells, the same thread of life of the original cell, the same protoplasm, continues in every cell in the body. Since the *sex* cells are also included in this ultimate diversification of a single original cell, the act of reproduction carries this came thread on in the offspring, combined with the equivalent thread of protoplasm from the other parent. Thus your children, while spatially distinct from you, are in fact as much a. part of your growing, evolving organism as your blood cells (which can easily be extracted and survive independently of your collective body) or tissue cells (which can also be extracted and grown in independent cultures). Your children are still "you"—your own living protoplasm continues on in their cellularly-diversified bodies. And in your children's children for all generations to come. All the cells in all your descendents will still comprise but ONE LIVING BEING!

Tracing our evolution back two billion years, through mammals, reptiles, amphibians, fish, and so on, *we* eventually wind up with ONE SINGLE CELL that was the ANCESTOR OF ALL LIFE ON EARTH. Even though there were undoubtedly many proto-cells formed in the early seas, the first one to develop the capacity to reproduce would have quickly consumed all the available free proteins and amino acids floating in the sea, effectively preventing the development of any competitors. Cell reproduction occurs at a fantastic geometrical rate, which, unchecked, Would result in all the planet being buried beneath the progeny of a single cell within months. Obviously, what checked this fantastic reproductive potential was a limited food supply, which would have included any not-yet-formed or newly-formed competitive cells. But when this call reproduced itself, and continued to do so for aeons, some of its daughter cells mutating and evolving into new forms, it still, as in the human body, continued to, comprise but a SINGLE total organism. When a cell divides and subdivides, NO MATTER HOW OFTEN, the same cellular material, the same protoplasm, the same life, passes into the daughter cells, and the granddaughter cells, and the great-granddaughter cells, FOREVER. NO MATTER HOW OFTEN or for how long this subdivision goes on, the aggregate total of the new cells continues to comprise ONE SINGLE LIVING ORGANISM!

Now, every amino acid (except glycine) found in the proteins of living organisms can exist in *two* forms, each one the mirror image of the other. Since they have the same spatial relationship as a pair of gloves, one type is arbitrarily designated "right-handed" (D, *dextro*) and the other "left-handed" (L, *levo*). The two forms are identical in chemical composition and physical properties. Were it not for the fact that they rotate a beam of polarized light in opposite directions, they would be indistinguishable. Now, when amino acids are synthesized in the laboratory, an equal amount of D and L forms are produced. Moreover, NASA recently reported the discovery of 17 different amino acids in a meteorite, with an almost equal number of D and L forms.

In any given cell, or course, only one of the two variant forms can exist; either all the cell's protein would contain D-acids, or they would all contain L-acids. And when the cell divides, whichever form was contained in the mother cell would be perpetuated in the daughter cells. If all life on Earth did not originate with a single cell, we would expect to find various creatures and plants with D-acids, and others with L-acids. However, this is not the case: it is an established biochemical fact that ALL LIFE ON EARTH CONTAINS ONLY L-AMINO ACIDS! The equivalent D-

acids are simply not found in any living organisms on this planet! Therefore, it is a biological fact (not a theory, not an opinion) that ALL LIFE ON EARTH COMPRISES ONE SINGLE LIVING ORGANISM! Literally, we are *all* "One."

The blue whale and the redwood tree are not the largest living organisms on Earth; the ENTIRE PLANETARY BIOSPHERE is.

Let us consider the following corollaries: An organism is composed of many organs—more, obviously, in complex organisms than in simple ones. As an embryo develops, groups of cells specialize into each of the organs that the adult organism will require. At early stages in cell differentiation, unspecialized cells can be moved from one part of the embryo to another, and the transplanted cells will still develop into whatever organs are needed in their new locations. Just so, the Planetary Organism (to which I will hereby give the scientific name of "Terabits") needs various organs in order to function properly. Continuing the analogy with the human body, each animal and plant on Earth *is* the equivalent of a single cell in the vast body of Terabits. Each biome, such as pine forest, coral reef, desert, prairies, marsh, etc., complete with all its plants and animals, is the equivalent of an organ in the body of our biospheric Being, sub-organs and tissues consisting of types of plants and animals, such as trees, insects, grasses, predators, grazing herbivores, etc.

ALL the components of a biome are essential to its proper functioning, and each biome is essential to the proper functioning of Terabios. If a biome is missing some essential elements, it is possible for relatively unspecialized "cells" of plants and animals to differentiate out by adaptive radiation to *become* all the required components. The most classic case of this is the radiation of marsupials in Australia to fill all the ecological niches occupied elsewhere by placentals with creatures virtually identical in structure and habits with their placental equivalents. Moreover, recent papers and books on the genetics of evolution, including *Biophilosophy*, stress that modern Darwinian theory has abandoned the notion of individuals determining the direction of the evolution of a species. Rather, the entire species, migrates towards a fortuitous ecological niche as if it had a sense of whither it needed to go. If all the mutations in the direction of such a change are destroyed, the species will produce more.

The non-living components of the planetary structure of the Earth itself serve the developing organism of Terrabios much as the nonliving components of the human body serve it. These components are the Lithosphere, the Hydrosphere, and the Atmosphere. The Lithosphere, the rock and mineral foundation of our planet, functions in the body of Terrabios much as the skeleton functions in the human body—as foundation and structural support (like the Lithosphere, our skeleton is largely mineral). The Hydrosphere, the water of oceans, lakes and rivers that covers three quarters of the surface of the globe, functions homologously with the plasma in the blood of the human body, which, incidentally, has a composition very like the water in those primeval seas wherein life first appeared. The Atmosphere serves the great organism of Terrabios much as it does us, as individual "cells"—in a carbon-cycle respiratory process, involving breaking carbon dioxide down into carbon and oxygen by plants and building carbon and oxygen back up into carbon dioxide by animals. What is the ultimate source of energy for Terrabios—its "food?" Sunlight, which, through photosynthesis in green plants, converts materials of the Lithosphere, Hydrosphere and Atmosphere into the materials of life.

Now, it follows that if a bionic component occupies a particular ecological niche in a given biome, it does so because it belongs there and is necessary to the proper functioning of that biome, and hence of Terrabios. Further, if some plant or animal is missing from a particular biome, it is because it *doesn't* belong there. Now, everybody realizes that the human body Will not function properly if one removes, replaces or rearranges parts of it. You will survive if your leg is amputated, but you certainly won't walk as well as beforc. This same principle of coher-

ency applies to Terrabios, as we are beginning to learn only too well. You can't kill all the bison in North America, import rabbits to Australia, cut or burn off whole forests, or plow and plant the Great Plains with wheat without seriously disrupting the ecology. Remember the dust bowl? Australia's plague of rabbits? Mississippi basin floods? The present drought in the Southwestern U.S.? Terrabios is a SINGLE LIVING ORGANISM, and its parts are not to be removed, replaced, or rearranged.

Just as in the human body the brain and nervous system is the last organ to develop, so in Terrabios the last biome to develop is the Noosphere, composed of Earth's aggregate population of *Homo sapiens*. What function does Man, as the Noospheric organ, perform? It would seem that at the present stage of evolution, the function of a biome of awareness would be to act as steward of the planetary ecology. Man's purpose in Terrabios, his responsibility, is to see that the whole organism functions at its highest potential and that none of its vital systems become disrupted or impaired. We might judge the state of Man's functioning in the macrocosmic realm by evaluating his performance of this organic responsibility.

When in the human body some cells start multiplying all out of control and excreting toxins into the bloodstream, we have a cancer. One of the ways cancer can be controlled is by radiation treatment. At this moment, Man himself is multiplying out of control and excreting vast quantities of deadly pollutants into the air, water and soil. If Man's cancerous population growth is not halted, his numbers and poisons will severely cripple or kill our planetary organism, Terrabios. Perhaps nuclear war—a global "radiation treatment"—will be needed.... But it is still to be hoped that it is not too late for us to wake up to our responsibility of stewardship.

Terrabios is nearing maturity. All the physical ecological niches have been filled, and the recently developed Noosphere now extends over the entire globe. Even the extinction of the dinosaurs, until now a total mystery to science, can be explained by an understanding of the maturation process of organisms. For just as certain organs, such as the thymus gland and baby teeth, are essential in early phases of human development but disappear as we approach maturity, so certain organs in the organism of Terrabios must disappear when they are outgrown (in the case of the dinosaurs, when it was time for mammals to move into the position of their ecological destiny).

But Terrabios has still not reached the adult stage of its species (*Biospherus planetarius*). Projecting a bit, it would seem most reasonable that Teilhard de Chardin was correct in his vision of an emerging planetary consciousness, what he called the "Omega Point" (*The Phenomenon of Man*) and Carlton Berenda calls "The First Coming of God" (*The New Genesis*). The maturation of a Planetary Biosphere requires the evolution of total telepathic union among the "cells" of its Noosphere (its most intelligent species: Man). When such an intelligent species ultimately develops telepathy to the extent that it eventually shares a single global consciousness, a PLANETARY MIND awakens in the "brain" (noosphere) of the Biosphere. This is our Human destiny—our ultimate function in the organism of Terrabios. And just as the brain in the human body is capable, via the conscious mind, of controlling virtually everything that goes on in the body and a good deal that goes on outside it, so a planetary consciousness would be in complete control of *everything* that goes on in the planet—from earthquakes to rainfall to ice ages to mountain building to hurricanes—and perhaps influence the rest of its local stellar system as well.

At this point it becomes necessary to define Divinity:

Divinity is the highest level of aware consciousness accessible to each living being, manifesting itself in the self-actualization of that being. Thus we can truly say, "All that groks is God." Divinity is a cat being fully feline (as all cats are!), grass being grassy, and Man being fully Human. Collective Divinity emerges when a number of people (a culture or society) share enough values, beliefs and aspects of a common life-style that they conceptualize a tribal God or Goddess, which takes on the character (and the

gender) of the dominant elements of that culture. Thus the masculine God of the Western Monotheists (Jews, Christians, Moslems) may be seen to have arisen out of the values, ideals and principles of a nomadic, patriarchal culture; the ancient Hebrews.

Matriarchal agrarian cultures, on the other hand, personified their values of fertility, sensuality, peace and the arts in the conceptualization of Goddesses. As small tribes coalesced into states and nations, their Gods and Goddesses battled for supremacy through their respective devotees. In some circumstances, various tribal divinities were joined peaceably into a polytheistic pantheon, being ranked in status as their followers' respective influences determined. In other circumstances, one particularly fanatic tribe was able to completely dominate others and eliminate their own deities, elevating its God to the status of a solitary ruler over all creation, and enforcing His worship upon the people.

However, no matter to what rank a single tribal deity may be exalted by its followers, it still could be no other than a tribal divinity, existing only as an embodiment of the values of that tribe. "Gods are only as strong as those who believe in them think they are." (*Alley Oop*) When the planetary consciousness of Terrabios awakens, it too will be Divinity—but on an entirely new level: the emergent deity Berenda postulates in *The New Genesis.* Indeed, even though yet unawakened, the embryonic slumbering subconscious mind of Terrabios is experienced intuitively by us all, and has been referred to instinctively by us as Mother Earth, Mother Nature (The Goddess, The Lady). Indeed, this intuitive conceptualization of feminine gender for our planetary Divinity is scientifically valid, for biologically unisexual organisms (such as amoeba or hydra) are always considered female; in the act of reproduction they are referred to as mothers and their offspring as daughters.

Thus we find that "God" is in reality, Goddess, and that our Paleo-Pagan ancestors had an intuitive understanding of what we are now able to prove scientifically. Thus also we expose the logical absurdity of a concept of cosmic Divinity in the masculine gender. These few pages, however, have only been the briefest of introductions to the implications of a discovery *so* vast that its impact on the world's thinking will ultimately surpass the impact of the discovery of the Heliocentric structure of the solar system. This discovery, which we shall explore in more detail in future articles, is the discovery that the entire Biosphere of the Earth comprises a single living Organism. Blessed Be!

GE Vo. IV, No. 40 (Litha 1971) 7–10

Evocation of the Goddess

*by **Oothoon** (Candace Hadad Campbell)*

in the name of the earth, and the sun,
and the rainbow which bridges them.

1
your counsel is in the cowrie
you engrave sand dollars with your runes
you flower forth in daisies
and teach oaks to twist in the sun
cows learn from you to lick their calves
women to spin flax and clay
the yeasty moon to double
and the sky to turn

2
at dusk, in my kitchen
i strip the onion of its layers
gouge out potatoe's eyes
hack off the carrot's head

forgive me this violence
i am blood of your blood
this is my body, too
and my sister the pomegranate
is the kiss of my mouth

3
lover, sweet lady
couch your love in my mother tongue
speak me the language of mirrors
show me how to maiden you, mother you,
crone you, as you, at my flesh's altar,
do to me

4
mother, i swear by my navel
how i swam like a fish
in your underground lake
sister, our lyric round
of tide, phase, and the womb's atlantis
overlays endlessly
charms the world out of time
daughter, i'd feed you at my veins
if my breasts ran dry
or bury me in the wheatfield
where i'll rot patiently under your breakfast
and my corpuscles will crumble
into vitamins you need

5
architect of the cell's alphabet
navigator of blood's latitudes
keeper of the archives of fire

my heritage unwinds inside me
uncoils like a long galaxy
through the dark nucleoplasm

like a snake gone opaque
she hides in the jungles of the chromosome
she lies at the hydrocarbon's heart
she is the black hole itself
between her thighs
the universe is squeezed from spirit

GE Vol. VIII, No. 69 (Ostara 1975) 24

Queen of All the Magics

by **Michael Hurley,** *Church of All Worlds (edited by Tim Zell, CAW)*

AGANISM, WITCHCRAFT, THE White Goddess and Druidism ere all bound-up in a complex cultural-religious-mythic structure. To study the whole structure is a task of great dimension. In this study, Robert Graves' *The White Goddess*[1] is to be recommended above all else. Graves pulls together a lot of research done in religion, mythology, anthropology and classical literature to draw a portrait of the origins of our Western Civilization.

Being a poet, Graves started out his research to answer poetic questions: "Why do poets call on the Muse?" "Whence comes true inspiration?" "What is true poetry?" In searching for the answers he ran across many threads of myth, religion and poetry which he wove into the tapestry of *The White Goddess.*

Graves was one of the first to synthesize the myths of Northern-Europe, the Mediterranean area and the Middle East. His hypothesis is that all three cultural areas share a common mytho-religious, background that runs deeper than was formerly suspected. This background has influenced the shape and direction of all Western religion and art.

Basically he contends that the original inhabitants of Western Europe were an agricultural people with a matriarchal society. They personified Mother Earth into their prime deity and made the Sun and Moon Her principal children. Sometimes the Sun was also Her husband.

The worship of nature in all forms was the main principle of prehistoric Paganism. Trees and animals (boar, deer and bull) were especially venerated. The whole calendar of the Druids was based on the trees. Many Pagan tree festivals became Christianized, of which Christmas and Easter are prime examples.

This culture seems to be one of the oldest in the world. Most recent archaeological studies have indicated that this European culture may pre-date Sumeria and Egypt.

These early peoples venerated nature. From primitive animism this nature worship evolved into a more complex system of religious traditions, myths and art (graphic, musical and dramatic). While some of these customs were rather bloody at first, the concept of symbolic sacrifice was eventually introduced.

This concept is one of the basic elements of magical theory. The ideas of Paganism are integral with magical practice. Three basic principles are:

1. All of Nature is alive or shares the same life force. In theological terms, Creator and Creation are One. This is simple Pantheism.

2. It follows from #1 that since all life is of the same essence it should have the same potential nature. Those patterns which we see around us influence and reflect our own lives. This principle is usually stated, "As above, so below."

3. Conversely, since we share the same life force as the rest of Nature, this force can be accumulated and channeled and controlled, thus allowing individuals to exert influence over Nature. This is the basis of all magic.

From these general principles come several specific patterns of action, motifs in myths, and rituals in religion. The first principle leads to veneration of the elements and personification of them in the complex myth systems of the more advanced civilizations (Sumer, Rome, Egypt, Greece, Britain, Germania, Ireland). Also there remained a reverence for the natural world and for the natural processes among the Pagan peoples.

In magic this pantheistic universe was an easy one to manipulate. Inert matter cannot be controlled; only that which is alive can be controlled. By assuming a living universe, by giving the various aspects of Nature names and personalities, magicians made it easier to assert their power over the universe. It is a principle of magic that only by learning someone's name can you assert control over that person. Thus in olden days people would have two names—a social one and a secret one. Magic uses this principle in the Names of Power: by learning the true names of the various spirits, gods and demons, one can assume control over them.

But this assumption of power cannot happen at will. The conditions of the universe must be right to allow magic to be worked. Here the second principle comes in. The various methods of fortune telling, soothsaying, oracling and divination are made use of. When one delves into magic one is learning basically a set of rules by which the universe runs. Once one understands the rules one can start playing the game and winning. Becoming a magician simply means putting yourself in tune with the functions and rhythms of the universe. Once you tune in you can move with and assert some control over the flow and pattern.

Thus one learns to read the signs of the universe to grok when it would be best to do a certain act. Astrology, palmistry, numerology, etc all grew out of this principle.

Once one has grokked the rules and learned to read the signs one is ready to assert his influence over that portion of the universe available to him. Since ell nature functions in the same general way and shares a common pattern and life force, one tuned-in can make use of this pattern to shape the direction of the flow. To do this one practices sympathetic magic.

The shaman in his hunting rituals symbolically slays a bison in hopes that his people will really kill one tomorrow. The magician, through his studying and preparation, has placed himself in contact with the functions and flows of the universe. As he becomes more skilled in his perceptions and can learn to anticipate trends, he can learn to manipulate situations so things work out his way. He puts himself in sympathy (empathy =grokking) with the world and asserts a gentle nudge to help it along his way. This is much like the stock investor who can foresee trends and manages his buying and selling to influence the rise or fall of the stock market. He is not "controlling" the market; his actions merely influence events to go his way.

Most of what we call magic is ritual magick—sympathetic magic used to influence events. This influence can be for the better or the worse. The goodness of evilness of magic—its Whiteness or blackness—depends on the motives, not the magic itself. Just like atomic energy, which can cure cancer or destroy the world, magic is a tool in man's hands.

These briefly are the principles of magical theory and practice end how they grew out of primitive Paganism.

Graves' book deals with these concepts in passing: His principle concern is in the application of certain of these patterns and principles in ancient culture and art.

Art by Van Dam

As we said, Graves gives evidence of a matriarchal culture that pre-dates written history. He gives further evidence of the survival of some of this culture down to modern times, particularly in the arts.

His basic contention is that the Mother-centered society was a more stable peaceful time, a time when true poetry first flowered. His purpose in exploring this world was to discover the language of true poetry and to apply it to his own work.

From his scholarship Graves demonstrates that the Earth. Mother, the Eternal Woman has several distinct traits that endear and en-fear her in the minds of men. She is gentle but absolutely just; she is kind and loving, but to her enemies she is a wild boar who will chop them in pieces; she is wise and fair and merciful; she has a deep insight into the natural order; she is at once a beautiful virgin daughter, a silver-haired mother full with child, and a decrepit old hag who is ugliness and terror: Freya, Frigg and Hel; Ishtar, Arram and Tiamat.

Graves' conclusion is that this image of Woman is the sublime subject of poetry. The eternal quest for Her love is the stuff of epic: The hero's search for Her is the concern of all literature.

In the ancient days when the Queens ruled, men had two special duties: one was to be the queen's consort to insure fertility and produce children; the other was to be the queen's poet and councilor. Thus the true poet was one who eternally sought the love of his Lady, yet was doomed to die when he received it. When the poet won the love of Her, She would take him for consort, but traditionally and mythically the queen's consort was sacrificed every spring after the Vernal Rites to insure not only a pregnant queen but a pregnant soil. On the artistic level, an artist can only produce one "greatest" work. Since the White Goddess is the subject and inspiration of this single great work, it was done at a moment of full sexual-like empathy-in-love (a deep grokking in fullness) which can only happen once.

This experience is so completely fulfilling yet so completely shattering (can one stand in the Light of the Face of Goddess for more than an instant? Can one be gripped in the love ecstasy of Her for more than a second?) that the true artist is broken afterwards. His greatest work is done. He can never attain such heights again. The quest is over.

All art, all religion aims at such a union, such an insight. Graves maintains that because no one realizes the true aim of art/religion (the Holy White Goddess), our art and reli-gions can never be fully satisfying. He has sought to practice his art in a quest for the Lady and to, do Her homage.

One of the corruptions that crept into our civilization and thus into magic and Witchcraft was patriarchalism. About 10,000 BCE Aryan invaders moved into Europe, the Middle East and India from the central plains of Asia. They were horse-mounted nomads; their religion was totemistic and emphasized the sky and war deities; and their culture was patriarchal.

These people, being warriors, quickly installed themselves in the areas they invaded. Major cultural changes can be observed in the myths that originated during those times. The Aryan war and sky gods "married" the various forms of the Mother and love goddesses. Patriarchal values crept into the myths. The paternalistic concerns with fatherhood, history, science and war emerged. Our whole sexual ethic stems from this shift.

Matriarchal societies tend not be concerned with determining exactly the male parenthood of an individual. Sex customs tend to be free, orgiastic, "liberal" by current standards.

Under a father-dominated system the paternity of each child is of vital importance. The father's siring of the children is the only link the man has with the family. A mother always knows her children, but a father has to take special steps to insure his link with mother and child.

From this compulsion stems our Western desire to know history, to keep records, to explore, to develop natural science. Indeed these drives have produced a civilization which is now on the threshold of the stars. But in Graves' thought, our culture has suffered some spiritual/emotional deprivation because of a paternal dominance. Graves' contention is that a return to more humanistic values in art and religion and our social structure, changes based on the Mother Deity's Way, would correct the spiritual imbalance.

---

1. *The White Goddess,* Robert Graves, Noonday FS&G, 1966

The Divine Maiden

*by **Frederick MacLauren Adams** (1928–2008), Feraferia*

1. HOLOCAUST OF THE FISHES

N AD 395 THE GATES OF GREECE were opened to Alaric the Goth by what Eunapios called "the Godlessness of those who in their dark garments entered with him unhindered." These "Godless men" were Christian monks. They drove straight for Athens and Eleusis, the Sanctuary of Demeter and Kore, Divine Mother and Maiden of The Mysteries.

In the sacred precincts of Eleusis, already a Mithraic father had sacrilegiously pre-empted the office of Hierophant. But in conspiracy with Godless monks, the Goths closed the woefully Romanized sanctuary for the remainder of the Piscean Age.

In AD 389, the great Pagan library of Alexandria was deliberately destroyed by a Christian mob. Also in Alexandria, and also instigated by monks, beautiful Hypatia, a Pagan Lady philosopher and geometer of the first rank, was flayed alive in a church by Christians.

In the late 4th century AD, again due to the Edict against Pagan worship promulgated by the Christian Emperor Theodosius, the Sanctuary of The Great Gods on island Samothrace, in which the Kabeirian Mysteries accorded prominence to Demeter and Kore, was systematically looted. The Hall of Votive Gifts was completely emptied of its offerings from grateful Initiates, perhaps by Cilecian pirates.

Between 401 and 402 AD, the eight Pagan temples of Gaza, among which was the famous Marneion of Cretan Zeus, were plundered and demolished by followers of Christ. The homes of Pagan devotees were searched for the sacred books of Magic used in their rites of initiation. These were destroyed.

The iconoclastic zeal of the new religion, when it gained political supremacy over the Roman sphere in the 4th century AD, resolved to eliminate every masterpiece of Pagan religious art. Thus many statues of Eros and of Aphrodite, such as the incomparable Venus De Milo, exhibit mutilations inflicted by pious mobs, whose company always numbered ego-maniacs actively seeking martyrdom. Paul Carus wrote, "It is the fanaticism of ascetic frenzy in the bitterness of its wrath against Nature in general and love in particular that showed itself in these iconoclastic demonstrations."

After some temple of Aphrodite was attacked by the votaries of "The Prince of Peace," and the Holy Icon of The Goddess lay prone beneath Her pedestal, Carus suggests the possibility that well-to-do friends of doomed Paganism returned to the sacked temple after dark, removed the sculpture, placed on shipboard, and sailed for Melos (= Milo). Here the Icon may have been hastily buried on the farm of a family still loyal to The Goddess.

"And as soon as Christianity fairly got the upper hand in the Fourth Century, the wrecking of temples and the smashing of the idols of the demons became a most popular amusement with which to grace a Christian festival. As we turn over the pages of the martyrologies, we wonder that any ancient statues at all escaped those senseless outbursts of zealotry."

But the Christians were only intensifying the Patriarchal heroics of their mentors Roman militarists and engineers, admired for their thrift and systematic thoroughness. At the beginning of their imperial career the Romans had committed merciless genocide against the more joyful Etruscans, and then the Carthaginians.

In AD 61, the Roman governor of Britain invaded the last refuge of the Druids, on the Island of Anglesey (Mona) off Wales. As Druids chanted among the Keltic warriors, "black garbed, wild-haired Druidesses rushed about with torches." However, the Romans won. They razed Druid libraries, filled with precious records of the age-old Nature religion; just as the Spanish Conquistadors obliterated the codices of Aztecs, Mayans, and Incas, just as the Red Chinese have recently destroyed the magical libraries of Lamaist

Monasteries in Tibet. In that same early year of Our Lord, the Brythonic Queen Boadiceia was cheated of her realm, publicly flogged, and her daughters raped by Roman legionaries.

Today we may discern that Christian persecution continued the Roman pattern through the Middle Ages. After the infamous Bull of Innocent VIII, promulgated in 1484, about eleven-hundred years after the holocaust of the Fourth Century, it is estimated that ten million men, women, and children were executed for the crime of adhering to the Old Religion, which had survived in abraided, fragmentary forms in rural regions of Europe as the various Culti of The Witches. Very possibly most of the victims were not members of bona fide enclaves of archaic Nature Religions, but that did not deter the Witch hunters. The repression and constant re-repression of their own negated instincts by the suppression of those upon whom they projected these instincts, became an irresistable necessity.

2. DAMNATION OF THE DAUGHTER

The extirpation of Pagan Faiths, especially Goddess-centered ones, is motivated by the power drive generated from the Father Archetype to dominate the Mother Archetype, and thus marshal the energies of Her Sons for the conquest and exploitation of Nature. Of course this motivation is rationalized as the glorious transcendence of Spirit over Matter. Now, even this motivation is not primary. The fundamental mainspring of the Patriarchal Revolution is a much more complex, obscure, and paradoxical matter: The suppressive objectives of Father-focused cults and cultures consists in some mysterious, ambivalent fear of the DAUGHTER Archetype. It is the Nymph or even the defenseless Maiden Who is defensively vilified and permitted progressively less and less influence in the archetypal transactions of the historical process. She is turned into a whore, an evil Witch, a cultural saboteur, if She does not submit to acting the role of the darling plaything, an unsubstantial frill, apprenticed to Her honored Mother, that no-nonsense vessel of procreation, after which She had better pattern Herself. As clinging vine, the proper Daughter is expected to espalier Herself against the befitting pendant of Her suitor, the heroic Son, who is groomed to cut a splendid figure in the Patriarchal order: protector and sustainer, "go-getter," rugged pioneer, admirably dashing and impetuous.

Of course, in our times at long last, real mothers and daughters, in the big cities at least, are deciding to reject these roles. The Lysistratan Revolution of Woman's Liberation must be enlarged. But so far this revolt is only outward, and in some ways could be construed as a possible advancement of the Patriarchal enterprise toward its ultimate goal: the eventual eradication of all organismic values. Militant women may be liberating themselves only to become men, to manipulate the means of the masculine establishment, and thus gain their places in the archetypal Sun of the historical constructions of the Patriarchy. Now what about women's places in the Mansions of the Moon? In the Moon and twinkling archetypal constellations of their aeonic instincts and superbly tuned magical sensibilities, to which men have no comparable approaches? Have ideals of masculine ego-consciousness finally converted feminine psycho-cosmic consciousness to patriarchal narrow-alley, no-exit power games? If it has, there remains no chance for human culture creatively to rejoin Ecological process and initiate the Age of The Daughter. The Divine Maiden is the true promise of the Equinoctal Point now precessing from the last 2200± years of Pisces into the next 2200± years of Aquarius.

When the star mill of Aquarius really begins to grind, the new measure of all things will be the paragon of daintiness and lyrical erotic exuberance: KORE SOTEIRA, the Maiden Savioress.

But who is The Daughter and why has She seemed so fearsome within the contexts of most historical societies? It is noteworthy that one tribal people of Tierra Del Fuego tell a story to the effect that women led by the Moon Lady established The Mysteries. But the men, led by the Sun Man, killed all the women and usurped their sacerdotal offices. However, these priests by right of gynocide were careful to preserve the little girls so they might perpetuate the race. Also, the girls could be "trained" to conform to the will of their masters.

Now, the males of the Hamadras Baboons, a species held sacred in ancient Egypt, have the intriguing habit of kidnapping immature females. These males then patronizingly feed and raise these girl children so that they will turn out to be good harem ladies.

It does not lie within the scope of this short essay to multiply scores of examples like the foregoing. There are many works currently in print that explore the complexities of woman's eclipse. What now demands attention are the religious and psychic potentials of the archetypal realm of The Daughter, Maiden and Nymph, She Who, among other things, inclines women and men to venerate romantic love. For often people will continue to invest tremendous amounts of libido in fantastic models of romantic amour even though their external lives grant them little or no return on that investment. In the "Engulfed Cathedral" of Eros and Psyche lies the perennially repressed values of the mystic Daughter, and some absolutely terrifying set of moral and metaphysical coordinates She alone can assemble and energize. Perhaps the buried standards of The Daughter present a whole new spectrum of evolutional possibilities very contrary to the one that is now terminating in a precipice.

(*Korythalia*, Vol. IV, No. 7, © 1973, Feraferia)
GE Vol. VI, No. 54 (Beltane 1973) 17–18

I Am the Lady of the Dance
by Svetlana Butyrin & Frederick Adams

I am the Lady of the Dance;
All Nature feels My emerald glance;
All Lovers join Me in their magic trance
For I am the Mistress of Romance!

When trees and grasses make pilgrimage
And fill the glens with Life,
I lead the jingling rout of Nymphs,
     The Faerie Companionage,
     The Faerie Companionage! *(Spring)*

I am the goddess of the Night;
I grant all Stars their diamond light;
I let all Worlds unwind their spiral sight
For I am the Enchantress of Delight!

In the heat of the shimmering days,
The Sun and Moon shall fuse.
And in the Ocean of glowing rays,
     My Flesh of Love diffuse,
     My Flesh of Love diffuse! *(Summer)*

I am the Lady of the Dance;
All Nature feels My emerald glance;
All Lovers join Me in their magic trance
For I am the Mistress of Romance!

From the flickering Grail of Night,
Seeds of Gold I bestow
On those who Wisdom of Koré sow
     Among the Dreams of Light,
     Among the Dreams of Light! *(Autumn)*

I am the goddess of the Night;
I grant all Stars their diamond light;
I let all Worlds unwind their spiral sight
For am the Enchantress of Delight!

Those who lift My Skirts of Flame
May stairs of Stars reveal,
Then mount to the bounds of Space surreal
     And burst the Seal of Time,
     And burst the Seal of Time! *(Winter)*

I am the Lady of the Dance;
All Nature feels My emerald glance;
All Lovers join Me in their magic trance
For I am the Mistress of Romance!

The Lord of Light

*by **Morning Glory Zell**, CAW (illustrated by Oberon Zell)*

I AM WRITING THIS IN RESPONSE TO what I feel is a growing tendency among the matristic elements of Neo-Paganism. There exists at this time a...dare I call it an obsession (wholly justifiable) with the Goddess. After many thousand years of patrist oppression, women and Woman worship are coming into their own again. Consequently, you hear a lot about Our Lady: poems, prayers, and promises all to Her and about Her but rarely a word is said in matrist Pagan groups and publications about tier partner and Her consort. I feel that this is not an entirely egalitarian approach. It seems that one Diety or another predominates in different Covens and different Trads. But why not both? Let's not make the same mistake that the Yahvists have made. Let's not become unbalanced in the other direction. Harmony and the perfect balance of both Yin and Yang should he our goal as free and healthy Pagan spirits.

Much of the lack of emphasis on the male Deity aspects are the symptom of a confusion about the role of the male at this time. Women seem to be more and more liberating themselves from their traditional roles and many sympathetic Pagan men find themselves wondering where that leaves them and what they can do to help. With all the talk of Mother Goddess there is little in the way of a male image for a self respecting Goddess-loving Pagan man to identify himself with. Mostly identification is of a negative sort: They know the kind of masculine values and the kind of Gods they abhor, but what does that leave you with?

In the midst of so much anxiety and turmoil in the world at large, it is a dangerous thing that men and women should be estranged from each others' comfort by pride and despair. "A house divided against itself cannot stand." We've all heard this many times, but it has taken on a new significance for the children of Aquarius. We cannot have an age of peace without love; and what is love without equality? I have not been exempt from this problem either. Though my own house is not divided, there is dissention in our community of friends and I frequently find myself on the defensive. The fact of my Witchhood is enough to insure my understanding about the nature of the male role, but at the same time it creates a lot of misunderstanding on the part of the average person to whom I talk. For instance, I find it almost impossible to discuss any kind of philosophy or theology concerning divinity and/or supreme being. I keep running into these incredible semantic snags: Number one, "God" is male; one always uses the pronoun "he." People say "God...He," never God...It, or God...She. Number two: the concept of supreme being is separate from humanity. There is "Me" standing (here) and then there is "God" over...(there) separate, see? But I am unable to conceive of being separate from "God." That's ridiculous! I am God, and so are you! I am the Goddess and you are the God (sometimes it works the other way around). The concept of supreme being, what most people call "God," is complete and total "isness." It is all there is, and was, and ever will be, and you are a piece of it. It is composed of many parts which can be divided into yang and yin, male and female, dark and light, etc. ad infinitum. This is duality. Yet beyond even duality is "Oneness" which is All. Part of getting into the All is digging the many parts, i.e. duality, so in Witchcraft there are these subheadings to the supreme being: *the* God, and the Goddess. I have italicized "the" to differentiate the God from His Judeo-Christian counterpart.

So now that I've tried to clarify who exactly I am talking about, and why, I want to discuss the Pagan divinity we call the Horned God (Old Horny), Cernunnos, Sylvanus, Pan, Herne, Tammuz, Dionysos, Amon Ra, Lucifer. He, like the Goddess, has many names and his devotees are scattered over much time and many places. He is the Sun who gives light; He is the bringer of knowledge which is also light. He is the divine lover, musician, magician. He is the Father of all creatures. Animal husbandry is in His care as gardening and plants are in the care of the Goddess. He is also the Great Hunter. This last image is His first incarnation. He came to us through the practice of Totemism. When men and women held equal status in the Paleolithic community, it was the God they invoked to give them good hunting. He was usually worshipped in the form of some totem animal which was identified with that particular tribe. The totem animal was worshipped and in some degree held sacred, but this did not always give it immunity from appearing on the tribal menu. However, the totem animal could not be killed without its permission. This was one of the duties of the shaman, who was a priest of the God. It was he, through the intervention of the God, who obtained this permission.

Next, historically, the God became identified with death and rebirth. This idea, which is rooted in the worship of the sun, is the basis for many legends and branch beliefs. It is a constantly recurring theme throughout human histories. He is Osiris, slain by Set; Tammuz taken by Nergal the Dark; and of course the Christ crucified on the cross. The God is the Sun who dies in Winter, is reborn of the Goddess and becomes Her lover in Spring, impregnates Her in Summer, and dies in Autumn to be incarnated in Her womb when Winter comes again. Thus the Sun who is the God is also the Son who is the God.

I am getting an idea that as our Mother Earth, Terrebia, is one living organism, so is our Father, the Sun, Solarvirens. Together They created us: His warm unfailing radiant energy on Her steady stream of liquid and solid matter created the miracle we know as Life. Though we are still carried in Her womb and are totally dependent on the Mother for our sustenance, are we any less dependant on Him? Where would *we* or our Mother be without His radiance? The answer of course is...lifeless.

I have discussed and argued this point with many different people and it always gets to the same point. If we see the Mother as an evolving, potentially conscious entity, then why not the Father? True, he is 93 million miles away, but his energy reaches us in minutes. As for being impersonal, that is something we have no conception of. The level of consciousness that it would take to be literally a Star is one that we would find incomprehensible. But perhaps not entirely, for though He gives birth to no life Himself, does He not nourish Life as does a true father to his child? Is not His never-failing warmth a parable that teaches us of love? The very electrical energy that pulses through our nerve cells and leaps the micro-abyss of our synapses, isn't this parallel to the same Divine solar energy that leaps outward from the corona of Solarvirens? And who is to say that Crowley was wrong: "Every man and woman is a star." We are the microcosm which reflects the macrocosm. Energy can neither be created nor destroyed, it merely changes form. As John Denver says, "Sunshine always makes us high." Even the concept of Sunshine makes us high; we don't have to see it or feel it - sometimes just thinking about the Solar fire is enough to cut through the drearyness of a grey day. Or the symbol of a single burning candle against the darkness will lighten our hearts considerably as it has done since we huddled together in caves for warmth. Finally, our Lady the Moon is like a reflection of Our Mother the Earth, so it is that a shadow is the mirror image of a light, and the Lord of Shadows is the other face of the Lord of Light.

I feel impelled to talk about the Horned One because this is His time of year, the season for holidays connected with rebirth. In December 17th there is Saturnalia, the traditional Roman feast that saw much orgiastic festivities in honor of Saturn and Dionysos. The winter solstice was the major holiday of the Druids, who celebrated the rebirth of the Solar fire carried into the sacred Grove in the Ark of Hu Gadarn. And last of all there is Christmas. As much disparity as appears at first between these holidays, they all celebrate the same thing; the rebirth of this Son who is the God.

The Pagans' view of their God is not a set role but a manifestation of the multidimensional ways of Nature. The God is wild and strong, overflowing with laughter and joy; filled with an insatiable energy. He is the fountainhead of passion. He has the four elemental faces of the Guardian of the Four Watchtowers; the Lord of Misrule. As Janicott, the two faced God, He is the epitome of pure sex and at the same time the wise old Ascetic. As Lucifer the Sun, he is brother and lover to Diana the Moon and father to the avatar Aradia. In all things He is present as teacher and lover. When you seek Him he is everywhere and everyone. Baba Ram Mass says, "When you know how to listen everybody is the Guru." In Buffy St. Marie's song *Eyes of Amber,* the God, the Eternal Lover, appears as "the heart of firelight... heart of snow, you come again. You are the midnight wind. With hands of moonbeams and clouds you call me...and though I'll never know you, wistful lover, until you're gone, you're here to teach me how to love...."

So these are the many faces of the God of the Pagani: the lusty laughing goat-footed God; the tender ephemeral Adonis, Friend, Brother, Lover, Teacher, Partner of the Goddess—not the servant or the master, but the necessary other half of a divine Whole. If you would like to tune into this aspect of the God within you, whether to strengthen your own understanding of the roots of true masculinity or to prevent losing perspective and becoming reactionary toward men instead of experiencing the reality of man as the vessel of the God, I've included a rite at the end of this article. I hope the readers of this feature can use its contents to achieve a more harmonious relationship with their brothers and sisters.

"For now is the time for your loving, and the time for your company. Now that the light of reason fails, and fires burn on the sea. For we are the Children of Darkness...."

Blessed Be.

Cernunnos Invocation & Meditation

Draw a large circle on the floor and place a yellow or orange candle in the center. Light some Cedar, Pine, or Patchouli incense and with it and a small amount of red wine mingled with salt, walk clockwise (deosil) around the circle. Start in the East, sprinkle the wine and hold the incense. Chant the Invocation. When you return to the East, turn clock-wise on your own axis and spin around seven times, saying "Harrahya!" Then kneel staring into the candle flame. Let your imagination flow. See Him coming through the dark forest; hear the trampling of the underbrush; smell the pungent scent on the wind. The light gets brighter and brighter as He bursts into view: Lord Cernunnos

Himself - the Horned One crowned with the living Sun! Feel His magnetism surround you. Bathe in His energy. Merge with Him.

Invocation:

Eko; Eko Azarak!
Eko; Eko Zomelak!
Eko; Eko Cernunnos!
Eko; Eko Arada!
Bagabi lacha bachabe;
Lamac cahi achababa,
Karellyos!
Lamac Lamac
Bachalyas;
Cabahagy Sabalyas,
Baryolas!
Lagoz atha
Cabyolas;
Samahac atha
femyolas,
Harrahya!

Libations at the Labrys

B'ng various mental meanderings
of a Neo-Pagan High Priest

by **Tony Spurlock (Brian Dragon)**, *The Pagan Way*

I.

NOW, THE WITAN DO NOT THINK ALL these Great Thoughts about the Gods and sit about arguing as to Her true nature, as do so many leaders and thinkers of the organized religions. There is no need to explain Her to others. The Pagani merely accept the beauty which is the Triple Lady.

Yet, the moonchild "accepts" so easily and so sincerely because of a knowledge and love which is...instinctive. Intrinsic. A part of the Pagan's being!

The others, therefore, argue to prove their knowledge...when actually those with the loudest mouths have none to prove.

However, their insecurity is not the topic of these writings, but rather, it comes to my attention that this Pagan "instinct" is truly a miraculous and wonderful thing...a gift from the Goddess. This simple acceptance and wordless knowledge is far more wonderful than all the magicks and powers, for it holds at its base the greatest magick—Love. Only the true Pagan, in this case a male Pagan, can feel the love of a child for the warmth of his Mother, and a sexual desire for the perfected female archetype at the same time. Only he groks the connection between the two.

What all this is about is a Pagan's feelings toward the Lady explained in *words*. I began trying to explain to a person and found that, to be understood by a complete outsider takes many *words* I had never thought before. These explanations could cover Pages, yet, before I began these words I held in my heart ONE emotion; an emotion which I think is given to Pagans alone. This emotion is knowledge of many things at once, and many emotions. Yet it is one emotion and I know no name for it.

This attitude toward the Lady is so simple, so direct, that compared to the complicated philosophies of religious thinkers through the ages, it seems primitive and worthy only of contempt. But try to fully put all the bases, and reasons, and proofs (which I never worried about until now) into words. To explain fully...WOW!

Example. Woman. To explain this divinity of woman.

ALL THINGS are but echoes of greater happenings on the higher planes. Woman is the focusing point for the greatest majority of echoes which are the Goddess. Ahh! If I could but say! If I say "Chalice" (a holy object/symbol of our Order) to a man of the grey god Technology he gets only CHALICE: A CUP. But if I say "Chalice" to you and you see: the yawning dark bowl of heaven...the great endless place of all origin; the great dark universal Womb, with those serene 'waters;' when you understand why the Cauldron of Cerridwen is the Holy Grail of Immortality; when your mind hints at the whereabouts of that Cup...but you know there is more to it. When you see and feel and experience all these things—and there are suggestions of others at the far reaches of your mind...when all this happens simultaneously without your conscious mind explaining it to you, then you are nearing that nameless emotion granted the Pagani.

II.

They say we are bound to this world (this plane; this sphere?). And yet we are bound merely by the imagination of the mind of man—an imagination which is, itself, bound by the shackles of individual experience...or the experience of others, whether real or philosophical.

He who knows no other is content with his personal sphere of existence, no matter how meager and frugal it may be. But...one who has seen within himself the limitless vistas of greater awareness, but is held in check by the preformed conceptions of the masses...is the most truly tortured of souls.

The oranges, the blues, the blacks, the whites, the greys. How pitiful is this excuse for life which is handed us at birth on a synthetic platter by the children of the Sky Father. This myth, this legend that has become reality for so many "people." They base their conceptions of reality and unreality upon but the tiniest backwashes of truth...as if even the greatest Earthian artist could show the entire structure and form of a mountain range by merely gazing at a pebble.

There are colors beyond that which the human eye can imagine. Spheres, planes ("realities") beyond the conception of modern man. Yet he denies their very existence! Too long have we gazed at the pebble.

The Kore
A Vision of Goddess as Woman to Be
by Penelope Novack

She is full-lipped and newly wakened
    to her legacy
Of being female and well aware that
    her breasts are round
With new-grown womanhood and that
    her waist is small
Against the symmetry and invitation
    which is swaying, found
In every wide-hipped step she takes
    on graceful feet.
Her laugh is marked by a back-ward
    swing of the head
Which throws her shining hair back
    to her shoulders
And reveals the tempting whiteness
    of a throat that is said
To drive the most faithful men to
    dream a little more
Than is their wont. She is woman
    and all young
All filled with more contradictions
    than a peace talk
And as gay as the half-filled beauty
    of a song.

III.

There are Christians who pray to their god with gratitude in their hearts, thanking him. And this is good.

Yet there are those who will say, "Our Father, who art in Heaven, I thank you for this new house," or "my raise in salary," or "my new car," and this is not so good, for a man or woman must learn to bear his responsibilities like a god, or he remains naught but a Karmic child, no matter his age.

What happens to a (wo)man in his life is entirely his own doing, whether as the Karmic result of a past action or because of his present endeavors. A person may work or fight (physically, mentally, emotionally or spiritually) to get a new house, or a raise, or a new car...or a friend may give him any of these things out of love.

Therefore does the Pagan say, "Shining Lord, who art Chief of all Creation, I thank you for giving me the will to work and the strength to fight; 0 Holy Lady of the silvery void, I thank you for the love by which I have these friends."

(1970-73 CE)

GE Vol. VII, No. 67 (Yule 1974) 13–14

Tony Spurlock (now also well-known as **Brian Dragon**) began to contribute material to *Green Egg* when he was around 14 or 15. As of 2008, he is 50 years old. He was initiated into the Feri Tradition of Witchcraft on 1977 at the Pagan sanctuary Coeden Brith, and is widely respected for his contributions to the poetic liturgy and theoretical literature of that Tradition. As Brian Dragon, he was singer-songwriter in the rock groups ELF and the Faces of Time. He founded the First Church of the Doors in 1984 to promote the study of Jim Morrison's writings, as was profiled in *Newsweek*. For the last 20 years he has made a special study of Dark Age Britain with an emphasis on the Picts of Scotland. *http://pictdom.org*

As regards the piece, "Libations at the Labrys," he reminds the reader that it is probably better for a person to have actually had sex *before* attempting to teach the mysteries of a sex cult.

Gods and Goddesses: Are They Real?

by *"Robert" (Fred Lamond), CAW, Gardnerian Wicca*

JUST WHAT ARE THE PAGAN GOD-desses, Her many manifestations, and the Jewish-Christian Jehovah? Images of the human mind created by our ancestors millennia ago? Archetypal images of the collective human unconscious? Planetary spirits that rule life on Earth? Or cosmic forces that antedate the human race, or indeed the appearance of life on Earth?

The question is anything but academic. The answer determines the power that we may hope to draw from invoking the Goddess, compared to the power that all varieties of Jew and Christian, from the most moderate to rabid Fundamentalists, draw from praying to Jehovah.

The Image and the Reality

When we represent the Goddess as a beautiful woman rising naked from the sea, or as an enthroned figure wearing the horns of Isis, these are of course humanly created images. So is the traditional Christian picture of God the Father as a fierce Hebrew patriarch with a long beard and flowing hair. But is that all that they are, or are these images just gateways to human understanding of eternal forces?

It is certainly possible for magicians, poets and marketing consultants to create new images and embed these in the collective unconscious of a TV audience, a nation or a whole culture. Old Glory is an abstract pattern whose symbolism would have been meaningless to an American colonist living 250 years ago, but which has enthused the U.S. Army in countless wars since the War of Independence. Trademarks become recognizable over time, and are the focus for considerable loyalty from both the staff who work for the owner firm and its satisfied customers.

When a god or great prophet image is created in this way, it can become a spiritual bank account into which worshippers deposit part of their spiritual energy, so that they and fellow worshippers may draw on it when in need through their prayers.

Some gods and goddesses are more than this, however. Their names and images are but gateways to human communication with timeless planetary or cosmic forces, and it is these forces that their priests and worshippers can tap directly if their conviction is strong enough to establish the required link.

The Goddess, Gateway to Planetary and Cosmic Love

Pagans who have first encountered the power of the Goddess within a circle may wonder which type of power they are experiencing: the spiritual bank account, or the cosmic force. But to those who like me first experienced Her in a spontaneous mystical experience before any initiation into a Pagan group there can be no such doubt. It was the cosmic power of Love that I experienced in the arms of my first girl friend, and that I recognised at my Wiccan initiation three years later.

A lithe reasoning may lead the remainder of us to the same conclusion. All Goddess-worshipping cultures have worshipped Her in three aspects: maiden, mother, and hag. She has thus always represented the cyclicity of life, which gives each solar year, plant or animal a birth, growth to maturity, union with a mate to reproduce the species, nurture of the next generation, decline into old age, and finally death.

These are not uniquely individual, nor even just human experiences, but universal experiences of at least all plant and animal species. There is clearly a power independent of and antedating the human mind that keeps this cycle going, on which the perpetuation of all plant and animal life depends. That same power drives all our human loves, in both their emotional and sexual aspects: why else do we tend to feel sexier and emotionally more intense in the springtime, when the whole of

Nature awakens from its winter sleep, flowers and trees blossom, most animals mate?

This is the power which we can reach magically, and from which we can draw solace, encouragement or the power we need when we invoke our Goddess. It is a profoundly conservative power. For all that we chant:

"She changes everything she touches,
And everything She touches changes!"

The changes She favors are those that take place strictly within a never-changing cycle of birth-growth-reproduction-death for the same species within the same ecological balance.

Jehovah, a Tribal Image Conceived by Moses?

What then of Her great rival and oppressor of the last two millennia: the male God of Creation, whom Jews, Christians and Moslems proclaim the only god there is?

Feminist historians from Merlin Stone onwards have pointed out that He is a comparatively young deity, little more that 3,000 years old against the tens if not hundreds of thousands of years that the Earth Mother was previously worshipped. From there to conclude that He is a humanly created image rather than a cosmic force is but a short step. Like Alice blowing the Red Queen's soldiers over with the words: "You are nothing but a pack of cards!" Feminists tell Jehovah: "You are nothing but an image conceived by Moses!"

Many Pagans of both sexes go along with this analysis, because we have kept from our Christian upbringing the idea that the deity ruling the Universe can only be good, and that all evil in the world is the product of human sinfulness. Now the Jehovah of the Old Testament is a fierce and rather nasty deity, who commands Joshua to kill all the inhabitants of Jericho, and Saul all the Amalekites, men, women, children and even sheep. How could such an unpleasant figure be anything but the projection of an authoritarian and genocidal tribal leader?

There are, however, several flaws in this argument. If Jehovah were no more than a tribal-totem-image first programmed by Moses, then He could be reprogrammed into something different by later generations. This is precisely what moderate Christian Church leaders have tried to do for most of the last hundred years, if not before. They find the genocidal deity of the Book of Exodus and Book of Samuel profoundly embarrassing, and dismiss Him as the product of the imperfect religious understanding of warlike desert tribes. Instead they give their own Father-God the quality of Love, albeit a somewhat anaemic Love, from which the sexual dimension is excluded.

But Jehovah has resisted this attempted reprogramming. Those who worship Him by obeying His Ten Commandments tend to this very day to be as aggressive and predatory as the Israelite tribes of Joshua's and Samuel's day: be they the settlers of the American West "a gun in one hand, the Bible in the other," the profoundly religious Afrikaners who quote biblical chapter and verse to justify apartheid, the Zionists who rob Palestinians of their ancestral lands, or the Fundamentalist American Protestants who support an aggressive U.S. foreign policy and armed intervention in Central America.

Besides, if Jehovah were no more than a humanly created image, could He have succeeded in displacing the cosmic power of Love from human worship in a single tribe for decades, let alone in the greater part of the world for two millenia? The power disparity would have been far too great.

And who says that cosmic powers are always beneficent? Predators that keep another animal species from overpopulating its feeding grounds may be good for that species as a whole, but nonetheless cause fear and suffering to the individuals which they catch and kill. And how much suffering was caused by the climactic changes that caused whole species to become extinct, like the dinosaurs 65 million years ago?

Jehovah/Shiva, Cosmic Power of Creation and Destruction?

It is much more likely that the Jewish-Christian Jehovah, like the Pagan Goddess, is a gateway image to a planetary or cosmic power equal to the power of Love, albeit not the only power as the Jews, Christians and Moslems believe. If so, what kind of power?

Read Genesis. He is the Creative power,

who separated the waters from the dry land, and both from the surrounding air, and created the plant and animal species that we know today. He did not, of course, do this in seven days, a poetic myth that was never meant by its distant author to be taken literally. Physics, archaeology and biology tell us that the world we know today was the product of a slow but continuous process of evolution, or—in the words of one British physicist—"continuous evolution."

This evolution took place in the face of Nature's (our Goddess) profound conservatism, which seeks to keep existing ecological balances always exactly as they are. If the power of Love were the only cosmic power ruling the Earth, the universe would never have progressed beyond primeval chaos, let alone reached today's level of complexity on Earth.

Geological discoveries do indeed tell us that for most of Earth's known history, ecological balances were maintained. Evolution only occured in response to cataclysmic climactic changes, produced by sunspots or the impact of a meteor, like the one which five million years ago wiped out the dinosaurs and gave mammals their chance to dominate the Earth.

All phases of Evolution and Creation were thus preceded by a cataclysmic period of Destruction of the previous ecological balance, on the principle that you cannot make omelettes without breaking eggs. Whatever power initiated these was not a gentle, loving or "nice" deity, but an immensely powerful Will to push life into ever more complex forms. What could be Its motive? The joy of creativity for its own sake is the only tenable explanation: Shiva's dance.

Until a hundred thousand

or so years ago, sunspots and meteors were the only relatively crude means that this creative power could use to upset Earth's ecological balance to spur another phase of evolution. But then, on the "sixth day" of life's evolution on Earth, God resolved to "create humanity in His own image" by endowing us with the left side of our brains, able to detatch itself from its environment sufficiently to destroy its existing balance, as the first step to transforming it into something different. He shared His power with us in this way that we might become His instruments in transforming the Earth faster, continuously but also in finer, more detailed ways than genetic mutation had achieved.

Far from contradicting each other, Pagan and biblical myths complement each other. The

Goddess, representing Life-Force on Earth, has always been represented as incarnate in every human being, animal, plant and even stone, just as we share our emotional instincts with all the higher animals. But the analytical detached left side of our brains is an exclusively human feature, the "image" within us of the Father-God of cosmic Creation through Destruction.

A Dialectical Divine Struggle

If I have correctly identified the two great cosmic powers represented respectively by the Pagan Goddess and Jewish-Christian God image, then the inherent antagonism between the two becomes apparent. He seeks forever to subvert ecological balances that She seeks to preserve. Far from being the result of alienated human bigotry, the persecution of magical Pagan cultures by the rational scientific Father God worshippers is but the microcosm within human religious consciousness of the cosmic struggle between conservative Love of things as they are and the creative-destructive Will.

But the clash between the Goddess and God is not dualistic but dialectical. It has always resulted hitherto in a synthesis: the slow process of evolution of life on Earth, to which humanity owes its existence. By contrast, little ever seems to change on the surface of the Moon and many distant planets, which are wholly within the domain of the conservative Mother (=matter). The Sun, which is wholly within the domain of the Creative-Destructive Father, is a fiery furnace on which an endless series of thermo-nuclear explosions constantly creates new gasses, elements and shapes, but dissolves them again immediately in the fire.

We cannot, therefore, call either the Goddess or the Father-God a "good" or "evil" power. We need them both but in a harmonious balance with each other, both within our own minds and through our efforts in the world around us. The destructive aggressive industrial society in which we live is the product of nearly two thousand years of unbalanced worship of the Creative-Destructive power to the exclusion of the conservative Goddess of Nature and Love. If it continues unchecked,

it will cause as great an ecological cataclysm as that which killed off the dinosaurs.

Fortunately, we still have some time to reestablish a sense of balance in our minds and those of our contemporaries. But we must be aware that our opponent in this endeavor is not just the military-industrial complex, some redneck Fundamentalist and cynical televangelists. It is none other than the cosmic power of Creation and Destruction acting through the collective human unconscious and His conscious worshippers to make us cause constant change on Earth.

We cannot fight this cosmic deity by pitting just our human wills against His in single-issue feminist, ecological and peace movements. We must use our religious convictions and magical knowledge to put the power of the equally strong cosmic goddess of Love and Preservation, by reestablishing Her worship on Earth after a two thousand year break.

Eventually, Pagan worship will have to be evenly balanced between the two deities. But as long as the majority in contemporary society continue to worship the Father exclusively, we can best reestablish the balance by putting the main emphasis of our worship on the Mother Goddess.

The dialectical struggle between the God and the Goddess is the subject of my book, *The Divine Struggle.*

GE, Vol. XXI, No. 84 (Oimelc 1989) 14–15

"Robert" (Frederick Lamond in mundane life) has been a Pagan all his life, consciously since a mystical experience in the arms of his first girlfriend over 50 years ago, He was initiated into Gerald Gardner's first coven at Brigid 1957 and has remained a member since then.

The dialectical interpretation of evolution on Earth and of human religious history, described in this article, came to Robert in a brainstorm shortly after his initiation, but is hardly novel. It is a development of the Taoist Yin-Yang and Tantric Shakti-Shiva dialectics, and gives an explanation of the split between thinking and feeling in the West diagnosed by C.F. Jung.

The Horned God:
Why the Wildman Is Not Enough
by John Rowan

 OBERT BLY SAYS THAT MEN HAVE lost their way: they have seen though the nonsense of traditional male chauvinisn and have in some cases taken on the equally misleading notion of the New Man, who is gentle, caring, nurturing and involved with child care, etc. Bly offers instead the model of the Wildman, who is in touch with the original deep masculinity which is his birthright. Bly gives a parable, the fairy tale Iron John, from the brothers Grimm.

In this fairy tale there is no information at all about how the wildman relates to women. He is apparently alone. In the first part of the story he lives at the bottom of a lake, and in the latter part of the story, which Bly does not quote, he is a great king followed by an impressive retinue. But we never hear anything about a queen, or any other female in relation to the wildman.

I am suspicious of an archetype of the Male which does not include some account of how he is related to the Female. Bly says quite correctly that male energy is different from female energy and that one cannot substitute one for the other. Men cannot get their models of masculinity from women. But without anything about relationship with the female, how can we avoid slipping back into the old ways? The wildman can be as oppressive to women as the models we have learned to question.

If a man gets in touch with his deep masculinity in a context which is patriarchal, he is going to be imprinted by that. What we must question is the patriarchal context, and Bly says not a word about that. In fact, what he does say about the goodness of the father, and the importance of the father to men, actually cuts right across the notion that we live in a patriarchal culture.

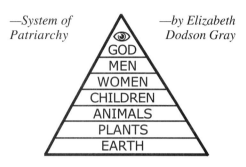

—System of Patriarchy

—by Elizabeth Dodson Gray

GOD / MEN / WOMEN / CHILDREN / ANIMALS / PLANTS / EARTH

Patriarchy

Since the word "patriarchy" may have already become jargon, let us take a moment to spell it out. Patriarchy is a form of hierarchy, arranged (as in the diagram) such that each level is allowed to exploit all the levels below it without criticism. Thus, if you want to know what God thinks, ask a man. Patriarchy is a system of society which gives all the power to the conventional masculine identity, granting privileges to those who reflect and respect it. This masculine iden tity is socially determined rather than biological. In patriarchy, the intellect and the dominating, controlling, aggressive tendencies within each individual are given sway. This results in a society dominated by violence, exploitation, a reverence for the scientific and a systematic rape of nature for man's benefit. In such a society the fear of homosexuality and the fear of the female are closely linked to the fear of softness and being "wet."

As Bly rightly points out, the moral which many modern men have tended to draw from all this is that it is OK to be female, and not OK to be male. But this a false conclusion: that women are good and men are bad and for the New Man it is good to be as much like a woman as possible. Bly is right to contest this. But patriarchy is really there, and really hurtful. It is an historical structure which came into being and can go out of being and has internal dynamics which are changing all the time. It is nothing to do with

111

biological determinism, as some critics suggest. It is about socially and historically defined gender. Recent analyses, such as the excellent book by Bob Connell, *Gender and Power*, show with a wealth of detail just what an oppressive system it is.

So "patriarchy" is essentially a unifying term, which enables us to see a single pattern underlying many apparently separate struggles. How then does a man begin to question such a system, which, on the one hand, gives him a privileged position, and on the other entraps him in a rigid role which is hard to escape from? We have to move to a different model again, one which is similar to Bly's wildman in a number of ways, yet does have an explicit relation to the female.

The Horned God

Imagine a stone circle with a tall stone in the center, an image of the healthy relationship of male with female. The female circle forms the matrix or context in which the male pillar can be filled with power. As long as that male power is contained within the circle, it is safe and usable, but if it tries to be self-sufficient, it comes to grief.

If we hold a violin string between our two hands, so that the hands are close together, then the string will hang loose and, if plucked, no note will emerge. If the left hand represents the female pole of experience and the right hand the male, this illustrates the way in which if the male gets too close to the female—becomes too much alike—no music can come out of that relationship. This Robert Bly has argued very well.

If, however, we pull the hands apart so far that the string snaps, the female and male hands have separated, become isolated, too different. Neither can music come of this. This possibility Bly has not ruled out—indeed it may be that his formulation makes such an outcome hard to avoid.

But if we hold the hands in tension, so that the male hand is in a creative relationship with the female hand, the string can be plucked and a musical note will emerge. This is the range of creative tension—not too slack, and not so tight as to snap. Depending upon what notes we want, the appropriate

tension may vary. In this way the relationship between the female and the male can be safe, because the continuing dialogue is guaranteed. This living kind of difference, as the feminist Audre Lord tells us, is

> a fund of necessary polarities between which our creativity can spark like a dialectic.... Only within that interdependency of different strengths. acknowledged and equal. can the power to seek new ways to actively "be" in the world generate. as well as the courage and sustenance to act where there are no charters.... Difference is that raw and powerful connection from which our personal power is forged.

This is a powerful statement of a great truth: we do not find answers by seeking one-sided truths (which then must defended), but by engaging in the creative tension of dialogue.

Another way of putting this is a quote from Arthur Avalon about the Eastern discipline of Tantra:

> The fully Real, therefore, has two aspects: one called Siva, the static aspect of Consciousness, and the other called Sakti, the kinetic aspect of the same. Kali Sakti, dark as a thundercloud, is represented standing and moving on the white inert body of Siva. He is white as Illumination. He is inert, for Pure Consciousness is without action and at rest. It is She, His Power, who moves.

This again is clear about the relationship. All power is first of all female power, and the God can only act by relating to her and being with her. But this God is male without a doubt—there is no question about his masculinity, which goes to the very depths of his being. Avalon remarks one of the basic Tantric beliefs is that honour should be paid to women; even female animals should not be sacrificed. If a man in that tradition speaks rudely to his wife, he has to fast for one day. To ill-treat a woman is a crime and women can be gurus or spiritual directors.

Western Paganism can be just as good as this, because it holds firmly to the primacy of the Goddess and the essential relationship of the Horned God. The Horned God is a consort. As a son, as a lover, sometimes even as a husband, he relates to the Great Goddess.

Particularly in the work of Starhawk, a feminist witch, we find some very strong and valuable suggestions about this relationship. In the work of Janet and Stuart Farrar, who are much more orthodox Pagans, we find this sort of statement: "Woman is the gateway to Witchcraft, and man is her 'guardian and student.'" I have gone into this difficult matter at much greater length in my book *The Horned God: Feminism and Men as Wounding and Healing* (Routledge, 1987).

Three Levels

Let us now draw the threads together and see where we have got to. There are at least three models of maleness: first there is the standard social model, where the male has to be a proper man, and not effeminate or cowardly. If one strays outside it in the feminine direction, one notices that this model is suspect and condemnable. We need not say much—it is too familiar.

Secondly there is what one might call the monistic model, where the man has to go down into his depths, finding perhaps first a layer of cliches, then a layer of self-putdowns, and then a layer of pain, and then a layer of deeper truth where it is OK to be male, and just a question of finding the deeper, truer version of it. This is the model which Robert Bly is still using, in a fresh and sophisticated way.

Thirdly there is what one might call a dualistic model, which is much more rare, where male power is found to be bad or harmful only because it is separated from female energy and female power. Connected up again in a proper relationship, that transforms into a deeper truth which is OK.

These three levels of understanding of the male are not necessarily contradictory. They correspond to three different levels of work in this area. The one level, which uses the model of adjustment to social reality, is the level of most of the counseling and psychotherapy which is generally available. The highest aim is to be able to play one's roles in society properly.

The second, the monistic approach, is the level of personal growth. Here the aim is not adjustment, but authenticity and real change. One is interested in the personal unconscious,

in the healing of the splits (in particular the split between the male and female), and generally in the integration of the person as a social and psychological being, what Ken Wilber calls the Centaur level, the level of the existential self or the real self. Robert Bly goes no further than this.

The other level, which uses the dualistic approach, is spirituality and the transpersonal, seen through the eyes of Paganism. It says that the male and the female must be related through the *hieros gamos* (the sacred marriage) if the male is not to be destructive. This is not about healing the split between the male and the female, but about enabling them to relate together as polarities in an appropriate way that actually works in today's world. This refers also to what goes on within the person—the internal male and female energies. It does not exclude the gay, the lesbian, the bisexual.

So we have three levels of working: at the first level we stick to adjustment, helping the person to make changes at the conscious level to make life more bearable and successful; at the second level we are concerned with the unconscious and with deeper changes which involve real self-discovery and owning up to one's inner reality; and at the third level we are concerned with the spiritual and the transpersonal, adopting the Tantric or Pagan approaches as being the safest for today's world.

I think it is this aspect of safety which speaks to me most. In a world where nuclear weapons are spreading to more and more countries, we need desperately to revise our notions of masculinity and power. It is this aspect which Robert Bly, in spite of all the good things he has to say, ultimately fails to address.

GE, Vol. XXIV, No. 94 (Mabon 1991) 4–5

John Rowan is a psychotherapist in private practice in London, England. He co-founded (with Jocelyn Chaplin) the Serpent Institute, a training centre for therapists based on a framework of Goddess spirituality. He wrote *The Horned God,* which is mainly about men and their spiritual nature. He is a member of the Pagan Federation and of the Integral Institute. *www.johnrowan.org.uk*

To/Ward Neo-Pagan Theology:
A Guideline for Navigating the Underworld of Our Divinity
by *Grant Potts*

HE PRACTICE OF NEO-PAGAN THE-ology is increasingly present in our community. Whether we find it in the thorough researches and reconstructions of the Asatru or Druidic communities, the ecumenical bleedings of the rising crop of Pagan Unitarian Universalists seminarians, or the columnal musings of our leaders in editorials, we are experiencing a growing interest in this sort of inquiry. Yet something strikes me as uniquely inappropriate and terrifying about the development of such a discourse. While, on one hand, it signifies the maturation of our community to the point where metaphysical, social, and speculative analysis can manifest as a full-fledged conversation; on the other hand, as much as we might attempt to avoid it, the systematizing and interpretation that theology requires begins that awful process of forging dogma.

Inevitably, if theology gains any credibility, people might begin to turn to their Jurist-Priest Theologians for an understanding of their experience instead of living it and constructing it themselves. It seems for good reason that Starhawk states in *The Spiral Dance* that "Witchcraft has always been a religion of poetry, not theology." So while this article represents an attempt to flesh out the beginnings of a methodology for performing Neo-Pagan theology, I also hope that it will explore how, if we must do theology in the Neo-Pagan context, (which now seems an inevitable development) we might offset its worst effects.

While no one has yet to develop and publish a widely distributed Neo-Pagan theology, parallel enterprises abound. They suggest a wealth of paths that we might follow in developing a general methodology. We might, as many seminarians I've spoken with suggest, simply build out of the rich tradition of Christian theology, borrowing its methodologies for analysis of our own specific issues.

Yet, when we examine even the most liberal and unorthodox Christian theological tradition, we find it immersed in an examination of scripture, tradition, and social context which just doesn't necessarily form a valid or coherent matrix in which to examine Neo-Pagan spirituality. The most fruitful exceptions seem to be Creation Theology (Matthew Fox) and Feminist thealogies which seek an understanding of Goddess external to, if in dialogue with, the Christian tradition (Mary Daly, Carol Christ). Yet even these theologies remain trapped in an attempt to form a dialogue primarily with the Christian theological community, and therefore often become so infiltrated with Christian assumptions that we end up with something that looks like Neo-Pagan theology, but remains Christian.

We might alternatively scrape through the Pagan past and attempt to find the types of metaphysical speculations that parallel theological discourse. Or we might turn to a rich contemporary Pagan tradition, like Hinduism. Yet, when we search through those fragmented records, we find nothing that really matches the contemporary practice of theology. So deriving methodology becomes a highly problematic venture. Additionally, our Pagan ancestors had a completely different set of issues to deal with when examining the intersection of their spiritual and cultural realms; the most apparent seems the lack of a need to understand their religion in the context of cultures as active, multiplicitous, and transforming as our own.

As a result, research and exploration of specific ancient Pagan traditions presents better avenues for developing specific theological explorations within in a particular tradition than for developing methodologies for the general practice of Neo-Pagan theology

As seems so often the case in our community, through a process of stripping away we discover that we must rely primarily on ourselves. Instead of searching for some external authority, Christian or Pagan, I suggest we look to our hearts, our community, and the types of issues that face us to develop a truly Neo-Pagan theological methodology. Over the past few years I have developed five guides for doing theology in the Neo-Pagan context. While other traditions might have norms like scripture, tradition, or church, we do not seem to have the blessing of such solidity. So, while I suggest these as guides, I would hope that they remain important considerations and never dogmatic rules.

The first guide arises out of the very process which we have been engaging in Neo-Pagan theology must maintain a firm sense of its place and loyalty to the active, living community out of which it emerges. This doesn't mean that Neo-Pagan theology should bow to every whim and fancy that we find in Neo-Pagan periodicals, but it does mean that it requires a thorough examination and engagement with the community itself The types of assumptions we, as theologians, should make, should be those which Neo-Pagans can accept. The stories, rituals, and myths we use for our theology should all be ones that we already find present in the Neo-Pagan community or at least those that would be interesting to it. And when we deviate strongly from the Neo-Pagan community, we must do it out of a sense of the importance of making such an alternative felt present. We have no standard, no document, no list of values, no law that can capture the Neo-Pagan experience and articulate the issues that Neo-Pagans wonder about. If we have any text to refer to, it is only the text of our own experience. This means, practically, that our theology must come out of a real world experience of interaction with the Neo-Pagan community, a thorough reading of NeoPagan periodicals and literature, an examination of the small body of anthropological literature about the Neo-Pagan community (which should be treated with some caution), and conversations and discourse with other Neo-Pagans.

As a second guideline, I would like to suggest that while theology does represent a mode of analysis, we should not abandon the premise of Neo-Paganism as a "religion of poetry." The mythic narrative of the bardic ceremony, of storytelling and entertaining, ought to frame our approach to theological discourse. We should try to avoid, first and foremost, writing dry and boring pontifications about the universe when we can encapsulate the same point in a tale. The best example we have to turn to remains Starhawk, who combines myth, ritual, personal narrative, and analysis together in a brilliant expository texture. But above simply being interesting, through this focus on theology as a mode of mythic narrative, we can begin to recognize how even purely analytical theology contributes to the narrative framework that people use to tell stories about their lives, their community, and their gods and goddesses.

Parallel to this, we should recognize the degree to which our theology embodies itself as a specific, magickal act. In other traditions, theology often remains a point of interpretation, understanding, and analysis within a highly mental pattern. Neo-Pagan theology must understand its presence as an activity, and form an intersection between the realm of gods and of humans. Even further, I would suggest that any Neo-Pagan theologan should understand her writings as having the intent, concern, and understanding of result that is implicit in any spell. Neo-Pagan theology represents an act itself, not simply a way of understanding, informing, and spurring action. Hakim Bey has suggested that while Sorcery parallels art, it "refuses to be a metaphor for mere literature" and "insists that symbols must cause events as well as private epiphanies." We would do well to make the same demands of our theologies.

The implicit understanding of theology as an act suggests a fourth guidepost. Neo-Pagan theology see as best done with an explicit understanding of its source. Although it may speak to a general audience, it arises from a particular framework of assumptions, understandings, political leanings, and socio-economic viewpoints. Theology by Druids will always bear a Druidic flavor. My own theological productions will be flavored by my involvement with Graeco-Roman Paganism, the Church of All Worlds, and Thelemic and Chaos ceremonial magick. This fuels the confrontation and dance between the particular and the general that creates the rich cultural texture which so many of us have grown to love in our community—and I find precisely this dynamic the most promising aspect of Neo-Pagan theology.

Finally, and in some ways most importantly, I strongly feel that we must abandon the category of belief as in any way necessary for developing theology. Not only do many abandon the category themselves, but those who do admit to beliefs cover such a wide range that it would be impossible, if not fallacious, to try to classify any "Neo-Pagan" set of beliefs. We often continue with a desire to move toward the category of belief when understanding religious sensibilities, particularly in a context of analysis and thought—which is where, structurally, theology remains centered. Instead of attempting to arrive at a set of common assumptions or beliefs, I suggest that Neo-Pagan theology will find better fruit through an exploration of the discourse arenas through which they can understand their relations with their gods, their world, and themselves. This maintains a focus on the types of issues that find important and considers the multiple reference points that exist around an issue even within the mind and soul of a single individual.

While we could find many other significant guides, these seem some of the most important to an active and engaged dialogue around the development of Neo-Pagan theology. Again, the theology can:

- use the Neo-Pagan community itself as its primary reference point;
- understand itself as a mythic act of narrative;
- recognize the way it functions as a magickal act or spell;
- avoid attempts to disguise, emphasizing and developing from the partic ular location from which it emerges;
- de-emphasize, if not abandon, the category of belief for more appropriate means of discussing Neo-Pagan viewpoints.

Hopefully, with these guides through the underworld of theological discourse, we can avoid some of the pitfalls that come from on the one hand having to carve out an entirely new discourse and on the other having to wrestle with a long Christian tradition that remains, in so many ways, foreign to the specific goals of our community.

Vol. XXVIX, No. 117 (Jan.-Feb. 1997) 28–29; 50

Grant Potts was born in Monrovia, Liberia, the son of an engineer and a schoolteacher. After a few young years traveling the world, he spent most of his childhood in rural Ohio, where he developed a strong love for the woods. He has a PhD in religious studies from the University of Pennsylvania, is an initiate of the Ordo Templi Orientis, and currently resides in Austin, Texas, where he gardens, works, and makes his home with his beloveds.

GOD THE CREATOR?

by **Matt Clark**, CAW (age 9½)

How could God have created the world if no man can give birth?

The answer is: God didn't. Oh, he played an important part. But the Goddess gave birth to the world. For the Goddess is a woman. Because only a woman can give birth. In all life they both (God and Goddess) play an important part. But the woman plays the most important part by giving birth, for if it weren't for the woman there wouldn't be any life. So the creator must be the Goddess.

You should listen to the Goddess. When you listen for the Goddess you may hear yourself, for the Goddess may use your mind to tell you. The same applies to when you see the Goddess or God. For They may use your own image for you to see.

GE Vol. VI, No. 60 (Oimelc 1974)

Chapter 5.
Nature, Evolution,
& Ecospirituality
Introduction
by *Chas S. Clifton*

LANCE CHRISTIE, CO-FOUNDER OF THE CHURCH OF ALL WORLDS, WRITES, "WE PROPOSE a world where man is conscious of his role as the 'cortex' of the planetary Biosphere, and therefore as the steward of Nature—rather than an enemy/exploiter/victim of Nature." His essay, "Neo-Paganism: An Alternative Reality" and others in this chapter deal with humanity's role as the thinking part of planet Earth with the job of care-taking, restoring, and celebrating the planetary biosphere. More recently this attitude has been called "eco-spirituality," but I think that it is fair to say that *Green Egg* contributors were among the first to articulate it in multiple forms.

These writers embody a powerful do-it-yourself ethos, recognizing that we live in a world through which we are connected on a cellular and psychic level, not in a disposable playground or schoolroom created by a stand-off God who is grading us all the while. Jesse Hardin Wolf, a powerful and prolific ecospiritual writer, diagnoses the problem with much environmental activism as the lack of an articulated spiritual connection to the planet: Overpopulation, habitat destruction, clearcuts, oil-tanker spills, classism, sexism and war are all symptoms of humanity's internal *dis-ease*, our cognitive (imagined) distance from our own essential natures, separation from the beings and processes of the natural work, from a distance and institutionalized Spirit." Rejecting the failed models of Creation, the writers seek new concepts of planet Earth and our place on it, not as its exploiters but as Her voice.

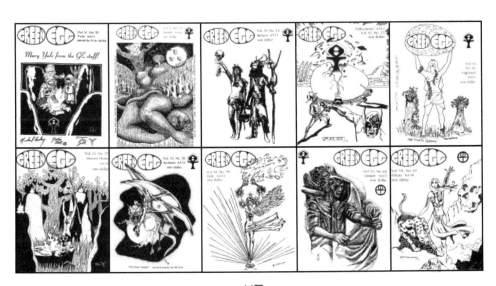

...And the Trees Shall Triumph

by *Tom Williams,* Church of All Worlds

 ACRILEGE IS ALWAYS AVENGED BY the offended deity. Man has committed a tremendous sacrilege against the Goddess of Wildness and is even now reaping the fury of Her just wrath. The present concern over pollution in enlightened scientific circles shows the awakening of the scientific mind to the dangers which it itself is guilty of bringing about. The scientific mind is slowly, gropingly beginning to counteract the injuries which it, in alliance with industrial avarice, has wreaked upon our planet. This is a positive, a hopeful sign—but it is not enough, not nearly enough.

Man is perhaps by nature a scientific, rational creature as evidenced by his mathematics and technology. But that is merely one side of his being and one which, since the Enlightenment, has been overly emphasized... perhaps to the detriment of our entire world. Man has another side which is equally valid. He has irrational desires, passions and fears which often cause him to act in ways which his cold reason would never allow. Who could rationally explain love (it has been attempted) but who could deny its validity? Romeo and Juliet die in a rationally absurd way of their love for one another, but can the emotional beauty of that love leave us unmoved? Thus man cannot be grasped from one side but must be accepted as a totality. Any attempt at a one-sided view separates man from himself and divorces him from his cohesion with Nature.

When man yet lived in a primal state and a perfect ecological balance, trees were gods. The Forest was a place of reverence, mystery and not a little fear. Man did not then rationally realize his dependence on trees for holding the soil, breaking rainfall, replacing carbon dioxide with life-giving oxygen or their importance for rainfall and climate control. But he *sensed* all this and knew in his irrational way that his fate was intimately involved with that of the trees. Later, with the growth of civilization, deities were still closely bound with nature and had their own sacred groves of trees. Two phenomena changed all this: the development of herdsman cultures with the contemporaneous rise of the art of warfare, and the spiritualization of Deity away from the nature gods to an all-pervasive god of pure spirit.

Herdsman civilizations demanded land for the grazing of their food animals. These animals could not graze on land occupied by forests or fields belonging to agricultural peoples. Trees got in the way. They were felled. Those agricultural peoples who got in the way were likewise cut down by the war chariots of the herdsmen. But the trees have exacted and will continue to exact their vengeance in terms of floods, erosion and famine against those who failed to recognize their importance in the total environment.

At about the same time as his war upon the forests, man declared war on the nature deities of vegetation and fertility. The sacred groves were hewn down and the altars were toppled. The gods of forest and stream were replaced by an omnipresent spirit, divorced from all material. The Mother Goddess was transformed into a paternalistic righteous father. Man had by stages cut himself off from an identification with his Earth. He could thus observe nature as something in a sphere apart from himself—he even learned to base his own existence solely on the existence of spirit: *Cogito ergo sum...* I think therefore I am.

In time man learned to view nature as an economic quantity; something to be used and exploited. Certain men found that they could exploit their fellow men as tools for the ravishing of nature. But nature's wealth is not inexhaustible, nor is the patience of men. Both will in time revolt against their exploiter.

The story of the trees is but an example of the result of man's lack of identity with himself and—with his world. Black, stifling carbon which over the course of millions of years had been removed from the atmosphere by the joint action of sun and trees, and deposited safely beneath the surface of an Earth made fertile and life-giving by the bodies of countless millions of trees, is in the space of barely two hundred years being ripped from the breast of the Earth and released back into the atmosphere. The high carbon atmosphere, deadly to animal life, which prevailed before the coming of the trees is returning.

Man's rational mind and his greed are at fault. His rational mind—being rational—is slowly becoming aware of the peril. Because of this, eminent scientists are calling loudly for positive, radical action to meet the danger. Various lay and civil groups are forming to help spread the awareness and protect our planet. The means will have to be extreme, including the abolition of the internal combustion engine and its associated polluting monster, the petroleum industry.

As gratifying as this growing awareness is, it is still insufficient, for it is yet the product of a one-sided view of man and the world. In order to save himself man must also within him. He must overcome the mind-body dichotomy under which he has so long labored and cry joyously with Nietzsche's Zarathustra, "I am body entirely and nothing else; and soul is but a word for something in the body!" We must change the *"Cogito ergo sum"* to *"Spiro ergo sum"*—I breathe therefore I, am. We must relearn our mystical involvement with our environment and celebrate nature as an eternal religion. We must feel within our veins the tidal surging of ancient seas and see in the skies the grandure of the eternal symphony of the cosmos. Only by seeing ourselves as a total entity—rational and irrational at once—within a total environment can we see our true place in it and function at our maximum potential.

We must stop measuring our development in terms of the ability of our reason to divert the course of nature to our immediate ends and regard it in terms of the maximum development of our individual mind-body organism in harmony with its environment. To do this we must constantly remind ourselves of the deity of Great Nature; of Her all-embracing presence and beauty. We must celebrate the rhythm of the heavens and the Earth and bring ourselves into harmony with the seasons and the days. Only through awareness on rational and irrational levels at once, through total identification with the

Earth and with all life can we hope to avoid the wrath of the offended Goddess; the Mother of Earth and all wild things.

We must build temples in the wild celebrating the union of Earth and Sky and Man with Plant and Animal. We must envision ourselves hanging on the ray of the North Star, bathed in the light of Sun and Moon and vibrantly drinking the intoxicating elixer of Life. Be joyous, lave, celebrate Life, drink of pure water and breathe clean air. Share with your fellow siblings of the Goddess the rapture of living and despoil not the abode of Gods.

GE Vol. IV, No. 44 (Yule 1971) 24-25

--Pendragon

If There Has to be a Shadow over Our Land, We're Going to Make Certain That It's Cast by Trees

Neo-Paganism: An Alternative Reality

*by **Lance Christie**, CAW (art by Susan Seddon Boullet)*

THE MODERN ACCEPTANCE of technical progress as man's highest good is not the result of mechanical inventions by themselves but of a Mechanical World Picture—a subjective reality which views the universe and man in Mechanistic terms. Most men live in fear of an unknown, malevolent, capricious universe (as for why, see Immanuel Velikovsky's theory). The discovery that patterns of cause and effect exist in Nature led to the ability to predict events and to build tools—machines—to manipulate and control Nature. To primitive man, this discovery was the key to the development of technology—a reliable, potent form of magic which held the promise of ultimate omnipotence over Nature and therefore freedom from the fear born of insecurity due to impotence. The scientist, engineer and craftsman became modern wizards whose magic never fails. Science evolved a picture of a mechanistic, orderly, predictable cosmos operating by the logic of machines: linear, Aristotelian, mathematical, digital, yes-no, absolutist, reductionist logic.

The mechanistic world-view, evolved from experience with matter and electromagnetic energy, was applied beyond the bounds of physics to biological, social, and human phenomena. This misapplication of linear, systematic forms of thought has resulted in absolutist political doctrines, social "sciences," the rule of law over justice, and the increasing worship of power, speed, size and efficiency to the exclusion of human emotional considerations and the welfare of the Biosphere, Thus mankind has developed a technological culture which functions according to the principles inherent in the mechanistic world picture. The function of this cultural system flea led to our present situation of megapopulation, megapollution, mega-alienation, and megadeaths. Lewis Mum-ford calls this cultural system "The Mega-technic Monster."

Against this "Megatechnic Monster" and "Mechanical World Picture," Mumford, Rene Dubois, and many others propose the "Organic World Picture," based on the eco-logic of Nature. This is the logic of energy flow, adaptation, experimentation, and check-and-balance which is studied under the name "ecology." It is the sloshing about which manages to attain a balance of pinpoint accuracy in human thought and natural adaptation despite incredible "inefficiency" and "error" on the part of individual components.

In classic scientific thinking, the whole must be interpreted in terms of the part, deliberately isolated. In ecological thinking, it is the whole that reveals the nature, function, and purpose of the part. The machine myth holds that only by such reductionism and isolation can "objectivity" be realized. The vitalist replies that, "In organisms, power is always related to function and purpose." What is the function and purpose of "objectivity?" Life does not flourish under a regime of compulsive dynamism and change for its own sake; life flourishes in a subtle, holistic interplay of organism, environment, and function.

The Church of All Worlds is evolving a vitalistic religious philosophy which subscribes to and develops the "Organic World Picture." We perceive that the 22 billion year process of evolution of life on Earth may be recognized as the developmental process of maturation of a single vast living entity: the planetary Biosphere itself. Just as a single original cell, the zygote, divides and subdivides into the billions of cells of the adult human body while yet retaining its coherent organic identity as a single living being, so has our planetary Biosphere developed from a single original cell into the billions of plants and animals of which it is now composed. We perceive the human race to be the "nerve cells" of this planetary Being—what paleontologist Teilhard de Chardin termed the Noosphere. And further, we equate the identity of our great living Biosphere (which we refer to as "Terrebia") with the ancient archetypal image of the Great Goddess: Mother Earth; Mother Nature.

We propose a world where man is conscious of his role as the "cortex" of the planetary Biosphere, and therefore as the steward of Nature—rather than an enemy/exploiter/victim of Nature. We propose a fresh vision of the cosmic process as more than clockwork. We wish to re-introduce the "qualitative attribute of life: its expectancy, its inner impetus, its insurgency, its creativity, its ability at singular points to transcend either physical or organic limitations." We point to the reality that where there is incipient life there is incipient mind—the roots of awareness, the fountains of wonder. We are not aliens thrust into a hostile cosmos. We belong here; our roots are all around us and within us in the throb and flow of life.

We preach Nature as a self-organizing system from which man has emerged through neural development which provided images and symbols for his unconscious life and conscious understanding. The pattern of change that we see is constant—an interminable succession of limited efforts and improvisations that in time re-enforce each other and become more coherent and purposeful. This is the model for evolution, whether biological, social, or that of our religious philosophy and activities. Man can act as steward to the evolutionary process by his ability to unify in symbol and in action; to display sensitive emotional reactions to complex wholes, yet to engage in linear analysis when appropriate.

We conceive of time as the flux of organic continuity. This stands in frontal opposition to the mechanistic notion of time as a function of the motion of bodies in space, which leads to the idea that one can "save time" by accelerating motion. We remember that only

destructive processes in Nature are swift, and only entropy comes easy. Organic growth proceeds on its own form of appointed time; it is never uniform, consistent, or automatic.

Insofar as the organism—individual or corporate/social—has achieved the necessary preconditions for stability, continuity, dynamic balance, and self-replenishment, further creativity is assured. Thus an organismic base for judgments of good and ill is established, without dictating the results desired but rather simply specifying healthy Conditions for growth and change. When these healthy preconditions are attained, transcendence from conditions becomes possible. It is in these moments of transcendence from the dynamic, aesthetic balance of the healthful. immanent that what we call the "Divine" is visible. In man, these moments are called "peak" or "transcendental" or "mystical" or "religious" experiences. On a planetary basis, such a transcendent moment attained by Terrebia *as a whole* would be the "Omega Point" described by Teilhard de Chardin. Thus, the path to a transcendence foreseen throughout the history of human consciousness is revealed. Man's mechanistic error has damaged the evolution of Terrebia; man can set Nature's immanent systems straight again, and when this is done the entire Biosphere system will continue its evolutionary creativity towards the point of systemic transcendence. This is our point of faith.

Whether or not you share this point of faith at this time, look at the "Organic World Picture" and examine the advantages here-and-now of a world governed by this reality vs. the "Mechanical World Picture" in dominion today. There is nothing but death to lose, and nothing but life to gain.

GE Vol. V, No. 51 (Yule 1972) 17-18

Wilhelm Reich & Neo-Paganism

*by **Geneva Steinberg**, co-editor of* Caveat Emptor

I HAD BECOME AN ADMIRER OF Wilhelm Reich quite awhile ago, but it still came as a surprise to me when I found references to Neo-Paganism in one of his books! There was a chart in the back showing the evolution of religion toward life-affirmation, and Neo-Paganism was listed toward the top. Even here, the chart showed a deflection to the life-negative side, and I understood why when I read through the text and learned that the Neo-Paganism Reich had in mind was the German National Socialism of the WWII era! It's a shame that Reich couldn't be around to see the real Neo-Paganism come into its own - I think he would have heartily approved.

Reich makes the point that there is a vast difference between merely *tolerating* our natural impulses, and actively affirming them and celebrating them. The former can be cone be a conscious decision, an act of will; but the latter requires a drastic change in our whole way of being.

Reich wrote of two types of thinking: "Armored" thinking and "functional" thinking If we re-label these as Mechanical thinking and Organic thinking, it may be a little easier to see the difference. Mechanical thinking works like a machine; it goes in a straight line, using information and goals fed to it from the outside, and it is totally predictable. Organic thinking is a living process; it modifies its data by direct perception, it can move in most any direction, and its results are unexpected and creative. Mechanical thought eventually grinds to a dead halt, for which we should be thankful. Organic thought can wander on indefinitely.

Reich never used the words "Thou Art God," but he recognized the concept. He repeatedly said that "God" was to be found in the Life Energy of our own bodies, which most people learn to block off at an early age, and perceive to be "out there" in the heavens somewhere instead of within themselves. While he was still being acclaimed as a genius (before he went one step too far and became widely denounced), Reich made no secret of the fact that *everybody* would have the ability to think like him if only they had the courage to accept responsibility for their own lives instead of looking to some outside authority. Nobody has a monopoly on creativity; it is inherent in our structure as living organisms. Some people block it off and others don't.

"Anybody could have done the same." How often do we hear these words from people noted for some unusual accomplishment? We seldom believe it, though. We prefer to imagine that they have some special quality that we lack. Because otherwise, if we really *could* have done something similar ourselves, that doesn't leave us much excuse for wasting our lives away!

If Reich was even partially-correct in the characteristics he attributed to biological, or "Orgone" energy, we have access to a science and technology that need not be at variance with the planet's eco-systems. Reichian contraptions are absurdly simple and easy to construct—maybe that's why Establishment "scientists" are so much inclined to dismiss them without trial. "Free energy" would become not a fantastic dream, but a reality.

Evohe

We are the Point within the Circle
We are the God within the Goddess
We are the Children of the Horned One
Our Dreams and Drives,
Our Fears and Fancies,
Our Essence like His, is Animal.
We greet the Wolf as Brother;
The Owl as Sister.
Father of Love and Light,
Father of Lust and Life,
We sing Your praise, Great Faunus!

— Morning G'Zell

GE Vol. VII, No. 67 (Yule 1974) 38

Individuals could become more self-sufficient. The principles of orgonomy would make for increased crop yields, and weather control. The all but lifeless deserts (many of which were created by the ravages of humanity—read *Our Plundered Planet*) could become fertile again. WE COULD HAVE THE COMFORTS OF CIVILIZATION WITHOUT AN INDUSTRIAL ECO-NOMY! (Maybe that is the secret of some of those impossible artifacts left by ancient "primitive" cultures!)

Reich pointed out that the same forces at work in living beings are also at work in the Universe at large. Pagans were not "anthropomorphizing" when they detected intelligent forces at work in Nature. Probably we are "misanthro-pomorphizing" when we *fail* to see them! Reich emphasized that all life operates by a single principle, which is the same in human beings as in the lower life forms. The only special quality we possess is the ability to armor ourselves against the flow of our own life-force.

Knowing that "intelligence" and "emotion," far from being uniquely human attributes, are operating in all the functions of the planet, it becomes easier to understand the concept of the natural forces sometimes called "Elementals."

And Reich came very close to grasping the idea of a planetary con-sciousness when he wrote: "The ocean of human life has begun to stir, this is certain; and nobody can do anything about it, or direct it, or prevent it from happening. Nor can anybody reasonably complain that the ocean began to stir. It is not the com-munists who make the stir. It is the stir that makes the communists..."

..And this will be when men will feel and know God, when the ripple on the surface of the ocean will become aware that it is a tiny bit of the great ocean, coming from it and returning to it, a beautiful passing event..."

GE Vol. VII, No. 63 (Litha 1974) 25-26

Declaration of the Four Sacred Things

by Starhawk

The Earth is a living, conscious being. In company with cultures of many different times and places, we name these things as sacred: **Air, Fire, Water** and **Earth.**

Whether we see them as the Breath, Energy, Blood and Body of the Mother, or as the blessed gifts of a Creator, or as symbols of the interconnected systems that sustain life, we know that nothing can live without them.

To call these things sacred is to say that they have a value beyond their usefulness for human ends, that they themselves become the standards by which our acts, our economics, our laws and our purposes must be judged. No one has the right to appropriate them or profit from them at the expense of others. Any government which fails to protect them forfeits its legitimacy. For it is everyone's re-sponsibility to sustain, heal and preserve the soil, the air, the fresh and salt waters, and the energy resources that can support diverse and flourishing life.

All people, all living things, are part of the Earth-life, and so sacred. No one of us stands higher or lower than any other. Only justice can assure balance; only ecological balance can sustain freedom. Only in freedom can that fifth sacred thing we call Spirit flour-ish in its full diversity.

To honor the sacred is to create condi-tions in which nourishment, sustenance, hab-itat, knowledge, freedom and beauty can thrive. To honor the sacred is to make love possible.

To this we dedicate our curiosity, our will, our courage, our silences and our voic-es. To this we dedicate our lives.

GE Vol. XXIII, No. 91 (Samhain 1991) 7

The Primal Energy
And a Possible Reality Construct
by *Penny of the House of Novack*

PROLOGUE

ANY, IF NOT ALL OF YOU, ARE aware of that old idea of the "primal energy." In recent years even our modern scientists are taking the notion seriously, though they seldom are found equating it with the energy the mystics have spoken of through the ages.

Again, you are all aware of our "material" reality's atomic structure; in composition being varying charges of energy held in certain patterns which relate in certain ways with similarly patterned compositions. At first glance, this seems amazingly close to the energy we experience our intuited awareness of the inner structure of matter is probably the reason some kinds of magic can work for those who have not, as yet, intuited the transtemporal nature of the eternal primal energy.

So what *is* this "primal energy"? I hardly imagine putting a name, a simple symbol of sound and print to it could reproduce or inform of its nature. I hope you also are aware of the ludicrousness of such an endeavor. However, I hope to be able to suggest at least a few things about the nature of this quite experiencable but incomprehensible (because I'll comprehend one thing and you'll quite correctly comprehend another) Source. I ask that you forgive me if I treat the subject and the ensuing reality construct in definitive and absolute terms. I wrestled with the problem of communicating some of these ideas to an unseen audience who, presumably, have experienced the many patterns, facades and archetypal images inherent in personal apprehension of the truly inexpressible and decided that if I overqualified it would merely muddy the message. I hope to use very stark language and would appreciate it if your response to this inadequate attempt would be to recognize what does, in fact, correspond with your experience and forgive me for not comprehending or interpreting as you do.

II

The Source of all things, seen and unseen, material and non-material is One and is, conceivably, best described as Energy, though common experiences with fire and *electricity* will not convey it. I am formed of energy in certain patterns. The obvious patterns are the ones forming my atomic structure, but while those in greater or lesser degree are the same as all other "matter," it is not this obvious energy I am referring to. That energy is neither timed nor untimed, neither matter nor not-matter. These things; both time and matter, do not exist as we see them but as very slight waves, patterns in the weave of the Unmoving One.

What we so obviously perceive as separation (the word "separation" and similar terms don't apply) between "things" does not exist. As the whole body follows the shape of the action of the limbs and the limbs express the attitude of the torso, thus also our thoughts, our acts and our emotions are both push and pull in some flowing universal motion. Divination is workable (for those skilled to read the signs) because of this factor.

Destruction, also, is not a valid concept though patterns within the One "change." There is still no loss/destruction since all that ever was, Is, as all that could ever *have* been (from our- temporal viewpoint) Is. So, also, are the future and possible futures. Nothing is impossible within the One. If we can imagine beasts we have no evidence of ever having existed in this reality system, could not there be not only these realities (whatever the reason: perception of close loops of the time-coils, alternate universes, etc.) but others which we would never imagine, not even apprehend were we to be placed in the middle of one?

However, as a friend of mine complained, seen from the womb of the Eternal Source (if I may use a familiar term), vacuum has the equal value of matter, shit is the same meaning as the rose. Even harder to accept; the kindly person, the shining, loving souls we find so beautiful, have the same value as the dull, hating, destructive souls. All is perfect, has equal value within the cosmic egg. If we *could* perceive this without having achieved in our own growth of Being some kind of esthetic sense, then perhaps we would simply accept that sameness—find it meaningless and of no spiritual value to prefer creation of beauty, warmth and lovingness in personal relations and all the other patterns in which humankind has traditionally taken the greatest delight. Perhaps some of our children who become very early catatonic were children born with no will to choose.

Of course, none of the children I've seen were like that, but it seems to me simple awareness of the Energy without some love of the weave, or, more simply, the Dance which describes our individuated patterns, would of necessity either immediately remove the being as part of the Dance (a goal many Eastern religions purport to aspire to) or create a simple counter-point to the rhythm of our constant Creation. For what we perceive as destruction is simply a natural part of some inward motion. And the psyche of our Earth, while more slowly playing harmonies to the Dance, so often counterpoints our own species' changes that it seems to me likely that both the desire to end as a pattern in the Dance and that desires' corollaries—amazing destruction and amazing indifference—are keyed by our Earth's own Dance within the spheres of the entire universe.

III

I am obviously now speaking of a need for a "reality construct," i.e. an interpretation of our own Beings and a method of relating to the individuated patterns within the Dance.

Our sense of Selfhood can be either very limited (often; for instance, situated in a part of the body or even somewhat removed from that awareness) or very great—it is the latter for which I hope to suggest a possible vision.

An infant, finding itself in an environment unfamiliar both in terms of body and habitat, "finds" itself by trial and error through self-examination. Presumably, learning to identify our first obvious environment, the body itself, is a prerequisite to learning how much more of this Dance fabric is also available to us, in this life, as part of our Self. If this identification is not developed, a strongly psychic individual may imagine, much as an infant just discovering his toes or a kitten its tail, that the phenomenon with which he/she is interacting is truly separate.

I have had the honor of knowing a yogi whose development in the joyous realms of bhakti yoga has resulted in much shining light emanating from her. Yet, since she denied herself complete Selfhood (in essence, cutting herself off from the lower chakras prior to even taking training) she is often troubled by intestinal and lower spinal trouble. Others may cut themselves off from other part of recognizing themselves, but the result is always the same: malfunction of the deserted areas of self-hood. The theory that the physical is not part of the spiritual has probably done more than any other factor (including curiosity) to cause our current pollution crisis and the terrible tensions of Life-denial in our present era.

A friend of mine who is teaching a Free U course in Paganism was asked by one of the people in her class if it would be ok to make an attempt to "create" her own deity; one consistent with the "modern" world. I found the idea interesting. If this student is willing to search honestly for an essence, a face of the original religious impulse which is completely meaningful to her—if she can find one which is consistent and which will explain the world as she is conscious of it, then not only will she have come a long way (though perhaps the hard way) but when she finally does get it together, I think I could guarantee to name the deity and give her the history of and land/lands in which the deity has been known. So long as our particular wave-thread-pattern-species is defined by those characteristics we call "human," our personal apprehension of the Eternal will take certain patterns, appear in certain archetypal forms because of our understanding of ourselves. The Goddess is the Eternal Female; Mother of All, Dancer, Eternal Spring Maiden because we, as humans, perceive those qualities of the mystic experience in such a light. The God as well is seen in His attributes coherent with the vision of the individual, psyche. The important part of the experience is the initial perception, not the rationalization and the important result is usually a kind of ultra-human growth and greater awareness.

Earth, moon and sun are primary manifestations (for us), on the material level of expression, of extremely important "powers;" powers which are implicit in *our* individuated existence and which are a constant source of meaning. When we perceive (in all the ways any manifestation of the Source may perceive) these powers, our inner personal response takes shape eventually in a kind of esthetic poetic expression in which we convey—in an outward flow of the original experience—a conceptualized vision. Since there are no words which are either true or untrue, since nothing is imperfect at the level of the One, the striving to portray our personal visions are as true as we can communicate them, but some have been better inspired to such an end.

Thus, the poets, the painters, those who create—either biologically or by conscious wedding of self-hood with some other factor in our environment (from cultivating gardens to painting bison and deer on the walls and ceilings of the caves of Lascaux) have molded and formed the pre-existent religions into which most of humankind has been born. And these poetic visions are remarkable in their similarity in all the parts of this world. Some of them are almost static: representations of the Eternal as Goddess or God—or as a pattern which somehow seems to mean a similar thing wherever one looks. A symbol? Or a key. For these artists were creating signposts, clearing paths (or trying to) for those who would come after them. And since this seems to be another universal—that the mystic vision causes a spontaneous urge to create-recreate something of that inner essence in outer form—I suspect we can recognize such to be an imperative inherent in our meaning as a species, as a part of the One Thing.

For the Dance is very beautiful!

GE Vol. VII, No. 68 (Oimelc 1975) 19-21

A Mother's Love

Words & music by
Gwydion Pendderwen
(for Z.)

A mother came unto her children,
And told them why she'd gone away.
She said the world was full of evil,
And all her sons had gone astray.

But she's returned to lead her children
Into a place of peace and love,
And as a sign, she's lit a rainbow
And changed a raven into a dove.

"I've watched you grow, but from afar;
I've seen your meanness and your pride.
But though you thought you were forsaken,
You felt my love deep down inside.

"Your father tried to raise this family;
For all these years he's worked in vain.
But do not blame him for this failure,
Just try to be my babes again.

"Now you may think that you don't need me;
You've done without me through the years.
But in a secret place inside of you
You've stored a lot of bitter tears.

"On your sisters, put chains of slavery,
And on your brothers, put chains of hate.
It won't make your days or nights secure
Or change the fabric of your fate.

"Now place your head upon my shoulder
And cry away your guilt and shame.
There is no place for shame or sorrow
When you have cried aloud my name.

"For I've returned to lead my children
Into a place of peace and love,
And as a sign here is my rainbow,
And for your raven, here is my dove."

GE Vol. XXV, No. 97 (Summer 1992) 24

Our Identity as Children of the Earth

by *Anasa Woodsorrel*

I FEEL INHIBITED WRITING THIS mainly for one reason; I'm male. It is as essential for men who are interested in freeing themselves from the fetters of sexism to resist the temptation of defining themselves in relationship to women as it is to refuse to identify themselves with their societal pseudo-identity. In other words, the non-sexist male is not a feminist male. Our unity is contingent upon our polarity.

The time has come that we move beyond the simple understanding of confining cultural and personal constructs. We must rather define an alternative construct that most closely approximates who we are individually and collectively.

The question that confronts us is, "what are the characteristics of such a construct?"

Patriarchal religious traditions are characterized by puritanical seriousness, by the notion that our essence is encased in the prison of our bodies, by negation. In classical Christian terms it is religion 'by the law.'

Mother religions are characterized by affirmation, by singing and dancing, by orgiastic delight and a relationship of erotic exuberance with the Earth Mother. It is religion of the Spirit. It is the religion of the resurrected body.

The ideal of Father religions is to adhere perfectly to a set of constructs (for example, the Ten Commandments); to deviate is sin. The ideal of Mother religions is to adhere perfectly to ones own direction and to be in tune with the flux of Nature, which necessarily entails casting aside the sobriety and repression of a civilization which is not based upon a model of Nature but rather a body of abstractions.

Father religion is of stone. Mother religion is of water and clouds.

Father religion is of gravity. Mother religion is of levity, of simplicity—light and free.

Mother religion is the void from which images arise. Father religion is the image.

Arthur Darby Nock wrote, "Primitive religion is not believed. It is danced." Mother religion is dancing, most wonderful dancing. Fluid, unstructured, simple—feet two inches above the ground.

The Universe as feminine. As Mother. Spontaneity vs. rationality. Woman clothed with the sun. The sixth Dalai Lama writes:

Drawing diagrams I measured
Movements of the stars
Though her tender flesh is near
Her mind I cannot measure

Womanspirit. Such are the Inuit (Eskimo) shamans who dress like women to be receptive to the natural power women represent—the power of regeneration, of change, of birth and nurturing, and of the congruency of the menstrual-lunar cycle. And such is Christianity at its very seed-roots where Jesus (Yehoshua) becomes its etymological origin 'semen, that which saves;' such is Christianity which affirms at its very roots the life-principal, the spiritual/sexual intercourse of the male-female polarity. And again, such is Christianity which celebrates the Vernal Equinox in the guise of Easter (Soft white-seeded greensprout from moist fertile ground/ A year at rest/ The Lord has risen).

Spirituality is the vehicle of human liberation. Of woman's liberation and of man's liberation. Native American cosmologies recognize the dichotomy of Earth-people and Sky-people. Mother religions are of the Earth, of practicality, the practicality of being human, the practicality of love and freedom. To verify the possibility of love and freedom in ones experience and expression is to directly intervene in the ontological constitution of the societal Universe.

But where to start? Can we do this?

The BaMbuti pygmies live in the dense African forest. They feel free with themselves by laughing uncontrollably and by singing about the virtues of their mother, the forest. One of their songs goes: "There is darkness all around us; but if darkness is, and the darkness is of the forest, then the darkness must be good."

Songs. Songs of the forest. Inebriating songs. To a forest that is dark.

Our forest is equally dark. Song-voice quivers bespeaking suspicions that our forest is not so friendly; bespeaking absurd pretensions that we are of virgin birth, that the world of people is not our Mother.

But our pretensions are by nature self-frustrating, and if we let them happen they are self-exhausting. Flow. Accept and move around. The forest must be good.

GE Vol. VIII, No. 71 (Litha 1975) 9

Paganized Hymns
by *Ed Fitch*, The Pagan Way

When Christianity was first spreading it was a most common practice to take existing music that traditionally had been sung in honor of Pagan deities and alter the words so that what had been sung in honor of some aspect of the Goddess or of the God became instead purely Christian hymns.

But now the times are changing, and Paganism has started returning once more...so why not reverse the process? The following were most enjoyable to write, and they are a lot of fun to sing. Try it!

O Goddess Great
(Tune: Amazing Grace)

O Goddess great, how sweet thy name
That calms the stormy sea.
O Goddess great, to us return,
We'll give the world to thee.

O Goddess great, let peace now come
We seek thy wondrous love,
Let forests grow, let streams be pure
And skies be clear above.

O Goddess great, this world now falls
The harsh ways pass away.
We'll build anew a world more true.
We'll know a finer day.

O Goddess great, We ask thee come.
Bring mysteries ever new
Send forth thy song into the world
Spread far thy mantle blue.

GE Vol. VI, No. 56 (Lughnasadh 1973) 16

With Spell and Chant and Song
(Tune: Battle Hymn of the Republic)

Mine eyes have seen the loveliness
Of mountains, seas, and stream.
I have seen majestic stormclouds
And the lightning's brilliant gleam.
I have seen the silent beauty
Of the moonlight's silv'ry beam.
She has returned again!

Chorus: Glory, glory, praise the Lady
Glory, glory, praise the Lady
Glory, glory, praise the Lady
With spell and chant and song.

I have seen Her in the circle
Of the need-fire's silent call,
I have seen Her at the altars
That lie hidden, one and all.
I can know Her magic beauty
And be held within its thrall.
She has returned again!

Seek for Her in the music
Of the wild bird's plaintive calls,
Search for Her in the vastness
Of the canyon's cloudswept halls;
The clouds and sky above you
In a temple without walls.
She has returned again!

In the beauty of the Ancient Ways
She's known as yet to few,
But the loving of the Goddess
Still is ever warm and true.
As we live Her magic wisdom
Shall we build the world anew.
She has returned again!

GROK

by Rev. Dr. M.S. Medley

WHAT'S IT ALL ABOUT? WHY ARE we here? Where are we going? What, exactly, are we trying to accomplish? The answer is both simple and difficult. We are trying to teach ourselves and the rest of the human race to grok.

Fine, but what does that mean? This is why I said 'both simple and difficult.' The word is simple, but the meaning is difficult to express.

Grok. A most peculiar word. It is taken from a science-fiction story: *Stranger in a Strange Land,* by Robert Heinlein. In the book, it was once defined as 'drink,' though it was used in conversation as meaning 'understand' most often.

To grok, then, is to absorb, love, understand, become one with, grow, live, and to enjoy all of it.

To grok is to live the Golden Rule; not as a duty or from fear of punishment, but because it is the most natural thing to do.

To grok is to be fully affirmative, optimistic, positive, loving, growing, being aware, being creative.

To grok is to realize your potential as fully as possible. It means becoming and being as fully, completely, and wonderfully, the very best that you can be.

To grok is to know yourself, accept yourself, love yourself, believe in yourself, and be true to yourself. Only when you truly have respect for yourself can you have any real respect for other people or the world around you.

To grok is to accept responsibility for yourself and be totally free. This is the only real freedom: responsible freedom. You can only be held responsible for the choices you make if you are free to make those choices. You can only be free to make choices when you can be held responsible for them. Orders and rules with some form of punishment to back them up may make for order and progress, but you can take no credit for the good you do in obeying them.

Ultimately, grokking is acceptance and belief in the innate divinity of all the universe, including yourself. Our expression of this is summed up in the statement: "Thou art God." Everything that exists is God. God is both creator and creation. God is both left and right. God is both male and female. God is both life and death.

We are not concerned with theologies, religious traditions, or the afterlife. Our chief concern is with the full, complete, aware living of this here-and-now life. The past is dead and gone, the future is unknown, only this moment truly exists. As only this instant exists or can exist, now, at this point of time, it must be accepted as unchangeable, the very best of all possible worlds. It must be lived in joyous awareness of its perfection. Yet the unknown future can be looked to with hope for its possibility of even better moments, and plans may be made to make those better moments come into existence.

We hope, in learning to grok, we shall all 'grow closer' to one another, and to the universe. In grokking, we become natural. The natural man has cast off all forms of artificiality. He has become honest, sincere, free of artificial hang-ups and false repressions imposed from without. In grokking nature and growing closer to it, we lose our artificial sense of time and live in the eternal instant of now. The events of man-made history and his artificial measurement of time are seen as the imposed system they are, no more real than inches, pounds, dollars, or national boundaries. We come to measure our lives in a natural way. We grok that experiences are measurable truly only in how they affect us, and our tithe is counted by the eternal cycles of the sun and stars.

To grok is to realize and accept the wonder, the delight, the full potential for good, the very divinity of our human nature. "I am God, and Thou art God, and All that Groks is God." Drink deeply of life. Laugh. Love. Accept. Grow. Grok.

GE Vol. IV, No. 37 (Ostara, 1971) 7

The Gaean Conspiracy

by *Anodea Judith*, CAW

Conspire: (*from spiritus, or spirit*) *to concur or work to one end; act in harmony; co-operate; to plot together; breathe together.*
Gaea: Earth Mother Goddess of pre-classical Greece, creator of the Heavens.
Gaean Conspiracy: a movement to connect the subsystems of Gaea into harmonious coopera-tion through mutual recognition of their identity as part of an evolving planetary deity.

E ARE ALL PART OF THE **GAEan Conspiracy.** Based on the scientific and thealogical premise that the Earth is an enormous multi-systemic living creature—a planetary deity we call *Gaea*—the Gaean Conspiracy is a movement to reconnect our social, economic, scientific, religious and political systems into harmoni-ous co-creation with the larger, long stand-ing bio-geological Gaean system. It is a rec-ognition of the evolutionary process that must take place as our planetary being awakens to a more integrated, self-reflexive state of glo-bal consciousness. The coordination of this planetary harmony is the next evolutionary step that we face as a species and as a planet.

The Gaean Conspiracy is based on the fol-lowing major premises:

A scientific principle with religious over-tones, this thesis states what ancient Pagans knew instinctively: that the Earth and all life upon it are an interpenetrating system of di-vine proportion. Earth's ability to resist en-tropy and to regulate temperature, oxygen, ocean salinity and other qualities necessary for life indicates that She is a biological super-organism having consciousness. This dynamic homeostasis (self-regulation) of living organ-isms and their environment is the interface that human beings are currently threatening.

In 1971, an article by Otter Zell entitled "TheaGenesis: The Birth of the Goddess" *(GE #40)* contained the first published de-scriptions of the Earth as a living Goddess. Otter's vision was based on the fact that all life in the biosphere began with a single or-ganism, which has divided infinitely to form the incredible diversity of life that has evolved thus far. Much as a fertilized ovum divides again and again to make up the many organs of a human body, all life in the biosphere is part of a single living organism, of which we and the plants and animals are like cells and perhaps, collectively, organs.

The *Gaia Hypothesis* has been popular-ized by James Lovelock, an atomospheric scientist. Through his observation of atmos-pheric fluctuations, Lovelock discovered that the atmosphere of Gaea maintains a consis-tent composition, defying the behavior of re-active gases. Such a homeostatic balance of oxygen, nitrogen, and carbon dioxide is an anomaly in our solar system. Oxygen, highly reactive, should combine with the reducing gas of methane or react with the 78% nitro-gen and fall to the ground. Instead, oxygen remains at a constant 21%. In addition, de-spite a 25% warming of the sun over geolog-ical time, there are homeostatic balances of world temperature and of the constant salin-ity of the ocean, which logically, should get saltier as it evaporates. In the words of Love-lock, "It must take a lot of work to keep up such a wild disequilibrium."

And who is doing the work? It is our biosphere, that arose over 3.5 billion years ago: the microbes and the plants and animals which interact with the seemingly solid or-gan of Gaea's crust. Thin as a spider's web, this delicate miracle of life is the chemical and climatic thermostat of the Goddess.

But Gaea is not the biosphere alone. Just as a living redwood tree is 97% inanimate matter, just as a snail includes its shell, so Gaea is a total organism, comprising Her crust, Her flowing mantle and Her radioac-tive metallic core. Her changing biosphere is a thin layer of expression on Her beautiful face—the visage of the One of Whom we are a part and upon Whom we depend to survive.

Gaea is not only alive, She is conscious.

An organism that is alive changes. As a thing changes it either moves towards entro-py, increasing disorder, or towards or-ganization and greater complexity. We see in every untouched wilderness that Gaea keeps Her house beautiful and balanced. We know by the proliferation of species and the perfection of untampered ecosystems that Gaea resists entropy.

The ability to resist the natural entropy of open systems implies the influence of consciousness or intelligence. Gaea's ability to sustain the wild disequilibrium of which Lovelock speaks is indicative of a feedback process that elicits a self-correcting response. She is able to sense and to change accordingly to maintain the exact conditions needed for life—operative intelligence at work.

While Lovelock was strongly criticized for implying that Gaea's intelligence had purpose, by definition a thing that is moving toward greater organization is evolving. Since She is alive and evolving, we watch for the pattern and ask the questions, "What is She evolving into?" and "How can we help?"

The basic evolutionary pattern in biological organisms is movement toward greater consciousness. Since the animals with the largest brains are the most recent additions, this progression is called *cephalization*. Simple homeostasis does not require a great deal of consciousness—our bodies maintain their inner temperature and chemical balance with little if any attention from our conscious mind. But as circumstances require greater effort to maintain balance, greater consciousness is also required: when it gets really cold, we put a coat on or make a fire.

Teilhard de Chardin, apocalyptic theologian, spoke of the Earth growing a new organ of consciousness which he called the *noosphere*. The noosphere is made up of creatures who are capable of sharing and spreading consciousness. It can be thought of as Gaea's cerebral cortex. Humans and animals may be the neurons of Gaea, growing neural networks via our wondrous communications systems, which are themselves only seconds old. This means Her consciousness is growing very rapidly.

What does a being do as it becomes conscious? Many spiritual systems, especially the older ones, have risen from the very fabric of this world. Gaea's evolutionary thrust is reflected in the spiritual goals of *self-realization*.

To realize one's self means to awaken to whom you are in your entirety, to harmoniously integrate your inner parts. Based on models of modern psychology, systems thinking and spiritual enlightenment, the next stage of planetary evolution will involve a reclamation of lost and severed parts; a reintegration and increased functionality of interdependent systems; and a continual self-examination and self-correction aiming toward complete identity as part of a planetary being.

Realization on a planetary scale means that a critical mass of the conscious aspects of Gaea realize the absolute importance of all the other Gaean components and unite with them. To come to understand that there is no "other," only a very large self that is highly diversified within, is a global process of epic proportions which will extend far beyond our lifetimes.

Put simply, this means:

Gaea is trying to wake up!

The noosphere is all sentient creatures as well as the interconnecting nerve fibers of the media and telecommunications networks. Even animals are part of this network: as we watch movies and documentaries about them, we bring them into our consciousness. In the same way that the occipital nerve of our central nervous system influences our consciousness by bringing visual information to the brain, the international communications medium is a neural network that affects our global consciousness.

While we sleep, we are unaware of external visual input and instead dwell in the archetypal realm. The process of awakening from sleep is reflected in an increasing ability to connect quickly and directly with what is going on around us.

So, too, is the planet awakening through the development of the noosphere. Once upon a time, war could rage in Europe without anyone in America having any knowledge of it. Then the noosphere grew and we could know, but with a time lag, a buffering separation between the reality of the war and our consciousness of it. Now the planetary nervous system is awakening ever more and information about significant events reaches a much larger body of consciousness more quickly. The experience is also a fuller one of sight and sound together. The noosphere is evolving, its body of consciousness self-organizing into an elaborate neural network.

When an injured person falls into unconsciousness, they cease to be aware of their wounds. As they come to, they first become aware of sensations and sounds. Then they open their eyes to their surroundings and next try to sit up, only to find their body racked with pain. Working toward awareness of the situation as a whole, they attempt to connect the sensory information impacting their groggy consciousness; they begin to remember who they are, where they are, and what happened.

Gaea is awakening now, as Her various members realize that they are part of a larger divine system. She got a look at Her face in the mirror when the pictures of Earth from space were broadcast into the minds of Her children. When all the parts of Gaea recognize each other as participants in parallel growth heading for an Omega point of coalescence and integrative harmony, then the global consciousness of this planet will have awakened to a realization of identity as a global being.

We who are aware of this process are privileged to have a ringside seat. We are Her eyes and ears, Her voice and hands. Human beings, with our instruments of science and global communication, are in a unique position to understand the direction of this change and help it or thwart it—at our own liberation or peril. Asking and perhaps discovering in what direction Her evolutionary thrust is moving, in answering, we become partners in it.

Teilhard de Chardin observed: "Man is not the center of the universe, as once we thought in our simplicity, but something much more wonderful—that arrow pointing the way to the final unification of the world in terms of life."[1]

But in our rush towards planetary realization, we are creating a paralysis of greedlock.[2] Since everything on this planet is part of Gaea, what in the world is She doing to Herself? Is destruction of our own habitat part of Her plan? Is She trying to get rid of us as a failed experiment? Or are we hurrying Her own awakening? If we are She, and we are also destroying the most living aspect of Her, does that mean She is engaged in self-destruction? If so, why?

Gaea is reacting to a deep psychic wound.

I return again to human beings as a mod-el. People come to me in my healing practice to deal with self-destructive activities that they are unable to stop: drinking, eating, scratching themselves raw, ruining their relationships, hurting their children. They don't want to be doing these things and they aren't fully conscious of why they do. Our culture is full of this kind of addictive self-destruction.

In every case, the behavior was the result of one wound or several that had been glossed over, forgotten, discounted or distorted. An unhealed wound of any magnitude is an event that thwarts the evolutionary progress of the afflicted. Until the wound is healed. the organism cannot go on to become what it is meant to be.

Human addictive destruction of the biosphere can he understood as a systemic reaction on the part of Gaea to escape from a wound. It is a sign of something having gone awry, a self-sabotage reflex, a circuit breaker. If this is so, then *what is the wound?*

The wound that Gaea sustained is the wound of Her children turning away from Her. If her children were to be the arrow pointing the way to unification, then we are surely missing the mark. Instead of unity, our separation from Nature has resulted in a fragmentation of Her energy. Culture is severed from planet, much as mind is "severed" from body, the ongoing condition from wounds suffered. As a result, we are living with a biospheric amnesia and Gaea is living in a state of partial dissociation. The noosphere has become what Theodore Roszak calls *the neurosisphere.*

The imposition of patriarchal dominator values, which destroyed the religions and cultural models that revered the Earth, was the original infliction of this wound. It has been a 6,000 year process of separation of human beings from Nature (long to us, but moments to Gaea). In this time we have moved away from biological models for our cultural structure, replacing them with mechanistic ones. Powerful, but out of step with Gaea, they take us away from Her and from ourselves as biological beings.

But in reality this separation is not actually possible—we are utterly dependent upon Gaea. Our separation is an illusion that unfortunately has us firmly in its grip. Joanna Macy points out:

"Trying to escape from something that

we are dependent on breeds a love-hate relationship with it. This love-hate relationship with matter permeates our culture and inflames a twofold desire—to destroy and to possess. These two impulses, craving and aversion, inflame each other in a kind of vicious circle."[3]

So our culture compulsively seeks to possess and destroy the very deity that gives us life.

We are each part of Gaea. Her wound is our own wound. As we are separated from Mother Nature, we are simultaneously separated from our own nature. Our self-destruction is her destruction. As the face of our planet breaks out in biospheric acne,our social systems break down, our economic systems decline, our political systems wage war and our immune systems fail. Our despair is Her despair. Her pain is our doom.

But as we are a microcosmic reflection of Her, so is our vision and our hope. Herein lies the good news.

What can we do?

Get rid of the illusion of separateness between yourself and other parts of the planet-"us-and-them" thinking. Look to heal the wounds within yourself and others—even your enemies are part of Gaea. Connect again with Nature, walk in the wilderness, immerse your consciousness in places where She is still whole and healthy. Help others to recognize the vision of global consciousness. Promote awareness of the Earth as awareness of our very selves and of our purpose in this amazing cosmic creation story.

Conduct rituals that strengthen the connection of human and Gaean consciousness. Recycle. Pray. Give money to environmental organizations. Write letters to your newspaper. Learn to love each other and appreciate the beauty and diversity She has created. Help to bring about the critical mass that can carry us on to global awakening. *Wake up!*

Ben Franklin once said that his greatest invention was the word "American" to describe the melting pot of cultures that were forming this country. It erased the differences emphasized by such labels as "Dutch," "Italian," "Virginian," "New Yorker," "Catholic,"or "Protestant." Otter Zell has suggested we begin to think of ourselves as "Gaeans," a word that further transcends our races, religions, or nationalities. As Gaeans we can join together in this global conspiracy to awaken our Mother.

Humanity stands poised on the brink of a quantum leap in evolution. The effects of a global change in consciousness are truly cosmic, shrinking by comparison the fall of the Berlin Wall, the end of the Cold War, and the advent of computers. We have an enormous opportunity if we can recognize it before we destroy our chance.

The Gaean Conspiracy is based on the belief that planetary awakening will occur through the mutual recognition and coordination of *all* our major systems: from individuals and families to cities and continents; from politics and economics to religion and science. As Al Gore stated at the Democratic Convention, "The environment must be the central organizing principle for civilization."

As we balance our mechanistic models by integrating them with spiritual and biological models, we make the first steps in this transformation. This process extends beyond our lifetime. For this reason, it is difficult for us to conceive and implement it. But if *homo sapiens* is indeed the animal privileged to point the arrow, let us reflect deeply upon its direction.

Footnotes

1. Teilhard de Chardin, *Phenomenon of Man,* translated by Bernard Wall, Harper Torch Books. 1959 pp. 154-157
2. A term coined byTheodore Roszak, *Voice of the Earth,* Simon and Schuster. 1992
3. Joanna Macy, *World as Lover, World as Self* Parallax Press, 1991 p. 7

Anodea Judith, Ph.D. is a long time member and former High Priestess of the Church of All Worlds (1987-'97) and the author of many books on personal and global transformation, including the classic *Wheels of Life* (1987) and the dual award-winning *Waking the Global Heart* (2006). She is also an award-winning filmmaker of *The Illuminated Chakras* (2003) and an international workshop leader and speaker. Her books have sold over half a million copies and been translated into 13 languages.
www.sacredcenters.com;
www.wakingtheglobalheart.com

GE Vol. XXVI, No. 100 (Spring 1993) 16-18

Gaian Ministry:
Reclaiming Earth and Spirit

by *Jesse Wolf Hardin* (art by Daniel Blair Stewart)

"We must remember the chemical connections between our cells and the stars, between the beginning and now. We must remember and reactivate the primal consciousness of oneness between all living things. We must return to that time, in our genetic memory, in our dreams, when we were one species born to live together on Earth as her magic children." —Barbara Mor

"You will speak and act with the courage and endurance that has been yours through the long, beautiful aeons of your life story as Gaia." —Joanna Macy

 E ARE BORN INTO IT, ALL OF US, and some remember the time before the first forgetting— the complete and constant experiencing of *Spirit*. But by age five the soulful and physical sensation of God's imminence had begun to give way to the reality the glaring television described, succumbing to an early cynicism fostered by intent observation and exacerbated by experience. But the feeling still returned from time to time, always at special moments and in hallowed places, an interpenetration of all-inclusive Spirit and inspirited boy, overcoming the rapidly developing hegemony of my rational mind. While I can easily recall my resistance to the formality of the few Lutheran services we attended, It happened in church as well, as even the walls seemed to dissolve around me. When the pastor called on us to "feel the presence of the Holy Ghost entering you" I was indeed entered, and all the magic of blessed childhood returned in the wake of its passage. Entered and filled, for a moment as long as a slow breath, and as long as eternity. The words of the sermon faded into an incomprehensible roar, and I again felt the ecstatic sense of oneness. I was one with my father, my hand melting into his. I was one with every kid in the aisles short enough to be hidden amongst the standing suits and dresses, with the little old lady with the strange accent and tears in her eyes when the talk came to love and devotion. I was one, even, with the distracted hypocrites fidgeting to my right, and the birds I hadn't noticed before cavorting in and out of the open upper-story windows. I was one with the bench I'd thought too hard, which is to say that a part of its energetic being seemed to extend up into me, and I into it, and thus into the ground as well. I was swallowed by, encompassed by, internalized by, *accepted* by the oneness I experienced as God.

My deepest communion with the sacred came, nonetheless, in the citadels of uncut forest, alongside the choir-voiced creeks just north of the sullied city, exploring my authenticity as I explored the hidden spaces among and beneath the bushes and flowers of my own backyards. I found little to fear or mistrust in the honest fertile soil of my youth, the dirt sprouting flowers where I played and prayed on chubby knees. The toddler never thought of the earth as a house of future punishment, fought against the perception of it as an impurity to be scraped from underneath the fingernails or fairly covered with suffocating asphalt. Like the amazing swallowtail butterflies, like the blossoms they fed from, to this child the soil was alive and inspirited: *Hallowed Ground.* The earth hadn't yet to be demonized for me, and there was nothing to indicate a separation or schism between what I sensed as creator and creation.

Perhaps this was but one example of what came to be described by child psychologists as an "emotional indulgence." Labeled "gifted" but "overly sensitive and willful," they prescribed the academia and conformity of a private school. While my well-intentioned mother worked an extra job to pay the tuition, I found myself in a boarding military school. While I thrived for awhile on the opportunities to excel, the thrill of competition faded when I saw how sad were the losers of the spelling bees, the cadets facing their parent's unreasonable expectations for promotions and honors. I was taught to "get over" my feelings, set up by my peers to never shed tears in public or laugh too loud. "God" often seemed reduced to an intellectual concept, a word stamped on the coins everyone hustled for, the moniker of an authority higher than but in the same hierarchical structure as our parents, the "Colonel" that was headmaster of the school, the policemen who patrolled the alley behind us, the army flying its jets overhead, and the president we though told them where to fly. Yet never did I fail to find relief in time alone on the grass or counsel in the ways of the birds, fail to take communion with the resident insects or make physical contact with the entire world just by opening to the touch of its globe-circling winds.

They talk about the "Tree of Life," and for me it was the magnificent avocado growing on one side of the field where we held our "dress rehearsals." It lifted its weighty trunk towards a hazy sky, right next to one of the ten foot high concrete walls that surrounded the school field. I have to smile, even now, imagining high-voiced preteens barking at even younger kids, squeaking as they shout their commands, "Left face! Forward march! Right oblique, march!" One of my continuing "indulgences" was to wait until just the right moment and drop away from the staggered column, scurrying up the sides of the botanical giant until secreted away in its foliage. While my brethren formed and reformed variations on the straight line below my perch, I allowed my mind to wander after the flying ants winding there way up its branches, fed my little hands through the canyons of raised bark, and pondered the polar worlds on either side of the wall. On one side were kids like myself inculcated with restraint, putting manners ahead of expressing our true feelings, convention ahead of caprice. I was witness on the other side to delinquents and "dally-ers," ditching classes at the nearby public school with the barbed wire fence, rewilding in the jungle and oasis of what could

well have been the last undeveloped lot in that part of the city, kicking off their shoes and doing all the joyous things children do whenever they've found a place free of an adult's watchful eyes. Unlike we cadets, the kids on the other side leaped on each other with abandon, squawked and howled with no concern for propriety or pretense, the dictates of machismo or the grass stains that won't come out. They laughed and they cried, true to the events and feelings of the ever-transient moment, and with an intensity I found enviable. With the few beyond the parapets, my days of structured learning were all but over, and my real education was about to begin.

Much of my life since has been dedicated to the dissolution of those walls, barriers erected to conceal and to hold back the threat of the unknown, constructed to provide some sense of safety in a world of challenge, stability in a universe of change and surprise. These same walls block sight of those endless vistas of our uniquely human potential, and of the encompassing Nature that houses and defines our being, the evolving land and flux that is our context, our extended greater self, our place and our home. They are the tools of separation and segregation, the servants of societal control, and the roots of racism and sexism, classism and biophobia, distortion and loneliness. At the encouragement of our modern society, we find ourselves raising or envisioning barriers between parts of a sacred, contiguous whole: walls between humans and Nature, male and female, young and old, black and white, rich and poor... walls between the left-brain and the right-brain, between thought and emotion, body and soul, self and other, Earth and Spirit. Here lies the basis for a revitalized theology, a "liberation theology" that frees us from both those divisive walls society places around us, and more importantly, the walls in our minds. I'd come to think of the "original sin" as being humankind's first imagined separation, their conscious and willful divorce from an integrated Spirit and Earth. As such, true liberation is a pivotal process or *re-membering,* becoming conscious members again. It is the rejoining of all the constituent parts, consuming and consumed by Spirit—made whole again. It was not transcendence I sought and experienced, but a reimmersion into that enlivening current I'd known as a child as the "Holy Ghost."

I soon realized how our dogma, our actual vocabularies can act as walls, terms dividing one denomination from another, one religion from another, one human from the next. While some biblical scholars separate into camps around the interpretation of a single term, we forget the unifying intention of all of the world's religions— increasing humankind's actual *experiencing* of God. For a period as a teenage runaway I couldn't bring myself to say words like "God" or "Spirit," substituting the wider-defined "magic." Yet even at the peak of my rebellious phase, I knew that the best of what I was somehow extended well past the sheath of skin that supposedly defined my being, sensed that there was an intrinsic holiness to every element of unperverted Nature, and knew that every valid truism in my life came not as conclusion, but as revelation, as *epiphany.*

What is it, I wondered, that allows us as children growing into adults to begin to ignore our visions, to brand our godly instruction as intuition or instinct, to choose concept over experience, to pull back from the pain that attends the great joy and deliberately feel less? How can it be that every child is not "called," and if so, then how can they ever forget to listen, or fail to respond? How is that we can ever deny the responsibility to mourn and celebrate, nurture and expose, awaken and heal?

Homeless and "on the road," earning my food by performing street poetry at the beach, I somehow remained contracted to a purpose. Without the benefits and disadvantages of intermediaries, free of the distortion of translators, I continued my assignment to listen and counsel, to open myself and serve. Everything that followed— traveling, art career, writing, playing music, working with kids— were part of my search for the root-cause and cure for so much disenchantment and destruction,

providing an outlet for my often painful awareness, and my unremitting love. Against the forces that would divide, I am called to help bring the parts back together.

It's now clear that every social and environmental calamity can be traced to this single root condition: our perceived separation from (and superiority over) distinct parts of our self, from other people, and other creatures. Overpopulation, habitat destruction, clearcuts, oil-tanker spills, classism, sexism and war are all symptoms of humanity's internal *dis-ease,* our cognitive (imagined) distance from our own essential natures, separation from the beings and processes of the natural world, from a distanced and institutionalized Spirit. Given this frighteningly simple fact, could there be any more important ministry than teaching the arts of awareness and reconnection, of empathy and compassion, prayer and personal response? In my twenty years as an activist I saw how any cultural, political or environmental relief was doomed to long-range failure in the absence of spiritual consciousness and likewise, that no spiritual sensibility is complete until it is manifested in the physical.

We live in a trying age, some believing we are the last generations with a chance of initiating a human-engineered cure for this distressed planet. While we live in a culture of distraction, abstraction, and articulate denial, we can *choose* to be fully aware. Being willing to feel the pain as well as the ecstasy, of both personal and planetary grief contributes to our participation and makes way for our redemption. With personal trauma comes a window of opportunity, a chance for trans-

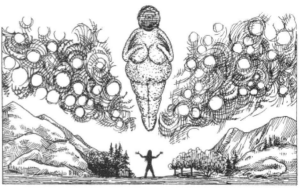

formation as we willingly carry our own cross for a time. And it is no less so for us as a species, facing both a pandemic loss of meaning and the plausible extinction of humankind itself. The techno-industrial society may be largely agnostic and materialist, but in times of personal or societal tribulation the majority turn at last to whatever they've come to know as "Spirit," to that which outlasts its every form. If we look for this Spirit embodied in ourselves, in the songs of the birds and the wind on our cheeks, if we seek it in the Earth of which we are a part— we won't have far to turn. The religiosity that matters (*mater*, matter, mother) is both experiential, and *now*.

It may also be that our multiracial tribal ancestors and many of the surviving primal peoples of today were right, and the only ultimately *survivable* religiosity is one that honors the sacred spirit embodied in the Earth and all of creation. We, and every other lifeform are paying the price for our belief systems, for the transgressions of those with no belief in God at all, and of those positing Spirit outside rather than inside themselves, the only Heaven detached from this Earth.

Looking towards my adulthood, I began appraising my ability to affect others in a positive way. I looked ahead, knowing full well that a future of artifice and ruin, or of diversity and sacrament, would always be a direct outgrowth of our coveted *beliefs*.

Much of what we all called on by Spirit to do conflicts with the modern edicts and reasoning we were brought up with. People tend to behave "righteously" while in church and do what they want on the days between. Think of the changes if we were to envision the entire planet as our church, with every day a Sabbath, every daily, natural process recognized as the miracles they truly are. What would it take for us to begin to consciously acknowledge every bite of food as a communion with inspirited life, recognizing the sin of failing to taste, failing to glorify? Are we capable like a native, like a child, like a saint— to experience the entire Earth as the Eucharist, as the body of wolf and flower, of beggar and mountain? Can we serve our greater selves, our experience of God, as sensitized participants instead of directors or even shepherds, plain participants in the liturgy of evolving creation?

I've now lived in the wilds of the Gila mountains for many years, long enough to feel allegiance, long enough to really listen and belong. Spirit speaks to me through this river canyon my wife and I so love, and it may be that God always speaks through *place*. Answering dozens of questioning letters every week, writing books and magazine articles, coediting *Talking Leaves,* speaking at any conference, church or college that will have me— I've been greatly moved by the power of these truths I've been given. "Talks" end with unrestrained animal howls, tears, laughter and mass hugs. It is always a great coming together, into a shared self, *Oikos,* home. Directing the *Earthen Spirituality Project,* I've come to think of this calling as my "Gaian Ministry."

> *"We must not expect that we can simply use the…image of Gaia to meet emotional,religious (or) political needs without allowing it to transform us in unexpected and radical ways. The spirituality of the Earth is more than a slogan. It is an invitation to initiation, to the death of what we have been and the birth of something new."*
> —*David Spangler*

"Gaia" was the Greek name for the Earth as living being, born out of Chaos. I am not Greek, nor do I experience the living world as exclusively female, but in a time of desacrelization and patriarchy the symbol of Gaia is a strong one indeed. It is the balance to, not a replacement for the worshiping of a male-imaged God. The scientists Lynn Marguellis and James Lovelock seized on this ancient metaphor to illustrate their premise that the Earth functions as a living entity, a body of self-regulating systems dependent on the balanced interaction of all its constituent parts, the atmosphere its breath, the cleansing forests its lungs. They called this notion the "Gaia Hypothesis," as if the truths honored by virtually every primal culture, by our ancestors of nearly every race, and by all children before the age of their disenchantment— as if the truth of an inspirited planet, sacred, indivisible and directed were merely theory, the invention or conclusion of modern minds! Before the advent of technology, before toxic agribusiness and skyscrapers, these were the truths we held "self-evident":

1) However we know God, that God exists within us, and within all of creation. We are each an inseparable part of, a dancing cell of that living planet body. All parts of that planet body are inspirited, with an intrinsic value and integrity of being worthy of our respect.

2) Our survival and well-being is utterly dependent on our practical and ritual demonstrations of that respect.

3) We serve the inspirited whole as celebrants and sensors, as the nerve endings of the Gaian body, conscious receptors channeling sensory input, communicating the anguish and jubilance of aware lives.

4) As aware, conscious members of the planet body, we must act on our innate responsibilities, our *ability-to-respond.*

While Lovelock argued for his Gaia Hypothesis he was defensive about any spiritual implications, insisting the process is unconscious and mechanical. Yet any deep knowing of the way energy moves on and through this planet, and through *us,* works to trigger an innate spiritual recognition: resonance. They can avoid using such loaded expressions as "Spirit," but any promotion of interdependence and wholeness is invariably a spiritual endeavor. A Gaian Ministry is founded in the deepest experiencing of the human-body as an integral part of the inspirited planet-body, a perceptual and instinctual recognition. We come to realize that the degradation of our mental and physical environs is largely the product of how we each perceive, and thus act on the world around us. And in time we may come to realize that as conscious beings our own sacredness is conditional, dependent on our *mindful* ecological presence.

I know now that we are not secular pilots of a dead Spaceship-Earth, nor have we been sentenced by God to a trial period on a disrupted Eden. We are blessed participants in the dance of embodied spirit. Singers. Dreamers. *Praise givers.* Our rightful ministry is the one which inspires and invokes awareness, reconnection, prayer and response. It offers everyone an opportunity for a Rite-of-Passage, opens up the door and invites us into a sacred space. As from a birthing hut we rise, forever changed, re-formed into our original selves, revealed as responsible celebrants of miraculous life, agents of Godly/Gaian process, playmates and vehicles for omnipresent Spirit.

I speak to congregations and religious leaders about the practical results of the cosmologies we teach, and to activist groups about how essential it is for them to feel the inherently sacred nature of that which they would protect. I ask them all to remember their own childhood and adult experiences of those moments when the walls collapsed, when all things appeared connected by luminous threads of pulsing energy, when like St. Francis of Assisi or the enraptured John Muir—the Holy Spirit appeared to them in all things, and they knew all things through their love.

In Gaian Ministry we plant our seeds, in the heart and in the earth, regardless of the chances of fruit. The immediate results, as I've witnessed again and again, are Visions...

And every aware minute, the glad recognition of the miraculous.

Jesse Wolf Hardin is founder and teacher of Animá earth-inspired practice, and the author of five books including *Gaia Eros* (New Page 2004). He and his partners offer inspiring online Animá correspondence courses, as well as host students and guests at their enchanted canyon and true ancient place of power. Opportunities include weekend retreats, personal counsel, shamanic vision quests, resident internships, and special Apprenticeships for the most dedicated. Annual events include the Wild Womens Gathering, and the Medicine Woman and Shaman Path intensives. Contact: The Animá Wilderness Learning Center & Medicine Woman Tradition, Box 688, Reserve, NM 87830. www.animacenter.org;   mail@animacenter.org.
Portions of this article appeared in *Earthlight,* the newsletter for Earth-centered Christians, 1558 Mercy St., Mt View, CA 94041.

Vol. XXX, No. 125 (Nov.-Dec. 1998) 22-25, 56

Chapter 6.
Ritual, Celebration, & Worship
Introduction
by Chas S. Clifton

THE ESSENCE OF PAGAN RELIGIOUS PRACTICE IS CELEBRATION, NOT SUPPLICATION. Pagans love talking about ritual almost as much as doing it—including producing sparkling but instructive parodies of Pagan rituals (see "Lord Moonwhistle's Guide to Perfectly Wretched Ritual"). The reason that ritual is so important is that Pagan religions are about *doing*, not about reading holy books or sitting still while the official holy man lectures you about what the holy book really means. In Wicca, for instance, blowing a kiss to the new crescent Moon the first evening that you see Her is a small form of ritual. Rituals are a natural form of human activity: we understand and remember them almost without trying. Children invent them spontaneously.

By contrast, religions that rely heavily on doctrine require that elaborate concepts be stored in what psychologists call "semantic memory" and constantly reinforced and re-explained—hence those long sermons. Doctrinal religions require official "explainers," and from that need arise hierarchies, schisms, persecution of heretics, holy wars, and the *whole megillah* as the Jews say humorously, *megillah* originally meaning scroll—the holy book again.

Pagan religions are *imagistic* rather than doctrinal. Our rituals appeal to the senses and arouse "episodic memory." Smells of incense, flicker of candles, rhythmic drumming, sexual desire, trancing and dancing, colorful costumes or naked skin—all of those produce what the psychologists call "flashbulb memories." Thirty years later I can still remember particular rituals from my first coven when the magical current flowed and I was zapped by it. The particular meaning of a Pagan ritual, while generally agreed on by the participants, might vary in its particulars from one person to another. When we supply the meaning, we remember it better than when the official explainer tells us what something is all about.

Besides humorous takes on what not to do, some of the topics in this chapter include new understandings of "sacrifice" in ritual, discussions of using masks in ritual (one of the quickest ways to get "out of yourself," believe me), and the personal altar. Also included is an essay about a Pagan event held at a municipally owned building that (don't tell!) is a functioning Pagan shrine: the recreated Parthenon in Nashville, Tennessee. Built in 1897 as part of a celebration of the centennial of Tennessee statehood—and incidentally to showcase the region's recovery from the Civil War—it was originally intended as a temporary building, but people liked it (funny about that). It was rebuilt in 1920, but the colossal statue of Athena was not added until 1990. The statue was gilded in 2002. If you ever pass through Nashville, be sure to visit Her—it is best if you can arrive when the Parthenon first opens in the morning. You will experience with all your senses how the temple of an imagistic religion works.

The Dance of Life

by *Carolyn Clark, CAW*

HE RITUAL CHAMBER IS HUSHED. Time passes in quiet meditation as ocean waves are heard crashing upon a distant shore. Members of the circle can see two priestess seated in the North, behind the Altar.

The older priestess speaks as she lights candles at the four quarters of the circle:

Seasons pass in rhythmic measure in the turning of the Cosmic Wheel. Spring flowers into Summer. Summer mellows into Autumn. Autumn dies into Winter, and Winter buds again into Spring, revealing the marvelous harmony of the Dance of Life.

The young priestess answers:

The same stream of life that runs through my veins night and day runs through the world and dances in rhythmic measure. It is the same life that shoots in joy through the dust of the Earth in numberless waves of grass and breaks into tumultuous waves of leaves and flowers. It is the same life that is rocked in the ocean-cradle of birth and death. I feel my limbs are made glorious by the touch of ages dancing in my blood this moment.

The older priestess takes from the Altar a small stone. Holding it, she strokes it and turns it over and over in her hand, looking at all sides, touching it to her third eye.

Stone reveals to the sensitive hand and eye the pressures that formed it in the womb of Mother Earth. Touch it, see it, hold the stone in your hands until you can hold it in your mind and unite with it to feel the rhythms of its forming and its birth.

She passes the stone to the person sitting on her left hand and waits as each person meditates briefly with it. As the stone returns to her, she reads *Stones* by Leslie Norris.

Upon the Altar stands a seedling tree, perhaps a lemon tree or a young Norfolk Pine. The young priestess now gathers the tree in her arms, touching gently its leaves and trunk, tuning to its bio-rhythms. At last she speaks:

A tree reveals in beauty the secret rhythm of all plants. See it, feel it, smell its fragrance, unite with its rhythms. Think of its beginning—the bursting seed, the thrusting shoot—think of its present glory and of its ending—leaves falling, branches withering, trunk decaying. Its individual rhythm moves it in harmony with all else that lives and dies, on the hills, in cities, in rivers and lakes, in the air, and in the ocean.

She sends the seedling around the circle as each member meditates on the rhythms of trees. She reads *The Tree*, by Andrew Young. Again, moments of quietness pass to the whisper of distant waves upon the shore. Softly, the old priestess speaks, her voice barely audible:

Life itself bears the ocean's rhythm.

Her voice gathers strength as she goes on:

Waves rise, each to its individual height in a seeming attitude of unrelenting competition, but only up to a certain point: and thus we know of the great repose of the sea to which they are all related and to which they all return in a rhythm which is marvelously beautiful. In fact, these undulations and vibrations, these risings and fallings, are not due to the erratic contortions of disparate bodies, they are a rhythmic dance. Rhythm can never be born of the haphazard struggle of combat. Its underlying principle must be unity, not opposition.

Only the ocean's voice is heard as the members contemplate this thought. Then the young priestess muses:

Rhythm—the touch of hand in hand, the same life force pulsing through the fibres of each.

The old priestess smiles as she replies:

Unity—the touching, the merging, of mind with mind, the same consciousness suffusion each, awakening each to the other, to grok in fullness.

Exultantly, the young priestess asks the group:

> Is it beyond thee to be glad with the gladness of this rhythm? To be tossed and lost and broken in the whirl of this fearful joy?

She lifts from the Altar a silver tray upon which lies a loaf of home-baked bread.

> The bread of life is the fruit of the Mother's body. Blessed be in Her name this gift by which our bodies are fed.

The old priestess raises the chalice and blesses it, saying:

> The water of life is our Mother's blood Blessed be the cup of consciousness which we share to unite with one another.

GE Vol. IX, No. 77 (Ostara 1976) 23

Be Pagan Once Again!

(to tune of "A Nation Once Again")

by P.E.I. Bonewits (Copyright © 1972)

GE Vol. VI, No. 59 (Yule 1973) 18

When boyhood's fire was in my blood
I dreamed of ancient dreemen,
Against the Church who boldly stood
As Pagans and as Freemen.
And then I prayed I yet might see
The Druids in the glen,
And Ireland long the Churches' toy,
Be Pagan once again!

> Be Pagan once again!
> Be Pagan once again!
> Oh Eire too long the churches' toy,
> Be Pagan once again!!

The Old Gods only sleep you know,
Although betrayed and slandered.
They guarded us from every woe
And blessed each crop and fine herd.
Then Patrick drove the snakes away
And brought the churches in—
'Twas a bloody poor bargain I would say!
Be Pagan once again!

> Be Pagan once again!
> Be Pagan once again!
> 'Twas a bloody poor bargain,
>   I would say—
> Be Pagan once again!!

And ever since that wretched day,
When first Ireland went Christian,
We've suffered woe in every way,,
With our Freedom made the worst "sin."
They set us at each other's throats,
To murder kith and kin.
Too long we've been their starving goats!
Be Pagan once again!

> Be Pagan once again!
> Be Pagan once again!
> Too long we've been their
>   starving goats—
> Be Pagan once again!!

Both Catholic and Protestant
Lead us round by our noses,
Distracting from the deadly scent
Of England's bleedin' roses!
Kick every preacher 'cross the sea,
Burn out their golden dens!
It's the only way we'll ever be free!
Be Pagan once again!

> Be Pagan once again!
> Be Pagan once again!
> It's the only way we'll ever be free—
> Be Pagan once again!!

How Athena Came to Nashville
The 1993 Panathenaia Festival
by *Shawn Eyer* and *David Fideler*

Amidst the leafy trees of Centennial Park, like some figment of times long behind us, but solid to the touch and certainly no mirage in the bright Tennessee sun, the Nashville Parthenon is real. One approaches it for the first time with a bewildering sense of elation, awe, mirth and familiarity. Every aspect bespeaks majesty and skill, and every gleaming surface or falling shadow adds its note to the visual symphony of this astonishing and enduring achievement of the genius of ancient Greece.

 ASHVILLE'S EDIFICE IS AN ACCurate, full-scale restoration, built for the 1896 Centennial Fair, of the fifth-century BCE Temple of Athena Parthenos (now in ruins on the Athenian Acropolis). Long considered the most perfect example of the Doric order of architecture, the Parthenon is one of the most famous structures ever built by human effort. In the large sanctuary, at its geometrical center, stood the masterpiece of Phidias the sculptor: an ivory and gold statue of the Goddess Athena, 42 feet tall, arrayed in all Her armor and attended by Nike, Goddess of Victory. The original disappeared after the Emperor Theodosius issued a ban on all Pagan religions. Now its counterpart—completed in 1990—stands with an air of immortal dignity in the *naos* of the Nashville temple. Eight years in the making, Nashville sculptor Alan LeQuire's magnificent Athena is the largest indoor statue in the Western world.

Running along the top of the outer columns on every side of the Parthenon, highlighted with a red background, the row of *metopes* shows battles between *lapiths* and centaurs, giants and gods, Amazons and Greeks and Trojans. If one stands on the steps and peers up into the space between the rows of columns, one beholds a continuous frieze which, though hidden, also runs along every side of the temple. It shows a procession: youths on horseback and bearers of sacrifices making their way up to the Acropolis. One follows the frieze around the temple to discover, over the main doors on the eastern porch, its culmination: the ritual cleansing and changing of the garment of the

Athena Parthenos in Nashville, Tennessee

statue of Athena. The frieze depicts the ancient festival of the Panathenaia.

It was perhaps inevitable that the Panathenaia should return, as it did the weekend of August 13-15, 1993. Thanks to the vision, skill and perseverance of organizers from the Church of All Worlds and Avalon Isle, the first Nashville Panathenaia festival fulfilled and exceeded every expectation. Though the festival generated controversy during its planning, nothing could stop the driving force of so many good and creative leaders.

The festival was based in the Holiday Inn across from the Parthenon. On Friday afternoon and early evening, athletes and spectators were shuttled to Temple Track at nearby Tennessee State University to compete in the games. The pentathlon consisted of a foot race, javelin throw, discus throw, long jump and wrestling. Even those who don't normally participate in such activities were prompted by Athena—through Her charismatic and persuasive priest, Jon DeClesto join in the action. The games were exhilarating and a great deal of fun. Participants were rubbed with olive oil in the ancient style, and then dusted with red clay in the case of the men, and white for the women. Although in ancient times athletes performed in the nude, in Nashville we wore what the Greeks called *perizomai,* essentially loincloths.

Later that evening attendees gathered in the conference room at the hotel to hear "When the Goddess Smiles, She Bares Her Teeth," presented by Patricia Monaghan, guest of honor. Her talk and slide show demonstrated that the Medusa is a complex figure which incorporates many earlier levels of symbolism that are not fully reflected in the surviving classical myths.

One of the fondest memories I have of the weekend is of the bardic contest later that night. Meant to balance the physical competition with an intellectual one, it allowed anyone to sing or recite whatever the Muses inspired. I sat astonished at the talent displayed as each person performed. It was especially amazing in that many of us had no advance notice that such a contest was to be held. Bruce MacLennan took the laurels with his original poetry. Deborah Kest, one of the guest speakers, chanted the Homeric Hymn to Athena, in the original Greek, from memory! Morning Glory Zell read her powerful invocations to Poseidon and other Greek deities.

There were four workshops presented the next day. I presented my research in a session called "The Eleusinian Mysteries and Psychedelic Effects." Morning Glory used her famous collection of goddess figurines to illustrate a talk on "Indo-European Roots of the Olympic Goddesses." Deborah Kest from

Brown University spoke on "Greek Magic and Mysticism." Jon DeCles spoke on "The Spiritual Content of Sport" in Greek culture and the value of athletics in the education of the whole person. At midday there was a panel discussion centered on the continuing relevance of Greek religion, myth, and spirituality.

On Saturday night participants took a step back in time as they became celebrants. The organizers had distributed guidelines for making authentic costumes, and soon the hotel was thick with colorful, extravagant Greek-looking characters, much to the confusion of ordinary guests. At 6:00 p.m., everyone assembled, and the procession of seventy, led by priests, priestesses and dancers, moving to the sound of drums, tambourines, and finger cymbals, left the hotel and began to wind through the trees of Centennial Park.

The first part of the ceremony was the *Plynteria.* The Athenians had a wooden figure of Athena much older than the one in the Parthenon, the Athena *Polias,* Guardian of the City. Annually she was brought out on a wooden craft and publicly cleansed and dressed in a new garment *(peplos)* made by the women of Athens. In Centennial Park, the procession was met by a small group carrying a life-size wooden statue of Athena Polias from the direction of the Parthenon. After a prayer to Athena, two priestesses ceremonially cleansed the primitive statue and covered her with a new peplos. During the cleansing, the women circled around the statue and sang a hymn to Athena, while the surrounding men faced outwards, averting their eyes from the unclad figure of the Goddess. All were chanting:

> *Athena, grant us wisdom*
> *Bright-eyed Lady, lend us courage!*
> *We are your joyous people*
> *Guide us in our lives!*

While spectators looked curiously on, the procession, led by the newly-robed Athena, approached the Parthenon. Once at the Parthenon, celebrants solemnly filed into the temple one by one. Each carried a handful of barley, held close to his or her heart, as a sacrifice to the Goddess. Celebrants were asked to close their eyes at the threshold of the sanctuary as they were led into the nave of the temple, which contributed greatly to the power of the ritual. It marked the transition into another reality, another space and time. Once the celebrants stood in the central sanctuary with their eyes closed and a fistful of barley held against their hearts, the ceremony proper began. To the accompaniment of a musical score in ancient Hellenic style, Athena was invoked.

Standing in the Parthenon, we heard the voice of Poseidon (Nybor) and Athena (Morning Glory) as each described their nature and what they offered Athenians. We were witnessing the famous contest between Athena and Poseidon for the land of Attica, depicted on the pedimental sculptures at the east end of the temple. Hearing the voices of the divinities reverberate throughout the temple as the contest unfolded before us made me feel we were in the presence of the gods. After the contest was completed, the voice of a priestess offered a prayer to Athena which contained all of Her classical epithets and described Her nature as the goddess of civilization, democracy, wisdom, the arts, law and justice.

After the prayer, and having stood within the sanctuary for perhaps fifteen minutes, we were instructed to open our eyes and behold the Goddess. We discovered ourselves in the heart of the Parthenon, arranged in a semicircle, facing the colossal Athena; it was an awe-inspiring experience; for many it was the first time that they had witnessed the towering image. The voice of the Goddess rang out, exhorting Her celebrants to strive for a life of goodness and excellence. The speech was followed by a hymn in Greek to Athena (composed by Deborah Kest especially for the Nashville Panathenaia) performed by Deborah, Lord Taliesin, and Cat of Weaversong, with synthesizer accompaniment by Dwani, wholly in the style of the ancient Greeks.

Following the hymn, the victors of the athletic and bardic com-

petitions were called forward by the priestess. Standing before Athena and her celebrants, the winners were crowned with laurel wreaths by a beautiful, winged priestess (CAW's May Queen, Sun) who assumed the role of Nike, Victory herself. Grand Champion Ann Darragh received the *amphora* trophy cup. The victors consumed an olive, sacred fruit of Athena and offered their barley to Athena by placing it in an urn which stood before Her great statue. Then they drank from a chalice of consecrated water. Two dancers, Cat and Shanti of Weaversong, came forward and removed two long, curved swords from the altar; everyone took a step back as they performed a dramatic sword dance to musical accompaniment. Following the dance, the other celebrants held hands and formed a line, moving to Athena to partake of Her olives, offer their barley, and receive the water.

Processional Athena statue in front of Parthenon

Once everyone had both given and received from the Goddess, the formal ceremony came to an end and was followed by a delicious Greek banquet in the treasury of the Parthenon. The evening came to a close with an astonishing performance of music and dance performed in front of the statue, which drew on both ancient and futuristic styles.

The first Nashville Panathenaia was a historic event which exceeded all expectations. The ceremony will forever mark the memories of those who were present: brilliantly conceived, perfectly executed, all elements combined to create a transformative experience that dissolved the boundaries of time and space and, like all things mystical, could never be fully described in words. The festival seamlessly integrated the scholarly study and the experiential dimension of Greek spirituality. The ceremony before the colossal Athena gave everyone a first hand, realistic experience of classical Greek spirituality.

If the pulse of a religion is the proliferation of legends, the Panathenaia has a definite heartbeat. A group of initiates, on their way back to the hotel, were questioned by a motorist: Why were they dressed like Greeks? They replied they had just come from the Parthenon. The woman explained that she was not a local resident, but from Greece. When they told her about the dedication of the statue, she remarked, "Oh? My name is Athena."and the car wheeled away into the lights of the city.

This article is a synthesis of articles by Shawn Eyer (Summer, 1993 *The Lyre: Journal of the Thiasos Orphikos,* $2.50, Box 674, Defiance, OH 43512); and by David Fideler from a special Panathenaia issue of Phanes Press. To obtain a copy of Fideler's illustrated article on Athena in the classical world and the Parthenon in Athens and Nashville, send $1 to Phanes Press, Box 6114, Grand Rapids, MI 49516.

Cycles and Seasons on the Canvas of Life
by Alene Wildgrube, CAW

The canvas is ready—come forth from the womb and paint your dreams, your thoughts, and realities of life. She has set up the easel and awaits your arrival.

Begin with the Spring offering of Youth:

Delicate pastels, warm, soft and gentle. Tender shoots, fragile blossoms surrounded by gentle breezes. Inner stirrings, shy blushing glances, let the brush begin. Let the need overcome your shyness. Dip from the Springs of Life. Begin testing shades and patterns, textures.

Release the Summer offering of Being:

Colors bright and gay on a lush emerald gown. Lush full growth, Dancing sensuous rhythms. Hot sultry temptations, Fiery clashes of thunder. Spicy tang, Lusty laughter. Passions rising, ecstasy and pain. Touch, taste, fulfillment. Refresh in the pools of your delight. Daring to be. Boldly leave your mark.

Blend to Fall Harvest of Gathering:

Blazing vibrant colors, Jewels of color added to Her emerald gown. Table laden with abundance. A mature strong final fling. Twirling, spinning pulsations, balance, richness of experience. Warm wines, sweet and tart nectars of life. Blending of tenderness and passion. Mix them all together; strokes of all seasons.

Fade to Winter of Restoring:

Faded hues, shadowed fond and haunting memories. Worn with time. Cold blustery harsh realities. The retreat, with stirrings of the childhood soul. Paint a white blanket in which to sleep and dream. A time to refresh and renew, to delve within the embers in the hearth and stir the flames so perhaps you will see the blanket slip first from the Mountain top into the valleys restoring the canvas of life fresh and new.

The Beginning!

Children, Pull Out Your Chickens!

by *Roland Nethaway,* Senior Editor *(art by Daniel Blair Stewart)*

ET'S QUIET DOWN, CHILDREN. Now that we've finally gotten rid of that terrible Supreme Court decision, I can again lead you in prayer. So children, let's get ready for our morning prayer. Did everyone remember to bring their chicken?

Mary, where is your chicken? That's all right, Mary. Don't cry. As I told you yesterday, if you can't afford a chicken, the school is required to provide one. I've got plenty of extra chickens up here by the prayer mats, meditation crystals, and peyote buds. Did anyone else forget to bring their chicken?

As you know from your schedule, children, today I will lead you in a Santeria prayer. It's a recognized, ancient religion. Now, I know some of you have complained that many of these prayers don't represent your beliefs. But remember, they do represent the sincere beliefs of many Americans. I promise you that eventually we will lead the class in a prayer representing your own religion.

But you'll have to be patient. There are hundreds of Christian denominations with all sorts of beliefs in the United States. And there are hundreds more non-Christian religions recognized in America. If your religion isn't on our list, just let us know and we'll make sure it's added. We don't want to leave anyone out. That's not the American way.

"Be thankful"

Everyone knows that you have never been prevented from praying in school, but for years you were denied having teachers and principals lead you in prayer. You should be thankful.

Johnnie, I don't know what you're doing to that chicken, but stop it. You need to straighten up and be serious. This is important. If it were not important, then why did 224 Texas counties and 51 Texas cities go to the trouble to pass resolutions supporting the reinstatement of state-sponsored prayer in our public schools? I'll tell you why, because lots and lots of people said the loss of state-sponsored prayers led to drug use, crime, violence, teenage pregnancy, dropouts, family disintegration, child-abuse, pornography, racism, poor academic achievement, overcrowded prisons and lots of other bad things.

Before we start, remember that tomorrow we will have a traditional Wicca prayer and we'll try to cast a spell on the press. Remember to bring a lock of your mother's hair.

Johnnie, keep that chicken quiet. What is it, Lucy? If you want me to tell you when I will lead you in a prayer of your religion, you'll have to tell me what it is. You can't look at someone and tell their personal beliefs. Unitarian?

What's coming up...

Let's see, coming up we have Christian Science, Amish, Tibetan Buddhism, Seventh-Day Adventist, Comanche,. Zoroastrianism, Druze, Calvinist Baptist, Unification, Hasidism, and Deliverance Pentecostal. That one should be interesting. I think that's when you bring a rattlesnake and a cup of poison.

I don't see it coming up right away, Lucy. Let's see, we have the Reformed Druids of North America, American Vegan, Shanti Yoga, Evangelical Presbyterian, Baha'i World Faith, Church of Satan, Gnostic Orthodox,

House of Yahweh, Agasha Temple of Wisdom, Church of Metaphysical Christianity, Jain Meditation, Catholic Charismatic, People of Destiny, Branch Davidian, Coptic Fellowship...

I don't know, Lucy. It doesn't look like Unitarian is coming up any time soon. But if we don't lead you in a prayer of your own church or religion this year, the government requires that we lead you in a prayer of your religion at least once before you graduate. This way, it's fair for everyone.

OK, kids, on the count of three, yank the heads off your chickens and I'll start today's prayer.

Altars & Ecology
by *Francesca DeGrandis, 3rd Road (art by Oberon Zell)*

 TOLD A FRIEND I WAS WRITING A piece on altars and ecology. She said "What do they have to do with one another?" so I asked her what an altar was. She answered "A sacred place." I received the same answer from her when I then queried, "And what is the Earth?"

If you worship the Earth as the Mother God, Gaia, and profess Her sacred nature, you tend the planet well because to do so honors the planet as a God. (I use the word "God" whether referring to a male or female Deity.)

In the ritual classes that I teach, I have sometimes suggested the following: set up a lovely altar under which you place a recycling bin. Consider this bin part of the altar. The Pagan religion is devotional, a two way street: if we pray at our altars for the old Gods to give us their help we had better give them ours. If we don't feed them and take good care of them, they don't have what they need to take care of us. Recycling is only one embodiment of this principle. For instance, we've not cared well for Father Sky's ozone layer. Now He cannot protect us from cancer producing rays. The ancients made sacrifice so that their Deities would be strong. Food and drink were placed on the altars because it was understood that the Gods need to be fed. This was neither stupid nor ignorant—the people of those times knew their responsibility. Though not a substitute for food, a recycling bin/altar embodies this same powerful sacrifice.

Furthermore, any religion, whether earth-based or not, needs to be a 'living' religion: part of daily life and always applicable to modern needs and dilemmas. The sacred and the profane can't be separate. So, in one of the classes I taught, part of the altar was a box for clothing donations. The clothes eventually were given to the homeless.

A witch's altar is a consecrated place for religious practices of love and worship, a place to meditate, just as ancients would meditate in sacred forest groves and caves, on mountains and high hills. I ask my students, "How can an altar be a place that helps you be in touch with your spiritual objectives and needs—similar to the way you feel at a favorite beach spot—if the shells on your altar were gathered by methods that caused ecological harm to the area from which they were harvested? Check your source of altar supplies."

The witch's altar is a place to take in God, just as a Roman Catholic receives the host kneeling at a cathedral altar. If you seek to receive the Goddess's divine energy and spiritual sustenance from crystals that you have placed on your altar, I ask again: check your source. Some crystals are gained by dynamiting mountains. We cannot receive God's grace through a practice that threatens Her well-being, the health of the Planet.

The altar is also each and every one of us, body and spirit. When we are attuned to our unique, inner nature we take in God's grace and healing better than from any crystal or at any Wiccan altar. When we listen to

SIÐHE

My love he is of Elvishkin;
  his people did not leave
This land, when distant voices called
  them cross the sundering seas.
Alone they tarried hither shore
  and numbered were their days,
Dwindling with their heritage
  and long forgotten ways.
For this is now the age of Men,
  and mortals rule the towns.
Mindkind raises kingdoms,
  and mankind casts them down.
Of Tir-na-Nog the Undying Land,
  never the tale is sung.
My love knows not his lineage,
  nor speaks the golden tongue.
But truth is told in noble heart
  and golden shadowed hair;
He walks in gentle wisdom,
  his bearing tall and fair.
For he's the last of Elven kind
  in Eastern lands to roam,
And never will the White Ship come
  to bear him safely home.
Though I am but a mortal maid,
  of mankind's flesh was born,
Yet I do love him deeply
  and my heart is sorely torn;
For though my people rule this day,
  my love wakes memories dear
Of golden times now passed away,
  when Faerie was near.

—*Morning Glory Zell*

GE Vol. VI, No. 60 (Oimelc 1974) 30

the sure voice within us we are more in touch with our spiritual objectives than when simply at a favorite beach spot or on a high mountain. Are you asking "What does a sense of selfhood have to do with ecology?" When we listen to our sure voice within, when we find this special nature in ourselves, we discover that we ourselves are sacred, and that each of us is a living part of the earth, a moving, breathing part of the Earth.

Which means that we each must receive the care we are struggling to find for our planet. So, I offer a simple ritual. Look at your specific commitments to the planet, and then see if you can make the same specific commitments to your own wellbeing. In other words, here are some questions that you might ask yourself as part of the ritual: what do you pollute your body with; what sort of pesticides and additives go into your meals; do you forget that you, yourself, are a nonrenewable resource (do you always figure there's no reason why you can't take on yet one more useful endeavor to help out your friends? Or maybe you are a political activist who is still burning yourself out?); do you struggle to promote farming methods that keep the soil rich yet live a lifestyle that is devoid of emotional nourishment? These were just examples. What do you pledge to the earth — do you need to pledge the same to yourself?

Francesca De Grandis, author of *Be a Goddess!*, *Goddess Initiation*, and *Be A Teen Goddess!*, lives midst the trees and sylphs of Pennsylvania. She provides professional spiritual counseling—renegade style—by phone for people all over the world, people of any spiritual tradition or happy lack thereof. A pivotal influence in the literary and spiritual culture of Goddess Spirituality, many of her poems have anonymously entered the oral and written literature of earth-centered and Goddess-centered spirituality. So, have her innovative magical techniques.
www.outlawbunny.com

This piece has also been published in the British magazine Quest *and in the* San Francisco Greens *newspaper.*

The Bullwinkian Tradition:
Ancient Secrets Now Revealed

by S.T. Crowe

THE EFFECTIVE PRACTICE OF THE Art Magical need not depend upon archetypes, symbology or accoutrements gleaned from ancient sources. Whatever wellspring produces the needed mindset is to be esteemed and respected.

While in an introspective mood I asked the Powers-That-Be to lead me to fresh sources of wisdom and meaning. Then it was that some discerning soul turned the channel on our communal television at work and I saw, with fresh insight, the new source of untapped power and knowledge!

Then it was that I saw...**The Bullwinkle Show.** Thus was born the **Bullwinkian Tradition** and its flagship organization, the Bullwinkle J. Moose Memorial Coven #1.

In order to fully appreciate the Tradition of the Moose, one must understand the archetypes. The following chart, simplified for the sake of space, will serve to explain the major Bullwinkian deities:

Bullwinkle the Horned God
Rocky the Messenger of the Gods
Boris Badenov the Trickster
Natasha Fatale the Devourer Goddess
Capt. Peter Peachfuzz the God of the Waters
Dudley Do-Right the God of Justice
Nell Fenwick the Goddess of Love
Inspector Fenwick the Divine Androgyne
Tom Slick the God of Quick Results
George Of The Jungle the Forest Lord
Super Chicken the Shapeshifter
Fearless Leader Marshaller of the Forces of the Left-Hand Path
Snidely Whiplash the God of Boundaries and Limitations

It should be noted that these archetypes are not without parallels in other Pagan and Neo-Pagan paths. Boris, for example, bears a strong resemblance to Coyote of Native American belief, while Capt. Peter Peachfuzz not only is akin to Cthulhu and other oceanic deities, but can he likened to the Divine Fool, common in most cultures. Tom Slick, as God of Quick Results, is virtually indistinguishable from Voodoo's Saint Expedite. And so it goes. The reader is invited to search for other parallels while meditating on the hidden meanings of Bella and Ursula; the Martians; and Roger Ramjet.

Ritual

In keeping with the simplistic nature of the original cartoons (which, legend has it, were instructional videos for the inner group, the Circle of Jay Ward), ritual is "bare bones" and purely symbolic.

Casting the circle: The Priestess dons the Kirwood Derby and walks the perimeter of the circle intoning the Holy Mantra: "Eeny Meeny Chili Beanie! The spirits ate about to speak!" Antiphonal chanting from a chorus discreetly hidden behind draperies sets the mood for the rite itself.

If the rite takes place in a waning moon, the Pottsylvanian National Anthem is next sung, led by a short man in a black fedora.

Cakes and Ale

This consists of Cheerios and Strawberry Milk. Lest it be thought that this represents an attempt by "boomers" to recapture the halcyon days of youth, realize that Cheerios have a deep and esoteric meaning. The central hole is emblematic of the Void of Chaos from which all things came in primordial times, while the hard and crusty exterior represents the hard nature of physical life, which only the will of the magician can transcend after years of spiritual discipline and practice. Strawberry Milk, on the other hand, is the physical reminder of life's sweetness which can be savored at leisure, yet returned to thc carth at last, for nothing is our own–it is only lent us. Hence the Cheerios, too, in *time* will transform into that which must to the earth be returned. Sometimes, it is said, in haste. (Origin of "Hush -A Boom??")

But on to the ritual of Cakes and Ale itself. The Priestess holds aloft the plate of cakes while the Man in Black, wearing the Holy Moosehorns, picks up one and says "Watch me pull a cake off the plate!"

The chorus: "What? Again?!"

Man in Black: "Nothing up my sleeve. Presto!" (Eats cake)

Priestess, passing around the cakes, says, "And now here's something we hope you'll *really* like."

Accoutrements

- The Kirwood Derby is worn by the Officiating Elder.
- The Holy Moosehorns are worn by the Man in Black when acting as the God.
- There is no knife, staff or pentacle, and the only cup upon the altar is that which holds the Strawberry Milk.

- The incense is known as the "Holy Smokes," although in recent years this has come to denote the favored activity of those who enjoy endless reruns of **The Bullwinkle Show.**
- There are no brooms used in the Bullwinkian Tradition, although sacred shovels are seen, especially when the forest lord is accompanied by his "good doggie Shep." Due to the size of Shep, snow shovels are the tools of preference.

Initiation

Like Seax Wicca, initiation is by personal decision to follow the Old Toons and no ritual acts by other parties are necessary or desirable. One simply kneels and says devoutly and loudly, "From head to toe do I devote myself utterly to moose and squeeril, dahling."

From that moment one is a Bullwinkian—and the odyssey begins.

GE Vol. XXVIX, No. 117 (Jan.-Feb.1997) 17

The Candles Are Blowin' Out Again

a filke song by **Bill Beattie,** *editor of* Shadowplay, Australia

How many robes can a Witch ignite
While dancing too close to the flame?
How many words from the Grimm
     Brothers' tales
Can you really expect to "reclaim"?
And how many chants fall as flat as a tack
When you mispronounce each Sacred
     Name?
The candles, my friend, are blowin'
     out again.
The candles are blowin' out again.

How many times can the incense go wild
And firemen break down your door?
How many times can athames get
     dropped
And spear peoples' feet to the floor?
Yes, and how many times can you
     brandish your wand

And whack the HP on the jaw?
The candles, my friend, are blowin'
     out again.
The candles are blowin' out again.

How many years can you do the same
     rite
And still get the words mostly wrong?
And how many spells of "Hereditary
     Craft"
Quote verses from Erica Jong?
And how many times can your Sabbat
     Great Rite
Last less than a half minute long?
The candles, my friend, are blowin'
     out again.
The candles are blowin' out again.

GE Vol. XXV, NO. 97 (Summer 1992) 2

Ritual: Ancient and Modern

*by **Ramfis S. Firethorn** (**John DeCles**) (art by István Kolonics)*

 HEN I BEGAN TO STUDY MAGIC and ritual, I took my teachers at their word and accepted the things they said and taught, and found that a pretty good way to proceed. The rituals worked and the magic achieved its purposes. But then I came to the point in my studies where religion became an important subject, not merely a corollary to the practice of magic, and a new set of parameters became the center of my attentions. I was lucky enough to have teachers who held the whole broad spectrum of knowledge to be suitable as source material, and the only restriction put upon my studies was that I should never close my mind to any idea or datum, and always be prepared to discover my conclusions insufficient.

That beginning of "graduate studies" was twenty five years ago, and the journey from the practice of ritual magic and basic earth religions to the present landscape of polymorphous magical and religious practice has been an odd one, to say the least. Looking back on the formal initiations of 1962, 1965, and the 70s, I am astonished at the growth of what has come to be called Neo-Paganism and the texture of the paradigm which has become established as a result of that growth.

I am also somewhat disturbed to discover what I have come to think of as a Wicker Curtain drawn across the landscape of scholarship and practice in that Neo-Pagan community; not as a deliberate act by any person or group, but rather as a result of a growing orthodoxy unwilling to consider some of the problems of a Neo-Pagan community within the Mega-Culture; an orthodoxy which seems to me to be accepting data from that cultural matrix which it avows to eschew as basis for further construction.

The single example I wish to examine here has to do with the structure of ritual, its significance to the mind and spirit, and the shifts which may have occurred between the times of general historical Paganism and contemporary Neo-Paganism. I would like to begin with what I consider to be an excellent analysis of the subject of structure, that in *Real Magic* by P. E. I. Bonewits.

While it is true that Bonewits is no Levy-Strauss or Malinowski, his analysis of the structure of ritual is sharp and incisive; and he is far more accessible to the reader concerned with actually *working with* the materials than with uncommitted learning. Perhaps more important than Bonewits' considerable scholarship, however, is the sheer practical value of his work. One need not accept his somewhat shaky ethical premises in order to make use of his analysis of the structure of ritual in today's world.

Stated briefly, that structure or pattern consists of: *Supplication-Introduction, Reply from the Deity, Identification of the Participants with the Deity, Statement of Requests and Statement of Success.*

Bonewits has given many examples of this pattern in his book, and I can commend his chapter on the fundamental patterns of ritual as excellent reading for anyone who is working on constructing a new ritual.

It should be understood, however, that this structure applies to the *overall structure,* and not to the 'particular parts' of ritual. There are, in addition to this pattern, particular structural elements that will be inter-culturally consistent in the construction of particular *types* of rituals. A *Mystery,* for instance, is a ritual which always contains certain specific elements which are not necessarily a part of the above cited overall structure. An *Initiation* is a particular kind of ritual, again containing elements which are consistent from culture to culture, but not requisite to the *overall* structure of ritual per se.

It should go without saying that various elements of various ritual forms may be part and parcel of one another, so long as they do not violate the overall structure; for that structure has particular significance to the human unconscious, and if it is not adhered to, the unconscious will not respond; any more than the unconscious will respond to tales meant as *myths* or *stories* if they do not adhere to the structures of those two recognizable patterns.

The section of the structure which I here wish to consider is the interface between the first and second, that is, between Supplication-Introduction and Reply from the Deity; and to some degree with the third, Identification with the Deity; for it is here, I feel, that the greatest differences are manifest between what we know of Ancient Pagan practice and Modern Neo-Pagan practice.

Bonewits' examples are all excellent (if somewhat colored by his views of the different religions which he cites), but they are all examples of religious rituals as practiced by religious groups in the latter half of the Twentieth Century. Even the most cursory examination of the rituals of those groups of whose practice we have records will show that major changes in the particular

contents of rituals have occurred over the past two millennia. Indeed, the central theses of worship have altered in some of those religions to the point where the historical adherents would not be able to recognize their own religions over the course of a century or so.

The most obvious, and significant, change comes in the matter of sacrifice.

Whatever details may be subject for argument, the single most incontrovertible practice of ancient religion is that of sacrifice: the giving back of some portion of what one has to the Deity(ies) with Whom one is spiritually and physically connected. I leave to others the discussion of the significance of this practice. I have read many good and reasonable

explanations for the practice, from the point of view of anthropologists, psychologists, archaeologists, and lots of other ologists as well; it must be left to the reader to decide to which to subscribe. The bottom line is that the practice is generally regarded as positive for a culture by any not committed to what I shall here call the Post Palestinian Heresy. (Note that the scholar who originated the term *Palestinian Heresy* meant by it the absurd idea that there is only one God. I am referring here to the usage of *Post Palestinian Heresy* as meaning those beliefs which come after the advent and cultural dominance of the one God belief systems.)

Sacrifice, in general, comes in two forms. That which is usually placed first is the offering of First Fruits: *aparchai, primitae,* or *premices.* The second is animal sacrifice.

The offering of Premices is an act of ritual abandonment and its psychological significance to the group is usually clear. It can also be quite powerful, as in the example set by Alexander the Great in the Gedrosian desert, when he poured out the last helmet full of water in offering; and thereby placed the entire army on a sudden and equal footing in the matter of survival; an act which revived hope and solidarity and got everyone through a particularly desperate time.

The sacrifice of Premices is not unfamiliar to Neo-Pagans, and I think most have little difficulty with its practice in various forms.

The offering of Animal Sacrifice is another matter. Very few people are ready to anthropomorphize a carrot to the point where they are unwilling to see it die; yet the same people who eat burgers as often as possible are terrified at the idea of killing a bull in honor of their choice Deity.

It should be understood that in ancient times, or even in times as recent as the 1940s, meat was not an option offered at every meal. In an affluent society, one might expect to eat meat (unless one had ethical objections) perhaps once or twice in a week. In a less than affluent society the incidence was far less often. In pre-agricultural societies, the consumption of meat was a matter of the success of the tribal hunters, with the help of the Gods. The rationale of offering a portion of the spoils of the hunt back to the Deities who aided in the hunt is pretty clear. The precise nature of that offering, across a broad spectrum of cultures, is curious. On the one hand, thigh bones are most often burnt on the altar to the Deity. On the other, horns and skulls are set up in the sanctuary. I have encountered, as yet, no satisfactory explanation of the choice of thigh bones as the offering of choice. Horns and skulls would seem a little more explicable.

With the advent of the herding of animals, the probability of meat in the diet did increase; but the actual incidence of meat consumption was still fairly low, at least compared to the consumption of meat among modern Neo-Pagans. The rituals by which a portion was given back to the Gods remained quite similar, or even identical, to those rituals in cultures where meat was acquired primarily by hunting.

The important thing in the cases of both kinds of cultures was that Animal Sacrifice did occur, was the center and most prominent feature of religious ritual, and served a social as well as religiomagical purpose. That social purpose was, of course, the sharing amongst the community of the larger part of the animal sacrificed: the kill of the hunt in pre-agricultural communities, and the carefully raised and husbanded animal in herding cultures. (It is important to note here how really *difficult* it is to raise an animal for food. Keeping a bull alive to maturity is a matter of long-term commitment. You must protect and feed and care for domestic animals. They don't come quick to hand off a shelf, all neat-

ly wrapped: at least, not until very, very recently.) In such circumstances, ritual sacrifice of animals was not only a socially positive activity, but a necessary one, if the whole community should be served.

It is here that the precise nature of ritual structure must be examined, for it is here that the divergence between ancient and modern ritual structure becomes apparent.

When you kill a large animal there is still a lot of work to be done. The ululations of the women as the blow is struck demark the supreme emotional moment; there is still the business of cutting up the carcass and cooking it. The thigh bones go on the altar, with some of the fat, and that part is burned in offering. You still have eight hundred pounds of beef to process before the feasting happens, and that takes a lot of time and a lot of work: and that time and work *is part of the ritual.*

Even when the offering is of Premices, baskets of barley and other grains need to be processed before the portion allotted to the people is ready to consume. Many vegetables need simply to be cooked.

In short, a part of ritual time is *cooking* time.

When we move from the cooking being part of the ritual to a version in which the offerings are pre-prepared foodstuffs, we have lost an essential feature of ancient ritual, and, I would maintain, we have lost something valuable. The things consumed in the feast are *not* a part of what was offered up at the altar, or even if they are, it is largely a matter of symbol rather than gut-level reality.

Looking at the scriptures of Judaism, we find precise instructions for ritual sacrifice that match up pretty well to all the religions of the region in Historic Pagan times. In the New Testament of the Christians, we find Jesus clearly discussing the conditions of ritual sacrifice as a given. It is only *later* than the penning of these works, and their adaptation by followers, that both Christians and Jews abandon the ways of their ancestors and establish rituals which exclude ritual sacrifice. And only much later, with the suppression of Paganism in general, that the practice acquires any negative connotations whatever.

It is this *moment,* this *place* in religious

ritual that I think needs consideration. The sequence that begins with Supplication-Introduction, Reply from the Deity, should lead, if we consider the practices of our Cultural Ancestors, to the Sacrifice (whether of Premices or Animals) and thence to Identification with the Deity through ritual feasting.

Historically, the time needed to cook the bull (or the barley) was filled, at the very least, with music, dancing, and other celebratory activities, such as the singing, dancing, clapping, and so forth which Bonewits cites as moving the group toward the ecstatic trance state. It was in this state, after a considerable time with the bull over the barbecue, that the Identification with Deity, in the form of the feast, occurred.

This pattern, in which the preparation of the feast is given sacred status, is preserved in a number of religions: but in such a diminished, symbolic form as to require an esoteric scorecard to be noticeable. And then it is not the shared feast of tangible delicacies which are the medium of the festal moment, but tasteless, symbolic icons; or at the best, good bread and wine, or good cakes and ale; neither of which is likely to have been prepared, except symbolically by a blessing, during the ritual.

The logic of the Dominant Paradigm has it that the Sacrifice is no longer necessary. In one form or another, this is a view held by all but a few of those who subscribe to the Post Palestinian Heresy. But I would ask: who has so much or so little that giving a part back is not a reasonable act in attaining Identification with the Deity?

I would suggest that continuity between Ancient Historical Paganism and Modern Neo-Paganism is a thing which may perhaps be of some value. And I would suggest that the efficacy of ritual might well be enhanced greatly by the restoration to ritual structure of that most central of Ancient Pagan religious activities, the Sacrifice.

I do not mean that you must all rush out and sacrifice a goat at your next sabat. I *do* mean that there is a place in the ritual structure for *giving back,* and for the preparation of the foods of the feast. A basket in which are placed things of use to the populace (which in our times may mean the poor and homeless of your community) can be a suitable sacrificial altar, so long as you take care to put in it the *best _portion ,* and put it there first. If you must content yourselves with short rituals, then learn to cook quickly; this, to some degree, will determine the nature of the sacrifice. Chiefly, the biggest change in ritual practice which this activity will bring about will be a greater awareness of the nature and value of the food of the sacral feast, and a greater honoring of those who prepare the food; who in many Ancient Cultures *were* the priests and priestesses.

In this manner I believe the structure which P.E.I. Bonewits has set forth from observation of modern religious ritual can be completed and linked back to that of ancient religious ritual, so that the form becomes: *Supplication-Introduction, Sacrifice, Reply from the Deity (During the Preparation of the Sacrifice for Consumption), Identification of the Participants with the Deity, Statement of Requests and Statement of Success.* It will be noted that in this format the reading, dancing, singing, etc., of the Reply From Deity become an upward movement toward the Identification With Deity, ecstasis, rather than an interruption, which so often occurs.

In closing, let me offer the following images: that of the sacrificial altar of the Ancients, with its small (or sometimes large) fire, the smoke of the offering and the incense rising up to the bright heavens while the worshipers join in the festal moment, waiting a turn at the barbecue, exhausted from their dancing: and the cauldron of the Witches, over the fire at the center of the Circle, filled not with abstract symbols but with the simmering tasty stew which has been concocted by priestess and community together, a scrumptious repast under the brightness of the moon where all have danced with the same spirits who dwelt in the wood and accepted offerings in Ancient Times.

This, too, is a circle which has been broken, and which can be retraced in the dancing sands of time.

GE Vol. XXX, No. 125 (Nov.-Dec. 1998) 8–11

Lord Moonwhistle's
Guide
to Perfectly Wretched Ritual (or How to Have a BAD Ritual)

written by **Lord Moonwhistle**
(illustrated by **David Ball***)*

Lord Moonwhistle is a 13ᵗʰ degree ipsissimus of a tradition so ancient and secret that a mere beginner like you *cannot possibly have even heard of it. Sit back and prepare to be enlightened.*

IRST OF ALL, WHATEVER YOU DO, don't send out flyers more than a few days in advance. This will ensure that there will be a lot of last minute confusion. (Real Witches should be psychic enough to know about the ritual without any notice.) The flyer should not have a contact number—who wants to get all those crank calls? And directions to the site should either be omitted or be confusing.

Tell people once they arrive that they have to change into ritual robes, and get out some odd item needed for the ritual not mentioned in advance. This will keep people off base. Some will not have a robe, most will not have red and green ribbons, or whatever other macguffin you have thought up. Don't warn people if your ritual will be skyclad. Just start taking off your clothes.

The script should be in 9 point type so it all fits on one page. It should be written in great detail, leaving nothing to be spontaneous. It should be passed out just before the ritual, or, at the earliest, at 5 pm for a 7 pm ritual. (It won't start on time anyway. See below.) You can also write the ritual out on 3 by 5 cards, which can be dropped, necessitating a search similar to one for a contact lens, and ensuring the cards will be put out of order, and thus the ritual will skip from end to beginning to middle. You and your coven and other friends should be the ones to take the main parts in ritual.

If you thought it up, you should be able to decide who should be in it. Since it is good to involve people, have as many parts as possible, so that everyone *can* participate. Having 13 people put on a ritual for 2 standing around in the circle watching is about right.

Don't tell people until the last minute that a potluck is planned. Some people will pick something up on route; others will bring nothing and be embarrassed. This is a good way to get an assortment of chips and dip, with no substantial food to ground people. Don't bother to remind people to bring dishes and such—just provide cheap flimsy paper plates. It's so much fun to watch people spill food on their ritual robes, or better yet, hot food on their bare skin. Don't bother to mention that some people are vegetarians, or that some have food allergies. Make sure there are no labels on the foods, or what labels there are can't be read. This is good for a laugh when one of the vegetarians realizes the chili has beef in it, and some excitement when someone goes into anaphylactic shock.

Start late. The later the better. Not just Pagan Standard Time, but really, really late. After all, none of these people have anything better to do. The record currently stands at starting at noon for a ritual which was supposed to begin at 7:30 the previous evening.

Have interminable announcements, begun by asking, "Does anyone have anything to announce?" and letting anyone who wants to get up and natter on and on, preferably in a voice low enough to be inaudible to half of the people present.

Make sure people have to stand for a long time, preferably while one person is doing all the talking. Foreign languages are good for this. The more obscure the ritual is the better. This is a mystery religion, after all. If people understand what's going on, they might be able to criticize you. Be sure to mix in as many different cultures, deities from different pantheons, and motifs as possible. Don't bother to find out how to pronounce any of these names. (After all, these deities and symbols don't really exist—it's all psychological, isn't it?)

You may prefer to hold a monocultural ritual to a deity of your choice in an ancient language that nobody—including yourself—knows how to pronounce. This is perfect for a public ritual to which beginners are invited—let them see a really powerful ritual for their first time.

Be sure to preach and harangue people at some point in the ritual, preferably about some obscure political or ethical issue. Pagans all agree on everything, shouldn't they? If you bring up nuclear energy or animal rights during the ritual, everyone will naturally concur with your opinions.

Put strong wine in all the chalices—that is the only good symbol for whatever it is the stuff in the chalice is supposed to represent. But don't tell everyone—a little wine never hurt anyone. Make sure whatever you are using for cakes is dry and crumbly, and goes around *after* the wine.

There is no need to bother matching the ritual to the place, time of year, or number of people attending. If it worked for your coven of five, it will work for 250. Why shouldn't the same ritual work for Spring Equinox as did the one for Fall Equinox? Be sure that any

ritual in which the central moment involves the significant lighting of one or more candles is held outdoors, preferably someplace windy. And remember there is no need to look over an outdoor site at night for an evening ritual. There won't be that much difference between full daylight and full dark, will there?

Don't be concerned about whether people can hear what you say or see what you do. What's important is that they are there, witnessing your great ritual. When you do have enough space outdoors to have a really large circle of people, standing one deep, holding hands, so that the circle is at least an acre, make sure that all the working is done at the middle of the circle, with voices and gestures appropriate to the living room in your apartment. It's also fine to say your stage directions out loud or even better, whisper them loudly to other ritual participants in such a way that they are more confused than when you began. It can also be useful to explain everything aloud in great detail. The best way to handle this is to explain what is going to happen, then, as it is happening, explain it further, and then reiterate what has just happened. If necessary, use a bullhorn.

Your job is to be High Priestess, which means you should have a good time, and derive profound spiritual meaning from what you are doing. Whether anyone else does is his or her business. You can't do it for them anyway. If you go into trance and space out completely, so much the better—people will have a vicarious experience of ecstasy. You can also have all the priestesses aspect, leaving no one designated to bring them out of trance. People who are aspecting don't need anyone to look after them, bring them back, get them food, etc, afterwards. After all, they are experienced Priestesses, and should know how to do this.

Each person should have a private audience with the Goddess; this is as true for large groups as it is for small ones. There is no reason to provide anything for everyone else to do besides witnessing these chats from afar. They are supposed to be private, after all. The other people in the ritual can chant, of course, but they may tire of this after the first hour or so.

For a guided meditation, have inconsistent background music, or even better yet, background noise, like traffic and train crossings. Use the guided meditation to go someplace grim, like the underworld, and leave people there for a long time. Go out for a beer.

Steep, high hills are holy to many people, and thus an ideal spot for a ritual. Even a very large ritual where the circle will have to go up and down the hill is suitable.

One charming way to do a ritual is to lead people deep into the woods, stand in whatever clearing you can find, hold hands, and wait for the Goddess to inspire you. At the present writing, Fall, 1999, mutterings about the Blair Witch will add to the thrill.

Candles and bonfires are sacred fires and you do not need to take safety precautions. You do not have to worry about long hair, trailing sleeves and the like, because sacred fires never get out of hand.

If you make a mistake, STOP. Call attention to your flub. Apologize. Start over. If you make several mistakes, blow up and refuse to finish the ritual. Leave people hanging.

You get extra points for thoroughness if you have the plumbing, electricity, or heat break down just before the ritual starts. Try to fix it while other people are doing the ritual. Of course the ultimate for public rituals is to arrive to find the door to the rented space locked, and be unable to find out who has a key. However, this means the ritual may not actually happen at all, and you will not be able to show off your expertise. You can console yourself with dramatic and important histrionics and chewing out the employees present who have no idea where the key might be.

In public, rented space, you can use chalk to draw diagrams on the carpet. These will of course be sealed later by having candle wax

dripped on them. This insures that you can use this place again and again. By the way, a ritual in public rented space does *not* need gatekeepers—it is after all *public*. Drunks, fundies, and passers-by should be able to come in freely, so as to experience the Love of the Goddess. If you find that the public space you have arranged for in a park or other open space adjoins another event, such as a family reunion or a group picnic, go ahead and do your ritual. You have as much right to be there as they do. Do not change any of your plans. Another good idea for location is, if you can, schedule your Samhain ritual half a block from the local Halloween "Haunted House" or some such. You may even get a few new people out of this arrangement.

Invite reporters; even better yet, a TV crew. Don't tell people in advance, so that the ritual will be natural and spontaneous. Flash attachments should be used, because most rituals are too dimly lit for good photographs otherwise.

There is no need to turn off your phone, answering machine, cell phone, fax or beeper. You have to stay connected, don't you? People need to learn to ignore these sounds, as well as those of babies crying, sirens, and foghorns. However, avoid any place within the sound of church bells—we don't want you to disappear in a puff of smoke, do we?

If, in your tradition, you, as high priest, are the only one who can take down the circle, drink until you pass out so people will have to wait until you wake and or sober up enough to open the circle and leave. You do not need to dismiss or banish everything that was called up. Grounding is optional, and there is no need for any kind of closure, because you want to see these people again. If the ritual is over, they might feel free to leave and never come back.

Blow up the altar at the end. A grand finale is always dramatic. This can be accomplished with the generous use of flash powder, sparklers and the like.

If all else fails, blame anything that goes wrong on Mercury retrograde, or the Moon void-of-course.

GE Vol. XXXII, No. 134 (May-June 2000) 12–14

The Magic of the Mask

by Lauren Raine, MFA

"Making a mask is a way of finding our faces before we were born."
—Stephen Larsen, The Mythic Imagination

IN RECENT YEARS, THERE HAS BEEN a growing interest in ritual theatre, not only within the Pagan world, but in many different kinds of communities. Within these events the Gods and Goddesses are reclaimed, elemental forces of nature are personified, and collective and planetary archetypes are invoked and voiced in new ways. Beyond the specific intent of these sacred dramas, what I also see being reclaimed is a conversant world, an ecology of many kinds of lives, some manifest, some more subtle. We seek communion, which is the endeavor in all sacred arts: to commune with our deepest selves, with each other and all our Relations, and with the living Earth. Ultimately, in a powerful ritual or a grace-filled work of art, that conversation is a circle that holds all of these presences.

The art of the mask is a potent tool. Over the years, as a maskmaker, I've learned to view my art with a great deal of awe. A mask, in traditional cultures, enabled performers to wear the face of a deity, a totem spirit, an ancestor; to invite those archetypal intelligences to enter them. Masks were never made lightly; there were many proscribed procedures to be followed in fashioning a sacred mask, and a great deal of psychic preparation was necessary before a ceremony was performed. Like all consecrated ritual tools, masks were activated and deactivated with great respect.

Among native peoples of central Mexico, for example, masks used for corn and rain dances were destroyed after a number of years, as it was believed that they accrued over time too much power, and could become dangerous, as the spirit of the deity increasingly inhabited the mask. This same sensibility is found in Noh Theatre; Noh masks are created according to traditions that go back many generations, and represent stories that have firmly become animated by the mask. Actors will often sit for days with a mask, allowing the persona to enter them, to create fusion.

An artist I know once told me of an African mask at the Museum of Art in Milwaukee that, legend had it, sweated. She said she went to view it over a number of days, and sure enough, there it was, if carefully observed, sweating away. How is it possible something like that can occur in a glass case before hundreds of people, unnoticed? Magic is literally on display.

Today, masks are generally created for fun or as "art objects." Or perhaps in workshops, as therapeutic tools to help participants express unclaimed aspects of themselves. A profound exercise for a group that can make the psychological commitment to such a project is to make a series of "Masks of Self"—masks that might be named "the Inner Child," "the Monster," "the Judge," "The Crone," or "The Warrior" are created, and their stories are revealed both within their creation, and in the performance and use of the mask.

To perform, in a ritual context, the great archetypes, the Goddesses and the Gods, the Power Animals, the Ancestors, is to call those qualities into oneself. Be warned: these are magical tools which become infused with the energy they are given; it's equally important to "devoke," to release the archetypes, to return to the grace of the mundane. Otherwise, we risk inappropriate inflation. Be warned as well; masks have a way of manifesting in our inner selves, and our outer lives, and transforming us if we allow it to happen. Or sometimes even if we don't.

I had an affirmation of this with a mask I made for Kali, inspired by a Kali puja I attended. Kali began to figure in my dreams—a great, laughing Being with Her sword and Her flames, helping me to cut away threads of the past I needed to release. At the time, I had just opened a gallery in California, and wanted to use the mask in some way, but, being new in town, I knew no dancers who would perform with it. I did, however, hang Kali in our opening show. At the opening, I noticed a young woman standing enraptured before the mask. As we talked, I learned she was a professional dancer. Her specialty was dancing with fire. She also had Kali tattooed quite prominently on her navel. Would I be interested in doing something with her, she asked? The result—Serene danced the Kali mask exquisitely at our next opening, flames bursting from all of her fingers.

I have experienced, as a maskmaker for collectors, theatre and ritual events, too many wonders to approach this creative mystery as theory. The masks, whether I want them to be or not, are alive. And like all worthy works of art and Craft, they commune in ways visible and invisible. I can't begin to say I understand it. I don't think, as artists/magicians, we necessarily have to comprehend it—maybe we only have to move over and let these forces work through us.

While making a Green man mask a few years ago, I had several nights when I felt a sensual male presence around me. If I closed my eyes, I saw eyes peering at me from among rustling leaves. When the mask was finished, that mysterious persona left me, going, I believe, to the man I made it for, who now is a 12-foot-tall Greenman on stilts at festivals, planting trees as he goes. I believe the radiant presence of the Greenman is more potent in his work than either of us imagine.

To make a mask, to wear a mask and find its inner voice, and to remove it as well, are ways of entering the Dream, with all of its mystery, contradictions, and revelations. Masks are tools that can help us to enter the house of our multi-dimensional selves.

Lauren Raine: "After studying temple mask traditions in Bali, I created 30 multicultural "Masks of the Goddess", a project that lasted for 10 years and traveled throughout the U.S. I found myself in a grand conversation that continually grew as others used the collection, filling them with energy and new meaning. I'm still making masks in 2008—many of them can be seen on my website." *www.rainewalker.com*

GE Vol. XXXII, No. 134 (May-June 2000) 20–21

Hymn to Gaia

by *Tom Williams, CAW*

When o'er your dreaming hills the
    dawning day ignites its fire,
And on your seas the light's caress
    awakens wind and spray,
Your breath bids branch and bud push
    forth to echo your desire,
And in a womb a heart begins your
    rhythmic hymn to play.
The eye that opens upon itself, an eye
    that's opened before,
Seeks knowledge deep with each repeat,
    the better to adore.

> *So Yes! Yes! to the beating heart,*
> *That echoes the surge of the sea,*
> *And sends blood's course,*
> *With primal force,*
> *Urged on by the will to be.*
> *And Yes! Yes! to the pulse that flows,*
> *The stream of life's rebirth,*
> *The sacred flame,*
> *Intones your name,*
> *Oh Gaia, soul of the Earth.*

When out of seed and spore and shoot and
    egg your song is raised,
From lovers' bliss your holy kiss awakens
    flesh anew
To feel and search and to behold and find a
    voice for praise,
And then to sing beneath your sky one
    sacred hymn to you.
A song of life begat from death that only
    life can give,
Begins and ends with one refrain that
    heralds the ages: "I'll Live!"

> *So Yes! Yes! to the song of life, Where*
> *all the voices are one,*
> *The pulse and beat,*
> *That all repeat,*
> *"What's ended is begun!"*
> *And Yes! Yes! to the quick'ning heart,*
> *That bids the darkness be spurned,*
> *A wild tattoo,*
> *That shouts anew,*
> *"Great Goddess, I have returned!"*

You dance upon the spiral stair of
    chromosome and gene,
Oh soft of eye and red of maw you pare
    and prune the tree.
In many forms I've sung your song,
    through many eyes I've seen,
In many forms I'll wake again, more fully
    yours to be.
Many's the dance I've danced with you,
    one round a pale cold mask,
The next a glow in a mother's eye as into
    Earth I'm cast.

> *So Yes! Yes! to the dance of death,*
> *Oh Kali devour me whole,*
> *Take me home,*
> *Consume my bones,*
> *And sing your song to my soul.*
> *And Yes! Yes! to the Wheel of Life,*
> *Oh Isis restore me anew,*
> *Return my breath,*
> *To laugh at death,*
> *And revel, oh Gaia, in you.*

When from your warm embrace I'm torn,
    in fields of stars to dwell,
Your voice, a sigh on cosmic dust, calls
    after your lover, "Return!
Embrace my green and loam-filled breast,
    drink of my scented well,
Ignite my fire with love's desire, shout
    through my winds, 'Return!'"
Then longing for my lover's arms will draw
    me back to you,
And in a cloak of soil-born flesh I'll swear
    my troth anew.

> *And Yes! Yes! I will dance with you,*
> *And forsake the fields of stars,*
> *And plunge me deep,*
> *In the Earth to keep,*
> *My vow to Lady and Lord,*
> *And Yes! Yes! I will live again,*
> *And ensoul the greening Earth,*
> *At my Mother's breast,*
> *In the hour of death,*
> *I pledge you my rebirth.*

Vol. XXV, No. 96 (Ostara 1992) inside front

Chapter 7.
Magick, Arts,
& Crafts
Introduction
by *Chas S. Clifton*

ACK IN THE 1970S, THE IDEA WAS PUT FORTH THAT A WITCH WAS A "BENDER" OF FATE, because "witch" supposedly came from an older word meaning "to bend." Actually, this assertion is not true: the "witch" of witch-hazel (which is a pliable shrub) and the "witch" of Witchcraft have completely different English language roots. (And if you don't believe me, look them up yourself in the *Oxford English Dictionary* at your local library.) But the people who made that false connection were still trying to express an idea about magic—or "magick" to those who wish to preserve Aleister Crowley's distinction between stage magic (tricks) and "creating change in accordance with the Will." Some forms of Paganism are about "doing things," beyond just celebration or attunement with nature's cycles.

In this chapter, Frater Khedmel of the Ordo Templi Astartes discusses what magick is and what sort of person can succeed as a ceremonial magician. Magick at base is a solo procedure, and famed fantasy writer Marion Zimmer Bradley describes how a home altar plays an important part in the Craft as a miniature temple: "It is only those affluent householders who have inherited, or acquired, an enormous ancestral mansion, who can be reasonably expected to devote an entire room to a household Temple. For everyone else, a table, folding desk or bureau makes an excellent altar. It can be kept in a small corner of the bedroom, a niche in a sewing room, a convenient closet, or what have you."

Another well-known writer, Robert Anton Wilson, explores the uncertain boundary between magic and science, asserting for example that,

> the instruments used by these early researchers [shamans] appear to have been the human nervous system itself and, in many cases, certain funny fungi, *i.e.*, mushrooms.... With the aid of these magick brews, evidently, the Witch-doctors were able to imprint, re-imprint and serially imprint their own nervous systems until they became calibrated to the reception of knowledge unavailable to the "normal" untrained human nervous system. In short, the primordial magician did not "guess" the souls of the trees: she (or he) communicated with them directly.

And he cheerfully goes on to suggest that some aspects of magick might be explainable through mathematics, although, as Crowley said, magick is "as dependent on the personal equation as Love."

Other writers explore traditions of handicrafts as magick, and of making a common Halloween jack o'lanterrn but with a difference. To the Pagan, it's not just a pumpkin! Larry Cornett's essay on nature spirits—what some Pagans call *wights*—contains a great deal of useful information in a short space. After all, if you are going to "do things," don't you want all the help that you can get?

What and Why of Magick

by Frater Khedmel, O:.T:.A:.

HENEVER I MEET SOMEONE THAT I really like, and during the course of the conversation, the fact comes to light that I am a practicing Magician, and an Officer in a Magickal Order, I find myself going to great extremes to explain what magick is and why I find it necessary (much less beneficial) to practice it. I will attempt to condense my explanation thus:

Basically, Magick is the Western counterpart to Yoga. One would go into it for much the same reasons that persons today study Yoga. Self improvement, self knowledge, and so on.

These statements are, of course, vast oversimplifications, but they will at least give. us a point from which to discuss the subject.

Perhaps the greatest difference between Magick and Yoga is the matter of the end result which is sought. As with most Eastern Mystical or Magickal systems, Yoga, and the people who really practice it in the Eastern sense, *seek oblivion.* The Western Magician, on the other hand, seeks to expand his identity, or to *identify himself* with "God," rather than to *lose himself* in the ultimate.

The second greatest difference between Eastern and Western Mystical Thought, is in the emphasis placed upon time. To the Western Man, time is of the essence. Not so in the Eastern traditions.

In my opinion, the third greatest difference between these two systems, is the emphasis placed upon "Real World" problems and solutions. The Western Magician seeks to become *a* more effective person in the real world about him. He is not attempting to deny the world as it actually exists, with all its faults. Neither is he attempting to ignore Science, *as* is usually the case with Eastern systems.

These basic differences continue throughout the two systems.

It is for these reasons (and many others) that most Westerners do not find Yoga (or other Eastern systems) as easy or as satisfying as the person from the Oriental traditions would.

Magick is in the Western Mystical Tradition. Magick exalts the Ego, expands the consciousness, and focuses on the uniqueness of the individual.

Magick (in the non-mystical sense) is the application of self-knowledge, self-discipline, and self-control, in order to control other things and (consenting) people. The practice of this control brings more self knowledge, more knowledge about other people, and the universe about you, leading to more control, and so on.

Usually, one's ability expands faster than the average magickal student's available time does. The common complaint is not "I can't" but rather "I haven't gotten to that yet" or "I don't have the time to explore that" or usually, "I'm too busy."

Magick takes time, study and work. It is not easy. It is occasionally dangerous. It requires intelligence and a good education. A strong grounding in any one of the following fields would be very helpful: Ancient History, Anthropology, Archaeology, English or European Literature or Religion (preferably with emphasis on the Old Testament), Psychology, Medicine, most languages (Hebrew, Greek, Latin, Sanskrit, etc.), Statistics, Spherical Trig.... The list is quite long, but I think you can see the general trend. From this you might assume that not everyone could be an "adept" in Magick. Such an assumption is quite correct.

Generally, persons who claim to have had many "mystical experiences" of their own, while not in some training program, *DO NOT* make good High Magick adepts. In other words, kooks, acidheads, and the like need not apply. The reason for this is not what you might expect. Magick is done by the exercise of the practitioner's *will.* Anything which interferes with that willpower means no Magick. It makes no difference what the cause of the loss of willpower is, the results are the same. Nothing happens. There are several additional, lesser reasons, which I will not go into here.

One of the first benefits derived from a study of Magick is the establishment of an awake, conscious, two-way communication link with your sub-conscious (or deep mind). The method is simple, and is not hypnotic. The result is an objective (physical) manifestation. This manifestation is photographable. The method is fairly slow (at first), and requires privacy, peace and quiet, and almost no equipment. The exact method is not a very well kept secret, but I will not aid in revealing it to the un-initiated.

If you like meeting odd people, then being on a recruiting team would give you quite a bit of fun. In this field, one is constantly meeting other persons who believe themselves to be "Mighty magicians before the Lord," Witches, Kahunas, and such, as well as various hangers-on.

We seek, meet, and communicate with these people (or try to) because every once in a while we will find someone who isn't crazy, and who has that certain something which tells us that he or she would make an adept. This winnowing process is slow, and in some cases (when working with Satanists, and other assorted nuts) dangerous physically, emotionally, and spiritually. This is the reason why we usually interview people with a team.

After going through several hundred potential recruits in order to find one or two acceptable people, the really hard part is convincing them that they should join our Order.

The reason for having a Magical Order (also called a Hermetic Lodge) is that such an Order can greatly speed up the training process, while reducing to a very large extent the risk and wasted energy, time, and money. Stated bluntly: This is where it is at, we have it and we know it. We can teach it. We do teach it. It works, and we can prove it.

We are a responsible organization, with responsible people. We want to keep it that way.

Please note that up to now, I have not. mentioned "faith," a common requirement in "low magic" and "witchcraft," etc. I would like to point out also, that I have not loaded a bunch of mystic double-talk on you. The usual blather is of no use, and conceals the simple fact that we mean exactly what we say.

"Faith" is not a requirement for a Magickal student. In fact, "blind faith" would be a great hindrance. It is not necessary for a Magickal student to "believe" anything.

A religious background is important, however that background need not be particularly strong or even consistent, so long as there is either Jewish, Christian, or Moslem exposure during the student's childhood. In this regard, the important factor is that the student has *not* renounced whatever religious training he did receive as a child, however tenuous it may have been.

An O∴T∴A∴ Magickal student is invited, at frequent intervals, to test that which he has learned, and to record such results in his Magickal Record. This record is reviewed at intervals by his instructors. The student is invited to speculate upon the results (or lack of them) which he obtains. Experiments are then suggested. The only "belief" which is encouraged, is in the student's own ability to produce a given result by following a given procedure.

This is not to suggest that there *is* no mystical or religious atmosphere about the practice of Magick. Such practice is often quite an intense experience, however we have attempted (and to some extent succeeded) in deleting the needlessly over-mystical aspects in the practice of the Art, because such excess baggage gets in the way of honest achievement and progress.

The tendency to over-mysticise the practice of Magick was the result of a (largely) defensive mechanism on the part of some very superstitious people who did not understand what and how they were getting the results they did get. In addition, there was an intense propaganda campaign conducted at that time by the Church, which also tended to confuse the issue and becloud the attempts at understanding the principles underlying the practice of the Art.

It is unfortunate that our admittedly clinical approach to the Art sometimes tends to turn away people who have useable talent, but who are so heavily structured that they are unable to accept (and reconcile with their religious views) the scientific method.

The Magician takes a general view. To him, there is no conflict between Science and

Religion, or between Religion and Magick. Others may be creating misunderstandings and conflicts, for whatever reasons they may have.

This is one of the reasons why a Magician has need for tact and diplomacy. He realizes that others are unable or unwilling to adopt such a general view, and may be disturbed, alarmed, or enraged at him for his Art. This is the real reason for the traditional secrecy which usually surrounds the practice of the Art. Such secrecy itself will alarm some people, but usually not as much as if the secrecy was not employed. The simple fact is that what a basically superstitious person does not understand, that person will fear or hate.

This is also one of the reasons for forming a Magickal Lodge. An individual Magician is frequently at the *mercy* of such hate and fear on the part of persons (many of which are in positions of power, of one sort or another), and that such persons may attempt to take forceful measures to suppress or harass that which they fear from lack of understanding. The individual Magician, of ethical persuasion, is at a severe disadvantage in situations of this type. If, however, there is a Magickal Lodge, which the Magician can join or affiliate with in some way, AND IF that Lodge is a legal, responsible organization, such an organization can greatly reduce the hazard to the individual practitioner on several levels. Such a Lodge can also act as a moderating influence in the case of intramagickal disputes.

It is for these reasons (as well as several others) that the O∴T∴A∴ was formed. We seek to take Magick out of the back alleys of the 'occult,' and make it a positive, socially responsible, accepted, functioning part of society, for the betterment of the Country in its present spiritual crisis, and for Western Man in general.

GREEN EGG, VOL. XXII, No. 88

The Household Altar

by *Marion Zimmer Bradley*

LMOST EVERYONE IN WHAT MANY Pagans and Neo-Pagans call the Craft—which I and mine prefer to call the Path—knows that his/her transition from dilettante and apprentice to serious student comes when they are willing to commit themselves to having and maintaining, in their domicile, a permanent altar to that facet of the Mysteries which he/she has chosen as his/her own. (This double pronoun nonsense is getting too much for me. As a woman, I am one half of mankind, and therefore I feel that male pronouns can include me, too. When I think what we lady writers went through to get rid of such designations as poetess and authoress and be referred to simply as poets and authors, I am appalled when I see a lady chairman demanding to be called a chairwoman, or, even more barbarous, a chairperson.)

To return to our muttons—or, rather, our altars. There have been times when I have brought this up, and the budding priest or priestess will say to me, "Keep a Temple in my house? I don't have the room."

This, of course, is nonsense and deserves no answer other than the old cliché, "Where there's a will, there's a way." I can imagine no one except the Army private, in boot camp, whose living space consists of a cot or bunk, and whose personal possessions are all kept in a footlocker, open to inspection by his sergeant, who would be completely incapable of keeping the tiniest of altars. (And I knew one of those who kept his personal altar in a folding stationary case, with his paraphernalia symbolically suggested by careful drawings of his Gods and all tucked up inside, which he could open for a private moment or two of his devotions.)

It is only those affluent householders who have inherited, or acquired, an enormous ancestral mansion, who can be reasonably expected to devote an entire room to a household Temple. For everyone else, a table, folding desk or bureau makes an excellent altar. It can be kept in a small corner of the bedroom, a niche in a sewing room, a convenient closet, or what have you.

My partner and I keep our altar in a niche behind the chimney in our bedroom. We impose a severe discipline upon ourselves that no secular item, however innocuous, must ever be laid on the altar. Since our altar is between a bookcase and a laundry hamper, and neither of us is by nature a tidy or orderly person, this isn't as easy as it sounds, but since the accidental tossing of a pair of socks or the novel I was reading on the altar involves us, by agreement, in various purifications, we're learning. (Let me hasten to add that I am not superstitious enough to think that a pair of socks, however grubby, or a novel, however trivial, could "contaminate" the altar. The prohibition, and the lustrations, are for our benefit, not the altar's. It is to emphasize the whole point of an altar—its psychological and suggestive effect on us; that in this mundane room devoted to mundane life and the daily round, a tiny corner protrudes, like the tip of an iceberg above the ocean, a doorway into the Unseen; that by approaching the altar, kept carefully apart from our all-too-trivial daily lives, we step emotionally and psychologically into a whole other dimension, as if we were stepping through a gateway; leaving the bedroom behind and entering an astral Temple which we have built here, with the doorway kept uncluttered.)

Size does not matter. I have a dear woman friend who lives in a house trailer with three daughters and four large dogs. Her altar is a folding shelf which she has fastened to the wall of her bedroom. When the trailer is moved, or mundane types are about, she folds up the altar and there is nothing but a shelf folded against the wall. When there is privacy and time the shelf comes down; the Godforms behind it are revealed and she sets up her chosen decorations—usually flowers which she has grown herself. A tiny altar but a beautiful one.

It need not be large, or expensive, but it

should be as lovely as you can manage to make it. Its beauty or lack of it reveals the part which your Work plays in your life. If you are only trifling, playing games with occultism, and you choose for your altar only a few cheap and shabby things, by them you will be judged. On the other hand. expensive and fancy things bought in "occult gift shops" are often mass-produced trash.

Altar furniture will vary according to the Path you have chosen. Some people who are on one of the Eastern Paths find it sufficient to place a portrait of their Guru there and wreath it about with flowers.

My own Order suggests that the Four Elements—Earth, Water, Fire, and Air—be present on the altar. Once you have chosen your altar (and if you buy it at a second-hand shop be certain that you wash, clean, polish, and garnish it first, following this with whatever exorcism you see fit—there is no need to take someone else's personal magnetism into your sphere of intimate contact) you may do as you like about an altar cloth, although if you choose to have one, it is well to make it yourself and preferably to embroider it with such symbols as you choose. One thing I do consider absolutely necessary, if you ever work with the element of fire, is an asbestos pad, or one of those metallic table protectors. Incense burners, especially those which burn charcoal, get very hot. So do candles when they are in metal or ceramic holders and are allowed to burn down to their cups or sockets. The leather top of our altar (which began life as a beautiful library table probably, from its size, intended to hold *Webster's Unabridged*) has an ugly charred ring from the time when my espoused priest/husband and I fell asleep after working an extended and weary ritual, leaving our ten colored Cabalistic lights burning in their candle cups. Any device sold in a kitchenware department intended to protect your tabletop from hot pans and dishes will serve your purpose. Ours is an attractive copper-colored one (the metal of Venus).

The element of water can be represented by your chalice, which can be anything large enough to hold water and/or drink from. Stained glass ones are sold by local craft shops and are beautiful. Mine is a silver communion cup from some church, and I am sure it wonders sometimes what it is doing on a Pagan altar. Despite its recognizable origins it was too beautiful to resist. Your chalice should obviously be the most beautiful vessel you can afford, or one with a deep meaning to you. I know a married couple on the Path who use their first child's christening mug as a chalice, and why not? You could even go into a bridal silver shop, buy a silver goblet or wine-glass and have it engraved (silver engraving is often included in the price) with your initials or those of your order or coven. This would indeed personalize it to its intended use.

The element of fire is, of course, found in your candle. Some lodges always have two candles present on their altar: a black and a white one for the Twin Pillars of the Great Temple (see the High Priestess card in the Waite Pack of Tarot cards). Others prefer a single candle in the chosen color associated with their ritual. If you choose to use colorless beeswax candles (we do, not for ritual purposes but because I detest the smell of paraffin which comes from non-wax candles, even when covered with cheap perfumes) you can put them into colored vigil light cups of the proper colors. Candleholders can be cheap, dime store ones or hand-made pottery ones fashioned in symbolic shapes. I was lucky enough to find a set of six brass pentagram candleholders in an import shop.

The simplest way to represent the element earth is a pottery dish with coarse rock salt in it. Another way is a geode or a beautiful crystal from a rock shop. Other ways will doubtless occur to those who work in other traditions.

The element of air is often controversial. Some feel that incense represents the

element air. Others dislike incense and burn it only when necessary to cover up the smell of marijuana or something. I own three incense burners. One is brass for burning resin or gum incenses on charcoal. (Note what I said about asbestos protectors if you use this kind.) The second is also a small brass one, shaped like a symbolic female organ, for burning powder incense or cones or pastilles. The third is a glass ball with a hole in the top to serve as a holder for the kind of stick incense which the Hari Krishna people give away on the street. This simplifies the daily tending of the altar, since no matter how busy or fussed I am I can light a stick of incense. Another air symbol is the magical weapon known as the Air Dagger. Some covens refer to it as an athame, and if you work that tradition you probably have one and know how to display it. Obviously keeping a dagger on display is impractical if you have small, meddlesome children, cats (and if someone could work out a ritual to keep cats off altars I would welcome it), or many mundane types passing in and out of your temple.

My own Air Dagger is a small knife which a friend wrapped for me in Samurai-sword fashion with a tiny green dragon (another air symbol) resin-cast from a Samurai *minuke* on the hilt. It is truly a thing of beauty but I keep it in our cabinet unless I am alone in the house. Another friend had a beautiful and valuable Malay kris stolen from his household altar. Knives attract thieves more than anything else except cash, typewriters, drugs or guns. An obviously valuable antique is an open invitation to a sneak thief.

In addition to the symbolic four elements, your altar should have items of deep emotional meaning to you which you wish to consecrate to your Work. Some groups feel that symbols of the Great Polarities—the male and female principles—should be present. The black and white "pillar" candles will serve for this, if desired. Our own symbols include a cowrie shell for the female principle. I've seen everything from a sword to a package of "Trojans" laid on altars to symbolize the male principle. One man I know, of Indian ancestry, has a group of Indian totem items on his altar and it is one of the most powerful I know; it feels like a great electric force-field when your palms are held flat, two feet above the surface. I know a woman who kept her first husband's wedding ring on her altar as a magical object; since he had been her initiator this was obviously reasonable. (And I heard of, although I do not know her personally, a witch versed in sex magic who kept on her altar a lock of hair from every lover. I don't know whether she asked her lovers for them, in a spasm of passion, or clipped them surreptitiously while their attention was elsewhere.)

Unless you are working in a completely Christian tradition, you will want God-forms on your altar. Reproductions of the Greek Gods can be had from many museums. The same, I understand, is true of the Egyptian Gods. If you have the slightest artistic ability it is well to draw or paint your own. Even without artistic ability most people can make a drawing of the Tree of Life or the signs of the Zodiac, which can be used as a reminder of the multiplicity of the created Universe and Nature. Our Triple Goddess consists of a detail from the Botticelli Venus, a painting of a young girl by an artist friend, and an imitation ivory-on-black-velvet Kwan Yin from Chinatown hung up three-in-a-row. One woman from my own order chose as her sign of the Great Goddess three snapshots matted side-by-side in a large frame: her mother, her sister, her twelve-year-old daughter. Since a portion of our consecration vow runs "that in the name of the Mother, every woman shall be to me as my own mother, my sister, or my child..." this is obviously a valid representation. Another woman I know uses only a mirror as a symbol of the God-Within. Certain saints used in the Catholic Church—the Virgin of Guadalupe, Saint Brigid—are obviously more Pagan than Christian. I am not exactly recommending the use of these images, but they are easily come by and no one is going to ask you, when you buy them, what use you will make of them. (Examine the symbols on conventional pictures of the Virgin of Guadalupe and then ask yourself if you can still consider her Christian, or if the Catholics haven't simply stolen the Great Mother for their own rituals!)

My own altar contains a simple head of Christ, without halo, because our Order regards Christ as one of the Initiated Masters. No virtuous Pagan could quarrel with the simple teachings of the Sermon on the Mount, and if Christianity had gone no further, repeating the simple ethic of love of God and one's fellow man, the various sects, schisms and stupidities of the Church would never have happened.

I do not personally care for Buddhist symbols in my Temple, and when a few have found their way in, they have found their way out again almost as quickly. (Some workers prefer them. I have seen a Temple elaborately furbished with Nepalese temple gongs, etc.) My own feeling on this matter is that I was born in the Western world for the purposes appointed by the Lords of Karma and if it had been intended that I should follow the Lord Buddha. I would have been born somewhere east of Suez. More than half the human race lives in the Orient and I could easily have incarnated there. But this is, of course, a matter for everyone on the Path (or, if you prefer, in the Craft) to choose for himself.

Marion Zimmer was born in 1930, and married Robert Bradley in 1949. She received her B.A. from Hardin Simmons University and did graduate work at the University of California, Berkeley. She wrote everything from science fiction to Gothics, but is probably best known for her *Darkover* novels. She also edited many magazines and an annual anthology called *Sword and Sorceress*. She wrote *The Mists of Avalon*, a novel of the women in the Arthurian legends, and *Firebrand*, a novel about the women of the Trojan War. She died in Berkeley on September 25, 1999.
www.mzbworks.com

GE Vol. VI, No. 59 (Yule 1973) 15–17
Reprinted in GE Vol. XXI, No. 84 (Oimelc 1989) 4–5

Lady Day

The Wheel of the Year turns,
The delicate balance of
The Solstice is now past.
The light daily grows.
The Sun-Child born at Yule
Gathers new strength with
Each earlier dawn, with
Each longer day.

The Wheel of the Year turns
To the quiet music of
Wind through bare trees
And the unheard poetry
Of green shoots stirring
Beneath frosty ground.

The Wheel turns,
The Lady of all fertility
Sits quietly singing.
Rocking Her young children
Resting after the birth,
Resting before the joyous surge
Of bursting light
That will transform the
Frozen wasteland
Into the Garden of Hope.

The Wheel turns,
Cows calve;
Soon the sap will run in the Maple,
The groundhog peers out of his den.

—Cara Whiteowl
of Circle Oakhaven

GE Vol. XXVI, No. 103 (Winter 1993-94) 14

The Origins of Magick

by Robert Anton Wilson

Magick begins in superstition, and ends in science. —Will Durant,
The Story of Civilization: I: Our Oriental Heritage

The magician does not doubt that the same cause will always produce the same effects.... Thus the analogy between the magical and the scientific conceptions of the world is close. —Sir James George Frazer, The Golden Bough

Magic is worked by the working. —Norman Mailer, Marilyn

Lie down on the floor and keep calm. —John Herbert Dillinger

ER CONTRA, MR. DURANT: MAGICK begins in science, and sometimes degenerates into superstition.

Every religion is a degenerated, i.e., frozen, i.e., dead form of magick. If magick is the natural working of the normal human mind (an "all-purpose computer," in the estimation of Dr. John Lilly), then religion is the stereotype machine that is left when the computer stops working.

The street-corner Krishna Freak or Jesus Freak is a clear-cut case of possession, i.e., of failed magick and/or "black" magick (brainwashing); but the theologians of Buddhism, Islam, Vedanta, Christianity *et al.* represent the same arrested neurological development on a more verbally dextrous level. Laughter at their expense is cruel and unjustified: many a yogin or Witch gets frozen or "stuck" at a higher plateau and moves no further.

"Many people stay here all their lives through," the Holy Guardian Angel tells the magician in Crowley's great allegory, *The Wake World.* The joke is that the Angel says this not just at the first stage (normal illusion) but also at each of the higher stages along the way.

All of which wise and pithy comment, the reader will be relieved to hear, is not code nor even *coda,* but only overture; the libretto begins now.

Will Durant, echoing Frazer and the anthropology of the pre-Castaneda epoch (B.C.), assumes that magick begins in ignorance, guesswork, delusion, "superstition," and similar mental ineptness. I suggest that it begins with genius.

I will not bore you with citations from contemporary studies of shamanism. For every ethnographer I could quote in support of my hunch (or bias) that shamans are the neurological elite of their societies, there's another investigator who claims they're recruited exclusively from the epileptic or sexually deviated classes. So much obvious prejudice goes into these "impartial scientific" judgments that they are worthless.

Let us look, instead, at the **historical** record.

One of the first "guesses" or "superstitions" of the first shamans and/or witchwomen was the notion that trees have souls and respond to our love and admiration. Considering that these primitive investigators lacked Cleve Backster's polygraph equipment, one must pronounce this a very lucky guess indeed, unless one assumes that their scientific instruments were at least as good as Dr. Backster's modern electronic equipment.

The instruments used by these early researchers appear to have been: the human nervous system itself and, in many cases, certain funny fungi, i.e., mushrooms containing the sort of alkaloids that Dr. John Lilly was later to call "metaprogramming substances." With the aid of these magick brews, evidently, the Witch-doctors were able to imprint, re-imprint and serially imprint their own nervous systems until they became calibrated to the reception of knowledge unavailable to the "normal" untrained human nervous system. In short, the primordial magician did not "guess" the souls of the trees: she (or he) communicated with them directly.

These "primitive" researchers also dreamed or intuited that the universe itself has a soul and is alive. This was a mind-blower to them, and it took a while before they were able to conceive this world-soul as a god similar to the local gods; they tended to consider it in a separate category and avoided it to some extent. This discovery, which underlies the frozen rigidities of monotheistic religions, is periodically re-discovered by individual scientists (Reichenback, Reich, Eddington, Leary, Lilly) who then become known as "mystics" or "philosophers."

(Oddly, it seems to be the unfortunate fact that Giordano Bruno and Theophrastus Bombastus Paracelsus were more gifted magically, i.e., as neurological empiricists, than they were verbally, i.e., as logicians-mathematicians. This is the PR side of why their animistic view of cosmology lost out in conflict with the mechanistic viewpoint of Newton and Descartes. See Francis Yates' *Giordano Bruno and the Hermetic Tradition* and Reich's *Cosmic Superimposition.*)

Having discovered "humanoid" or "anthropomorphic" (i.e., godly) personalities in trees and in nature generally, the first magicians also discovered means of differential calibration of transmission-reception of information with these beings.

Men Disguised as Chamois Hunting Magic

Hunting Magic - Trois Freres Cave France

Normal telepathy with the divinities was probably based on funny fungi, as suggested above. Higher definition was attained, the cave-paintings attest, by ritualized sexuality. It is an amusing note on the power of Christian bigotry in allegedly scientific circles that reproductions of these images are conspicuously absent from standard works on paleo-anthropology. Weston LeBarre does admit, in *The Ghost Dance: Origins of Religion,* that "bestiality" is the single most common theme in all cave art thus far unearthed; in fact, the similar magick use of human-animal sex is prominent in Egyptian, Greek, Chinese, Hindu and Oceanic art. Occidental (crypto-Christian) prejudice assumes that these depictions represent "sexual perversion"

in the modern sense. They are transparently magical in most cases.

In late Republican times the Romans still kept the functionary of "King of the Wood" (Rex Nemorensis)—hero of Frazer's *Golden Bough*—whose function as priest of vegetation was guaranteed by his "marriage" to an oak tree. Frazer never did understand that the sexual link was necessary for high-definition telepathy with the vegetative world, just as the sexual link with the bison was necessary for the shamans of our hunting ancestors.

Aleister Crowley's practise of this form of magick was one of the many facts which, gossiped about among the ignorant, created his reputation as a Monster-with-a capital-M. John Lilly remained respectable by skirting this issue; one of his assistants did masturbate dolphins occasionally, but only after retiring from such research did Dr. Lilly grant (in a *Penthouse* interview) that the way to true "species interlock" was by "fucking with them." (Presumably, he said it bluntly, instead of saying "copulating," because he really means to stay retired.

A word about human sacrifice, the first great stain of the record of the ur-magicians: however repellent we find this, it again does not show ignorance or stupidity. If you scatter a dead body around the field before planting, you *will* have better crops in the autumn. As Herbert Baily Stevens points out in *The Recovery of Culture,* this is because human (and animal) bodies contain lots of nitrogen.

The shaman who discovered that, for this purpose, an animal corpse will do as well as a human corpse thereby saved the life of many a Divine King (see Frazer); distorted portraits of this Great Leap Forward may be found in the legends of Cain-Abel and Abraham-Isaac, as recorded in *Genesis.*

Human-human sex magick, as distinguished

from paleolithic human-animal sex magick and its desiderata in the legends of Leda and the Swan, Mary and the Dove, etc. (where the formula for Higher Consciousness has been superimposed upon the animal-human pattern to reveal the DNA blueprint in detail: animal-human-Godling: the offspring of such unions represent the Great Work Complete)— or, since this sentence is out of whack already, let us note the *King Kong* parallels, Fay Wray=virgin, Kong=the god in beast-form, the Great Wall=crossing the Abyss of the Cabalists, etc.; see my "Even A Man Who Is Pure Of Heart: The American Horror Film as Folk-Art," *Journal of Human Relations,* Summer, 1970, and my forthcoming: *Babalon 156, a* study of Fay Wray, Marilyn Monroe and Linda Lovelace as archetypes of Crowley's Scarlet Woman—at which point we end this digression and proceed:

Human-human sex magick (which did not discover but created the Holy Guardian Angel of Sufic and Rosicrucian alchemy) is only now being recognized by mechanistic science, even though Freud long ago noted the sexual undercurrent in all "occult" happenings, the British psychic researchers realized the role of the repressed adolescent in 95% of poltergeist hauntings, and Rhine's statistics showed that spontaneous ESP happens most frequently between members of the same family. Again, it is hard to believe the shamans just "guessed" the truth; we must credit the possibility that they found it by magick forms of neurological research.

"Zulu medicine-men fried the genitals of a man who had died in full vigor, ground the mixture into a powder, and strewed it over the fields." (Durant) The formula of this fertilizer reads: nitrogen + magick, "energy," i.e., "orgone," kundalini, the force photographed by Kirlian cameras.

Ritual cannibalism, to turn to another sad case, is based on the self-evident fact that the "mind" (or soul) of the eaten *is* absorbed-by the eater, as Crowley had the guts to proclaim in the epoch of Victorian science. McConnell's research on cannibal worms, in which "memories" are transferred this way, leaves no doubt that the RNA molecule carries definite information between eaten and eater.

(The Aztecs made bloody nonsense of human sacrifice, just as the Christian Mass is a caricature of magick cannibalism. This is part of what we meant in saying every religion is a degenerate form of magick. Incidentally, it is now possible to obtain fertilizer or RNA without killing any living being.)

Most of the research we have been discussing occurred at least as early as 30,000-20,000 BCE. That the *amanita muscaria* mushroom was the chief tool of neurological investigation is supported by Allegro's *The Sacred Mushroom and the Cross,* Furst's *Flesh of the Gods* and Wasson's *Soma: Divine Mushroom of Immortality.* Around 18,000 B.C.E., the cannabis indica plant was discovered by shamans in the vicinity of the Caspian Sea; magick, and subsequent religion, took on a more philosophic and spacey character. Yoga, a complex but precise technique employing neuro-muscular gimmicks to trigger the internal chemistry, came along several centuries later, possibly during a famine when the magick plants were not available. Thereupon it became possible to focus the world-spirit more clearly and monotheism emerged. Taoism and Buddhism evidently appeared when super-yogis were able to transcend monotheism and confront the world-spirit without humanoid projections, whereupon the Void yawned... At this point, only the Mystic and the Magus (a magician trained also in mysticism) can talk meaningfully of the Next Step.

Meanwhile, most of humanity, including the theologians of all faiths from Catholicism to Mechanistic Scientism, represent a point where magick stopped, i.e., where the results of previous research inspired no further investigation but instead solidified into dogma.

As I point out in my novel, *The Sex Magicians* (Sheffield House), magick events have the structure of the mathematical Markoff Chain. This evidently triggered early witch-folk to create such emblems of hazard and chance as the trickster gods (Coyote, Loki, etc.), Eris, Goddess of Chaos, Hung Hung, spirit of anarchistic agnosticism, etc. and such practices as the *lila yoga* (ritual laughter) of the Sufis and Tantrists, Sufi gibberish, speaking with "tongues," etc. Art did not catch up with magick here until the invention of Dada, and Science didn't get into the act until Claud Shannon showed the reciprocity of information and entropy *(Mathematical Theory of Communication)* and von Neumann and Morgenstern investigated the merits of random strategies *(Theory of Games and Economic Behavior.)* Mullah Nasrudin, inspirer of Sufism and Gurdjieff, is identified (depending on which source you read) as either magician, mystic or clown.

As Uncle Aleister said truly, "Magick *is* as mysterious as mathematics, as empirical as poetry, as uncertain as golf, and as dependent on the personal equation as Love. That is no reason why we should not study, practice and enjoy it; for it is a Science in exactly the same sense as biology...."

GE Vol. VII, No. 63 (Litha 1974) pp. 5–7

Wild Harvest

by *Singing Flower/Roberta Lanphere (Melian)*, CAW

 WOULD LIKE TO DEVOTE THIS COLumn to the many delicious methods in which the ancients converted various edibles into intoxicating ambrosia. If you are wondering what I'm talking about—just hold onto your seat and grab your favorite drinking mug. As a Pagan, I favor fixing any food in the simplest, least chemically polluted manner possible. Therefore, all the following wine recipes do not use chemical yeast-killers, chemical starters, chemical clearing agents or fancy apparatus. Glass or crockery containers are used; coverings during fermentation, etc. are ordinary dish-towels (if a *drop* of liquid gets on the towel, you must immediately change that towel for a fresh one or risk turning your wine into vinegar). The yeast I use is ordinary baker's yeast. Although most of the original recipes were for barrelfuls of wine, you will find the proportions reduced to a gallon or two. Generally, to make one gallon of wine, use a 1 1/2 or 2 gallon crock, to make two gallons of finished product, use a 3 gallon container. This allows space for the bubbling and swelling of fermentation. One more thing before we move on to the actual recipes: Most of the recipes are created out of "by guess and by gum" measurements. Even though a recipe says "1 teaspoon" of (for example) cloves, if you just love cloves, add extra. If you just hate cloves, reduce the measurement or eliminate it. If you find your favorite wine is Daisy Wine, try that same recipe on some other edible flower. Always be creative. Modern living has nearly wiped out individualism and adventurous thinking, so let's re-discover the joy of life!

Let's start with three recipes using leaves. Grapes are well known for wine, but how many people can make Grape Leaf Wine? To make this wine, use 5 pounds of young leaves and stem tips. (The best are gathered from the first growths of the spring, but the new growth from any time of year will work quite satisfactorily.) Cover the grape leaves and stem tips with one gallon boiling water and allow to stand for three days. Strain. To the liquid, add 4 pounds sugar. Stir til dissolved, and then take a small cup of the liquid and heat to lukewarm. Stir one package dry yeast into lukewarm liquid and when dissolved, stir into remaining liquid in crock. Allow to ferment for 10 days, or until all fermentation has ceased. Skim, strain, and return to crock. Allow to set for one more week, then strain and bottle. Total time: 20 days.

Oak Leaf Wine takes 20 days to prepare, also. Pick 2 gallons of oak leaves in October when they are withered. Place in a crock and pour one gallon of boiling water over them. Let stand 3 days, then strain. To liquid add 4 pounds sugar, 1 ounce bruised ginger root, and boil for 10–20 minutes. Cool to lukewarm, strain, and add 1 package dry yeast, dissolved in a little of the liquid. Allow to set for 10 days, or until all fermentation has ceased. Strain, and return to the crock for another week. Strain again, and bottle.

For Walnut Leaf Wine, pick one large

bouquet of walnut leaves. Boil one gallon of water with 3 1/2 pounds sugar and pour over leaves. Let stand for 24 hrs, then squeeze out the leaves. Discard spent leaves and add 14 pounds chopped raisins and 1 package dry yeast dissolved in a small amount of the warmed liquid to the contents of the crock. Allow to ferment for the rest of the moon cycle. Strain, then bottle.

My favorite recipe follows. It is potent, but so mellow and smooth it sneaks up on the unwary. (I might add, however, the hangover is excruciating!) Boil 3 pounds honey with 1 gallon of water, 1 teaspoon ginger, 1 teaspoon cloves, 1 tablespoon mace and 2 tablespoon cinnamon for 10–20 min. (It will smell like pumpkin pie). Pour this into slightly less than one gal of cold water in a 2 gallon crock. When lukewarm, add 2 packages dry yeast, dissolved in a little of the warm liquid. Cover and ferment til it begins to clear, stirring once a day with a wooden spoon. Decant carefully into a clean crock and allow to ferment another 3 or 4 weeks, tasting to obtain potency desired. When fermentation is positively over, then bottle. This is fabulous when aged for a year or two, but make an extra batch, because if it is left in sight during aging, it disappears fast! What is it? Mead, of course!

A nice flower to brew is the Red Clover. Gather 4 quarts of Red Clover blossoms on a dry day. They must not have any dew or moisture on them. Pick over your flowers and keep only mature ones at their prime. Once they are measured and in the crock, pour 1 gal of boiling water over them. While it is cooling, slice 2 oranges and 3 lemons (peel and all). When liquid is lukewarm, add the fruit and 4 pounds sugar. Stir 'til sugar is dissolved. Stir in 1 package dry yeast dissolved in 1 cup warm water. Leave for 5 days, stirring twice daily. Strain again and leave for 3 days longer. Bottle, leaving the corks loose for 10 days. Allow to age for a month. Total time: approximately 2 months.

Daisy Wine is easy to make. Put 4 quarts small field daisies into a crock, and cover with 1 gallon boiling water. Let stand til next day; strain, squeezing pulp. Boil liquid and sugar for 10 minutes. Return to crock and cool to lukewarm. When it has cooled sufficiently, add 2 lemons and 2 oranges sliced (peel and all), 14 pounds chopped raisins, and 1 package dry yeast dissolved in warm water. Allow to work until all fermentation has ceased (about 14 days). Strain, and return to crock for a week. Strain again and bottle. Total time: 21 days.

You will notice that there is little difference between one wine recipe and another. The basic method remains the same, and what changes is the amount of sugar (how sweet whatever it is that you're brewing is to start with); the length of fermentation (how sweet or dry you like your wine. Short fermentation gives a sweet wine, and longer fermentation gives a drier wine); and amount and kind of spices added (personal taste and what harmonizes or accents what). Remember when you start making your own wines, to write down, right as you are doing it, what methods and what measurements you used. This is most difficult to remember accurately a month or so after the fact when you discover that you simply *love* that wine. If, after writing down carefully just what you did, you find that you do not like the wine, then before you throw that paper away, sit down and analyze just what about the taste it is, that you don't like; and see if some slight alteration in the recipe you invented would make it better. Don't give up on an idea just because the first try didn't work. Remember, be creative! Thou art God-dess!

Melian: First Wiccan Initiation 1974. Initiation Interdimensional Mysteries (European group melding Wicca, Magick, and other esoteric teachings) 1984. Ordained 3rd-level Priestess Gaian Life Church of Washington in 1999. Taught seminars in Europe in late 1980s. First degree Reiki in 1983, 2nd and 3rd degrees in March 2000, and Master/Teacher level in April, 2000. Certified in Neuro-Linguistics in 1985. Co-authored *Deva Tarot* deck with Herta Drnec, 1986. Taught classes online from 2000-2002 through Dracona. On Board of Directors of Professional Association of Holistic Arts and Sciences in Tolouca Lake, California, for two terms (four years), lectured at their 1st and 3rd Annual Psychic Expo. On Board of Directors of Church of All Worlds from 1995–1997.

GE Vol. VII, No. 65 (Mabon 1974) 25–26

JACK IN THE HEAP
A Song to the God
of Dying and Rotting Vegetation

A parody of "Jack in the Green," with apologies to Ian Anderson

*by **Melissa L. Pinol**, September 1991*

Now summer is over, I'm sorry to say
And we're all met again on our
    Composting Day
Yes, we're all met again by the garbage so
    deep
To pay our respects to old Jack in the Heap

    Jack in the Heap,
    He gives us the creeps
    But we'll dance through the compost
    For Jack in the Heap

He transforms the plants that have seen
    better times,
He breaks down potatoes and carrots and
    vines
He takes old grass clippings and changes
    them so
They turn into a substance that makes
    flowers grow

    Makes flowers grow
    Makes flowers grow
    They turn into a substance
    That makes flowers grow.

O come all you young maidens, I bid you
    beware
Of touching poor Jack, you'll get glop in
    your hair
And if you do touch him, then many can tell
Like old rotten mushrooms your body will
    smell

    Body will smell,
    Body will smell
    Like old rotten mushrooms
    Your body will smell.

The sun is half down and it heralds the hour
When we crown all the compost with last
    summer's flowers
And now let us sing as the fumes make us weep
And we'll offer some worms to dear Jack in
    the Heap

    Jack in the Heap,
    He gives us the creeps
    But we'll dance through the compost
    For Jack in the Heap.

(art by Daniel Blair Stewart)

GE Vol. XXVI, No. 102 (Autumn 1993) 30

Halloween and Old Jack

by Lady Gwen Thompson (Celtic-Trad. Wicca)

 HO OR WHAT IS OLD JACK? OLD Jack is another name for our Great Horned God of Wicca when he appears at the death of the year (Hallows) and takes complete charge over the winter months of the year. As God of Death and Rebirth he reigns over the Hallows festival as Old Jack, and often an effigy is made to represent him. The effigy takes the form of the well-known farmer's Scarecrow (and no doubt this is where the old farm folk originally got their inspiration for the Scarecrow).

A Covenstead need not be located in a rural area for the members of its coven to construct Old Jack. He can be made as any scarecrow is and placed in any part of an apartment, house or Circle Room. He can be as easily stuffed with old newspapers as old and dried leaves, and the project is fun. Making an effigy of Old Jack is sheer Wiccan-Pagan sport. May I say to the purists who may chance to read this: in no way is such an adventure insulting to our God. Being a God of death and rebirth does not diminish the fact that he is also a God of great joy, mirth and laughter. He

may be fierce or he may strike Panic wherever he appears, but he also also enjoys being acknowledged in happy ways. For us, All Hallows is not a somber time at all. It is a time to remember our ancestors and commemorate our beloved dead; a time to communicate with them and to let them know we are aware of their existence. It is a time to search into past lives and to gain knowledge from them…to learn from that which has gone before.

In order to construct Old Jack, one need only have on hand an ordinary broom, lots of leaves, newspaper or rags, an old pair of trousers with some sort of belt, an old shirt, a pair of gloves, and an old hat or cap (optional). There is no limit to the various ways in which an effigy of Old Jack may be constructed. Invert the broom, plunge it into the ground or prop it in the corner and take it from there. For the head, a pillow with a cover on it can be placed over the broom head with the pillow in front of the broom bristles and tied at the "neck" to make a large and suitable head. A happy face can be drawn on Jack with washable colors, and he's then ready for his hat or hair of straw. The shirt can be secured to the bottom of the pillow case or cover that forms his head until it is stuffed. No cross bar is needed since the stuffing will cause the arms to stretch out when

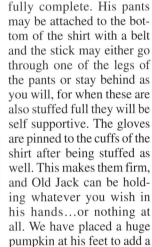

fully complete. His pants may be attached to the bottom of the shirt with a belt and the stick may either go through one of the legs of the pants or stay behind as you will, for when these are also stuffed full they will be self supportive. The gloves are pinned to the cuffs of the shirt after being stuffed as well. This makes them firm, and Old Jack can be holding whatever you wish in his hands…or nothing at all. We have placed a huge pumpkin at his feet to add a touch of color and additional support. He may be leaning on a corn stalk, standing at the edge of the garden patch or have his own special place in a room. He will create a friendly aura wherever you decide to place him, and if you have the space and the privacy— a dance around Old Jack can be very exhilarating and a cause for much merriment.

Old Jack can be given special vibratory Powers as he is constructed when this is done with song and rhyme. Such an effigy of Old Jack may produce some interesting Hallows effects for you. If you wish him to guard your Circle then impart this fact to him. If you wish him to help you with the art of necromancy, then also impart this fact to him. The God has a limitless ability to expand himself. At any rate, let him know of your joy in his presence.

There need be no fear of placing Old Jack in your yard. Cowans are used to scarecrows, and particularly at the Hallows season. Hallows is certainly one time of the year that Witches and Pagans can be themselves without the hassles that usually accompany a gathering that might be held too close to Cowans. There is absolutely no reason why you cannot enjoy a bit of trick or treating yourself before Circle time. We've had the fun of going incognito with sheets over our heads (playing ghost), and getting some very good pics of the local Cowans. One year we snapped a picture of the Deaconess of a very narrow local Xian church. She was in full "Witch drag," heavily made up, and wearing a long black wig. However, there was no doubt as to who she was. My, my…we certainly are not advocating blackmail.

Never gripe about the Hallows being "too commercial." Thank the Great God for it! Without it we might have the burnings again. Although, we do agree that certain perverts are desperately trying to do away with the Hallows...even make it evil and dangerous...by the placing of nasties in such things as our sacred Apple, for instance. If I say that a typically Xian pervert did such things, all the Xians from here to the Vatican would raise a howl, but it certainly was *not* one of us, now, was it? These people obviously wish to suppress Hallows and to degrade it. They wish to cast an aura of evil, hatred, and the so-called "devil" about it. Thus far, they've done a pretty good job in their efforts, but it is up to Witches and Pagans to end it where it began. And that is discovering just who these guilty parties are and of what religious persuasion, if any, they are. Obviously they are killer fanatics who will do anything to promote their cause…the destruction of Hallows and anyone who observes it. We have a real problem here, and we ought to face up to it with some well directed action. If we cannot physically deal with the perverts of Hallows, we can at least deal with them magickally. Before it's too late.

We do not sacrifice little children by having them swallow razor blades and pins; in fact, we do not sacrifice anything but our own lives for the ideals we believe in.

Let Old Jack guard well your Hallows Circle and impart to him the magicks that you wish. He will not fail you, and soon he will drawing snow and ice designs upon some windowpanes in his aspect as Jack Frost as he rides the mighty Northwinds.

GE Vol. VIII, No. 74 (Samhain 1975)

Matters of Life & Death

Came Death one early morning to Greenwood,
To speak with the healer there;
Death was a lord both dark and tall,
And wondrous, terrible fair.
Said He, "We've striven, you and I,
"Over some who approached my door;
"But I find you Pagans fear me less
"Than most I've seen before.
"Can you tell me why this is?" He asked.
And the healer, laughing, replied,
"Because, my Lord, we Pagans know
"That we can return when we die.
"You're the other half of Life," she said,
"No less, but nothing more;
"And all that lives must come, in time,
"To wait outside your door.
"But I heal, my Lord, in my Lady's name,
"And it's She Who guides my hand,
"That none I love will walk,
"Before their time, your shadowed land.
"And all that falls shall rise again—
"I know this to be true
"But none whose lives I hold in trust
"Shall early come to You."
Death smiled then and took his leave.
The healer, lingering, found
A single pomegranate seed
Beside her on the ground.
She planted it; and in the Spring,
When she returned to see
If anything had grown, she found
A slender apple tree.
—*Gale Perrigo* ©1985

Vol. XXV, No. 98 (Autumn 1992) inside front

Nature Spirit Magic

by *Larry Cornett*, CAW

ACH PLANT, ANIMAL, ROCK, AND other entity has a spirit (consciousness resonance matrix). These spirits can join together, in a hive-mind, as a spirit of an area. Nature spirits include real biological intelligences, are psychically powerful, and are much less abstract and controllable than the Elementals that many magical people who perform all of their rituals indoors are familiar with. They can be extremely powerful allies. It is possible to sense nature spirits, to determine if they are receptive to a ritual planned, and to have them actively participate in magical workings if they are.

Some Effects of Working With Nature Spirits

Spectacular physical manifestations can happen when working with nature spirits in the wild. I have personally seen actual foxfire mark the boundaries of a magic circle at a location that was identified as a receptive power spot and attuned to a planned ritual the day before. I have seen more than one site attuned for ritual be dry and comfortable, with a round hole in the clouds overhead, on days that were cold and rainy at other nearby locations. Birds have joined in rituals, flying around the circle when energy was being raised; and insects, birds and animals have joined in chants. In addition, the wind often responds to invocations. Generally, these spectacular manifestations happen unexpectedly.

With or without such manifestations, nature spirits often will channel tremendous amounts of power into the magic being performed. It is suggested that you do not consciously try for specific manifestations. Let Nature channel Her power into the magic in Her own way. If approached with respect, Nature may give you many pleasant surprises.

Spectacular physical manifestations are not a necessary sign of success. If you need a spectacular manifestation and nature spirits know this, you will get it. The best success in magic is on the inner planes and more subtle than such manifestations. This success involves beneficial changes in consciousness that last and helpful chains of synchronicity. In addition, working with Nature Spirits can also bring a deep sense of partnership with Nature, and bring new levels of attunement.

To get the best results, perform nature spirit attunement several hours to several days before the main ritual. The purposes of such attunement are to find suitable power spots and to get the help of friendly nature spirits. This timing gives Nature time to gather Her children and to prepare to actively participate in the main ritual.

What Not to Do

If nature spirits are approached with disrespect by attempting to command them rather than listening to them and inviting them to work with you, they may flee, rebel, or attack. I once attended a ritual by some pseudo-Crowleyites who attempted to perform the "Ritual of the Barbarous Names" at a power spot in a forest and then to extend the circle several hundred yards in all directions.

While the forest in general had loud insect and frog noises, the area at which the ritual took place got quiet immediately when the main ritualist declared that all spirits were subject unto him. The vibes from nature could best be characterized as "Oh yea, Motherfucker!" One participant was quickly possessed by an angry spirit and kept repeating "You killed my children, your children will never live in peace." When the priestess stepped out of the boundaries of the original circle, she was attacked by bees and bees covered the Book of the Law. Magicians should know better than to attempt to command spirits whose true names they do not know!

Calling Nature Spirits

To make the most out of working magical ritual in the wild, one should find power spots where nature spirits are receptive to the ritual planned and approach the spirits with respect, as equals. In my experience, the most effective power spots for working with the living intelligences of nature are located in wild areas with diverse, active ecologies.

When entering a wild area to find a site for a ritual, find a place that feels good. Then do the following, either individually or, if in a group, as a guided meditation:

- Relax, while standing upright, and focus on your breathing.
- Breathe deep breaths from the diaphragm. Breathe together if in a group.
- Feel the wind, and let it relax you and awaken your spirit within, as your deep breathing takes you into non-ordinary reality.
- Picture, in your mind's eye, a light inside you. As you breathe, feel the light expand, purify and energize you—as it expands to fill your aura.
- Feel yourself glowing, balanced, purified, and full of power.
- Connect with your inner self (your higher self), and feel your intuitive self operating. Feel yourself as:
- The wind, full of life and intelligence, communicating with all around.
- The Sunlight, warm, alive, channeling the power to communicate with nature and energizing all around.
- Water, emotional, intuitive, refreshing, and connected with nature.
- The Earth, and note how your physical body is able to wander while remaining part of Mother Earth.

Focus on your spiritual self, and:

- Note the light within and feel it as love.
- Expand the light and love beyond the immediate aura of your body to the surrounding area—where you will go to find a power spot and contact nature spirits.
- Telepathically (by thinking while channeling the love and light energy) send out signals to nature spirits to emerge and be aware of your presence.
- Say why you have come, and invite them to join in sharing, mutual celebration, and the work you intend.
- Visualize the light and love energy you are channeling extending out and merging with the light from distant places.
- Feel the power of the Earth flowing up through your body and feet.
- Feel the power from the sky, and channel this power also to further energize the carrier signal of light and love for communicating with nature.
- Visualize the light expanding and merging.
- Continue to send out telepathic signals. Now go deeper:
- Close your eyes, sit on the Earth, and feel your connection while you channel more light and love.
- Continue modulating the light and love with your thoughts, inviting receptive spirits to join with you and to make themselves known.
- If in a group, someone should start playing a drum at a rate of about one beat per second; listen to the drum and let the drum take you deeper.
- Affirm that you are a nature magician, a medicine person, who knows and communicates with nature. Let this part of yourself emerge to full consciousness. Let the drum and the connection to your inner self awaken that part of yourself that naturally communicates with other life forms. Let it awaken your telepathic senses.
- Continue sending telepathic signals to nature.

When you feel ready, and an inner urge to begin, open your eyes a crack and look around, while continuing to channel love and light and telepathically calling for a response.

You may see light coming from certain areas that are receptive. You may get other signals, such as a feeling of power or love returning in a certain direction. Perhaps the type of response to this work will be unexpected; follow your intuition in interpreting it.

You may test your connection by communicating (mentally) instructions for signals for yes/no responses (such as light getting brighter for yes and darker for no) and then mentally ask questions and observe the responses.

When you have found an area that seems to be responsive and receptive, begin walking to the area, while beaming love energy. Extend your aura to the area and sense the energy.

Entering a Power Spot

Before entering a power spot, ask permission to enter. If the response is good, enter; if not, locate another more receptive area.

When entering the power spot, look around. Perhaps the responsive energy will be concentrated around some singularity (a bush, a tree, a specific branch, a moss covered rock, or other entity that stands out). Perhaps the energy will be more general. Use your intuition and feedback from the spirits to guide your actions.

If it feels right, send out a signal that you would like to touch the singularity (or the ground) for better communication. If the response is good, approach beaming love energy, and then touch or hug the singularity (or the ground).

Treat the spirits as you would other Pagans you meet for the first time—be sensitive, open, and listen.

Deepening Communication With Nature Spirits

Now that you have made contact with spirits that seem receptive, deepen the communication:

- Breathe deep breaths from the diaphragm, and with each breath, feel more refreshed.
- Now imagine that your spine is the trunk of a tree; from its base, roots extend deep into the Earth. Deep into the rich moist Earth.
- With every breath, feel the roots extending deeper,
- Feel the energy deep within the Earth and within the waters of the Earth. Feel your roots absorbing nourishment from the Earth and from its waters.

- Feel the moist, warm energy rising.
- Feel it bursting up from the Earth and rising up your spine, like sap rises in a tree.
- Feel the energy rise to your crown chakra (at the top of your head).
- Now imagine that you have branches, branches that sweep up and then willow.
- Feel the branches extending and interweaving with your surroundings.
- Feel the warm, moist energy of the Earth flowing through your branches. As it flows, feel yourself being purified, centered, and connected to the Earth.
- Feel the power from the Earth flowing through your branches and then down back to the Earth, like a fountain.
- Note how your branches absorb energy from the air. Also, feel them receiving light (fire) from the sky.
- Feel the energy from above penetrating deep through your body into the Earth.
- Feel the warmth of the Earth rising also.
- Feel the energy circulating.
- Notice how your branches intertwine with the branches of energy surrounding you.
- Feel the energy dancing among your branches and the branches around you.
- Notice how your roots also intertwine with underground energy channels.
- Feel the energy dancing between your roots and the surrounding energy patterns.
- Notice how you and the life around you are rooted in the same Earth, breathing the same air, receiving the same fire, drinking the same water, sharing the same underlying essence.
- You are one with the magical grove.
- Telepathically mention the time in the past when nature spirits and people communicated regularly and the need to establish such communication now.
- Test your connection by asking questions and observing the responses.

Working with Nature Spirits

Explain to the spirits the purpose of your coming to them and the nature of the ritual you plan. If the spirits you contacted are receptive:

- Explain to them the details of the ritual and invite them to provide ideas.
- Listen, you may receive suggestions on how to improve the ritual. A Such suggestions may come in the form of hunches, visions, answers to yes/no questions using pre-arranged signals, or in other ways.
- Explain what type of space is needed and ask what the best place to perform the ritual is.
- You may see light or get other psychic signals leading you to other sites, or you may be at one of them. You may also ask what the best places for other aspects of the planned work are (picnicking, individual vision quests, etc.).
- If preparation of the site is needed (removing briars, preparing a fire circle, etc.) ask permission of the spirits before proceeding with such action.
- Before you leave the power spot, tell the spirits you have contacted when you plan to return to do the ritual (visualizing the associated lunar and solar aspects can help with this communication).
- Invite them to join in the ritual when you return and to bring their friends.
- Ask if it would be best to return silently, with drums, with chanting, or with some other form of approach.
- You can also ask the spirits to provide guidance for working in balance and to provide a teacher to provide further guidance.

Before you leave the power spot:
- Thank the spirits.
- Channel love energy.
- Trigger your memory of the experience.
- If it feels right, leave an offering of tobacco, or beer and honey poured on the ground (or other suitable material).
- Leave in peace and love.

Proceed to other sites that were indicated by the spirits, doing similar meditations at each site.

If you need something, like a staff, a Maypole, or a wand, you can also ask where you can find it and follow the guidance you receive (not slavishly, but as you would guidance from another Pagan).

Before leaving the general area in which you found power spots and contacted nature spirits:
- Channel love energy towards the receptive sites you found.
- Thank the spirits of the land.
- Pull back your roots and branches.
- Ground any excess energy into the Earth (placing your hands on the Earth, breathe in any excess energy, and channel the energy down your arms, while visualizing and feeling the energy going into the Earth).
- Leave in peace and love.

Naturally, you should leave the area at least as clean, and preferably cleaner, than you found it.

If you work with techniques of Wicca or Ceremonial Magic, you may find that by casting a circle, calling the Elements, the Goddess, the Gods, and the local nature spirits while you are at receptive sites, you may be able to greatly increase communication.

Through the use of drums and other power raising techniques, it is even possible to energize receptive nature spirits. The results can be very interesting. If with a coven, such circles can be done as part of a group attunement to a power spot you have located.

If you do not get good feelings in response to your explanation of the ritual and are unable to come up with a ritual that gives good responses, do not try to force a good response. You would only be fooling yourself.
- Thank the spirits for their attention. Ask them why they are not receptive (if it feels right and they are communicative).
- Trigger your memory.
- Pull back your roots and branches, return any excess energy you feel into the Earth.
- If it feels appropriate, leave an offering of tobacco or other appropriate material, out of respect for the spirits.
- Move to a more receptive site.

If it is hard to find a site that is really receptive, you should consider any impressions you got of why the nature spirits weren't receptive in the area you were in, and re-think your plans for a ritual, as necessary and appropriate. It may also be appropriate to look for another general area in which to find a suitable power site that is receptive to the work planned.

What to Do When Returning

It can be very powerful to purify and center yourself and to attune to the spirits of the land using the techniques previously described for calling nature spirits immediately upon returning to the site.

Often, individuals may have found small specific power spots to which they have a special attunement, where the spirits are interested in participating; but where the site is too small, has too much vegetation, or is otherwise unsuitable for the main ritual. Individual attunement to the spirits in such areas and inviting them to participate in the main ritual can be worthwhile.

Then approach the main ritual site using the previously arranged technique. You should have the details worked out with the spirits of the land. An exceptionally powerful technique involves doing a procession through or past receptive power spots, inviting nature spirits to join as you pass each power spot, and then moving to the central power spot for the main ritual. If participants are at individual power spots, they can join the procession as it passes nearby.

When consecrating space in the wild, or casting a circle, do not set up the perimeter as a barrier to all outside forces; it should be a beacon to attract friendly nature spirits, a container for holding magical power and a barrier to spirits who it isn't right to be with.

One thing that is fun and worthwhile in nature is to bring instruments, such as a rattle, a flute and/or a drum, to tune in to nature's sounds, and to make music in time to nature's sounds. You may be able to get some very interesting back and forth exchanges of music going with selected creatures of the wild, and get into an amazing jam session.

After the work is complete, be sure to thank the spirits for their participation. Libations and other offerings may also be left for the spirits during and/or after the ritual.

Acknowledgements

There are other ways of working with nature spirits. This is one approach. The author thanks Selena Fox for teaching the basic guided meditation technique for locating and contacting nature spirits at a tranceworking session sponsored by the Chameleon Club (part of the Association for Consciousness Exploration) in 1981, Vicky Smith for editorial review of this article, Isaac Bonewits for the outline of the expanded tree meditation, and Carlos Castenada, Black Eagle, Pasha, the Goddess, the Gods, and various nature spirits for teaching the rest of the good methods.

Rights to Distribute

Larry Cornett (*http://members.aol.com/lcorncalen/CORNETT.HTM*), known for his *Calendar of Events (*http://members.aol.com/lcorncalen/CAL-OHIO.htm*), is a founding member of the original ADF Mother Grove, as well as the Association for Consciousness Exploration (*www.rosencomet.com/about.html*), the Church of All Worlds Triskelion Nest, the Earth Religions Legal Assistance Network (*www.conjure.com/ERAL/eral.html*), the Sacred Earth Alliance (*http://members.aol.com/lcorncalen/SEAHomepage.htm*), and VisionWeavers Coven. He works as an environmental consultant on air pollution control, toxic and radioactive waste management, risk assessment, monitoring, and clean-up. *lcornett@en.com*

GE Vol. XXVI, No. 101 (Summer 1993) 8–9, 33

Chapter 8.
Pagan Culture:
Family & Tribe
Introduction
by *Chas S. Clifton*

O TODAY'S PAGANS CONSTITUTE A "TRIBE"? PARTICULARLY IN EASTERN EUROPE and Russia, much of the contemporary Pagan revival has been expressed in language about a deep ethnic identification with one's motherland. And as "ethnic" is a Greek word, the term *ethnotikos* is often used in that nation to translate "Pagan," which comes from the Latin language. The situation in North America is different because of the population's multiple points of origin. Nevertheless, the nature of Pagan religion does create a quasi-tribal bonding. As I discussed in the introduction to Chapter 6, our religion is "imagistic" rather than "doctrinal." It is based on experience. (For more information on these categories, read anthropologist Harvey Whitehouse's *Modes of Religiosity*.) Shared intense experience produces a special sort of bond. Consider that the Eleusinian Mysteries, a group initiation into the cults of the goddesses Demeter and Persephone, were celebrated in Greece for 2,000 years. Yet to this day, we do not know exactly what happened in them, despite partial accounts in art and literature, because most of the initiates kept their shared vow of secrecy about what happened in the ritual chamber.

It is this deep, quasi-tribal bonding that Miki Levenhagen invokes in "Water Brothers," describing a central ritual of the Church of All Worlds. Tribes, even (especially) deliberately created ones, require maintenance: Macha NightMare speaks to an important component of that process—the people who remember and maintain tradition and continuity. (Pete Davis puts the role of eldership into a magickal oath.) They and the other writers are concerned with passing this vision of ours on down through the generations, something that has already happened since many of these essays were first written. As Elizabeth Barrette wrote a decade ago, there has indeed been a Pagan baby boom, and issues of raising Pagan children (or children in a Pagan household) have come more and more to the forefront over the past years. The tribe definitely is continuing, both in blood and in affinity.

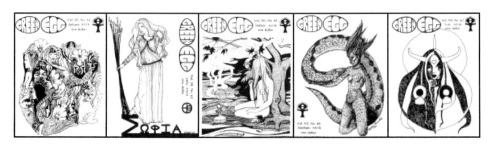

The CAW and Tribalism

by *Lewis Shieber, CAW*

EDITOR'S NOTE: This was a very significant essay, presented in the formative phase of the emerging Neo-Pagan religious movement. Lewis here articulated for the first time the clear distinctions between belief-based religions and tribal religions; a perspective that was subsequently adopted by much of the Pagan community, thus shaping the way modern Pagans came to view their own religion in comparison (and contrast) with others. OZ—2008

 T HAS LONG BEEN ASSUMED THAT the Church of All Worlds was, as it claims to be, a Neo-Pagan religion. The CAW has presented itself as such, a religion among religions, a way among many ways. But CAW's insistence upon complete eschewal of dogma makes the job of describing the differences between the CAW and any other Neo-Pagan religion rather difficult. While it is easy to say, "The CAW is not an Egyptian group or a Craft group or a Mycenean group," it is difficult to say what the CAW *is*. Describing just what the CAW religion positively advocates is a difficult task.

Admittedly, there are some practices and ideas which have been associated with the CAW. However, all these associated things are unofficial and not even accorded the name of tradition. Since the CAW has not defined its basis for distinguishing itself from all other Neo-Pagan religions and groups, it is perhaps time that this was done.

At this time, therefore, it would be well to examine the two types of religious bases available. All religions, ancient and modern, have used them and there are advantages and disadvantages to both. By exploring these qualities and comparing them with the evolved heritage of the CAW we may be able to arrive at a method of religious expression that is natural and well-adjusted to the CAW. Hopefully, after debate and discussion, a pattern of religious practices can be chosen that will differentiate in a positive manner the CAW from the rest of the Neo-Pagan religious groups-at-large.

The two religious bases are rather easily named and described by the terms Dogma/Belief and Tribal/Tradition. These terms can be examined for their meanings and religious uses.

Dogma/Belief systems are not based in a local cultural matrix. They are the large, often evangelistic, "universal" religions. They have a dogma, a set of statements, that must be believed in. Christianity is a prime example of this type of religion. Without belief in the dogma *no amount of action or religious practice* can support one's claim to be a member of the religion.

These systems have a great advantage: they can claim to have the One True Way for humankind and thus provide their adherents with a sense of superiority and confidence. An adherent to a Dogma/Belief based religion can feel better than anyone else *as long as their belief is strong.* These religions, because religious ritual and practice are secondary to the belief, can cross cultural boundaries with relative ease and have enormous numbers of avowed adherents.

In addition, because such religions must support the dogma, a cosmology, and, usually, a cosmogenesis must be devised. In this manner the dogma is woven into the very fabric of the universe itself. Because of this mechanism, belief in the dogma is nearly as important as the dogma itself and sometimes becomes part of the dogma. It becomes necessary to believe in "God" to believe in the "Word of God."

This weaving of dogma into the universe creates a powerful closed system of reality which can easily be accepted by large numbers of people. The practices and rules connected with such systems are not nearly as important as the belief.

Thus, systems with a Dogma/Belief base can be large and powerful. They are, however, not very flexible and stagnate rather quickly. In addition, their large populations link them inexorably to the machinations and problems of political governments. Finally, their only mechanism, belief, is easily shaken and hard to instill in generation after generation without appreciable change.

The other religious base, Tribal/Tradition, is quite different from the Dogma/Belief system. Instead of basing itself on belief in a dogma, this type religion is based on the traditions of tribal practice. It is not as important to believe in the myths and legends of the tribe as it is to *participate in tribal actions*. It is what you do and how you do it that counts, not what you believe. All "primitive" Pagan religions have this base. However, one of the most striking examples of a Tribal/Tradition religion is Judaism. In it, it is even permissible to disbelieve in God if you follow the precepts and rules of the tribe set down in the Talmud and the traditions of rabbinical leadership.

Systems of this sort are disadvantaged in their population size, which is relatively small, and in their cultural exclusivity, which requires the religion to be identified with a locale or to serve as the cultural matrix of a "guest people" living within a larger population. Again, Judaism has examples of both types.

Tribal/Tradition religions are usually rather flexible in their treatment of myth and especially of cosmology and cosmogenesis. This is a result of not being forced to weave any one belief pattern into the universal fabric.

Thus many sometimes contradictory beliefs may be held by individuals without harm to the religion as long as the *identification with the Tribe and tribal practices is strong.*

Because the tribal practices and loyalties are often not concrete and written down, it is difficult, if not impossible, to have conversions of large numbers of people. The small size of such religions and their locale-based character often brings them into conflict with political governments but seldom, if ever, links them with governmental rise and fall. Also, the emphasis on tribal identification is easy to maintain from one generation to another because these things create a sense of place-in-the-world for the child. This comfortable sense is created and maintained simply by maintaining traditional tribal practices. Thus it is to the individual's psychological benefit to maintain and support the Tribal/Tradition based religion. Lastly, these religions are highly social in nature, laying great stress on the personal interactions of their adherents to uphold the religious process.

Pagan religions have always been Tribal/Tradition based. This is not to say that they could not be Dogma/Belief based, only that they have not been so. Moreover, whenever a Pagan religion has come into contact with civilization, whether by evolution or invasion, the humanistic quality of the religion has disappeared relatively soon. By "civilization" I refer to those societies with a civil government, a state, as opposed to those societies with a kinship-based organization, a *familias*, a tribe. Tribal societies are basically anarchistic in that they maintain order without government. Tribal order is generally maintained by conventions and discussion leading to consensus.

A simple analysis of CAW evolution will reveal a definite but unofficial tendency toward the Tribal/Tradition religious base. The marked antipathy towards dogma should of itself convince anyone that the CAW is not a Dogma/Belief based religion.

In a publication of the CAW, *Neo-Paganism and the Church of All Worlds: Some Questions and Answers* by Tim Zell, the statement is made, "The Church of All Worlds doesn't believe anything. The people of the CAW try to avoid speaking of 'belief' or 'faith.'" This statement shows a definite antipathy towards a Dogma/Belief base. Also, from Tony Kelly's *Pagan Musings,* published and endorsed by the CAW, "Belief is the deceit of the credulous; it has no place in the heart of a Pagan."

In addition to the anti-dogma stand, the CAW heritage tends to espouse a strong current of tribalism. From *Pagan Musings,* "Our first work and our greatest wish is to come together, to be with each other in our tribe...." The conversations of CAW members are studded with remarks indicating strong interest in Tribal/Tradition based religions and religious practices. Indeed, it is almost unthinkable that the CAW should adopt a Dogma/Belief base.

There is, however, a strong urge to initiate a Dogma/Belief base, and often for what may seem to be good and beautiful reasons. The temptation to require belief in the poetic and useful vision of Tim Zell's 'TheaGenesis" theory is very strong. Indeed, one Neo-Pagan religion, Feraferia, has such a dogma by requiring acceptance and perhaps belief in the paradisal vision of Fred Adams.

The importance of the CAW's status as a Tribal/Tradition religion lies in the acceptance and use of that status. By accepting and using a Tribal/Tradition base for the CAW we formally commit ourselves to an avoidance of certain religious practices and embrace certain others. No longer can we claim to be a 'Universal' religion. No longer can we long for vast and powerful populations of members. Political governments cease to concern us except when we must of necessity deal with them. Above all we cannot claim Truth and the One True Way. We may not even imply these things and must watch our words both written and spoken to guard against a slip of this sort. We must assume that *we* are a "guest people" in a possibly unfriendly nation and act accordingly. We must ever hope and work for a land or lands of our own.

We must proudly lay claim to our own tradition and label it as such. We can, and perhaps should, direct our own religious evolution. We, being fully cognizant of who and what we are, can, as has no other Tribal/Tradition based religion before us, direct our own course and choose, with an eye to the future, those traditions we would wish to adopt as tribal practices.

As a tribe, we are simply the People, as every tribe has been to itself, and our religion is simply the practices of the People—what the People do. Let us choose carefully our tribal practices, that they may retain meaning and purpose over generations, thus becoming true Tradition. Let us always beware of Dogma and Belief. It is, I think, possible to grow traditions that change, to have practices that grow and promote growth while being hallowed by time and use. The tried and truthful can be ever changing and so, ever meaningful. Let us keep these things in mind and become what we potentially are, a tribe in the best and most hallowed sense of the word.

GE Vol. VIII, No. 75 (Yule 1975) 5–7

We Won't Shave Any Longer!

Lyrics © 1990 by
Jeff Kalmar & Isaac Bonewits
Music by Gwydion Pendderwen
("We Won't Wait Any Longer!")

We have trusted no man's razors;
We have nicked and cut ourselves;
We've been stung by all the aftershaves
Upon the drugstore shelves!
And our patience and endurance
From late puberty 'til now
Have given us the strength to make this vow:

Ch: We won't shave any longer;
Our beards are stronger than before!
We won't shave any longer;
Our beards are stronger!

We have shaved away our stubble
And have scraped away our skin;
We have cut and hacked and sliced and diced
And raised an awful din!
And on every weekday morning
We'd be bloody nervous wrecks
Sticking wads of toilet paper to our necks!

Now the ladies too have suffered
In their armpits and their legs
Just to wear those pantyhose
That come in little plastic eggs!
But we think it's time to tell 'em
That we Pagan men don't care
If they throw away their Zipwax and their Nair!

Through the ages many faces
Have arisen and have gone,
But the male ones all look better
With a beard and moustache on!
Now the time has come to throw
Our stiptic pencils on the floor
And refuse to wreck our faces any more!

Shick, Aquavelva, Norelco, Wilkenson,
Gillette, Bic, Mennen, Nox-ee-ma!

GE Vol. XXIV, No. 94 (Mabon 1991) 16

Circle of Life: Pagan Families
by *Elizabeth Barrette*

ELCOME TO THE PAGAN BABY boom. When the modern Pagan movement began, it consisted primarily of young folks—singles and couples who wanted to take the world in their teeth and shake some sense out of it. You didn't see too many little kids around, then. Today we have Elders from among those who helped build the Pagan community we know and love; and we also have children. Some of these folks have written books to help other Pagan parents, like *The Pagan Family: Handing the Old Ways Down* by Ceisiwr Smith, in which the author explains: "As the Pagan movement starts to leave its adolescence behind and its members raise children, the problems become more acute."[1] Those few who were children at the beginning of modern Paganism, and grew up in the rapidly developing Pagan community, are now ready to start their own families. Many who came to Paganism as adolescents or young adults a little later on are also ready to start families. Finally, people just discovering Paganism now include many folks who already have children or plan to soon. All that adds up, and Pagan parenting has become a hot issue in many magazines, mailing lists, and other forums.

RAISING THE ISSUE

Ideally, the time to start discussing how you want to raise your kids is before you have any. You and your mate(s) should reach an agreement on as many basic points (discipline, education, spirituality, etc.) as possible; better yet, extend the discussion to cover grandparents as well, so that everyone knows what to expect. Childraising technique is a great topic for long car rides. Of course, it isn't always possible to plan ahead, but even if you already have children you can anticipate many of the issues before they arise.

Do you want to raise your children in a Pagan context or not? Strong arguments support both sides, so your choice depends primarily on your tradition and tastes. Consider your circumstances and then decide. Either way can work. Margie McArthur puts it like this: "Our responsibility is to raise our children in a way that will heal the past and create a viable future."[2]

Some parents prefer to raise their children without any overt emphasis on religion at all. They only mention basic concepts of divinity, ethics, worship, etc. Parents may feel that children are not equipped to understand complex theological ideas and would find religion boring. Others come from a background of extreme indoctrination and wish to avoid making the same mistake. Certain traditions hold that serious religious study is inappropriate for young children, and do not begin teaching spiritual matters until adolescence when the child demonstrates a readiness to join the Circle of Women or the Circle of Men. Likewise, "Wicca's mysteries are the special rewards of study and discipline"[3] which is as good a reason for not teaching small children as for not sharing rituals with outsiders. Given the sad prevalence of religious harassment in some areas today, this course offers a measure of protection; families who must remain "in the broom closet" may choose not to raise their children within a Pagan tradition to reduce the chance of harassment.

Most parents raise their children to follow the parents' own faith. This offers a solid foundation in the tradition and gives children a strong sense of direction; it also makes explanation of key concepts easier within a Pagan context. One can avoid some of the nastier pitfalls of "mainstream" childraising this way. Some Pagan traditions celebrate children, welcoming their presence in all rituals and activities; children enjoy the festive trappings of many Pagan traditions. Another solution is to set up a Children's Circle with age-appropriate activities, popular at various festivals and other events.

"Simplicity and symbolism is the language best understood by children."[4] Children raised in a Pagan context often find it easier to develop not just their spiritual beliefs but their magical skills as well. Contrast this with the "mainstream" tendency to stamp out magical thought and curiosity, and you'll see the advantages of growing up Pagan. This also greatly reduces the child's vulnerability to negative social imprints, like distorted body image for girls and glorification of violence for boys; give them a clear, positive template and they can shake off bad influences.

One common challenge facing Pagan parents today is the prevalence of interfaith marriages. No figures were available for Earth-centered traditions, but I turned up the following numbers: "The proportion of Jews who married Gentiles...in this decade has leveled off at just over 50 percent. The comparable figure for Catholics...is 21 percent; for Mormons, 30 percent; and for Muslims, 40 percent."[5] Sometimes one parent agrees to raise the children solely in the other's religion. More often, though, parents either avoid the issue of religion entirely or introduce their children to both religions, assuming the children can make a choice later. Ignoring the issue tends to foster confusion and undermine belief in any type of spirituality. Experts sometimes argue that the same applies to raising children in both religions, but it doesn't have to. The key lies in making sure that children enjoy a variety of positive, vivid experiences in both traditions. Give them plenty of experience so they can make an informed choice! The same holds true in teaching children tolerance for other religions, especially since most Pagan children have some non-Pagan relatives. Ashleen O'Gaea handles it like this: "When the Explorer notices differences in our lifestyles, he asks us about them. This gives us yet another opportunity to point out what wonderful diversity there is in the world."[6] My partner and I plan to raise our children, when we have them, in both Pagan (mine) and Baha'i (his) traditions, along with introducing them to other systems whenever possible.

ANSWERING THE BIG QUESTIONS: SEX AND DEATH

Pagan religions of all stripes put forth a particularly good showing in this arena, where modern society often stumbles today. We mark the cycles of our lives along with the cycles of the seasons. "Pagans have developed distinctive ways of honouring birth, naming, first menstruation, sexuality, adulthood, marriage, giving birth, honouring the dead, and receiving death."[7] This cyclic viewpoint makes it easy to teach children our beliefs about important issues like sex and death—we can just show them through analogy and example. For instance, most traditions feature stories about a dying-and-reborn God and the eternal Goddess who is his mother and sometimes mate.

Acceptance of one's body and respect for its procreative powers are easier to learn in a supportive atmosphere, and most Pagan traditions celebrate rather than revile the human body. You can see this in the content of many rituals. Some covens or other ritual groups include a promise not to conceive or fertilize irresponsibly in their Womanhood and Manhood Ceremonies. Handfasting Ceremonies typically draw a connection between the bride and groom and the Goddess and God: "You are She, the One without beginning. You are the Mother of All, Who gives birth to the world. ...You are He, dying and rising again and again. You are the Father of All, born in every moment."[8]

It is important to give children a sense of joy, reverence, and celebration concerning matters physical because the generally toxic attitudes of the "mainstream" culture can and do cause serious problems if undiluted. Discuss your views (and reasoning) towards sexuality with your children early on, and if you present it as something positive and natural they will respect the inherent magic of the power to create new life. For a terrific demo-fieldtrip, take them to see baby tigers, bears, or ducklings at the zoo.

Likewise, respect for death as a natural transition appears in most Pagan traditions. "Death is a rite of passage for both those who die and for the family and friends left behind."[9]

We do not consider death something to be feared or hidden. Unfortunately, this in itself can create conflict with the dominant American culture, which attempts to sweep real death under the rug while simultaneously glorifying violence in the media. Many Pagans consider it advantageous to "practice" for death by enacting symbolic deaths in various ceremonies and meditations throughout their lives. For example, at Samhain rituals Pagans typically "honour their dead, both the ancestors and recently deceased loved-ones, and are given the opportunity to contemplate their own death."[10] According to popular belief, this reduces the chance that the newly dead, confused by their sudden change of state, may become lost or stuck; for Pagans, familiarity with the process and concepts can help smooth the passage. In dealing with the death of a loved one, "Ritual can be healing for children as well as adults, but kids need support and help to cope with the powerful emotions involved."[11]

Edain McCoy's excellent book *Entering the Summer-land: Customs and Rituals of Transition into the Afterlife* features a special section on explaining death to Pagan children. Presentation style varies according to the parents' beliefs: "Some Pagan parents try to discuss reincarnation, others the great cosmic oneness of all life, while others talk of the brevity of the human life span."[12] The author also points out that Pagan traditions help maintain a connection between the living and the dead, especially in families who keep an altar or hearth where the ancestors receive regular attention and honors. This reassures children by allowing them to "see for themselves the continuity of their family line and feel themselves a part of that great unbroken chain. They will grasp early on the abstractions of death by knowing that they can still share with Grandma the picture they drew in school and will better be able to feel her loving presence even though her physical shell is absent."[13] All of the systems I practice place at least a little emphasis on honoring one's ancestors and some of them feature it quite strongly, including the traditions of my own family. It does make a positive difference, and I'm grateful for the continued connection with my own beloved dead.

TEACHING BY EXAMPLE AND EXPERIENCE

Provide your children with information and answers upon request. They rely on you to show them the skills they need. If your children lead magical, spiritual lives then they need to know basic methods of handling energy, communicating with divine patrons and other friendly powers, caring for magical or sacred tools, and so forth. Fortunately, children respond readily to guidance when presented in a form that makes sense to them, so make use of their active imaginations to enhance the experience.

Let them browse your reference library, especially if they are precocious readers (I was), but also offer them books suited to their own level of development. *Spellcraft: A Primer for the Young Magician* by Lilith McLelland has a light conversational style; the author provides a great deal of useful information in an entertaining way, on a level kids can easily understand but without a condescending tone. For instance, she explains magic itself like this: "With the power of your mind, you can control the things that usually happen by natural law.... And in this way, you can change your life."[14] You can also give them books featuring magical fiction, mythology from various cultures, and other material likely to fuel thoughtful discussions about how the world works and why.

Besides book-learning, though, children benefit from hands-on experience. If they show interest in your rituals, let them watch or even participate or if your tradition restricts rituals to initiates, describe some of the details and ideas to your children. Children enjoy making arrangements of small meaningful objects and often create impromptu altars of their own; you can encourage this by providing age-appropriate items (stones, feathers, pictures, figurines, etc.) and a suitable display area like a special shelf or table.

Structure some games and other activities to develop an awareness of emotions, energy flows, and connections. These skills will serve your children well in any path, but especially apply to Pagan ones. *Teaching Children to Love: 80 Games & Fun Activities for Raising Balanced Children in Unbalanced Times* by Doc Lew Childre is a rich resource of ideas for fostering emotional skills and intuition, with entries for all age groups. For example, the game Heart Ball "teaches young children how to send and receive love and that learning to love is fun and feels good to the heart."[15] This lays a great foundation for casting spells later! There are also a number of books featuring cooperative rather than competitive games, such as *Everyone Wins! Cooperative Games and Activities* by Sambhava and Josette Luvmour. I like this one because it includes old favorites as well as new ideas, with a lot of extra data to make finding the right game easy. Many games include magical and/or nature elements sure to appeal to Pagan kids, like Giants-Wizards-Elves, Hawk & Mouse, and Inuit Ball Pass." Make learning fun.

Above all, you need one thing to make this work: trust. Trust yourself, your spouse(s), and your kids. Exercise your imagination and shape customs to suit your family, rather than taking them straight off the shelf. Believe that if you raise your kids in a Pagan context and teach them to think for themselves, their brains will not suddenly atrophy when Grandma and Grandpa start spouting Christian (or Jewish, or Muslim, or whatever) homilies.

The issue of Pagan parenting came up on the FIRE religious-freedom mailing list, in the context of holiday gatherings. I was delighted by the lively discussion that ensued, and some of the examples offered struck me as so relevant that I wanted to share them with you. The originators graciously gave me permission to reprint the following:

"My mom got out her Xmas decorations recently, including a nativity scene which she invited my five-year-old daughter to play with (grrrr...). My daughter said, 'Mommy, look at the Baby Jesus Playset I get to play with!'" [Saphire Mann]

"In our family, Yule comes first and the rest of the relatives (g'rups) celebrate Christmas (for whatever reason) send presents which are opened Christmas Day. A tree is decorated and stockings hung out. SANTA does not come. Father Christmas comes. He's Santa's older brother. These things come by subscription, like National Geographic, or the newspaper. Told the kids we had an older religion and so we subscribe to the older brother, Santa was for Christian kids.... One of the responsibilities of a parent is to create memories." [Avery]

So you see, in some very important ways, Paganism is what you make of it. Your children will absorb that from you. If you involve them in your spiritual life, they will grow and thrive within that context. Personalize it, make it real for them. Show them how wonderful it is, and why. Let them know that other people believe differently, give them at least a glimpse of that too, and they will learn tolerance from your good example.

PASSING ON TRADITIONS

We touch the past through our ancestors; we touch the future through our children. Ancient Pagan cultures depended heavily on a rich oral tradition—a key facet of the contemporary Pagan community as well. Traditions, stories, and customs: they all evolve over time. We must pass these things on to our children or risk losing much of the content. "Are we to remain a religion of converts?" asks Ceisiwr Smith.[17] Children raised in a Pagan context enjoy benefits many of us experienced only as adults.

Throughout history, different cultures have found different ways of raising and educating children. Most Pagan societies value children, so often the whole tribe would help take care of them. For instance, Native American tribes raised and taught children in the context of extensive family webs: "There were no special educational complexes—the whole village and tribal territory were her school."[18] In the modern "mainstream" world we see terrible problems caused by the breakdown of family ties, and many Pagan groups work to counteract that trend by cultivating relationships with coven members or others to serve as an extended family to each other. Children benefit from the stability and diversity of such an arrangement because there is always someone available to spend time with them, love them, and satisfy their endless hunger for knowledge.

Likewise, historical Pagan cultures often went into considerable detail in stipulating the responsibilities of parents to children (and vice versa). For instance, *The Rites of Odin* features a section on family life which mentions the following guidelines: "Always respect your children's tastes. Do not hurry them to be as adults, nor ridicule their tastes in stories and other literature. With proper upbringing, they will mature at their own individual times and ways.... Parents must care for their children, even when the young ones become mature.... Conversely, grown children are obligated to see that their parents are secure in old age, keeping them as honored elders of the family for the remainder of their natural lives."[19] These are typical of Pagan family values. A little research should turn up similar lists for whatever tradition you practice. If you can't find a list you like, feel free to draw up one of your own!

Remember that you are never alone. Other Pagan parents have faced, and continue to face, the same challenges and rewards that you do. Reach out and connect with them. Find Pagan playmates for your children when possible, even if you can only manage it a few times a year at special festivals or other events. Study and explore the Pagan cultures of past and present for inspiration. The resources cited in this installment make a good beginning. Practice your networking and communication skills so that you can follow up on good leads. Keep your sense of humor! We are all part of Life's web; let us celebrate that and find ways to nurture our children within our own belief systems.

Endnotes

1. *The Pagan Family: Handing the Old Ways Down* by Ceisiwr Serith. Llewellyn Publications, 1994. St. Paul, Minnesota. p ix.
2. *WiccaCraft for Families: The Path of the Hearthfire* by Margie McArthur. Phoenix Publishing, 1994. Custer, Washington. p 9.
3. *The Family Wicca Book: The Craft for Parents & Children* by Ashleen O'Gaea. Llewellyn Publications, 1994. St. Paul, Minnesota. p 17.
4. *WiccaCraft for Families.* p 18.
5. "A Matter of Faith" by Jerry Adler. Newsweek magazine December 15, 1997. p 50.
6. *The Family Wicca Book.* p 17.
7. *Contemporary Paganism: Listening People, Speaking Earth* by Graham Harvey. New York University Press, 1997. Washington Square, New York. p 197.
8. *The Pagan Family.* p 190.
9. *Contemporary Paganism.* p 203.
10. *Contemporary Paganism.* p 203.
11. *The Pagan Book of Living and Dying: Practical Rituals, Prayers, Blessings, and Meditations on Crossing Over* by Starhawk with M. Macha NightMare & the Reclaiming Collective. HarperCollins, 1997. New York, New York. p 213.
12. *Entering the Summerland: Customs and Rituals of Transition into the Afterlife* by Edain McCoy. Llewellyn Publications, 1996. St. Paul, Minnesota. p 88.
13. *Entering the Summerland.* p 90.
14. *Spellcraft: A Primer for the Young Magician* by Lilith McLelland. Eschaton Productions, 1997. Chicago, Illinois. p 2.
15. *Teaching Children to Love: 80 Games and Fun Activities for Raising Balanced Children in Unbalanced Times* by Doc Lew Childre. Planetary Publications, 1996. Boulder Creek, California. p 31.
16. *Everyone Wins! Cooperative Games and Activities* by Sambhava and Josette Luvmour. New Society Publishers, 1990. Philadelphia, Pennsylvania. pp 5, 18, and 47.
17. *The Pagan Family.* Page ix.
18. *Daughters of the Earth: The Lives and Legends of American Indian Women* by Carolyn Niethammer. Collier Books, 1977. New York, New York. p 23.
19. *The Rites of Odin* by Ed Fitch. Llewellyn Publications, 1996. St. Paul, Minnesota. p 30.

Elizabeth Barrette has published numerous articles, poetry and fiction in a number of Pagan publications including several pieces in *Green Egg*. She is currently Dean of Studies at the Grey School of Wizardry. This article originally appeared in *Moonbeams Journal* and we are delighted to reprint it with permission here.

Vol. XXXI, No. 131 (Nov.–Dec. 1999) 14–17, 26

Water Brothers

by Miki Levenhagen

ATER BROTHERS ARE CLOSER than perhaps even a mother and child. It is a stronger bond than marriage is today, and is accomplished by a very simple act.

When two wish to become water brothers, they first must be certain that they understand completely what they are getting into. There must be no doubt in either mind (and essence) about it. One is usually sure; (s)he is the one who usually asks the other. If the other is just as aware and willing, then they share a glass of water, and the seal is set.

There: now what was so hard about it? The best is yet to come. The first thing: once you have become someone's water brother, there is no backing out. It is for life (and then some), and that is why you *must* be *absolutely sure*. Now: water brothers must *never* do the following—steal from, lie, mislead, cheat, or be jealous of any water brother. They must never force any water brother *or* non-water brother to do anything they don't want to.

This is what water brothers *do:*

Water brothers revere the essence of *every* being. They trust completely, share completely, and love completely.

You, as a water brother, are eternally responsible for each person that you share water with.

You are obligated to advise each brother in need, but committed to "leave" them at point of cusp, for it is theirs alone.

Becoming water brothers is like getting married, in that you become as One with your brother. And it is like baptism in that you *are* symbolically reborn. It is such a serious matter, and yet I am *filled* with joy each time I find one who would share with me. Why? I am not completely sure why; however, perhaps *this* is why: To love is joy, to trust is happiness, to share is fulfillment. To know that there are people like this is what gives me joy. Perhaps in simply telling you what water brothers are, what they do and *do not* do may give you some idea about what it means to be a water brother and to have one—or two (three?).

But a few words of warning: Once done, it's forever. So be *sure.* It is not always a bed of posies. You no longer *own* anything; you *share it.* And if something is asked of you, you shall oblige your brother...or find someone who can. But, at least to me, no thought is ever to the contrary; it is automatic to me.

In being a water brother, you may find your lifestyle slowly changing. But it may not seem that way to you, only to those who don't know what you've become.

GE Vol. VII, No. 67 (Yule 1974) 38

Memories of the Goddess

by Fredda Kullman, CAW

HE OTHER NIGHT WHEN IT WAS raining I kept hearing a strange sound in the house. I couldn't figure out what it was until I went to bed. I was looking up at the ceiling and saw the hole to the attic was open. Coming through were the sounds of rain on the roof. I had almost forgotten. It reminded me of when I was a child. I had an upstairs room with a balcony to myself. The roof was not more than 6 or 8 inches from the ceiling. I could hear the rain falling on the roof with its own special sound. Many a night I was lulled to sleep by the pitter-patter on the roof. Some nights when the storm was at its height I would stand out in the rain on the balcony watching the trees lashing back and forth, getting wet but enjoying the storm.

On calm warm nights I could sleep on

the porch and watch the changing pictures in the treetops, listen to the night birds, let the breezes caress me with warm gentle smells as I looked at the stars and traveled among them lost in the wonder and glory of the aloneness in the multitudes.

I remember in the spring and early summer, early evening rains, how the grass seemed to get greener and more plants popped up through the soil to reach up towards the sun and life. How after the rain the very air had a beautiful green glow to it and the smell of the wet earth was so delicious. How I eagerly waited for the flowers to pop out of the ground, the scent of lilacs to fill the air, the birds busy making their nests of a day and frogs croaking of the night.

All these things I remembered and more. It made me realize how busy everyone is now days, how little time people have to notice the signs of the Goddess. I cry in my heart each time I see where bulldozers have come along and cleared all the trees and ground for another FANTABULOUS HOUSING DEVELOPMENT. More and more I wonder when will man stop fighting Nature—hating the Mother—and learn to work with Her. When will men learn not to isolate themselves in caves of concrete, steel and asphalt to get sick in the soul and spirit, then wonder why.

I have decided I must take more time to enjoy the many beautiful things that Mother has from now on. Why don't you too?

GE Vol. VII, No. 67 (Yule 1974) 20

Oath of Eldership
from the liturgy of the Aquarian Tabernacle Church
by *Pete Pathfinder Davis,* Arch Priest, ATC

How, my Sister (or Brother), as an elder in the decline of my years, to you who would begin your Eldership, I admonish you to heed my words at your direst peril, causing the destruction of this place of honor to which you now aspire before your peers and our beloved Goddess and Domed God.

Accept now the awesome responsibility and make your deepest commitment:

To KNOW; To WILL; To DARE; To KEEP SILENT.

In all things KNOW with certainty the source whereof you speak before you would inform and advise another from your position as Elder. If not, keep your silence.

Make strong your WILL to uphold the good of the Craft and of your Community over personal benefit and ego, for it is not your Craft lineage, but rather your actions that will mark you as an elder in the eyes of the brethren.

DARE to serve those of the Craft rather than to attempt mastery over others. Dare to be subservient to the will of the

community, for by doing so you will be seen as resourceful and wise rather than demanding and manipulative. the power of an Elder is power shared.

KEEP SILENT when the temptation comes to belittle or speak ill of the brethren. One's stature is never enhanced at the expense of another. Practice restraint, the most difficult of life's lessons, and others will honor you as a true Elder of the Craft.

Go now. KNOW, WILL, DARE, KEEP SILENT, and you shall be accorded the recognition of many more than attend here. You shall receive the recognition of many who know not of this ritual for by your deeds and actions they shall know you best. We cannot elevate you in the esteem of others; only by your own words and deeds can you truly attain that which we here seek to afford you. Dark ye to these words of old, and go now with our blessings and best wishes:

SO MOTE IT BE!

Vol. XXVIX, No. 115 (Sept.–Oct. 1996) 4–6; 50

The Role of Elders in the Pagan Community

by M. Macha NightMare

[AUTHOR'S NOTE: *I recently reviewed this essay with an eye to updating it, but found that my criteria remain valid ones.* –MMNM 5/10/08]

What Is An Elder?

 THINK THERE IS A DIFFERENCE BE-tween an Elder of a particular Craft or Pagan magical tradition, and an elder in the Pagan community at large.

I belong to, and have been active in, an organization of Witches called the Covenant of the Goddess (CoG). In CoG, an elder is defined technically as one who is qualified to carry on her tradition, i.e., to teach it to others, to lead a coven, to initiate others, one who has qualified and attained all degrees of her particular tradition.[1]

But, of course, there are many one-degree traditions. In those, the Witch takes vows and formally dedicates her life to walking the Lady's path and to worshiping Her, to celebrating Her seasons, phases, gifts. By the time one has received an initiation from her "elders" in these kinds of traditions, one has already demonstrated unmistakably and sincerely her abilities to conduct magickal work—to cast circles; to call quarters, invoke deities, cast spells, alter one's consciousness; to give strength, love and healing to others; to raise power; to ground; to conduct herself ethically. Presumably she is also able to transmit this body of knowledge to others, which indeed is a thing she may have been doing on an apprenticeship basis prior to her taking vows.

So in the most basic way, I use CoG's definition of an Elder of the Craft—one who is qualified to and capable of transmitting her tradition to others.

But on the other hand, are we not perhaps being a bit less than elevated about our standards when we use such a loose definition? You'll notice that it is a definition which has nothing to do with age. Nor, ultimately, with accountability.

I honestly have mixed feelings about lots of young and middle-aged Witches going around calling themselves elders, even though I myself did it in my younger years, since I was in my 30s.

While it's true that many of us may have highly developed magickal skills and may be quite competent at teaching those skills to others, what we do lack is life experience. No matter how much I hear of someone's past life experiences, I seldom see, in those who claim them, evidence of the maturity one might expect such past life experiences to afford.

For CoG's legal purposes, I accept its definition of Elder of the Craft. But I think this present exploration requires a deeper look into what elder means. So I move to my second question.

Who Is An Elder?

As I mentioned, I think a person who is described as being an elder, or who describes herself as being one, should have some mileage on her.

In "native cultures" (and I use the term very loosely to mean, in general, ethnic cultures which have not been over-cultivated or which have not been too transformed from their origins by so-called "civilization"), age seems to be one necessary and indispensable characteristic of elder status (as the word "elder" implies).[2] Perhaps one of the blessings of age is that one is still alive and of this world—the world of matter and Earth and material and substance—when most of one's contemporaries have crossed over to the other side.

The older I get, the broader my perspective. I don't know how one achieves this perspective without "doing time" in this game of life. Perhaps there are other ways of achieving it; one now and then encounters souls who seem very ancient, or wise beyond their years.

On the other hand, if these old souls are truly old souls, they have acquired patience and can comfortably wait till they're older in years. Those who are always in a rush, even though older, have yet to embrace the virtue of patience. But for me, the only way that I seem to have been able to achieve perspective is to have *lived*. You know the old word—experience. (Remember that old "best teacher"?)

So if we accept that an elder has the skill and knowledge to competently pass on her tradition—as Craft elder; and that an elder must have lived, with or without having practiced some magical tradition for all of that life, to some state at least beyond childbearing years, what other qualifications must she have to function as an elder? And what, in fact, *is* the function of an elder?

I propose the following qualifications:

♥ *Age and experience, not alone, but combined into "seasoning," or "ripening"*

We all know older people who seem not just youthful, but immature. Many of us in this culture are as affected (or perhaps "afflicted" is an apter word) by the youth culture which the media promote. We pathetically try to hold onto whatever semblance of youth we may retain: The middle-aged man who courts younger women and discards older women (or woman) with whom he has had a long relationship, presumably with a shared history; the frantically trendy woman who behaves like her daughters, who takes pride in being told she looks like her daughter's sister, who is truly flattered at being told, "you don't *look* 50." To that supposed compliment, I answer in the words of Gloria Steinem: "This is what 50 looks like."

A primary learning experience which contributes to our seasoning (i.e., having turned with the Wheel of Life many seasons; steeping in our experiences) is parenting—successful parenting of thriving offspring. I do not limit the definition of parenting herein to biological parenting, rather nurturing of young beings.

Other experiences which season our lives are: mistressing skills; suffering illness, loss, injury, mishap; hard labor; successes and losses; wide exposure to the creatures and sights and sounds of this world.

So age—with some grace and seasoning and humor and perspective—is one qualification. But age alone does not an elder make.

♥ *Grace under pressure*

No need to freak out; everything levels out in the long run. Calm, compassion and reason, in balance with wisdom. By this I don't mean aloofness and distance, but an understanding of a situation which is informed by the memories of one's own youth—and youthful follies, if you will—and by a certain compassion and empathy for the specific crisis being addressed, either to or by the "elder."

Other ways to express or conceive this quality are grounded adaptability, or centered pliancy.

♥ *Skill in crisis situations*

A "qualified" elder needs skills at defusing crises, while not trivializing them. She requires the ability to lessen the immediate heat of the situation, to keep the parties to a crisis from attacking one another. But she still must face the very real feelings of all parties, and she must hear them and help them to be heard by the other parties to the situation, something most parents learn in the course of their child-rearing.

♥ *Respect and trust of one's peers*

This is a much more difficult and elusive quality, both to define and to reach agreement upon. How does one acquire it? What does one do to earn it? What quality demonstrates that one has it?

Other than by taking a popularity poll (and, of course, popularity does not necessarily imply respect and trust), by what criteria can we judge the respect and trust in which a person is held by her community? After all, none of us is perfect. All of us have some kind of skeleton in our closet, or some kind of unpleasant experience with another co-religionist. We have all made mistakes. It is human to be flawed; we would be imperfect humans were we "perfect." So this particular quality must, of necessity, be relative.

Perhaps trust and respect can be held to have been earned by one having done years of community service, or years of competent, effective, potent, efficacious "priestessing" (creating appropriate, powerful rituals for specific magickal purposes, presiding at rituals).

Perhaps trust and respect are earned by having been consulted for counsel, and having been entrusted with private vulnerabilities, and not having broken that trust, but having helped the one in crisis to overcome the situation, to triumph over adversity; a parenting skill.

Perhaps trust and respect are earned by some merely by their having been a "good listener" and emanating "good vibes" in both ritual and non-ritual situations with one's co-religionists over a period of years.

Obviously, one's individual, personal history in our community(ies) has significant bearing on her acceptability to her co-religionists

to function in the capacity of elder.

Assuming that we as a community accept the definitions and qualifications put forth above, what do we do with it? Do we attempt to form a more formal eldership? Is the concept of eldership useful to all Craft organizations and Pagan traditions?

I believe it could be useful, particularly in light of the strong organization and solidarity of the Christian right. We Pagans need our own solidarity. We need our own organization (and I don't mean by that an organization, but being *organized*).[3] We need mutual trust and respect, both within traditions and inter-traditionally.

To complicate the issue, this presents

A Call to the Ancestors
by *Fathom Hummingbear*

Ho, you ancestors!
You whose faces swim from the
pages of family albums in my attic,
whose papers molder in my cellar,
whose DNA courses through
my blood and my loins
seeking eternal life;
Elders whose names are lost,
while your manners and visions persist
in the patterning of my brain;
You who dwelt in the cities of old
when even cities remembered Earth our Mother;
clever craftswomen and men, potters, weavers,
farmers, hunters, mothers,
cave-dwellers, tree-dwellers;
Ho, grandmothers, grandfathers,
from deeper in me!
Four-leggeds, furry ones;
feathered fliers, welcome!
Scaly ancestors with four legs or none,
I open my depths to you;
and you who mastered the change
from water to air breathing,
Hail!
Sea-swimmers, I honor the water deep in me.
And you of the many-jointed legs,
your exoskeleton is part of my fabric, too;
even the tiniest of mites who are with us now,
thriving on the food of my cast-off skin.

And you who were my ancestor
before legs were thought of,
gastropods and nematodes,
burrowers and swimmers and floaters
and all dwellers on the face of Gaea;
tiny creatures who drift in Her waters,
you deepest ancestors,
even you bacteria in all your billions,
Hail!
And hail to our green cousins
who snatch fire from the sky
and juices from the rock
to bring all into Gaea's dance:
tree and shrub and vine and grass,
moss and lichen
and all the vast webs of energy
collectors
in the lakes and oceans,
you are honored, too.
Family of life!
We sit on the dust of your bones
and dream with the vision of your life
still growing within us.
HAIL AND WELCOME!

Hummingbear is the founder of the Temple of Transformative Music. *www. hummingbear.net/~aayoung/Mission.html*

GE Vol. XXVII, No. 106 (Autumn 1994) 45

us with the problem of reconciling how pur- portedly non-hierarchal groups/traditions might deal with the concept of eldership? In non-hierarchical traditions such as my own, there may be an unacknowledged or unnamed eldership. If there is, how do we acknowledge this fact while still maintaining no official hierarchy?

In addition to the qualities I've suggest- ed for defining who is an elder in the wider community(ies) age, experience, grace, calm, compassion, reason, wisdom, grounded adaptability, centered pliancy, crisis skills, respect and trust of peers, perspective, per- sonal history in community—non-hierarchi- cal groups need to beware of separation, or unwarranted, unearned, undeserved eleva- tion. Our special skills and experience can benefit the community, yet they are nothing without community.

I don't feel prepared to propose any an- swers to the question of non-hierarchical el- derships in this writing. The subject has been brought up, and so far I, for one, have no ready solutions.

In the meantime, I would put forth the question of what is the value and purpose of having a Council of Elders? And my primary answer would be as above—to foster mutual trust and respect, intra- and inter-tradition- ally, throughout Neo-Pagandom.

Then what would this Council of Elders do? What kind of authority would these el- ders have? Moral authority? How would they function as a body? To whom would they be accountable?

A council of elders might be charged with resolving disputes, mediating "Witch wars." The elders might be convened to redress a misdeed, such as abuse of power (sexual or otherwise), to name an error and its perpetrator(s), then to recommend compen- sation to the wronged.

Elders' moral authority must come from within the individuals who comprise the coun- cil as well as from the empowerment of it by its community(ies). Elders might employ magic and/or divination techniques when appropriate. They must be willing to give free- ly of their highly developed specialized skills in service to council and community, with a

balance of both pride and humility. These offerings can only benefit our community(ies) insofar as community actually exists and sup- ports its elders—in decisions; in carrying out decisions; in honoring its collective wisdom, discrimination and judgment.

A council's functioning as a body must be determined by its members, from within the council, not by anyone outside, yet a council is ultimately responsible to its community(ies).

Though it is not too early to examine these questions within our community(ies), there is no way I, one Witch, can put forth the definitive solution to meet the needs of our growing subculture. I hope that the def- initions and qualifications that I have offered can be a stepping-off point for our continued collective self-definition, with the heartfelt prayer for mutual trust and respect, intra- and inter-traditionally, throughout Neo-Pagandom.

Footnotes

1. For purposes of this article, and as an acknowl- edgement of my Dianic tendencies, I will be using the feminine personal pronoun through- out.
2. This is even true of the institutions of the Chris- tian churches!
3. Which so far no one could ever accuse us of being—whatever else they might accuse of us, eating babies or whatever.

Macha NightMare is an internationally pub- lished author, ritualist and all-round Pagan webweaver. She is a member of the American Academy of Religion, the Marin Interfaith Council, the Nature Religion Scholars Net- work (www.paganstudies.org), the Board of Directors of the Foundation for the Advance- ment of Women in Religion, the Sacred Dy- ing Foundation (www.sacreddying.org), Ad- visory Council, the Covenant of the God- dess, and The Biodiversity Project Spiritual- ity Working Group. Macha speaks on behalf of Paganism to news media and academic re- searchers, and presents at colleges, universi- ties and seminaries, and teaches on the broom- stick circuit. She is Chair of the Public Min- istry Department at Cherry Hill Seminary (www.cherryhill seminary.org), the first and only seminary serving the Neopagan com- munity. www.machanightmare.com

Vol. XXVIX, No. 115 (Sept.–Oct. 1996) 4–6; 50

PNG: Pagans Next Generation

by Aurelea K. River

AN ANTHROPOLOGIST—OR A PSYCH-
ologist, for that matter—would
have a field day with my
childhood. I grew up in rural
Northern California, and I was
born solidly into the Neo-Pagan movement.
My father joined the Church of All Worlds
when he was younger than I am now. He's
been a Pagan priest since 1978. My mom isn't
an organized-religion type of person, but that
never stopped her from being a Witch. Almost
my entire extended family (and it's a pretty
extended family, as in dozens of people)
consists of greatly varied counterculture
types. I made my ritual debut at one month
old, under the Yule tree, and I've been going
to festivals ever since. Unlike some of the
other Pagan offspring that I know, I haven't
defected into either nihilism or stock-
brokerism. I am still a Pagan, eighteen and a
half years in the tradition. It's been weird.

My parents split up when I was two, but
it was an amicable separation, and they both
wanted to raise me Pagan. I've heard a lot of
horror stories about custody battles where the
Paganism of one parent became the defining
issue. I am, in that respect, very lucky.

When you're a little kid, having Pagan
parents is really cool. Everyone, when they're
young, thinks that their parents can do magic.
Mine really could, and they told me that I
could. It is tremendously empowering for a
child to have their parents listen when there
are monsters under the bed. I once explained
my aversion to Dungeons and Dragons to a
friend of mine thusly: "I don't have a problem
with D&D, but I don't need it. I can fight
with a sword and cast a spell for real." Then
we made up a role-playing game based on
situations that I really had never been in. "Roll
a D6 to see if Jeff will take you to the prom!"

In many ways, my parents were classic
hippies, and they raised me accordingly.
Environmentalism was a big part of my life,
which makes sense. Honor the Earth, right?
It's still very important to me. They also
taught me to not believe everything I heard
in school. I remember coming home and
telling Mom what we'd learned about

Christopher Columbus. This was before the
revisions of the curriculum that took place in
1992, the 500th anniversary of his landing. This
was warm 'n' fuzzy, isn't-imperialism- nifty,
Intrepid Explorer Columbus. "That's crap," said
my mother, and proceeded to tell me what had
actually happened. I got in trouble later on for
mentioning it in school. I think that in general
I was more politically aware than many small
children are. Once, I tried to build a spaceship,
so that we could leave the planet in the event
of nuclear war. I was about four years old. In
retrospect, that's pretty heavy.

I lived up on a mountain, with no hot
running water and no electricity, so even when
I was going to public school, a large portion
of my life took place in a rather unusual
environment.

School was hard. I was obviously a
weirdo, but I managed to avoid being outed
as a Pagan until the fifth grade. I didn't lie, I
just didn't bring it up. While I don't remember
a sense of shame, I did know from an early
age that I had to be careful. A friend of mine
who had, with her parents, just discovered
Paganism, announced at lunch that she was
one and so was I. As fifteen heads swiveled
my way, the following went through my ten-
year-old brain: *Oh, shit.* Actually, for most of
the kids it wasn't too big a deal. Most of
them had been raised by hippies, and they
didn't really care that much. There were a
few hyper-religious types though. They
really wanted to save our souls. We were the
hot topic of Room Three that week. The
teachers reacted very reasonably, and
suggested that my friend and I have a
mediated session with the girl who was most
upset to see if we could work it out. She
declined, we went back to our homework, and
things smoothed out pretty quickly. Until I
was in middle school and people kept asking
me if I was a devil worshipper. It was teasing,
though, not an organized campaign of
harassment. As I said before, people didn't
really care. I have met Pagan teens from other
parts of the country who have been suspended
or expelled, and one whose school counselor
told her she was going to Hell.

When I was about twelve I switched schools, to one that was even smaller and more rural. By this time I was sporting a motorcycle jacket and magenta hair, and I, um, didn't fit in. Everyone else had their perms and their pastels and their subscriptions to *Seventeen,* and there I was, this little proto-Goth art wench. I made friends with all the poets and metalheads (all six or seven of them) right away. A few hard-core born-again Christians hassled me a little when they didn't have anything else to do. Actually, the faculty was more of a problem than the students.

At the time, my stepmother was a computer teacher at my school. She was one of the better middle and high school teachers; also, all the kids liked her. This didn't stop the school superintendent from harassing her for her Paganism. For whatever reason, curiosity or stupidity or sheer rat-bastardness, he harassed me too. I remember when he was driving my stepmother to a remote school in the district to repair a few of their computers. I went along. As we sloshed down the interstate, he fixed me with his "official" stare and asked, "Are you a witch?" "Um, yeah." I replied. "Poof, you're a frog!" He must have felt a little dumb, because he didn't mention it to me again. Still, the religion issue wouldn't go away, and with the addition of a dispute over an injury received at work, my stepmom did eventually leave her job.

I switched schools again, back to my old one, for the last two years of high school. Both students and teachers there were a little more enlightened, and there were even some other Pagany types. I went there for two years before I ran off to Ireland, to live with different Pagans, see all the sites, and watch talk shows in pubs for a year. Ah, education.

As a small child, I got a lot of casual instruction, especially from my mother. She's always been very matter-of-fact about magic; not a lot of woo-woo involved. From her I learned house-blessings, faerie lore, and scraps of Russian folk magic. ("When I told my mom I was a Pagan," my mother says now of my Russian Orthodox grandmother, "she said, 'Oh, that reminds me of what we used to do back home,' and proceeded to reel off this list of ostensibly 'Christian' folk traditions. All totally witchy, of course.") She also told me stories, mostly Russian, English, and Irish, and read me *Grimm's Fairy Tales,* in all their symbolic goriness.

My father was much more involved with group rituals, gatherings and the like, so I'm also well versed in the arcane arts of camping, dressing for outdoor circles in the cold, and keeping the fire going (with diesel, just like the Druids). I saw a great deal of eclectic ritual theater and absorbed a fair bit of mythology, Greek and otherwise.

I certainly wasn't the only kid. There were a lot of other children around, almost all of whom are still my good friends. One of the best things about being brought up in contact with a Pagan group is that your friends can relate to your religion. The children of solitaries are usually the only ones in their schools, like I was, but they don't have the cushion of "festival friends" to fall back on.

Circles are an interesting thing; less like prayer, I think, more like church, at least in CAW, and not always child-friendly. They're long. They require listening. They're chilly, and the people in the flowing robes are always nearer to the fire. I wish that somebody had sat my friends and me down and told us what the point was. Our parents all knew why they were there; they had made a conscious choice to do this. We were along for the ride.

Not that I never enjoyed myself. Hardly. Some events were geared toward children, like the Egg Hunt at Ostara, and festivals are a great place to run around in the woods, get filthy and tangled, and stay up late. Beltane was a blast every year, barefoot and living on bagels, tearing through the trees with my crazy elfy friends. I always looked forward to it. The actual rituals, though, weren't really a big part of it for me. In fact, although my understanding of the aforementioned point and my attention span have both increased considerably, I still don't have a lot of affection for large rituals. They're too big and impersonal for me, they're too familiar, and they usually don't do anything for me, the way religious observance is supposed to. For most newcomers, a circle is something different from anything they've ever seen. For me it's just the way things are.

One of the problems with being young

and at festivals, especially Beltane, is that some people really don't like children, or don't feel that children should be there. Some times this is valid. There are legitimate legal concerns about involving minors, however peripherally, in practices that many people might consider misguided or "immoral." Children also can be disruptive, and people understandably don't want to baby-sit someone else's kids while there's a ritual going on. On the other hand, sometimes it's just bullshit. Paganism, by which I mean actual, Paleolithic, Venus-of-Willendorf-carving Earth worship, was a fertility religion. Neo-Paganism claims to be.

The Church of All Worlds in particular is big on sacred sexuality, espousing the fecund Goddess, what-have-you. Reality check: *fertility leads to babies.* That's what *fertility* means. I don't mean to imply that sex is only for reproduction, though that is one of its obvious purposes. But to say, "This is a sexuality festival, there shouldn't be children here," is missing a pretty damn important point. Of course the old Irish and British Beltane fires weren't all about reproduction. They also weren't all about jumping in the sack with that great person you met on-line. There is a whole family aspect to festivals, or there should be: Spring is about children and growth and potential and magic, not just single white career people screwing in the woods. Sorry.

There's a phrase that gets tossed around a lot: "We're a tribe." I don't think so. The Maori have tribes. What NeoPaganism has is something more diffuse; interconnect-edness, yes, but in the sense of common thought, rather than blood or time or tradition.

My parents' friends, my various aunt and uncle figures, did look out for me at festivals and send me birthday cards. Still, it was not so much because I was a child as because they knew my father. There's nothing at all wrong with that, but it isn't tribal. The potential is there, I think; 200 years from now, maybe it will be. It depends. A group of progressive-minded adults who've all read the same books may be an excellent basis for a religion, but I think tribes are more dynamic than that, and also much more insular. People

in a tribe live together, eat together, are related by blood. That's a bit more intense than subscribing to a magazine or two and getting together with other Pagans eight times a year.

That said, there is a real sense of extended family. For example, what is the relationship of my stepsister (daughter of the man my mother married) to my stepmother (the woman my father married)? There's a connection there somewhere. What is my relationship to my stepfather's former wife, my step-siblings' mother? One of my sisters calls it stair-relatives: more than one step.

It's nice to go to a gathering and know almost everyone there; there's a sense of belonging that you just don't get at your average PTA meeting. It may not be a tribe, but it certainly is a community. There are some really wonderful things about that.

There are also some bad things, i.e., the good old rumor mill. Because the Pagan community is the context in which everyone interacts, personal grievances have a way of becoming community-wide problems. I've lost count of the times that somebody's specific gripe has ended up the topic of widespread community gossip and sometimes even dissention. Why is it that just because the argument is between Pagans, it's "everybody in the pool"? Doesn't everybody have better things to do? It's like every time X complains about B on the Internet, everyone has to comment before the universe implodes or something. Who cares? I have been listening to this stuff since I was tiny. It doesn't fix things. It's pointless and exhausting and stupid and selfish, that there is so much wrong in our culture, so much energy needed, and people can sit around and snivel about the letter somebody wrote to *Magical Blend.* You want to contribute to the global community? Send blankets to Albania.

I think growing up with all the craggy old leftists that my parents knew gave me a rather unique perspective. The whole Pagan movement aspires to diversity, which is absolutely wonderful. I don't remember being particularly shocked—in fact, I hardly noticed—when my best friend had three mommies and no dad.

Shame seems to be rejected by Pagans,

especially those who grew up in strict Christian households and have a lot to work through. The whole concept of the body as evil, of the physical as the realm of temptation, baffles me completely. Lucky me. So many people have that Christian guilt, even if they weren't raised specifically as Christians. I once met a girl who said she was ashamed to take a bath.

Because I grew up attaching very little stigma to nudity, I'm sometimes surprised by the context people place it in. I recently saw a movie where nakedness was very sexualized, where it was employed for the shock value. It didn't shock me at all. I sort of thought, "Oh, a naked woman. Whatever." I was talking about it later to one of my younger sisters (also raised Pagan), and I discovered that we both associated nudity not with sexuality, but with swimming. Lingerie, we agreed, was sexual. Naked was just naked.

Some people in the Pagan community, though, don't seem to see it that way. Pagans, in their laudable quest for tolerance and new paradigms, appear to have a lot of confusion over boundaries, both their own and those of others. (Disclaimer: I was raised in CAW, and have only passing familiarity with other groups like the ADF, ATC, or member covens in the Covenant of the Goddess. I'm really talking about CAW here, though I've heard this can be a problem in other organizations as well.) There's a good line in the Festival Etiquette section of the CAW membership handbook: "Nudity is an affirmation, not an invitation." Damn straight.

Just because someone is beautiful, doesn't mean that they're being beautiful for public consumption; just because someone is sexy doesn't mean they're on the market. A very small percentage of people just do not seem to get this. It's not like there aren't predators in the office, but somehow the anything-goes vibe of Paganism makes them feel more justified, like just because Paganism is sex-positive, you should sleep with them. That's wrong, in the very deepest sense. It isn't respectful of humans, and it isn't respectful of sex.

Newbies are especially vulnerable to this kind of thing, because they aren't sure where the boundaries are in this new culture, and

Wε ᕼrε Onε ᖴamily

© *1983, 1994 by* **Isaac Bonewits**

We are the children of the Earth.
She is our Mother!
Offspring of the Sun-god's bright mirth.
He is our Father!
We have our siblings in the air,
On land, in the sea
We are one family!

Ch: We are one family!
    We are one family!
    Kin to the whale and the dove!
    We are one family!
    We are one family!
    Joined by the strength of our love!

The Dolphin so free and alive,
He is our brother!
The Wolf who must kill to survive,
She is our sister!
We are the cousins of the eagle
Who soars in ecstasy.
We are one family!

Sequoia and bristlecone pine,
They are ancestors!
The cactus and the mushroom divine,
We are related!
The DNA that runs
Through us all is the key
We are one family!

Throughout all of time and of space
Life has been granted!
Every intelligent race—
We have been planted!
And those who have sown the
Seeds now wait patiently
We are one family!

GE Vol. XXVIII, No. 108
(Spring 1995) inside front

because they've just got religion and they're blissed to the point of insensibility. If the new person (either male or female) is really gorgeous, people practically form a line. My friends and I (and we can all spot a pseudo-spiritual pickup line from twenty paces, let me tell you) have been observing this phenomenon for a good long time now, and it is seriously fucked up.

Being fabulous—wearing pretty clothes and makeup and just being out there—is most definitely something I wouldn't do at a Pagan festival, the same way I wouldn't feel comfortable being fabulous in a bar. It just doesn't feel safe.

I think there's a real generation gap—anyone who remembers the Sixties has this free love ideal, whereas I, and most people of my age group and subculture, grew up knowing that sex could kill you. Free love isn't realistic. Then there's the predator concept—the pervasive awareness that there are some really scary people out there. I think that young women especially are much more mindful of this, and from a much earlier age, than they were twenty years ago.

Having someone old enough to be your parent making the moves on you is far more threatening than it is flattering. It's probably correctable, but it says something that I have heard this complaint from every single one of my Pagan girlfriends and from a few of the boys. I personally haven't been hit on, but then I've spent nearly my whole conscious life publicly establishing my space.

There's already a culture of wariness around being female in America. Pagan girls do not need this, too. I know that I'm slightly paranoid, but so are all my girlfriends. I know more than one person who says that they felt like everyone was waiting for them to turn eighteen. I see this as being a real problem, albeit one we can most likely do something about. I don't know why everyone's so fuzzy about boundaries. I think it's getting better; years of objections seem to have finally made a dent. This year at Beltane there were people specifically designated to make sure nobody got, uh, too big for their britches. I think it worked.

So here I am. What has it been like, growing up Pagan? It's been genuinely odd, which is more than most people can say for their family church. I am blessed to have been raised to see the Earth as alive. I think that I've stuck to the spirit if not the letter of most of the things my family taught me, and they're probably happy about that. I love nature, though I also love cities. I can be completely blown away by beauty. I tilt my head all the way back to see the stars better.

Sometimes I run up against problems with my friends: a lot of people my age have at least temporarily lost their sense of joy. They don't (except for the few who are actively religious) quite get the faith thing.

It's rather common nowadays to break away from the religion of your parents, but I haven't, though I don't think I'd miss it if I never went to another big circle again. I'm an environmentalist, a writer, and a general freak, all of which I'd be proud of in my kid. My education (the unofficial one) has been pretty interesting, though I'm not sure how much I can do with it, besides foist weird legends off on my friends and do well at Trivial Pursuit. College, maybe.

I like the people I knew growing up, and I like my stair-family. I think that if I ever have children, I'll raise them Pagan. Right now, though, I'm a little burnt out on the "Pagan community," not because I dislike the people but because the infighting has kind of worn me down. I think I'll be taking a break from festivals and things, just to get some perspective. It would probably do me some good to get out in the real world and have a straight job.

I'm sure I'll be back.

Vol. XXXI, No. 131 (Nov.–Dec. 1999) 8–11

Aurelea River is a grown-up Pagan American Princess and former teenage writing prodigy. An early interest in folklore and mythology led her to study anthropology at UC Berkeley, where she knew way more about goddesses than all the other undergrads. She lives in glorious Oakland, California, where she fiddles, gardens, and puts a bowl of milk out for the Little People every May Eve.

Song of the Suburban Shaman

© 1991 **Arch-Druid Seamus O'Blivious** (revised 2008)

To the Irish tune "The Plowboy" or any good tune

O once I was a husband but now I am a man
It was in the fall of '89 that my new life began
I went out to find myself amid the mushrooms and the trees
Along with forty other Joseph Campbell wannabees.

Ch: With me rantin' toorin' addie fal de di do. *

O I went into my closet to see what I could find
My dacron and my polyester I did leave behind
I took down my goatskin drum with the Navajo design
And I borrowed Martha's silver fox to gird around my loins.

I drove up to the campsite on a Friday afternoon
I heard what sounded like coyotes howling at the moon
I took out my Diners' Club card to pay them what was due
They said, "you are a Cave Bear, you're in teepee number two."

They took away my glasses, my flashlight, and my watch
All they left me was the silver fox to cover up my crotch
I staggered through the bushes to try and find my clan
But instead I stumbled on another naked howling man.

I asked was he a Cave Bear and could he help me please?
But he said he was a Stag and we were mortal enemies
Then he gored me with his antlers, so I slashed him with my claws
And I grabbed him by the neck and held him in my mighty jaws.

I dropped him on the ground, and gave a mighty roar
For I heard a lusty chorus chanting hymns in praise of Thor!
There were half a dozen cave bears hunkered down around a rock
And two chickens wrapped in plastic from the Safeway down the block.

Now the patriarch of cave bears, he was six foot three or four
Covered head to foot in weird tattoos he'd gotten in the war
But he couldn't light the matches with his awesome furry paw
So he growled and said, "To hell with it, we'll have to eat 'em raw!"

We planned a rite of passage so we could be born anew
But we found we all were circumcised so what else could we do?
We set up a peyote rite, and brother it was deep
I could tell you more about it if I hadn't gone to sleep.

Now the weekend's over and I'm on the freeway home
Together with my bold comrades no longer can I roam
No more wading in the river, or leaping from the rocks
And there's mud and blood and chicken grease on Martha's silver fox

O once I was a husband, but a cave bear I am now.
And neither Martha nor the kids can make me break my vow
I'll no longer take the trash out, I'll do just as I please
I'll hibernate and eat and growl and scratch my hide for fleas.

* *Proto-Indo-European: "Let them go and mount upon themselves if they do not see the humour in it."*

Chapter 9.
Power & Politics:
Changing the World
Introduction
by **Chas S. Clifton**

 OM WILLIAMS' "OIL" WAS WRITTEN DURING THE OIL CRISIS OF THE MID-1970S, BUT IT seems oddly relevant again. That's typical of *Green Egg*: prophetic, as well as utopian. This chapter illustrates how *Green Egg*'s writers leapt early into a variety of social and political issues, such as how a Pagan might cope with a 12-step addiction program, or how Pagans could claim their place as a contemporary religious movement.

Oberon's essay "Niggers of the New Age," which appeared in 1990, was designed to ask some shocking questions, hence the shocking title. In one sense, it asks why Western Pagan traditions are denigrated in favor of something more exotic: "Weren't we practicing Witchcraft as European shamanism years before Carlos Castaneda and Lynn Andrews made Native American shamanism the 'in' thing for New Agers? Weren't we using herbs, crystals, incense, chanting, healing, dream- and trancework, psychic experiences for *decades* before their current popularity?"

Since he wrote the essay, the academic study of contemporary Paganism has indeed become somewhat established—in this country, the American Academy of Religion, the leading scholarly association for the study of religion, added a section for "contemporary Pagan Studies" in 2004. Yet one of the problems this essay identifies stays with us: to some extent, Paganism in its various forms remains an embarassment to a world able to accept the Middle Eastern monotheisms and (with reservations) Asian religions. Perhaps that reluctance that Oberon identifies comes from seeing Paganism as religions of the past, with all their multiple gods and goddesses, magics and mysteries. Only we are not of the past, but growing.

Indeed, as lawyer Phyliss Curott writes in "Pagans and Their Religious Rights," we are not merely growing but demanding our place in the religious "marketplace." Curott describes Pagans' struggles to be legally accepted as clergy, to worship in public, and to avoid having their religion used against them in child-custody cases and employment cases. Her essay was written before the multi-year struggle to get the Veterans Administration to accept a Wiccan grave marker for military service members, a quest now being carried forth by other Pagan traditions, such as Druids.

Over the years since Curott's essay has appeared, numerous Pagans have taken her advice to heart: "It has been my conviction that the only way for our community to be truly free and genuinely safe is to be visible in the public eye, at both a personal and social level. We must also insist upon, act upon and defend our right to religious freedom." As Isaac Bonewits (and others) have pointed out, Lady Liberty can be regarded as a goddess of freedom, even as the ancient Greeks could simultaneously treat Nike (Victory), Themis (Justice) and other abstract concepts as deities too.

Finally, if we are to be accepted, we must be honest about who we are and where we came from, which is the part of the rationale for Jenny Gibbons' "Fixing Your History in Nine Easy Steps."

by Tom Williams, CAW

S THE SOLAR SYSTEM INEXORABLY turns slowly and majestically into the Aquarian Age we witness one after one events taking place which we knew had to occur, but whose impact we were, with all our reason, unable to comprehend until they were upon us. For the past several years we have been publishing and supporting the warnings of ecologists and historians who decry the gluttonous consumption of fossil fuels and the unlimited increase of industrial production. Rape of Mother Earth! All falling on deaf ears until somewhere in the desert an Arabian hand shuts off the spigot...drip, drip, drip.

What had to happen eventually is finally taking place. The brown goo, cursed by conservationists and lovers of clean air and blue skies, is drying up. And with it will dry the machine industrial, overpopulated military world which has dominated the first three-quarters of the twentieth century. It is no longer merely a matter about which we write and read and talk about on long evenings in the circles of our own when the pipe is passed from hand to hand. The changes are here, the age is dawning and we, who were spawned into a clattering mechanical world, but whose hearts linger with melancholy longing in the green glades of the Goddess, are present to witness a new birth—a birth that will begin with moans of pain which imperceptivity merge into cries of ecstasy.

With a dramatic turn it is becoming clear to millions of people why the present society has been condemned as "plastic" by so many Earth-oriented persons and groups. Plastics are, for one thing, produced from petroleum. But far beyond that is "plastic" in the sense of "artificial." The whole of modern indust-rial society turns out to have been an idol with feet of carboniferous muck.

Petroleum-based fertilizers and insecticides allowed a runaway growth of population while hopelessly upsetting the balance of the eco-systems upon which the artificially increased food supply depended.

The resulting overpopulation was then busied with largely nonessential jobs and "creating needs" for such modern blessings as electric can openers and vaginal sprays. While this energy-swallowing world provided some of its members with a level of luxury never before dreamed of, it also led to the ruthless exploitation and extermination of most of the few remaining Pagan peoples of the Earth. Wars of staggering horror and destruction were fought over oil and fueled by it. Like the legendary Ring of Power, whose ownership meant certain death, it drew the nations after it.

And now the tank is running empty with a sort of last, sickening "slur-r-r-p!" leaving that well-oiled machine of modern technology stranded in the boondocks—out of gas (wanna neck?). The driver of that gas-gobbling dinosaur, the American automobile, now sees the tar pits yawning for the return of their own. The question is, who is going to be sucked into the mire with their auto?

Well, all of the above is well-known bullshit, but I daresay it will put many of our long-touted slogans to the test. Even Pagans enjoy hitchhiking or tooling about the country in the ol' camper or beetle. As I write this it is a Sunday in Germany and there's not a car running in most of Europe (except France, whose diplomats are busy kissing Arab asses). All this comes as a bit of a shock to one who's used to the workaday world. So it's really true what we've been saying all this time!? Oh well, what was so groovy about the workaday world? All of us who have written and said things against industrial society while at least partially enjoying its benefits (and I number myself among such) will soon be required to put their ass where their mouth is.

Those who are not intimately attached to "Plastic Land" will not be mortally affected by its demise...and it will no doubt go thru some really heavy death-throes which will temporarily further fuck things up: Alaska Pipeline (who's she?), renewed drilling in Santa Barbara Channel (goodbye, LA), increased construction of atomic plants, etc. But I am sustained by thoughts similar to those of Regis of Amithaine in his superb little article in GE 56. We *are* the Freemen and the fact that the Behemoth is in the process of croaking before our very eyes will not affect us as directly as those who are its direct servants.

It *will* affect us. We will no longer live our lives in this quasi-schizophrenia of recent years: "Drive down to the organic co-op for the groceries and get gas on the way home!" How many of us have rather *not* confronted the inconsistency? But it will in much more devastating fashion affect those millions whose lives are inexorably bound up in serving the industrial Moloch. There will be sorrow.... That is to be, that is Karma.

But keep in mind the "Timeless Land" as Regis calls it. We see but one more sign of what the Age of Aquarius has in store for the children of Earth. The new age will have its pangs of birth, but thru them we will emerge into a cleaner, greener life. We will pull our wings out of the cocoon; we will weep with the effort. But then they will dry in the smiling warmth of the Sun and as butterflies we will laugh together in the garden.

"We are stardust; we are golden
We are billion-year-old carbon!
And we've got to get ourselves
Back to the garden..."
—Joni Mitchell, *Woodstock*

GE Vol. VII, No. 61 (Ostara 1974) 21–22

The Oilman's Burden

Take up the oilman's burden,
Send forth the best we breed.
Commit our kids to slaughter,
In service of your greed.

The homes they shall not gladden,
The loves they shall not wed.
Tie on a yellow ribbon,
They'll be our "honored dead."

Take up the oilman's burden,
Ye dare not stoop to less,
Nor call on conservation,
To curb your avarice.

What lands will ye not plunder?
What waters ye not spoil?
What death of elk and otter,
What seabeds fouled for oil?

Take up the oilman's burden,
Think of the good it brings.
It gives us Ziploc baggies,
And lubes our piston rings.

And as the war-clouds rumble,
And fury fills the sky,
How many oilmen's children
Are marching off to die?

Take up the oilman's burden,
Are we the less to blame?
Have we not fed your habit,
And is this not our shame?

—Tom Williams, 1991

GE Vol. XXIV, No. 94 (Mabon 1991) 13

Niggers of the New Age
by Otter G'Zell

IS IT JUST ME? OR IS ANYONE ELSE out there getting the distinct impression that we Pagans are regarded as somehow not quite "respectable" by our fellow inhabitants of the New Age paradigm?

"Nigger" is a term that has outgrown its original usage of referring solely to Black people, and has come to mean any who are despised, derided, reviled, repudiated, distained and denigrated (from *de-nigrare,* to blacken). Many people besides Blacks have been treated as Niggers by Western society: Jews, Native Americans, Chinese, Mexicans, women, hippies—and always, it seems, Pagans.

I first got an inkling that Neo-Pagans were New Age Niggers when Marilyn Ferguson's vast encyclopedic compendium *The Aquarian Conspiracy* did not include a single Pagan organization among the many hundreds of groups lauded and catalogued. Lately I have encountered more of this Pagans-as-Guttersnipes attitude from a few New Age bookstore owners we have approached about carrying *Green Egg,* New Age Centers, and even radical environmental gatherings.

And yet—weren't we Pagans the ones to introduce many of the concepts that are now so much a part of the whole New Age stock-in-trade? Weren't we Pagans the ones who were promoting a return to the Goddess back in the late 60s, years before modern feminist scholars ever wrote about Her, when the feminist community was totally into being political and didn't want to hear about Her? Hadn't we adopted the "Gaea Thesis" as an operant thealogy years before the rest of the world had ever heard of it? Weren't we ordaining women as priestesses for decades before the Episcopal Church made headlines by ordaining women "priests?" Weren't we promoting religious ecology and sacred environmentalism years before Earth Day? Weren't we advocating healthy and celebratory approaches to sexuality years before Esalen and all these Tantric workshops

became a fad? Weren't we practicing Witchcraft as European shamanism years before Carlos Castaneda and Lynn Andrews made Native American shamanism the "in" thing for New Agers? Weren't we using herbs, crystals, incense, chanting, healing, dream- and trancework, psychic experiences for *decades* before their current popularity? And on and on....

So why are we not heralded as visionary pioneers, forerunners, revered ancestors of the New Age movement, instead of its untouchables? *Why is* Pagan *a dirty word?*

In the first chapter of *Drawing Down the Moon,* "Paganism and Prejudice," Margot Adler notes:

> If Neo-Paganism were presented as an intellectual and artistic movement whose adherents have new perceptions of the nature of reality, the place of sexuality, and the meaning of community, academics would flock to study it. Political philosophers would write articles on the Neo-Pagans' sense of wonder and the minority vision they represent. Literary critics would compare the poetic images in the small magazines published and distributed by the groups with images in the writings of Blake and Whitman. Jungian psychologists would rush to study the Neo-Pagans' use of ancient archetypes and their love of the classics and ancient lore.

Something strange is going on here, and we need to understand it if we are to deal with it. New Age liberalism embraces Native American shamanism, Greenpeace, spiritual environmentalism, Goddess worship, feminism, sexual liberation, reincarnation, women's spirituality, Third World self-determination, inter-racialism, animal rights, gay rights and crystal magic. So do we. We have always thought of the New Age as including us (remember: *"This is the dawning of the Age of Aquarius.... Harmony and understanding, sympathy and love abounding. No more tears and cruel derision; All that's living dream a vision! Mystic crystal revelation and the mind's true liberation...Aquarius!"*). So why do New Agers, Neo-Native Shamanics, Eco-feminists and others who embrace so much of what we *are,* seem to reject *us* as a religion and a movement?

Regarding those in both the New Age community and in academia who distain Pagans, Margot says: "Yet many of these people maintain a generous openness about visionaries, poets and artists, some of whom may be quite mad according to 'rational' standards. They are fascinated by people of diverse professions and life styles who have historical ties with, let us say, the Transcendantalists or the Surrealists, as long as the word [Pagan] is not mentioned."

This suggests that our terminology is at fault. Yet, as has been often discussed in these pages, both "Pagan" and "Witch" have a long and rich history, and these terms accurately describe who we in fact are. We are Nature-worshippers, lovers of the countryside, i.e., *pagani.* And we are practicing a shamanic tradition of European lineage, i.e., *wicce.*

In this light, it is of course no revelation that we have always been denigrated in Western civilization, at least since the Roman conquest. But then so have the Jews. From the Middle Ages through WW II, our Pagan history and the history of the persecution of Jews have been remarkably parallel. Even the bizarre accusations leveled at us by our tormenters have been similar. People love to blame the victim. Only in the past half-century have the Jews managed to turn their Nigger-ness around, and it would behoove us to learn how they did it.

Was it something we said or did? Or is it something we are? In overcoming prejudice, it is essential to know just what our antagonists are actually mad about. Usually what is stated is merely a smokescreen. Blacks have been called "lazy," Indians "drunks," women "silly," Jews "avaricious," Chinese "inscrutable," and Pagans "Satanic." But those accusations are bogus. Blacks were enslaved and abused, and Indians had their lands stolen out from under them. I suspect the prejudice against them was motivated by guilty conscience. Jews and Chinese were simply willing to work harder and study more than many outside their communities, and

therefore were apt to succeed, inciting jealousy. Women have been oppressed for millenia for innumerable "reasons," and perhaps the patriarchy fears a turning of the tables.

Could any of these factors be the reasons why Pagans today should be regarded as Niggers? Could the Christian churches, for instance, be suffering from a guilty conscience over the brutal persecution of the Burning Times? Are they jealous of our success and growth? That would explain Christian hostility towards us, but not New Age antipathy.... Could it be (dare we say it?) a class or money issue? Perhaps we're not perceived as Niggers, but as White Trash!

GE Vol. XXIII, No. 90 (Lughnasadh 1990) 2

The Curse of Greyface

In the year 1166 BC, a malcontented hunchbrain by the name of Greyface got it into his head that the universe was as humorless as he, and be began to teach that play was sinful because it contradicted the ways of Serious Order. "Look at all the order about you," he said. And from that, he deluded honest men to believe that reality was a straightjacket affair and not the merry romance as men had known it. It is not presently understood why men were so gullible at that particular time, for absolutely no one thought to observe all the *disorder* around them and conclude just the opposite. But anyway, Greyface and his followers took the game of playing at life more seriously than they took life itself and were known even to destroy other living beings whose ways of life differed from their own. The unfortunate result of this is that mankind has since been suffering from a psychological and spiritual imbalance. Imbalance causes frustration, and frustration causes fear. And fear makes a bad trip. Man has been on a bad trip for a long time now.

IT IS CALLED THE CURSE OF GREYFACE.

(—*Principia Discordia, 4th Ed.*)
GE Vol. VII, No. 63 (Litha 1974) 24

Gaian 12 Steps

by *Anodea Judith*, CAW

THE 12 STEPS OF ALCOHOLICS Anonymous have been used by millions of people for addressing a variety of habitual sins. The phenomena of addiction—being unable to do without something, until it severely alters your life—has been expanded from abuse of alcohol and other drugs, to food, sex and behaviors such as loving too much or having too little sense. We are, as Anne Wilson Schaef so aptly states, an addictive society.

Al Gore, in his phenomenal book *Earth in the Balance: Ecology and the Human Spirit,* states plainly that *as a civilization, we are wholly addicted to consuming Earth.* Piecemeal environmental solutions, such as recycling or carpooling, while useful, cannot begin to address the full scope of the problem. Like the wife hiding her husband's bottle, our denial and failure to confront the situation enables it to continue. Having already written a Pagan 12-Step alternative to the Christian context of the original 12 steps (GE 92, Ostara 1991), I here apply them on a planetary level:

1. Admitted that we were powerless over the culture's addictive consumption and destruction of the planet, and our environmental crises had become unmanageable.

2. Came to believe that the power of Gaea, the living Earth, could run the biosphere correctly and heal the destruction over time.

3. Made a decision to turn our will and the legislation of our lives over to the will of Gaea, as we understand Her needs through science and religion.

4. Made a searching and fearless moral inventory of the extent of the damage we have done to the planet.

5. Globally admitted the exact nature of our wrongs.

6. Were entirely ready to let the needs of Gaia override these short-sighted policies and behaviors.

7. Humbly returned to simpler ways allowing our connection with Gaia to erode our destructive habits.

8. Made a list of all systems we had harmed, and realized the need to make amends to them all.

9. Created direct policies, legislation, and practices to address such harm wherever possible, without endangering lives.

10. Continued to monitor the way we live upon the Earth, and when wrong, promptly exposed it.

11. Sought through appropriate activity and spiritual practice, our conscious connection with Gaia, seeking knowledge of the planet and the power to live collectively in harmony with Her.

12. Having experienced a global awakening as the result of these steps, celebrated and sought other systems to apply them to.

Anodea Judith, PhD is a long-time member and former High Priestess of the Church of All Worlds (1987–97) and the author of many books on personal and global transformation, including the classic *Wheels of Life* (1987) and the dual award-winning *Waking the Global Heart* (2006). She is also an award-winning filmmaker of *The Illuminated Chakras* (2003) and an international workshop leader and speaker. Her books have sold over half a million copies and been translated into 13 languages.
www.sacredcenters.com
www.wakingtheglobalheart.com

GE Vol. XXV, No. 99 (Winter 1992–93) 8

Goddess of Freedom: Lady Liberty Statue Consecration

*A Report from **Arch-Druid Isaac Bonewits**, ADF*

O N SEPTEMBER 18, 1993 CE, FORTY members of ADF, the Church of All Worlds and several local Wiccan groups, gathered in Washington, D.C. to consecrate the statue of Libertas, Goddess of Freedom, who stands atop the Capitol building's dome. There, on the Capitol's East Lawn, surrounded by old trees, on ground that felt sacred already, we were aware that this might be the first overtly Pagan ceremony done in sight of America's power center.

We stood and admired the bronze statue, 19.5 feet tall and very beautiful, with a noble bearing and a compassionate expression in her deep, loving eyes. She was being repaired and polished before Her return to the dome.

Ray, a local Wiccan, gave a rousing oratory, then we chanted *"We are a circle..."* while Patricia and Gwydion purified the statue with water and incense, which were brought to the center of the nemeton, becoming our well and sacred fire.

I sang *"O Earth Mother,"* the Tree Meditation was led by Will Pierson and Wiccan quarter invocations were done. The symbol ism of four directions that intersect everywhere defined the ritual's center as simultaneously the well and fire, the statue of Freedom, the Capitol Building, and the ceremonial center of the USA. I declared the Gates open and invoked the Three Kindreds of Four Regions from which Americans have come, as well as the Native ancestors of these lands. Deborah did a powerful Invocation of Lady Liberty:

We invoke you, Lady Liberty, and welcome you anew to the land of the free. America is... the place where you hare achieved your highest goals...where you have faced your worst enemies. America was founded

on your principles: freedom, democracy, and individuality. America was also founded on slavery, oppression and genocide of native peoples. Lady Liberty... You are the one who wipes out intolerance and tyranny. You are the bringer of freedom: freedom to speak...to gather...to publish, freedom of worship of whatever deities we choose...freedom to pursue happiness—loving whom we will, living as we choose.... Lady Liberty, now and always, here and everywhere, we invoke you by these words: let freedom ring!"

Praise offerings to Lady Liberty included a rewrite of "My Country 'Tis of Thee" by Don Meinshausen:

*Our Goddess, 'tis of thee,
incarnate Liberty,
of Thee we sing.
Our blessings far and wide,
strong as the rising tide,
Forever shall abide,
let freedom ring!*

Power was raised with drumming and singing *"We can rise with the fire of freedom!"* Power was fed steadily into the statue while I spoke the Consecration Spell:

In the Name of the Earth Mother, the ever-changing All Mother: and in the Names of all those deities who have ever been worshipped in this land, ancient or modern; and in the Name of our most holy Goddess Liberty Herself: We do charge and consecrate this sacred statue of Her. Let it be a constant influence On this ceremonial center of America. Let it cause all our public servants to make, enforce, and judge the laws and policies of this nation in accordance with Liberty's highest ideals of freedom and justice for all, ill America and the world. Let this statue, and our holy Goddess Liberty Herself he ever defended from the forces of evil and oppression. Let the fires of freedom burn bright! So mote it be!

We then thanked the entities and closed the Gates. In the excitement of the moment we forgot to reground, so we had to spend a few minutes afterwards hugging trees.

We found out that before we began, local Masons had celebrated the 200th anniversary of the laying of the cornerstone of the Capitol Building by re-enacting the original Masonic consecration. So now that building, and by extension the entire U.S. government, has been magically charged by the Goddess of Freedom from top to bottom: "As above, so below."

I suggest that every year, on the Fourth of July, American Goddess Worshippers reinforce the consecration we performed in September, and magically call forth the powers of Liberty and Freedom upon our government.

GE Vol. XXVI, No. 103 (Winter 1993–94) 37

Invocation to the Earth

*Blessed is the Earth -
Our Mother and our Home.
Blessed is She whose spirits dance
In the forests and grasslands
And in all living places.
Blessed is She who brings forth all
  things
Living and non-living;
Our sustenance, our comfort, our
  shelter,
To Whom we return when our living
  ceases,
With Whom we are One always
In the perpetual cycle of taking and
  giving back.
Blessed are we for we are Her
With all creatures and plants –
With all of Life*

—Julie Carter

GE Vol. VII, No. 65 (Mabon 1974) p. 26

Liberating Wisdom

by *Joy Williams, Scion,* CAW

AT THE SECOND NEW MOON NEST meeting, we participated in a ritual to release a Great Horned owl to the Wild. A wildlife rescue center that rehabilitates and releases wild predatory birds contacted me after reading a forwarded email message. I asked people around Eclectia (our intentional community) if they would agree to allow the rescue center to release a wild Great Horned owl (already trained to hunt) here. Our 28 acres, almost exclusively wild land—except for the 5 acres upon which we live—already had some Great Horned owls and other predatory birds present. In mid-September, the wildlife people arrived.

We held a brief circle to invoke the four directions, the Goddess and the God. The owl was placed in the center in its carrying box. We called upon Pallas Athene, Hellenic Goddess of Feminine Wisdom, with her sacred totem the owl. The God we called upon was Pan, God of the wild things, fertility, and the hunt (an appropriate God for an owl, we felt, since the owl is predatory). The owl, greatly agitated from the trip in the car, was clicking and hissing, but calmed down almost immediately upon being put in the circle. The wildlife rescuers were surprised and pleased with the result. We did a grounding meditation to get in touch with Mother Earth and the interconnectivity of all life. Then we opened a door in the circle and started to walk up the mountain to the release point. Children and other people from the ranch joined our few nest members. After about thirty minutes, we reached the release point and waited for dusk. We all grew quiet so Tom (Williams) and I and the person from the release center could undo the carrying box. A soft but lively wind began to roll down the mountain. I remember looking into the owls' eyes through the holes in the box. There was no fear in them, only ackn "OWL"edgement. What wondrous eyes it had! We tipped the box forward... forward...then the glorious Great Horned owl burst forth, hovering on the updrafting winds for a second. Looking

around to get its bearings, (and I vainly imagine that it looked at us) it swooped to the eastern trees to freedom and life. For the first time in it's life the owl was free to be free, no longer in a shelter or aviary. I felt tingles as it flew away to find a home, beautifully expressing its nature in body and flight.

We trudged back down the mountain and opened the circle, wishing this new friend on our ranch health, well-being, and plenty of food and love. "Stay if you will, go if you must, hail and farewell."

The center who brought the owl to us was so happy with the circle and the energy there, that they may bring us a companion owl. This one got to know the first owl in captivity. Hopefully, they are of opposite sexes and will mate and bring more blessings upon the land. When we got back, and were completing the ritual, I realized that the circle we had drawn was under the olive tree in our yard, sacred to Pallas Athene. I feel like I touched the sacred heart of Gaia through her granddaughter's totem, in this act and rite.

Gaia, the Greek Mother Earth and what we, as Neo-Pagans call our sacred Mother Earth, was the original primary deity at the Oracle of Delphi. Her sacred Priestesses disclosed oracular messages to the people who needed guidance. She was the Mother of Themis/Metis who was impregnated, and then eaten, by Zeus while she carried his seed. She gave birth into the mind of Zeus, who grew so agitated from this incredible Goddess of feminine wisdom, that

Art by Joann Powell Colbert

he asked Haepheastus to open his skull. Athena sprang forth in full battle armor. The Patriarchal Graeco-culture tried to say that this meant that women were not related to their children, though fathers were, because Pallas Athene was not born of woman, but of man.

This story, to me is a true metaphor for our age. From the intellectual thought processes of the patriarchal culture, the Goddess is emerging, with great pain. The Goddess of Justice had been truly removed from the picture, subjugated and buried, her knowledge hidden in the power-over paradigm of Western culture. But Gaia's pain, Her Mother, Our Mother, has given birth to our full blown, painful realization—we must address the injustices that the Earth is suffering. Athena has come forth from the confused brain of Patriarchal Culture as a full-armored Goddess, but Hers is not a war of violence, it's a war of Wisdom. This Wisdom knows that the answers lie in our re-connection to Gaia, our re-connection to each other and Her other magnificent children. This is why Athena is still in armour. The armor of Pallas Athene is Her protection against the onslaught, it is defensive, not offensive, protecting the Wisdom She holds from further abuse and attack. We need to understand that we are, as Gaians, still vulnerable to the onslaught of Zeus's Patriarchal anger over his pain in consciousness. This is of His own making, but He denies his responsibility. This is why he is in such pain—suffering such a migraine. Patriarchy has eaten justice. Hephaestos, invention and technology, is unconsciously aiding the birth of the Goddess. Zeus has been the fundamentalist seeking to silence what threatened his world view. Patriarchy is the bomber of the abortion clinic. Patriarchy is the corporate polluter who would seek to rob Gaia of clean places for Her children to live. Patriarchal Zeus is angry and afraid, because the migraine, the rebirth of the Goddess, threatens his rule and blinds him with suffering. He is beginning to realize that to heal, he must accept love, wisdom, and guidance. He must realize that he loses nothing, not status or anything else, by loving the Divine Feminine.

GE Vol. XXVII, No. 107 (Winter 1994–95) 51

The Word for "Woman" Was "Goddess"

The word for "Woman" was
      "Goddess" once
The word for "Goddess" was "Woman"
They were one and the same

When did we lose that primal
      knowledge?
When did we lose the link
Between "Mother" and "Magic"?

Somewhere between the years of stone
      and steel
We forgot where we came from,
We forgot Who we came from

But now we remember
That the First Fertility sprang from a
      Female place
From a Goddess unnamed—before
      naming—

Before anything but the pure power
Of Creation pouring out over the
      newly-greed planet
Dreaming us into being

In turn we created other things—some
      good,
Some bad—and gave names to our
      Goddess and
The Gods Who came after.

Now we remember where Love came
      from
And Fertility, and Family. Let us
      remember
To be thankful once again.

—Elizabeth Barrette

Vol. XXX, No. 122 (March–April 1998) 13

Fixing Your History in Nine Easy Steps

*by **Jenny Gibbons** (art by Scott Thomas)*

ISTORY—YOU CAN'T LIVE WITH IT, you can't live without it. Every religion needs a glorious and inspiring past, one that will warm the hearts of its adherents and reveal the agelessness of its philosophy. Unfortunately, history is composed of an almost impenetrable morass of inconclusive, inconsistent, and contradictory evidence and it's damned hard work to slog through the stuff. So what's a True Believer to do?

One solution is to leave it to the professionals, but scholars are fickle creatures, liable to change their minds at the drop of a hat. 150 years ago everybody knew that the Druids built Stonehenge, then somebody invents something called "radio-carbon dating" and the whole theory's blown out of the water without the least thought for the impact this is going to have on your liturgical practices! And what if your ancestors weren't as enlightened as modern minds might like? Academics often have no sense of what is and is not proper to say and they'll blather on and on about how the Celts worshipped severed heads when all you really wanted was a nice description of what Druids wore to their rituals.

Nope, if you want your history done right you've got to do it yourself. Fortunately that's not as hard as it may seem. By following these nine simple guidelines you can quickly make the most politically incorrect history produce a glorious past and eternal truths (modern ones, that is—outdated eternal truths require a lot of behavior modification, so they're best avoided).

RULE #1: Know What You're Going to Find Before You Go Looking for It

"Plan Ahead" is the Golden Rule. I cannot emphasize enough how important it is to know what happened before you go wandering into the wilderness of historical evidence. If you do your work backwards—looking at the evidence first and then trying to formulate theories from it—it'll take forever. Also, without a good Plan of History you're doomed to be overwhelmed by ambiguous evidence. Take those buxom Neolithic Venus figures, for instance. Are they evidence of widespread Goddess worship or the Stone Age equivalent of Playboy? You're not going to know for sure unless you've got your Plan of History worked out ahead of time.

RULE #2: Keep It Simple, Sweetheart

Nobody wants a complex history. Nobody wants to hear, "The Celts had a nature-focused religion, but they were head-hunters and practiced human sacrifice, though the human sacrifice was more like capital punishment and the evidence for it does come from hostile sources." No. What people want to know is, were the Celts Good Pagans or Bad Pagans? Keep the teams straight. Women, Celts, and Pagans are Good. Men, Romans, and Christians are Bad. And no, this isn't stereotyping: stereotyping is saying "Women, Celts, and Pagans are Bad." This is the exact opposite.

RULE #3: Think Positive!

Don't weeble with your history! Don't say, "I think Venus figures offer strong evidence that Neolithic people may have worshipped a goddess." Nobody wants to hear opinions—they want to know what history proves. No doubts! Say, "These figures prove that Neolithic people everywhere venerated the Great Goddess."

RULE #4: Don't Confuse Yourself With the Facts

The most important rule for historical research is: don't bother. Actual research is tedious and inexact—you're never sure what you're going to come up with. You could spend the rest of your life rummaging through archives trying to count how many Witches were killed in the Witch-hunts but why go through the effort, especially since you might end up with some unimpressive figure like 40,000. Be creative! Make it up! Say, "Nine million Goddess-loving women were killed in the Burning Times."

You frown, Gentle Reader. You think, perhaps, that people will question your fabrication? Not at all—for once history will actually aid you. History is located in the most inconvenient places—dingy libraries, distant monasteries, and the lowest shelves of museums. Nobody's going to bother double-checking you unless you goad them into it by saying something ridiculous like,

"Fourteen women got killed in the Burning Times, but they were all a bunch of Satanists, so who cares." People judge you on what you say, not why you say it, so as long as you sound plausible and don't offend anybody you'll do just fine.

Now if you follow these first four rules closely you don't have to read the rest of this article. However, I know some of you Adventurous Readers are going to ignore my warnings and try to use actual facts in your histories, so here are a few pointers to help you through the process.

RULE #5: What You Don't See Can't Hurt You

When in doubt, leave it out. The key to a good history is only using the parts that make sense. Are your medieval Witches employing the Eucharist in their spells? Well ixnay on atthay! If you drag that nonsense into your history you'll have to swap your heroic Pagan underground resistance religion for a bunch of fence-straddling syncretists who couldn't tell the difference between Christianity and Paganism.

RULE #6: Be Creative!

Sometimes you'll find evidence that's almost perfect—but not quite. A lovely description of the Sabbat, with the unfortunate addition that the Witch left her body home when she went. Three or four women who were accused of Witchcraft, but not a full coven's worth. At times like this let your creative juices flow! Trim down that oversized passage! Combine a few different trials to produce the requisite thirteen Witches! Obviously in an article this size I can't detail the hundreds of ways there are to sculpt the raw material of history, but if you really can't think of anything, Margaret Murray's works are very inspirational.

RULE #7: No Notes Is Good Notes

No footnotes! If you're going to be silly enough to use historical evidence don't compound your error by admitting what you did. Footnotes enable your critics to quickly spot any creative source use. Never, ever underestimate the malign power of footnotes—one careless citation can cripple the greatest of histories.

Take the Burning Times. For decades everyone knew that 9 million women were killed in the Witch Trials. Nobody knew how we knew, but everybody knew. Perhaps (shiver!) it was handed down by word of mouth from those horrible days. Then some careless feminist cited the original source: Matilda Jocelyn Gage's *Women, Church and State.* What a catastrophe!

Far from being the record of a demographically fixated medieval Witch, the 9 million figure was nothing more than a rough guess by a 19th-century writer.

Because of this you can't mention the Nine Million Martyrs these days without having half a dozen historical purists jump down your throat. Meditate on that the next time you're tempted to cite a source!

"Well," you may be thinking, "those rules sound easy enough. Why is Our Humble Narrator dead set against historical evidence?" Because, bunky, by trying to use facts you've set yourself up for a never-ending headache: criticism.

If you'd stuck to your imagination there wouldn't be much your opponents could do to you. I mean, do you know anybody who can prove that Merlin didn't get the secrets of Witchcraft from Atlantis? But by using real or semi-real evidence you've given your enemies a stable target and every amateur historian with a scholarly book in her library is going to feel qualified to try to poke holes in your lovely history.

Ah, now you begin to see the magnitude of your error. But don't despair—there are ways of handling criticism.

RULE #8: Repent!

It's never too late—just insist that any negative evidence doesn't apply to your theory. If someone says, "Look at all these medieval Witches cursing cows and babies! What ever happened to the Witches' Rede?" you simply reply, "Those weren't Real Witches." Were the Druids too political? Well, they weren't Witches. Romans and Germans exposing babies?

Not Witches either. By throwing out everything that contradicts your Plan of History you can eventually dispose of evidence entirely, and then you're safe again!

RULE #9: Attack the Weakest Part of the Theory— the Theorist

Never, ever let anyone goad you into attempting to counter facts with other facts— it's a sure way to spend the rest of your life arguing. Instead, cut right to the heart of the matter: the idiot who criticized you in the first place.

Is he a man? Well, we all know about Them, don't we? Christian? Bigots, every one. And don't be intimidated by academic credentials— they just prove how thoroughly an author's been inculcated in the Patriarchy's Hidden Agenda (and if someone compares your Plan of History to his Hidden Agenda, well that just shows he's prejudiced against Pagans).

But what if an uneducated lesbian Iroquois Clan Mother contradicts you? Obviously she's been subtly compromised. Otherwise why would she be disagreeing with you? Take advantage of the fact that nobody's perfect—and if they are, that's suspect too.

There you have it—a beautiful history in nine easy steps (or four, if you're really smart).

Vol. XXVIX, No. 121 (Nov.–Dec. 1997) 20–21

"'Hail ye Gods', the Priestess Prays, moonlit nights—and sunlit days, she shows us love, please, with eyes, hair breeze, and into her Goddess lives, divine, the message hands, into troubled lands, the Gods to rain-dripped blown by as we come shrine, the and is carry in your the hateful **GODDESS LIVES!**"

Reclaiming the Center: The Politics of Gaean Religion

*by **Richard W. Ely**, Priest, CAW*

OLITICS IS THE ART OF GOVERNING, not a swear word. Gaean religion is the modern manifestation of the oldest spiritual traditions on this planet, remnants of which survive in the Amazon and elsewhere around the margins of the industrialized world. These Earth-centered archaic traditions arose from the perception that the natural world is endowed with spirit, and that one can consciously interact with Nature in ways that are not purely physical. This is the path of the shaman, magic, and the way of the plant and animal powers. Earth-centered spirituality has reawakened in the Euro-centric cultural sphere in a variety of forms, including Witchcraft, NeoPaganism, Druidism, some Deep Ecologists, and the African Diaspora traditions. Collectively, these Earth-centered traditions will be referred to as Gaean religion, and the followers of such traditions as Gaeans. Incidentally, the spelling "Gaea" refers to the Greek name for the Earth Goddess, whereas the more familiar "Gaia" refers to the James Lovelock's scientific hypothesis that Earth's surface environment is controlled by the biosphere.

The revival of Earth-centered religion is part of a global fundamentalist resurgence that is a reaction against materialistic modernism, and the expression of a longing for enduring values in an era of accelerating cultural, economic, technological and environmental change. Gaean religion is marginalized at present, but will enter the mainstream political discourse as the global environmental cri sis worsens and more people reawaken to the importance of their roots. This is a true bottom-up religious revolution that will create the biggest political realignment since the American and French revolutions.

What follows is a summary of what I perceive to be some of the core beliefs of Gaean religion. Obviously, there will be many Gaeans who object to some of these beliefs, or would wish to see beliefs included that have been omitted. This is as it should be in this eclectic, ornery and opinionated group of co-religionists. Criticism and further discussion on these subjects are welcomed.

GAEAN VALUES

The sacred texts of Gaean religion are the Earth and the cosmos, and Gaean laws are the laws of Nature as revealed by science and magic. Gaean religious beliefs center on the concept that divinity is both immanent and transcendent, that there is no limit to the sacred. Restoration of the divine feminine, as symbolized by the Triple Goddess, and embodied in Mother Earth and all people, is a paramount goal in Gaean religion. As this restoration proceeds, the sacred masculine must be honored and not be neglected, because spiritual wholeness requires all polarities to be honored.

Rather than seeing creation as a pyramid with God or mankind on the top, Gaeans map creation as a multidimensional web of relationships, and each thing, be it living or inanimate, is a node in that web. It follows that an essential aspect of Gaean religion is holism, the belief that all of reality is an interconnected whole that has emergent properties the component parts lack.

Many Gaeans either are pantheists, believing that God is identical with everything, or are panentheists, believing that divine spirit is present in everything. Belief in reincarnation also is widespread in Gaean religion, as it is in Eastern religions. In the West, belief in reincarnation was found in Gnosticism and Manichaeanism, and passed from Pythagoras and Plato through Neoplatonism to Western occultism. Followers of the monotheistic Abrahamic religions—Samaratinism, Judaism, Christianity and Islam—are conspicuous in not espousing a formal belief in reincarnation. However, esoteric Judaism—the Kabbalahcontains numerous references to the transmigration of souls. Belief in reincarnation also is found in esoteric Islam, as in the writings of Rumi. Reincarnation has obvious moral implications for such contentious issues as abortion and the death penalty.

Gaeans believe the human body to be sacred; it is the temple of our Self. Because we hold complete spiritual autonomy over our person, the state has no right to control our beliefs, what we ingest, or our sexuality. Community concerns in these matters rightfully enter only when our behavior harms other parts of Gaea.

The Christian right is correct in believing that political values and religious beliefs are inextricably intertwined. Because Gaean religion has no formal code of ethics, a form of moral relativism is the norm: "And it harm none, do as you will." Moral relativism holds that there are no absolute ethical truths; morality is simply a collection of cultural norms. Gaeans make their own decisions on matters of ethics and morality, tempered by the awareness of the sacredness of the Earth.

THE POLITICAL AND MORAL NECESSITY OF COMPASSION

A logical consequence of the Glean belief that the Earth is sacred is that the enemies who bedevil us are sacred as well, because they are part of Coca no less than we are. Hitler, Stalin, Pol Pot, Saddam Hussein, all of them are sacred enemies. From the Gaean perspective, these men are parts of the Godhead that have forgotten their true nature. We are fully justified in using force to protect ourselves from such men, because when they harm us, they harm Gaea. Therefore, we have a moral imperative to minimize the use of force and temper it with compassion, so that healing the Earth will be facilitated when the conflict ends.

Ideally, Gaeans are people of good will who are willing to listen to contrary political opinions; every voice is part of Gaea. Some parts may be very confused, vicious and damaged, but it's all Gaea. When political programs are conceived in compassion and a sense of good will, there is much less chance that a vengeful opposition will eliminate them when it returns to power. This is why the American national park system has endured and grown, even during the Reagan and Gingrich eras, and why well meaning programs like the New Deal-Great Society welfare system persisted for decades in spite of obvious flaws.

ETHICAL DUALISM

Dualism is the belief that reality is irretrievably divided into two antithetical parts. These parts may be variously framed as mind and body, light and dark; spirit and matter, male or female, good and evil, positive and negative, above and below, or whatever pair you may choose. Ethical Dualism emphasizes warring of the opposites, and places positive value on one pole. The roots of ethical dualism lie in Zoroastrianism and its descendants, Manichaeanism and Gnosticism, which saw physical reality as the product of a divine struggle. On one side was the good, the kingdom of God, spirit and light. On the other side was evil, the realm of matter and darkness ruled by the Devil. Human souls were believed to be tiny fragments of the light trapped in matter.

Christian theology has a strongly dualistic bias and moral rigidity, identifying mind-light-spirit-male-above with the good and with God. These biases have their intellectual foundations in St. Augustine, whose youthful adherence to Manichaean dualism framed his adult intellect. Aristotle's either-or logic of the excluded middle, by way of Thomas Aquinas, was an essential aspect of that Medieval scholasticism. Therefore, one is saved or damned, a Christian or a Pagan, worships either the Trinity or the Devil, a woman is Madonna or whore, and spirit is idealized over matter and the flesh. Ethical dualism is a deeply ingrained and unquestioned operating principle of Eurocentric consciousness. It pervades Paganism, leading many to advocate matriarchy over patriarchy, which is simply the other side of the same unbalanced, oppressive coin. Riane Eisler's model of *partnership* between the genders is an expression of Gaean values.

A particularly troubling aspect of ethical dualism is the way that the *other* is treated. In mind of the ethical dualistic, the parts of the psyche correlated with the rejected polarities become *other* and are identified with the personal shadow. Once the psyche is divided in this manner, there is a strong psychological need to project the rejected shadow material upon others. This lot naturally has fallen to other races, particularly dark ones, the other gender, foreigners, subversives, and other religions.

A fixation on purity is characteristic of ethical dualism, as in the Nazi obsession with racial purity. Because contamination with the other gender is seen as especially corrupting, homosexuals and bisexuals are singled out for special attention. The collapse of Soviet hegemony temporarily left the American right without an appropriate demon to project their shadows upon; homosexuals and environmentalists have become the new targets of choice. One of the frequent charges leveled against Greens is that they are Pagan Earth worshippers sacrificing people's livelihoods on the altars of their religion. As Gaean religion continues to grow, more and more of these shadow projections will be directed at us. It is important for Gaeans to remain conscious and not play this game with those who revile us, for they are part of Gaea as well.

RECLAIMING THE CENTER

If ethical dualism is the root of the problem, then reclaiming the Center is the solution. The Center is a moral reference point that we all hold in common; it controls the balance of power and occupies the midpoint between opposites. The Center is the common point where *all* political and social dualities intersect. The political extremes are characterized by fanaticism; the Center is the place of moderation and justice. Metaphorically, the Center is the heart of the Tao, the divine fulcrum; it mediates the dance of Yin and Yang. The Center is the symbol of the Self, the archetype of wholeness in Jungian psychology. Opposites become complements where the Center is held, because the Center creates a bridge across the gulf between them. Instead of two opposing forces there is a continuum, black and white become the rainbow.

GOOD AND EVIL

Good and evil are terms that are bandied about quite freely in the political arena.

Gaeans have no Ten Commandments to provide us with an absolute map of this territory. Most of us might agree that evil has the quality of malevolence, that it creates unnecessary fear, pain and ugliness. Doing serious harm for selfish reasons is evil. Evil is like art, we know it when we see it, but not everyone agrees. Good has the qualities of generosity and benevolence, it nurtures and enhances life, and it creates beauty.

The mythic underpinnings of the European concepts of good and evil are found in Genesis, where human beings become as Gods by eating of the Tree of Knowledge. Godlike knowledge was a consequence of the evolution of human consciousness, symbolized by the arrival of Eve's feminine perspective, which allowed the classification of the parts of Gaea as morally clean or unclean. The discriminating mental process of ethical judgment—the identification of evil or unclean things—broke up the primal unity of the All. By evolving a discriminating mind, Adam and Eve transcended the natural state and were shamed by their animal bodies. This myth marks the end of humanity's unconscious *participation mystique* with Nature, which is the essence of the Fall.

Good and evil have no absolute meaning in the natural world. Tornados, earthquakes or floods simply are; they are incapable of malevolence. When people experience natural disasters, there is a tendency to attribute evil intent to Nature, but more than likely the disaster has resulted from their own greed or ignorance. A flood may destroy your home because the mountains were deforested, as happened during hurricane Mitch in Central America, or a poorly constructed dam failed, or you built on a floodplain. Moderate sized earthquakes kill thousands in the Middle East because the land has long been deforested, and homes are built of adobe and stone.

Christians might define evil as going against God's will, as Adam and Eve did when they ate from the Tree of Knowledge. The difficulty here is proving just what exactly is God's will. The Bible has only its own word that it is the ultimate moral authority, there is no objective proof exterior to the Bible, and much history to the contrary. No revealed system of ethics can demonstrate the proof of its own axioms; one either accepts them or rejects them as a matter of individual taste and preference. This situation is analogous to Gödel's Incompletability Theorem, which states that no mathematical procedure that demonstrates the truth of another mathematical theory can prove itself true. Another proof may be devised to prove the initial procedure, but this would simply force a regress of the incompleteness problem. Interestingly, because physics is based on mathematics, there can be no ultimate theory of everything because their will always remain a least one unproven mathematical postulate.

A Gaean definition of evil could be as follows: *a malevolent condition that comes about through the sustained and systematic oppression of a polar attribute by its opposite.* The classic example is the Burning Times, which was made possible by thousands of years of unbroken patriarchal, rule.

Consider the polarity of parent and child. If there is either too much parental involvement or too little, the child's spirit will be crushed. Parental neglect causes a child to grow up with severe psychiatric problems that in extreme cases can lead to institutionalization or suicide. A pathological outcome also will occur if the child is smothered and invaded by too much parental involvement. Such children have difficulty leading independent lives when they grow up, and typically are filled with paralyzing rage and self-loathing. Healthy children grow up in homes where they have a balance of personal autonomy and loving parental attention.

Evil sometimes results from excessive attempts to do good. A common pattern is that evil comes about through the misguided pursuit of purity. The pursuit of purity comes about generally because of the overvaluation of one member of a duality, and the concurrent denigration of the other. The Nazis were not doing evil in their own minds, but rather attempting to purify Europe of subhuman beings and protecting the racial purity of the master race. Similarly, the Khmer Rouge attempted to purify Cambodia of decadent western influences, as did Stalin in the Soviet Union. A less extreme example of purity obsession is the negative effect of a severe dietary regime, such as macrobiotics, on the bodies of people who practice them to excess. Child abuse frequently takes the form in the abuser's mind of a self-righteous attempt to purify the child of bad thoughts or behaviors, as in the case where a small child was placed in an oven to cook out the Devil.

AFTERWORD

Everywhere we find people independently coming to the Goddess and sharing the realization of the sacredness of the Earth. Gaean religion is a spontaneous movement rising from below, from the very Earth beneath our feet. As such, it is the natural religion of the Left, which draws its authority from below. It is tragic that the patriarchal religions have discredited spirituality in the minds of leftist progressives. By rejecting spirituality, leftists have unilaterally disarmed themselves in the political and ethical debates now shaping our future. Leftists will remain marginalized until they get over their problem with religion, and reclaim their spiritual common ground.

One thing is clear, there is no way that the billions of people on Earth are going to be able to live decent lives without most of them holding the belief in Earth's inherent sacredness. There are too many opportunities for ecological harm for there to be enough police to stop the despoliation of the planet if most people think they can get away with it. However, if Earth is held sacred, no police or laws are needed, only the knowledge of what causes harm. Ecologically sound behavior need not be compelled, because it is an intrinsic quality of Gaean religious ethics.

Richard Ely lives in Sonoma County, California, where he makes his living dong environmental geology. During the Vietnam War, he was an anti-war activist and has had a life-long interest in politics and environmentalism. He has walked the labyrinth and exper-ienced the mysteries of the Great Below. In 1994 he became a priest of the Church of All Worlds and retired in 2004.

Vol. XXXI, No. 126 (Jan.–Feb. 1999) 12–15, 48–49

Pagans & Their Religious Rights:
Past Victories & Future Challenges

*by **H.Ps. Phyllis Curott, J.D.**, Attorney at Law*

N THE TWENTY YEARS SINCE becoming an attorney and a Wiccan priestess, I have witnessed the Pagan community (for the purposes of this article I will use the term "Pagan" as a general term which includes Wiccans and all other practitioners of the Old Religion) grow from a few thousand practitioners, quietly hidden in the back of our broom closet, to the fastest growing spiritual movement in the United States. Current estimates place our numbers at approximately 3–5 million. (And this does not include the estimated 1.2 million teenage girls devotedly watching shows such as *Sabrina* and *Charmed,* who buy countless books and are showing up in increasing numbers at workshops and festivals).

As we approach the next Millennium CE, we have emerged from the broom closet in force with legally organized churches and temples, countless Websites receiving huge numbers of hits (the notable *Witches' Voice* already with over 5 million), workshops and courses offered through mainstream continuing education programs, university classes and degrees, divinity degrees in feminist theology, TV shows and movies that command number one positions in time slots and at the box office, and a publishing industry so successful that the New York Times called it the fastest growing and most lucrative area of publishing! And as someone who has been on the front line struggle to remedy negative stereotypes, I have seen a major shift in the mainstream media where informative, respectful and positive coverage now appears.

With this increasing visibility comes greater understanding and acceptance within mainstream American society. Yet countless practitioners of the Old Religions remain hidden, justifiably afraid that being public will lead to discrimination and even danger. A single parent worries that if her ex learns of her spiritual practice, she will lose custody of her child. A school teacher worries that he'll be fired if he appears on a TV show participating in a Sabbat ritual. A teenager is suspended from high school for wearing a Pentagram. The High Priestess and Priest of a coven find their home worship, something all practitioners engage in, outlawed by the municipal government. Unfortunately, people have reason to worry.

Concerns about violations of fundamental rights to religious freedom reach beyond the individual to that of our broader community, and to our place as American citizens. As Ira Glasser, Executive Director of the American Civil Liberties Union recently said, "Ever since the 1994 midterm elections, an extreme-right political force of New Puritans has been hammering away at the Bill of Rights with the intensity of a battering ram." In control of Congress and most state legislatures, they have mounted a concerted attack on our most fundamental civil liberties and personal freedoms. In 1998, they attempted a massive assault on the First Amendment guarantee of freedom of religion and the separation of church and state at both national and local levels. In Congress, they attempted to pass a Constitutional amendment that would have allowed the government to sponsor prayer in public schools, thereby imposing fundamentalist Christian religious beliefs on children of all faiths. And this was just one of many efforts by the religious right to indoctrinate children by usurping the power of the government and our tax dollars.

And make no mistake about it, when Jesse Helms sponsored an unsuccessful legislative amendment that would have made the practice of our religion illegal, he fired a warning shot across our bow. There are already Neo-Nazi websites publishing excerpts from the *Malleus Maleficarum* and calling for another Witchhunt. And Christian fundamentalists are a conspicuous presence in the media, aggressively attacking anyone who steps forward to challenge the negative stereotypes. The irony of our increasing size, visibility and acceptance in the mainstream is that we are coming under increasing scrutiny and attack by the extreme right.

As an attorney with a long history of civil liberties and social justice activism, and as a Wiccan priestess, I have chosen to be public—to use both the media and the law, and my spiritual practices, to battle against discrimination and persecution. In my memoir, *Book of Shadows,* recently published by Broadway Books, I used the story of my own life, that of an Ivy League lawyer becoming a Wiccan priestess, to explain not only the philosophy and practices of the Old Religion, but also the tremendous value of our spirituality to mainstream America. I also wrote *Book of Shadows* to fill a gap in our literature by explaining some of the most important aspects of our spiritual work: what it feels like to use these ancient practices and how they transform one's "mundane" life into a spiritual journey filled with divine magic, challenges, and changes. And I wrote it to hold up a mirror to our entire community—to use the ancient magic of story-telling to honor our experiences and hard-earned wisdom, to inspire others, and to show how, personally, the incorporation of my spiritual values with my professional life inspired my decision to be a public Witch and an activist attorney, devoted to the fight for the rights and freedoms of our community.

Has this decision damaged my ability to practice law and make a living? As an attorney with my own practice, the boss can't fire me. I became an attorney to fight for social justice. Like everyone else, however, I also need to make a living and so I developed a practice in an area of law that doesn't compromise my spiritual values (real estate). But it is certainly true that there are clients who no longer call. I continue to support myself, and consider my freedom to have been worth the price. It has been my

conviction that the only way for our community to be truly free and genuinely safe is to be visible in the public eye, at both a personal and social level. We must also insist upon, act upon and defend our right to religious freedom. It has been my experience that as greater numbers of our community adopt these strategies, the mainstream discovers who we really are and what our practices are really all about, and we are increasingly treated with greater tolerance. Our numbers also grow. And there is tremendous strength in numbers.

A common concern in the civil liberties community is that unless we are persistent in defending our civil liberties, we will lose them. In this religious community, it is more accurate to say that unless we act upon and assert our right to religious liberties, we will never be able to enjoy them. But as an attorney who has represented and advised Pagans in many cases of religious dis-crimination, I know that there are many circumstances that still require anonymity. The assertion of one's rights can come with a very high price tag. But I have also seen how often such a crisis of visibility may arise, not from a person's choice, but from circumstances. Whether you choose to be public, or are unexpectedly confronted with the need to protect yourself, or whether you wish to respond to the growing threat against our freedom at the level of social and political activism, awareness of our rights, and our success in securing those rights, is both empowering and liberating.

Over the years, members of the Wiccan and Pagan community have battled for and won rights to religious freedom in a variety of important areas. It is impossible to review them all in detail, but I have chosen to summarize a number of key cases which raise critical areas of practical, day-to-day concern and which are cases where I have perspective as an attorney who provided representation or advice, or who served as an expert witness or media commentator. I hope these examples of the successful use of the law by Wiccans and Pagans will illustrate what can be accomplished when we defend our religious liberties. I also hope they will provide encouragement, reassurance and inspiration to others.

CLERGY RECOGNITION

In 1985, with the assistance of the New York Civil Liberties Union, I represented a group of Wiccans who had been denied the right to register as clergy. Unless registered, they could not perform legally binding marriages within New York City. We fought City Hall and we won. This was an important step in the process of obtaining recognition, both legally and publicly, as a legitimate and genuine religion, entitled to all the protections afforded by the Constitution, and particularly the First Amendment of the Bill of Rights. It was also an important psychological step for our growing spiritual movement.

PUBLIC WORSHIP

In 1993, I was again engaged in another case where a major city had violated the civil and religious liberties of our community. This time I was involved not only as an attorney, but as a plaintiff, for I was the priestess who was supposed to lead a full moon Goddess ritual in a public park in the City of Chicago as part of the Parliament of the World's Religions. The city of Chicago denied our permit. Once again, with the assistance of the local ACLU, a major city was challenged and defeated. A permit was finally granted and the ritual occurred, attended by the media and over 700 clergy and practitioners of the world's many faiths.

In both of these cases, the combination of a clear violation of fundamental First Amendment rights to freedom of religion, a private attorney with a keen personal interest in the outcome, assistance from the American Civil Liberties Union, and positive press coverage which put additional pressure on the municipalities, all helped to secure positive settlements. The ACLU is a formidable ally in any religious liberty struggle, the kind of legal "muscle" that spurs a belligerent opponent to swifter settlement. The media can also be critical in a strategy of quick and successful settlement. It has been my experience that the media, once educated, are highly valuable allies in these struggles. The realm of the First Amendment is an area

where they share particular sensitivity and sympathy and press coverage is a source of tremendous pressure on politicians or businesses who hate bad publicity. What was also critical in both of these cases was the necessity of complying with all reasonable city requirements. This is a critical point for anyone involved in similar situations seeking to exercise their rights. Once complied with, any exceptional treatment becomes highly visible as discrimination and a clear violation of civil liberties and religious freedom. Under these circumstances, the threat of litigation alone was sufficient to resolve grave violations without ever having to go to court.

HOME WORSHIP

In the state of Florida, The Church of Iron Oak was engaged in a much lengthier and costlier battle to protect the rights of its members to engage in "home worship." They were ultimately successful, and the legal theories developed during their struggle will be of great value to anyone else confronted with similar persecution by municipalities using restrictive zoning ordinances to inhibit our freedom to worship in our own homes. An important strategic aspect of this case was the cultivation of support from other religious groups whose First Amendment rights were also at risk. As with the ACLU, cultivating a positive relationship with the Interfaith community can provide invaluable support in critical cases involving religious liberties. Even the most unlikely of religious allies can understand that a threat to the rights of any group is a threat to all. The legal questions regarding zoning, religious institutions and religious freedom is an area of growing concern as our community matures and expands—purchasing land, sponsoring festivals, building spiritual retreats and centers.

RELIGION & CHILD CUSTODY

It is rare that courts will consider religious differences as grounds for divorce, but there have been numerous instances where religion has been made an issue in child custody cases. Thus far, the United States Supreme Court has chosen not take any cases regarding this issue and state courts vary widely in their opinions.

In a recent New York case, a husband sought to win custody of the couple's children by raising as an issue the wife's Wiccan religious beliefs. The Judge refused to consider it in determining "the best interests of the child," the principal criterion for deciding which parent should be granted custody. Generally, most states adhere to a rule that religion will be considered in deciding upon custody only when specific religious beliefs or practices can be considered to impede a child's development and this can be articulated. Some states, such as New Hampshire, have taken the position that religion is never to be considered in a custody determination because it would improperly entangle the government, via the courts, in religious matters. Other states will include religious beliefs as one amongst many other considerations.

Many members of this spiritual community will not wear a Pentagram at work, nor will they discuss their beliefs, for fear of being fired. The Constitution does not provide protection for the employees of private (non-governmental) employers. However, employers may not discriminate against someone because of her religion. This protection is provided by Title VII of the 1964 Civil Rights Act. In fact, it requires an employer to accommodate an employee's religious practice so long as doing so would not cause any undue hardship to the employer. Title VII has been interpreted to include the right to take time off for observance of religious holidays and many states have enacted laws similar to and often stricter than Title VII. Local governmental human rights agencies are available to assist anyone who has suffered religious discrimination in the workplace.

It is certainly true, however, that individuals who "come out of the broom closet" at work can find themselves facing subtle forms of persecution and termination justified on other grounds such as poor performance, reduction in size of work force, etc. Still, it is important for individuals to know that they are not without some form of legal protection. In fact, where an employee has had a stellar employment history, and upon going public suddenly finds a pattern of harassment or criticism developing, a good offense can often be the best defense—and a threat of a Title VII complaint could remedy any persecution or possibility of termination.

Numerous other issues concerning Pagans and the law remain for consideration, such as the Free Exercise Clause, the Supreme Court case, Employment Division v. Smith, and the Religious Freedom Restoration Act; clergy confidentiality; clergy malpractice; religious displays; religion and public education; religious freedom and the military; defamation; and many others. Hopefully, these will be covered by other articles in this and future issues. What is critical in any consideration of Pagans and the law is our understanding of our entitlement to the full protection of the law as we exercise our religious liberties. Equally critical is a vigorous commitment to the defense of these rights. As a community, we must be aware of and supportive of those whose struggles affect not only their own personal liberties, but those of us all.

Over the years, numerous networks have developed to advise, support, and represent individuals who find themselves on the frontline of the struggle for religious liberties, and to inform the rest of the community, such as the Lady Liberty League, WADL, and The Witches' Voice. In addition to the various associations that have served this need, a group of Wiccan attorneys is currently discussing the creation of a lawyers' network to work with existing groups, provide speedy legal assessment and assistance, and heighten visibility, sensitivity, and respect in the mainstream.

Standing together, exercising and defending our rights under the law, we can turn back the assault which the New Puritans have launched not only against our liberties, but those of countless other Americans. The measure of our response to this threat will be the measure of our maturity, and our spiritual conviction. Witches, and Pagans, cannot live in fear. We can only live in freedom. To do so, we must have the courage of our convictions, the magic of our spirituality lived fully in our lives, and the power of our principles embodied in our actions.

GE Vol. XXXI, No. 129 (July–Aug. 1999) 4–8

Chapter 10.
Gender & Sexuality
Introduction
by Chas S. Clifton

AGANISM IS REALLY ALL ABOUT SEX, RIGHT? After all, to a lot of people, to be a "pagan" means to live a non-spiritual life of pleasure. When you experience the Pagan life, however, you know that Paganism does not separate the human body from so-called higher concerns. It's not like God is "up there" and we are "down here," all sweaty and miserable. In many Pagan traditions, the gods can briefly occupy a person's body—that process is called "drawing down" in Witchcraft. And in other situations, the people around us can manifest aspects of divine power. Sometimes those situations are sexual. Simply put, the body can be a place of worship. This "erotheology," as Oberon was calling it in the early 1970s, remains one of the fundamental principles of Pagan life.

The first members of the Church of All Worlds, inspired by Robert Heinlein's *Stranger in a Strange Land*, also were drawn to the book's concepts of "Nests," self-selected groups of compatible individuals who were able to share sexual partners. But this particular dream of a new cultural approach to sexuality did not start with CAW. Different sexual arrangements also marked some 19th-century American utopian experiments, such as the Oneida Colony, started in 1848 by John Humphrey Noyes, which had a similar practice called "complex marriage." Experiments in sexual relationships and new religious movements are often connected! Many *Green Egg* writers, in fact, examined alternatives to heterosexual monogamy, and this chapter presents a selection of their work—Morning Glory Zell's article "A Bouquet of Lovers," in which she coined the term *polyamorous,* became one of the foundational articles on polyamory and non-monogamous living relationships in the current era.

In addition, Ivo Dominguez in "A View from the Bridge" discussed connections between Wicca and homosexuality. When the dominant culture dismisses both someone's sexual identity and their religious identity, he urges great Pagan attention to the psychological problems that that dismissal provokes and sets out parallels between "coming out" as Pagan and as gay or lesbian.

While Tom Williams writes a hymn to Aphrodite, the goddess of love and beauty, one-time *Green Egg* editor Diane Darling is thinking about the attributes and needs of those women called to be her priestesses. In her essay "In Her Majesty's Sacred Service" she links sexual freedom to the reclaiming of magic, autonomy, and spirituality claimed by all contemporary Pagans.

Among Pagan traditions, Wicca in particular is criticized by some other Pagans for its focus on sexual duality and polarity, a criticism Darling rebuts by saying that a "sexual spark" and magical energy and flow between priest and priestess are not always the same thing (although of course they can be). It's important to understand that although traditional Wicca does emphasize polarity and fertility, it is not the measuring stick for all other Paganisms. Instead, it is a particular mystery religion for those persons who are drawn to it. Deborah Lipp writes of "joyous excitement" as another metaphor for creativity, and I get that feeling too from some of the writings of Jesse Wolf Hardin, who here celebrates his own masculinity as a child of Earth and asks that we not let squabbling over gender roles detract from the larger planetary mission: "In service to the living Earth, we have no time to indulge in stereotyping ourselves with predictable behavior, and little energy for defending ourselves from being stereotyped by others."

Erotheology: Sexual Communion as Worship

by *Julie Carter* & *Tim Zell*, *Church of All Worlds*

THE ISSUE OF SEXUALITY IN NEO-Pagan and especially Church of All Worlds thinking is one in which misconceptions are rife. Drawing conclusions from no other evidence than their own lurid fantasies and wet dreams, people have projected onto us all of their own repressed sexual obsessions and have conceived us to be the antithesis of their own carefully controlled sexual fears and hang-up. They imagine us to be lustful, orgiastic, sex-obsessed satyrs, much as they imagined our Pagan ancestors as justification for persecuting them. We observe, however, that obsession with sex is not a component of the liberated personality, but of the repressed one. After all, the primary market for the vast outpouring of visual and literary pornography in the U.S. is not found among the liberated youth, but among the pathetically hungup members of the older generation.

We are not interested in emphasizing or advocating any particular manifestations of sexuality, nor do we condemn any sexual expression shared among reasonably mature, mutually consenting persons, regardless of whether or not that expression is one with we personally would identify. We do, however, encourage the healthy approach to sexuality offered by Maslow, Gunther, Lowen and other transpersonal psychologists, by such humanistic philosophers as Bertrand Russell and A.S. Neill, and by a few novelists such as Robert Heinlein and Bob Rimmer. A common theme among these approaches is the possibility of sexual union as a religious experience—a direct communion with Divinity.

A full comprehension of the liberating potentiality of fully experienced sensuality and the communion with Divinity inherent in the sex act requires that we return to our previous discovery of the biologically organic unity of the planet Earth as a single vast living organism which we have decided to call by the name *Terrebia*. It is this entity, now approaching the emergence of consciousness referred to by Teilhard de Chardin as the "Omega Point," that has been identified by mankind from time immemorial as the Earth-Mother Divinity: "Mother Earth," "Mother Nature." Terrebia has in the past three billion years matured (evolved) from a single original cell to the vast complexity of the entire ecosystem of our planetary Biosphere. Within the greater macrocosm of Terrebia, each living plant and animal, including man, is as a single cell in our own microcosmic bodies.

A great deal of the difficulty we seem to have in developing a full appreciation of sexuality appears to stem from the common confusion of the sexual act with reproduction. This confusion has been augmented by the prevailing Christian morality, which teaches us that reproduction is the sole purpose of sex. The basis for this teaching is an attempt to separate the sensual from the sexual by removing the erotic element from sexuality. Yet any objective examination of sexuality, particularly among primates and especially among humans, indicates that the occasional reproductive consequences of the sex act have very little bearing on the act itself, which, when freed of the social components, is purely sensual and immediate. Indeed, we might observe laconically that, far from enjoying sex in order to reproduce, people and other animals reproduce in order to enjoy sex!

Interestingly enough, if we observe certain protozoa, among which reproduction occurs asexually by fission (mitosis), we find nevertheless a behavior pattern we would be tempted to regard as sexual. Among paramecia, two individuals will join together in a form of union (conjugation) in which an exchange of cell particles (micronuclei) transpires from one to the other. This union seems to have a rejuvenating effect on both individuals after separation.

Similarly, a cross-fertilization through an

exchange of biological energy ("bioplasma" or "prana") is the basic component of the sex act among ourselves. In psychoanalytic theory, the inherent energy of pleasure, creativity, and eroticism is known as libidinal energy. The flow of this positive energy is the essence of sensuality. All sensuality is thereby creative and thus life-affirming. Any act of sensuality has e positive energizing effect from which one emerges rejuvenated as our protozoa. Now in an organically whole body comprised of many cells, as Terrebia, each cell contributes to the whole what it does not need and receives from the whole in turn what it needs to live and grow. In the same manner, energies are given and received in the sex act; exchanged between both partners. So it is in our sensual communion with Nature that energies are offered and received on both sides. Sensuality, as our means of exchanging energies, is the essential life/growth force, necessary to our very existence.

To be liberated means to be free from external control—to have the center of one's control within oneself, rather than without. Before one can relate sensually one must be liberated have one's center within oneself. This is part of what we call being God. The energy of sensuality, of worship, can only flow from such a center. This energy cannot proceed from someone who is under the control of outside forces. To deprive people of their sensuality is therefore to deprive them of the capacity for true worship.

Philosophical religions, established in part for the purpose of obtaining control over the minds and actions of their adherents, have long since recognized the necessity of enjoining strict regulations over the free enjoyment of sensuality, and these regulations have taken the form of "divinely ordained" taboos. Sexuality specifically has felt the brunt of this suppression, for it is potentially the most liberating form of sensuality, enabling all to participate in the direct religious experience with no need of priestly intermediaries. The plain fact is, sexually and sensually fulfilled people simply cannot be controlled by irrational and arbitrary demagoguery. Hence, all institutions with a primary commitment to unquestioning

obedience on the part of the inmates have found it essential to create a state of sexual/sensual deprivation amounting to effective castration.

Sensuality has been so denigrated by Western "civilization" that is become a dire insult to call someone a sensualist. To an extent, this is a reaction against the prevailing sensuality of the old Paganism, but to a greater extent it may be seen in the context of exercising control over others by isolating them from competing realities. Thus guilt is promoted by Christianity to isolate one from oneself, and moral indignation to isolate one from others. When there is nothing else left, one becomes dependent upon the religious mythology of transcendent Divinity, sin, saviors, priests and confession as interpreted by the agents of authority, the churches. In this process, we see depriving man of his sensuality as functionally isolating him from the rest of the living Biosphere and the universe, for it is only through our senses that we remain in contact with that greater system of which we are a pert.

Our vocabulary is often inadequate to express significant concepts. We have the word "sex" to describe the process of relating sexually, but no equivalent word to describe the process of relating sensually. We propose the term "sens" to fill that gap. Sens involves the entire mind/body system, and is more general than mere sex. which is more-or-less genitally focused. As sex relations are considered erotic, so may we say that sens relations are ecotic.

Sex and sens are not, of course, distinct phenomena, but the former is rather a specific case of the latter. It is possible for the sex act to transcend the merely sexual experience and achieve a level of higher sensuality in which it becomes the ecstatic experience. The experience of "ex-stasis" ("out of stability") is the experience of communion with Divinity; of worship. The ecstasy of a full orgasm (one involving the entire body) is distinguishable only in degree from the ecstasy of a true cosmic union with Nature (the "oceanic feeling").

As macrocosmic Divinity is, in a literal and Pantheistic sense, our entire planet, so anything that brings us into communion with that vaster Being is by definition a religious experience; an act of worship. Ecotic sens relations, experienced, for example, when alone in the deep forest, are a direct communion with the forces of macrocosmic Divinity, and as such, are the essence of Pagan religious awareness.

The perception of Divinity on a microcosmic scale has been aptly expressed in the conceptual phrase "Thou art God," used by Robert Heinlein in *Stranger in a Strange Land*) and in the Bible (Psalm 82:6 and John 10:34). We have once defined Divinity as "the highest level of aware consciousness accessible to each living being, manifesting itself in the self-actualization of that being." God (or Goddess, if you will) is manifest at many levels of awareness, starting with the individual perceiver and moving outward into the universe. Through deep meditation, we can come to discover and commune with the aspect of Divinity that is we ourselves. Through sens, we can commune ecotically with the greater aspects of Divinity that are the biomes end Biosphere of Earth. And through sex, we can commune erotically with that aspect. of Divinity which is another person—another cell in the vaster body of Terrebia—much as unicellular paramecia merge protoplasm (and bioplasmic energy, perhaps?) in their microscopic world. Wilhelm Reich describes the capacity for sexual orgasm as "the capacity to surrender to the flow of biological energy." As we are integrated with Nature, indeed we *are* Nature; coming into complete harmony with our own energy flow as it joins with that of another *is* to enter also the flow of the Biospheric Organism Herself; to become One with Goddess.

Worship may be defined as the flow of positive energy (*eros* in psycholanalytic terminology; negative energy is *thanatos*) from subject to object; from the worshipper to the Divine. In the sex act, each participant is both the subject and the object of this flow; of worship. For most of us, the sexual communion will remain the primary, if not the only way in which true communion with Divinity can be realized, and it is certainly the most commonly accessible form for us all. Thus we should come to regard human sexuality not as man's greatest weakness, as Christianity would have us believe, but as our greatest strength and asset, for by it we may all come into true union with that immanent Divinity which is manifest in each of us and in each other. Thou art God(dess)!

GE Vol. IV, No. 45 (Oimelc 1972) 11–14

Hymn to Venus

Venus Amathusia!
Laughter-loving Aphrodite!
Come to me with laughing breast,
Come on waves of golden crest.
Come with doves and golden light
Drawn by swans and sparrows bright.
Alight! Alight!
I am thy man, I am thy mate!
Receive me til our storm abate!
Thy green glades echo with my calls,
Come to me from emerald halls,
Flanked by maidens winding there
Rose and myrtle in thy golden hair.
Come to me! To!
And mate with me upon the grass,
Laughing, lusty, oh ravishing lass!
Our bodies arch and strain and twine,
I am thine and thou art mine!
Come from heavens of azure hue,
Ocean born and ever new!
Pulsing, laughing, yearning, straining,
Pleasure, lust, all life containing.
Race with me through glades of green,
Exalting, loving, oh rapturous queen!
To me! To me!
Oh come to me!
And enter, merge, enfold, unite!
Suffuse desire with golden light!
Never sated in eons of time,
I am thine and thou art mine!

—Tom Williams

GE Vol. XXVII, No.104 (Spring 1994) 34

A Bouquet of Lovers: Strategies for Responsible Open Relationships

by *Morning Glory Zell*

You want to know how it will be,
Me and her, or you and me.
You both sit there, your long hair flowing,
Eyes alive, your mind still growing,
Saying to me: What can we do,
Now that we both love you?
I love you too. I don't really see,
Why can't we go on as three?
　　　　　—"Triad" by David Crosby

 ET US BEGIN WITH THE *A PRIORI* assumption that the reader is either currently practicing or firmly committed to the concept of Open Relationships as a conscious and loving lifestyle. If you are not in that category then this article will probably not be of interest to you. If you are full of curiosity about the potentials of Open Relationships, there are resources which deal with such soul-searching issues as jealousy management and theories about why the whole lifestyle is healthy and positive. Some of these resources will be given at the end and herein there will also be found considerable points of interest.

The goal of a responsible Open Relationship is to cultivate ongoing, long-term, complex relationships which are rooted in deep mutual friendships.

What elements enable an Open Relationship to be successful? Having been involved all my adult life in one or the other Open Marriages (the current Primary being 16 years long), I have seen a lot of ideas come and go and experimented with plans and rules to make these relationships work for everyone involved. There is as much variety in what different people require in a relationship as there are people involved in them. However, there are some sure-fire elements that *must be present* for the system to function at all and there are other elements that are strongly recommended on the basis that they have a very good track record. Let us refer to them collectively as the" Rules of the Road."

Rules of the Road

The first two are **essential.** I have never met anyone who has had a serious and healthy Open Marriage that omitted these first two principles. They are:

Honesty and Openness about the poly-amorous lifestyle. Having multiple sexual relations while lying to your partners or trying to pretend that each one is the "one true love" is a very superficial and selfishly destructive way to live.

There are marriages in which one of the partners will state: "If you ever have an affair, I never want to find out about it." I suppose some folks take that as tacit permission the same way a child will connive when the parent tells them, "Don't ever let me catch you doing such-and-so!" Without complete honesty, especially about sexual issues, the relationship is doomed. Some Open Relations have an agreement not to discuss the details of their satellite relations with their Primary partner or vice-versa, but there still must be the *fundamental honesty and agreement that other relations do exist and are important to maintain.*

The next principle mentioned is equally fundamental:

All partners involved in the Multiple Relations must fully and willingly embrace the basic commitment to a polyamorous lifestyle. A situation where one partner seeks polygamy and the other one insists upon monogamy or strongly politics for it will not work, for this is too much of a fundamental disagreement to allow the relationship to prosper. Sooner or later someone has got to give in and have it one way or the other. The truth is that people usually do have a strong preference.

Hogamus, higamus, men are polygamous.
Higamus, hogamus, women monogamous.

The only reason such mixed marriages have actually worked has been because there was an all powerful church/state taboo enforced on options other than monogamy. In a patriarchy, men's deviation from that norm is ignored and women's is punished, often by death. The first recorded gender-specific law, in the ancient code of Urukagina from 2400 BCE, was directed against women who practiced polyandry, specifying that their teeth be bashed in with bricks. Now that the social codes are being challenged, even though the state maintains laws against legal plural marriage, both men and women are more free to explore alternative preferences and relationships are conspicuously in a period of flux.

When I first met and fell in love with my present Primary partner, I roused myself sufficiently from my bedazzled emotional state to say: "I love you, but I hope that we can somehow have an Open Relationship because I am not really suited to monogamy and would be very unhappy in a monogamous relationship." Fortunately, Otter was delighted to hear this as he had been too afraid of losing the new-found bliss to broach the subject first.

Many a relationship has foundered on the rock of Higamus-Hogamus. Nevertheless, the sooner it gets dealt with the better chance for the relationship to survive. It also means a quicker and kinder death to a romance if this basic agreement cannot be reached. **Honesty and willing Polyamorous Commitment are the basic building blocks all partners must use to build a lasting Open Relationship.**

Once over that hurdle, next comes a set of ground rules for conducting the relationships. Any relationship profits by ground rules,

even a one night stand. Nowadays, the state of sexuality being risky, such considerations are more than a politeness; they can be a life-saver.

Never put energy into any Secondary relationships when there is an active conflict within the Primary. This has to be bedrock or the Primary will eventually fold.

The difficulty with this rule is that if both partners are not equally committed to the openness of the relationship, it can be used as a gun in their disagreements. By deliberately picking a fight just before Primary A goes to see a Secondary sweetie, Primary B can control her spouse and prevent him from ever having successful Secondary relations. This behavior is fraught with dishonesty and secret monogamous agendas; if it is persistently indulged in, it is symptomatic of a fundamental problem with the basic principles.

If Partner B plays this game with Partner A's satellite assignations while continuing to pursue his own, B is an out and out hypocrite and needs to be called on his bullshit in no uncertain terms!

Nevertheless, this rule is the safety valve for sanity and preservation of Primary relationships and should be followed with scrupulous integrity. It is a good idea for Primary partners to have an agreed upon set of signals or a formally stated phrase to politely request their Primary to postpone or cancel the secondary assignation so that the energy can be put into the Primary relationship for fence mending or bonding. This ritualized request can be structured so as to avoid loaded terminology and to decrease the negative emotional charge. Frivolous use of this signal is very destructive of it, as is refusal to participate in healing when access to the Primary partner has been obtained.

Territorial jealousy has no place in a polyamorous agreement. However *situational jealousy* can arise over issues in the relationship when one or more of the partners is feeling neglected. Obviously the best cure for neglect is to focus attention on what has been neglected; the relationship will prosper when all partners are feeling strong and positive about each other. From that strong and healthy center it becomes possible to extend the love to others.

Consult with the Primary partner before becoming sexually involved with a new long term Secondary lover. The Primary partner must approve of the new person and feel good about them and not feel threatened by the new relationship. Nothing can break up a relationship faster than bringing in a new person that is hostile or inconsiderate to the other Primary partner. On the other hand, the most precious people in my life are the lovers that my Primary partner has brought home to become our mutual life long friends.

The check and balance on this rule is *how often* it is invoked by the same person. If it is used all the time by one person, this is patently unfair and is symptomatic of a problem or need that must be addressed. This can be tricky and once again, if honesty is not impeccably observed, the rule can be abused. If a man has a hard time relating to other men for instance, he can use his alienation to pick apart every other lover his wife proposes on some ground or other, leaving her with no satellite relationship that is acceptable to him. The cure for this is for the person who has the problem relating to the same sex to seek a therapy group for people who want to overcome this alienation.

Different rules may be used to apply to one night stands or other temporary love affairs. One-night stands are not necessarily frowned upon and can be a memorable experience, but some Primaries choose to not allow any such brief flings as too risky, while others feel that such happenings add spice and are especially welcome during business trips or other enforced separations. The "ask first" rule may be suspended for the duration of the separation.

All new potential lovers are immediately told of any existing Primary relationship so that they genuinely understand the primacy of that existing relationship. None of this hiding your wedding ring business! Satellite lovers have a right to know where they truly stand and must not have any false illusions or hidden agendas of their own. For instance, in a triadic relationship of two women and one man, there is occasionally a solitary satellite lover who wants to "cut that little filly right out of the herd." If satellite lovers are really seeking a monogamous relationship then they will not be satisfied with the role of a long term Secondary relationship, and it is better that they find this out before any damage is done to either side.

If a Secondary becomes destructive to the Primary partnership, one of the Primary partners can ask the other to terminate the threatening Secondary relationship. It is wise to limit this veto to the initial phase of Secondary relationship formation. After a Secondary relationship has existed over a year and a day, any difficulties with the partner's Secondary must be worked out with everyone's cooperation. If you are not all friends by that time, then you are not conducting your relationships in a very cooperative and loving manner. When all is said and done, what we are creating is extended families based on the simple fact that lovers will come through for you more than friends will.

An additional complication can arise with the variable of alternate sexual preference. A bisexual woman I knew who was partnered to a man had to terminate a relationship with one of her female lovers because the Secondary lover was a lesbian who objected to the Primary relationship for political reasons. Another bisexual couple had a system whereby they were heterosexually monogamous and all their satellite relationships were with members of the same sex. This elegant solution underwent considerable stress and eventual alteration with the advent of AIDS.

Staying Healthy

Venereal diseases have been the thorn in the rose of erotic love for centuries, but recently the thorn has developed some fatal venom. If open relationships are to survive, we must develop an impeccable honesty that will brook no hiding behind false modesty or squeamishness. We must be able to have an unshakeable faith in our Primary partners and a very high level of trust with any Secondary or other satellite relationships. This demands a tight knit community of mutual trust among lovers who are friends. A recent study yielded some sobering statistics: over 80% of the men and women queried said they would lie to a potential sex partner both about whether they were married as well as whether they had herpes or other STDs. All it takes is one such liar and the results can be pathological to all. Nowadays, anyone who feels that total honesty is "just not romantic" is courting disaster and anybody unfortunate enough to trust a person like this can drag a lot of innocent people down with their poor judgment.

In order to cope with this level of risk, a system has been evolving that we call **The Condom Commitment.** It works like this: you may have sex without condoms only with the other members of your Condom Commitment Cadre. All members of the Cadre must wear condoms with any outside lovers. The Condom Commitment begins with the Primary relationship where trust is absolute. Long-term Secondary lovers can join *by mutual consent of both Primaries and any other Secondaries that already belong.* If a person slips up and has an unprotected fling then they must go through a lengthy quarantine period, be tested for all STDs, then accepted back in by complete consensus of the other members of the Cadre. The same drill applies if a condom breaks during intercourse with an outside lover.

Adherence to the Condom Commitment and to the other Rules of the Road may seem harsh and somewhat artificial at first, but they have evolved by way of floods of tears and many broken hearts. Alternative relationships can be filled with playful excitement, but it is not a game and people are not toys. The only

way the system works is if everyone gets what they need. The rewards are so rich and wonderful that I personally can't imagine living any other way.

I feel that this whole polyamorous lifestyle is the *avante garde* of the 21st Century. Expanded families will become a pattern with wider acceptance as the monogamous nuclear family system breaks apart under the impact of serial divorces. In many ways, polyamorous extended relationships mimic the old multi-generational families before the Industrial Revolution, but they are better because the ties are voluntary and are, by necessity, rooted in honesty, fairness, friendship and mutual interests. Eros is, after all, the primary force that binds the universe together; so we must be creative in the ways we use that force to evolve new and appropriate ways to solve our problems and to make each other and ourselves happy.

The magic words are still, after all: Perfect Love and Perfect Trust.

Recommended Resources and Reading:

The single best resource is *Loving More* magazine and its associated website: *www.LoveMore.com.*

Here's a few other Internet resources: *poly@polyamory.org;*

The news:alt.polyamory newsgroup; *www.polyamory.org;*

Sacred Space Institute, *www.lovewithoutlimits.com;*

Glendower: A Panfidelity Newsletter, *polyfi@aol.com.*

You can also type in the keyword "polyamory" into your search engine and find many more sites and references.

There are also a number of good books addressing this topic, both fiction and non-fiction. The great classic fiction is Robert A. Heinlein's *Stranger in a Strange Land* (1961)—as well as most of his subsequent books, culminating in *To Sail Beyond the Sunset* (1988). We Ravenhearts also highly recommend Donald Kingsbury's *Courtship Rite* (1982). See also Robert Rimmer.

For non-fiction books, see Deborah Anapol's *Love Without Limits* (1992) and *Polyamory; The New Love Without Limits.* See also *The Ethical Slut* by Dossie Easton & Catherine Liszt.

GE Vol. XXIII, No. 89 (Beltane 1990) 12–13

A View from the Bridge:
Gay/Lesbian & Pagan Emergence
by *Ivo Dominguez, Jr.*

Author's Note: I actually had a bit of trepidation when I heard that this was one of the pieces that had been selected since social concerns and contexts change swiftly in our communities. Upon rereading the essay, I found that though I would change some of the details and the wording, it was still a valid statement of need. The issues raised in the essay still need addressing and if anything are even more urgent more than two decades later. —ID

 S A GAY MAN AND A WICCAN, THE process of my growth and integration has meant in part the building of a Rainbow Bridge between these two parts of my life. There are many parallels that can be made between different oppressed and minority communities, but there are striking similarities between the Lesbian/Gay and the Neo-Pagan Communities. We share a deep history of joy and pain as both the Fey folk and as the faggots for the fire. In this time, our paths join again.

Changelings

Most Pagans and Gay/Lesbian people were not raised in households free from society's prejudice and blindness. For many there was a sense of being different in some special and central way and often there were no words, images, or role models to give form and substance to these feelings. For many the anguish was felt that there are no others like themselves. Like changelings, in time we come to know that, though we may love our families, someplace there are others like ourselves and we must find them.

Sometime after this realization the *coming out* process begins. Depending upon an individual's circumstances, this quest can be rapid or ponderous and the road may be rocky. Like the Gay/Lesbian community, the Neo-Pagan community suffers from insufficient awareness and understanding of this process and those seeking their changeling identity. Don Wert, from the Pride Institute (a drug/alcohol rehabilitation center for sexual minorities) outlines the coming out process for sexual minorities in five steps. I believe it is applicable to coming out of both

the closet and the broom closet and I present it here in a modified form.

As a young adult, I was fortunate to have access to a consciousness-raising group for men exploring their sexuality, which had a profound impact on my growth as a person. I wish there had been a similar group to explore the issues of my spirituality. Many of the Pagans enter the community through books, periodicals, study groups, circles, covens, and festivals. These are long on ideas and magickal instruction but short on space, encouragement, or structure to help newcomers process the creation of a new identity, though of late there has been greater attention to adding ideas from feminism, ecology, and Pagan politics to the training of newcomers and as discussion topics at festivals.

The rapid growth of the Pagan community has meant that the proportion of knowledgeable Neo-Pagans (with identities that have integrated their spirituality) has dropped precipitously relative to newcomers. This has also meant there are insufficient openings for those seeking entry into established groups, resulting in the formation of many new groups with no elders. On one hand, this has freed us from some of the limits of rigid traditions and will yield many new rich and beautiful traditions in years to come. On the other hand, the emotional and psychological cost to those newcomers may be high. Though a certain amount of pain and hardship is necessary, perhaps even desirable, in the process of establishing one's identity as a Neo-Pagan, too much can mar, harm, or prevent the completion of this soul sculpture. The lack of widespread conscious work by the community on the Neo-Pagan coming-out process is hurting all of us.

The dominant cultural values, images, and archetypes hold very strong negative messages for people who are Neo-Pagan and/or Gay/Lesbian. Spirituality and sexuality are taboo topics in this culture and much of the society's shadow is projected onto those peoples that live outside the narrow strictures of the socially accepted norms. In addition to this shadow that is projected onto the group soul/energy of non-mainstream communities, there is the shadow that becomes internalized and a part of an individual's personal shadow. As magickal people, consider what this means in terms of:

The nature of the shadow and its integration in the self.

Morphogenetic fields and the reality of thoughts as forms.

The stresses that are generated by the Great Work.

The psychological impacts of repression and low self-esteem.

I have heard people say that being Gay is just something they do in their bedrooms, and being Pagan is just their way of worship. However, elements as central to the web that forms the self as sexuality and spirituality, touch *all* aspects of life. Thus the compartmentalization of the self can be tremendously draining of the force for growth and joy that every being merits.

I propose that the Neo-Pagan community begin the process of developing resources and methods to help newcomers (and also elders who are stuck in their process) to integrate their identities. One way that the Lesbian/Gay community has addressed this issue is through the distribution of guidelines and topics for discussion for consciousness-raising and coming-out groups. The Neo-Pagan community could distribute such in the same vein as various *how to start a coven* and *how to design a ritual* booklets. Gatherings and festivals would be ideal places to distribute and to have demonstrations of how to run a group.

Some may feel the chill specter of dogma brush by your neck as you contemplate the distribution of guidelines for Neo-Pagan consciousness-raising and coming-out. This will probably not be a significant problem if we approach the development with borrowings from feminism, Gay/Lesbian activism, the peace movement, green politics and other peoples striving for wholeness. I have great confidence in the power of the trickster, a part of every Neo-Pagan I have met, to dispel unneeded authority.

Some may feel that this hand-holding and coddling of newcomers is not necessary because you've managed to find your way through on your own. But not everyone begins this process with the skills or emotional fortitude to continue and many leave before achieving clarity. Let us not fall into the snare of our own version of social Darwinism. In the face of the large influx of new people, some new responses *are* needed. Creating and implementing ways to integrate Pagan identity will help everyone, new and established, gain fresh insights. Taking this bull by the horns will also take the bull into the china shop of outmoded ideas!

Some of the benefits from widespread efforts to nurture those in their coming-out process include:

• Greater commitment to the future of the community as a whole. I have seen that Lesbian/Gay people who had access to coming-out groups are more likely to get involved in community service. All too many Fey folk find a lover and cocoon themselves away from the world just as many Pagans find a comfortable set of magical partners and weave a cocoon of a similar pattern.

• Greater strength and joy from the energy reclaimed from the integration of the individual selves that can be applied to growth.

• Greater depth of understanding of how the mainstream society affects us and others.

• A deepening of the meaning of our various forms of spirituality.

The Lesbian/Gay community is experiencing a new Burning Time with the health crisis of AIDS/HIV and with violence and oppression fueled by Right Wing forces in response to the gains of the past three decades. As the Neo-Pagan movement grows, becomes more visible and seeks recognition, those same forces will in their fear and insecurity attack Neo-Pagans. In part the

Right Wing is correct in believing that we seek to change the world. What they do not comprehend is that we seek healing, not conquest. We will need clarity of spirit and cohesion in the coming decades. Whatever form it may take, the time is *now* to seek and nurture the power within and the heart to hear the needs of others.

There are many other areas for dialogue and comparison between the Gay/Lesbian and the Neo-Pagan communities. The issues that parents face are similar. Both communities are grappling with the issues generated by their incredible internal diversity. What sorts of organizations, with what structures, and with what sources of funding, are needed as infrastructures vital to a community's health? This encompasses everything from lobbying, legal support, land/community center acquisition, nursing homes, schools, etc. and must be dealt with sooner or later.

We are living in a very important era for alternative and disenfranchised communities. Neo-Pagans are a diverse people and the time has come to weave this diversity into a cloak of comfort.

Can we talk?

Coming Out of the Closet— Five Steps to a Public Identity

• Step One—Denial

Lesbian/Gay

Homosexual feelings or thoughts cannot be recognized or admitted.

Cognitive: Information collection and processing is inhibited and fantasies are repressed.

Behavioral: Over-compensate in the imposed sexual role or inhibit all sexual activity or its enjoyment. May seek therapy or religious counseling for help.

Emotional: Restlessness, confusion, difficulty in focusing. There may be increased use of substances such as alcohol, nicotine, drugs, etc.

Neo-Pagan

Feelings and thoughts of a magickal or spiritual nature cannot be recognized or admitted.

Cognitive: Fantasies are repressed and psychic perceptions are inhibited or explained away.

Behavioral: Any connection to a mainstream religion is reinforced, or worship shifts to the altar of science and secular thought. If psychic experiences are strong, help may be sought from friends, counselors, or clergy.

Emotional: Restlessness, confusion, difficulty focusing. There may be increased use of substances such as alcohol, etc. Science fiction, fantasy, or role-playing games may be sought as an escape.

• Step Two—Encounter

Lesbian/Gay

The person has a homosexual experience that may not be their first but it marks a threshold.

Cognitive: Bargaining and rationalization about what the experience means.

Behavioral: Often a withdrawal from activities and relationships.

Emotional: Exhilaration usually followed by fear, shame, or a sense of being unclean. There may again be denial or regression.

Neo-Pagan

The person has a magickal experience, perhaps an open circle, that may not be their first experience but marks a transformation.

Cognitive: Bargaining and rationalization about what the experience means.

Behavioral: Avoidance of people or places that are identified as magickal.

Emotional: Exhilaration usually followed by fear, doubt or a sense of having broken some taboo. There may again be denial or regression.

• Step Three—Immersion

Lesbian/Gay

The person experiments with the Gay/Lesbian community, seeking out people and activities that strike a balance with needs and comfort level.

Cognitive: Acquires the language and the flavor of the Gay/Lesbian subcultures. Often thinks in dualities of Gay/Straight.

Behavioral: A whole-hearted exploration

of their sexual beings and of the Lesbian/Gay communities' activities. Separation from straight friends and activities.

Emotional: Relief at finding peers and a sense of belonging. Pride in growth, but anger and sadness in seeing the oppression of sexual minorities.

Neo-Pagan

The person experiments with the Neo-Pagan community seeking out study groups, circles and gatherings that strike a balance with the person's needs and comfort level.

Cognitive: Acquires the language and the flavor of the Neo-Pagan traditions. Often thinks in dualities of Magical/Mundane.

Behavioral: A whole-hearted exploration of their spiritual beings and of the Neo-Pagan communities' activities. Separation from mundane friends and activities.

Emotional: Relief at finding peers and a sense of belonging. Joy in freedom, but also anger and sadness in seeing the oppression of fundamentalist beliefs.

• Step Four–Internalization

Lesbian/Gay

The person develops a more stable self image and self definition.

Cognitive: A sense of personal power and capacity to change is gained.

Behavioral: A balance between Gay/Non-Gay friends and activities is sought. Identity as a Lesbian or Gay person occurs as needed or desired.

Emotional: Grief for the losses and guilt for disappointment to those hurt in the coming out process. Often an increased sense of focus and integrity.

Neo-Pagan

The person develops a more stable self image and self definition.

Cognitive: A sense of personal power and capacity to change is gained. Explores the relation to their other beliefs.

Behavioral: A balance between magickal/non-magickal friends and activities is sought. Identity as a Neo-Pagan person occurs as needed or desired.

Emotional: An increased sense of

purpose and center. Grief for the losses and guilt for disappointment to those hurt in the coming out process. Often an increased sense of focus and integrity.

• Step Five—Commitment

Lesbian/Gay

A more complete identity is embraced and life goals and directions are chosen that relate to this identity.

Cognitive: Accepts what is as a gift and recognizes diversity. Integrates various parts of the self and evaluates myths and stereotypes.

Behavioral: Explores personal interests and develops an individual style of life and relationships.

Emotional: Increased appreciation of trust, honesty, and gratitude. For some, a hunger for growth.

Neo-Pagan

A more complete identity is embraced and life goals and directions are chosen that relate to this identity.

Cognitive: Accepts what is as a gift and recognizes diversity. Integrates various parts of the self and evaluates myths and stereotypes.

Behavioral: Explores personal interests and develops an individual style of magick and relationships. Often commits to a circle or a tradition.

Emotional: Increased appreciation of trust, honesty, and gratitude. For some, a hunger for growth.

Ivo Dominguez has been active in Wicca and Paganism since 1978. Ivo was a founding member of Keepers of the Holly Chalice, the first coven of The Assembly of the Sacred Wheel, a Wiccan Tradition where he now serves as one of its Elders. Ivo is also a professional astrologer who has studied astrology since 1980 and has been offering consultations and readings since 1988. He is the author of *Spirit Speak*, *Castings: The Creation of Sacred Space*, and *Beneath the Skins*. www.ivodominguezjr.com

Agents of Aphrodite:
In Her Majesty's Sacred Service
by **Diane Darling**, CAW

 HE PRESENT-DAY RESURRECTION of worship and service to the Goddess of Love is essential to the survival of our Mother Earth. In the absence of Love we find ourselves over-whelmed by Death and Suffering, the sum of which is Destruction. So let us talk a bit about how a Gaian woman can manifest the Goddess Aphrodite in her present lifetime.

Long ago...

At other times in the history of humankind, contexts have existed for dedication to the service of the Goddess of Love in Her various forms. The environments of the women who served Her varied and some more than others were liberating, oppressive, sacred or corrupt.

Perhaps the best known of these forms is the temple priestesses who made love to men who had sacrificed to the Goddess and also made a donation to support the temple. In some times and places young woman did service at the temple before becoming eligible for marriage; in others it was a lifetime commitment, and an attractive option for widows and abused women. In *Gilgamesh, the King*, Robert Silverberg gives a vivid telling of the ancient epic with much on the hero's sacred marriage to Inanna. In it, the figure who acts at the pivot point of the story, who does what no other could do and does it well, professionally and joyously, is the temple priestess Abisimti. She tames the wildman, Enkidu:

"All unafraid and unashamed, Abisimti went to him and stood before him. He growled, he grunted, he frowned, not knowing what sort of creature she might be; but he did not snarl, he did not bare his teeth. She unfastened her robe and disclosed her breasts to him. I think he must never have seen a woman before, but the power al the Goddess is great, and the Goddess made the beauty of the holy whore Abisimti manifest to his understanding. She uncovered herself and showed him her soft ripe nakedness, and let him fill his nostrils with the rich perfume of her, and lay down with him and caressed him, and drew him down atop her so that lie might possess her.... Six days and seven nights they lay together coupling. I will testify myself to Abisimti's skills: I could have sent no one to him who was wiser in the ways of the flesh. When she lay with Enkidu—for that was the wild man's name, Enkidu—she surely must have made use of all her wisdom with him, and after that he could never be the same. In those hot days and nights the wildness was burned from him in the forge of Abisimiti's passion. He softened, he grew more gentle, he gave up his savage grunting and growling. The power of speech came into him; he became like a man."

Forty-five centuries intervene between us here today and Abisimti, Enkidu and Gilgamesh at Ur. The chasm across which we must reach to awaken this Goddess in ourselves and in other women and men is vast and deep and long. The near extinction by violence of Goddess-worshipping cultures by sexually twisted, male-dominated, monotheistic imperialists has left those who feel the call to Aphrodite with no temple, no elders, and no niche in the modern world.

In the 1960s, with the advent of the Pill, a new window of opportunity opened for the sexually-inspired women of the Western world: the choice to enjoy sex for the sake of itself, unencumbered by great expectations of joy and sorrow. The years when sexuality was a noose around each woman's neck are coming to an end. We live in a time when our sexuality is a garland of blossoms carressing our bare breasts. We are making a place for ourselves and those who love as worshippers and as healers.

Heeding Her Call

The calling to the service of Aphrodite must be different for every woman, but two essential attributes of the Aphrodite woman are *personal autonomy* and the *practice of unattached love*.

Personal autonomy is the Goddess-right of all Gaians. *Autonomy* translates as *self-naming*. All of us who struggle with the patriarchal master cultures understand how difficult and imperative it is to allow no other to name us against our will, thus assuming the *power over* that the magical act of naming brings. In our daily lives we notice and destroy the definitions imposed on us by the death cult which rules this land. When we choose Life and Love, naming ourselves Gaian, Witch, Pagan, we choose the context of our acts as sacred and free.

Whore. Harlot. (Harlow). Slut. Courtesan. Hetaira. Trollop. Wench. Lady of the Night. Goddess. Priestess. Prostitute. Hooker. Tart. Wanton Woman.

Our process of self-naming and reclaiming our sacred art includes plucking the barbs and draining the poison from words that rightfully belong to women of our ilk. The barbs are hate and fear, the poison is shame. The rendering harmless may be accomplished by several means, not the least of which is cultivating in ourselves a righteous rage at the imposition upon the Goddess of Love and her priestesses of vicious attitudes by the degraded creatures of malignant cultures.

Equally important is researching the ancient roots of these stolen words. By developing an understanding based on our ancestral languages, we can redefine these words correctly and replace shame and fear based definitions with wisdom. Then, when an unworthy person speaks our words with malice, the evil is his alone, three times three.

Further desensitization and resensitization may be accomplished by composing and singing a litany of words for sexually free women, interspersed with sacred names of Love Goddesses and Their avatars: *Aphrodite, Venus, Yolkai, Sappho, Shakti, Branwen, Oshun, Radha,*

Anat, Freya, Hathor, Ishtar, Jezebel, Lilith, Shiela na Gig, Mae West, Marilyn, Marlene, Annie Sprinkle, Mary Magdeline, Abisimti, Babylon, Phrynne, Lysistrata, Anais, Madonna, Eurydice, Uinnius, Galatea, Dierdre, Zipporah, Hero, Penelope, Psyche.

Unattached love: the ability, willingness and inclination of a free-standing woman to engage in love affairs of service to the gods, free from human hooks, strings and biologically-based expectations, in which there is healing, sowing of seeds, delight and insight.

Unattached love affairs are ones limited, in scope, duration, proximity or in some other important way. Thus they are seasoned with excruciating ephemerality, which awakens one to savour every moment. At a festival, for example, these boundaries are given, but when we engage with someone whom we can expect to know, perhaps circle with, over a greater span of time, it is very important that both lovers are in agreement and respectful of the finite nature of this love. Hidden agendas will distort and choke off the flow of tantric energy. In a sense, the lovers of Aphrodite are freed to manifest themselves as their best and highest and also as the humble seeker because this love is *outside* the

ASTARTE TO ASTAROTH

THE MOTHER GODDESS WAS WORSHIPPED UNDER MANY NAMES, ISHTAR, ASHTART, ASHERAH. THE GREEKS CALLED HER ASTARTE AND EQUATED HER WITH APHRODITE IN HER ORIGINAL FORM. SHE IS MENTIONED IN THE OLD TESTAMENT FREQUENTLY AND WITH VIOLENT DISAPPROVAL AND EVENTUALLY, LIKE MANY OF THE OLD GODS WHO RIVALED THE GOD OF THE CHRISTIANS AND JEWS WAS TRANSFORMED INTO DEMON

MORE LATER

realm of mundane love with its baggage of mate-seeking, shielding, posing and games.

Unattached is not the same as uncaring. On the contrary, the attitude of the Aphrodite woman is one of sincere concern for the well-being and self-realization of those whom she encounters in her practice. Her interplay with their personal development stays centered between deep emotional involvement and cold dispassion. The power of Aphrodite is wondrous, indeed, and the woman who carries it has great responsibility to her lovers and is accountable to the Goddess Herself. The Lady of the Morning Star is generous in Her rewards and equally ruthless in her punishment, as shown in this story from our long-ago:

There was a priestess of Ishtar, whose service was as a Lady of the Evening. The temple of Ishtar was built with windows above street level so that the sacred whores might show their faces to potential worshippers as they passed, enticing some to come within, make offerings and delight in the pleasures of the Goddess. This priestess of whom we speak was very beautiful but cruel. She tormented a particular man who, in anguish, cried out to Ishtar for justice. The outraged Goddess responded by turning her priestess to stone when next she stood at her window. This we see in the well-known stone carving "The Lady at the Window" iron Assurbanipal (8th century BCE).

The metaphor serves us well, for how many women, blessed with beauty by the Goddess, abuse Her power and find themselves turned to stone sexually? The service of Aphrodite is not to be taken lightly, nor may the mantle be shrugged off at will.

The Seasons of a Man

By what signs may we know a man to be ripe for the Goddess? There is little value in picking him when he's green, or riddled with insects. Some of the signs of worthiness are kindness, honesty, reverence for the Goddess and God Immanent, a certain hunger, and a willingness to be changed by the experience of the love shared, however fleeting or lasting.

There are modern Aphrodite women who will tame the wildman. Others may lay Beige to the walled fortress of the warrior and persuade him to throw open his gates to the Goddess. My particular specialty is men in flux. The period when a person is in the act of becoming a more refined, balanced, inspired version of self is a sacred time and a teachable moment, the most exciting opportunity to bring Aphrodite into a life. Adrift on the tides of his life, unsure of which current or wind will carry him onward, to such a man Aphrodite comes with her balm of sweet compassion, pleasure and support, sowing the seeds of Love for the Lady, the Mother, and all women. Such men may be opened up to the ecstasy of worship of the feminine, first in the women who are Aphrodite to him, and then in himself and the living planet. By mirroring to our lovers the higher self we see when we gaze upon them with our Aphrodite eyes, we may heal doubt, allowing them to shape and partake of their own transformations. Many men consciously and unconsciously solicit the aid and mercy of our Lady of Delight, and as we notice the petition of a particular man or contemplate a foray into his life, we owe it to ourselves to decline certain doomed and fruitless opportunities. Times are such that we no longer are at leisure to attempt to save every sparrow that falls. We must invest ourselves in strong, viable persons whose lives will help tip the scales towards the future we all pray for.

Some relatively bad investments of our time are the energy vampires, who have a ceaselessness to their need; process junkies, who are not really interested in being healed, just circling around, soaking up compassion and agonizing over it; and the hopelessly arrogant, who are unable to receive anything transformative from women. It is occasionally useful to engage in a brief affair with such ones for the purpose of gaining an understanding of the syndromes and for pleasure, but we should be open-eyed, come from a stance of solid strength, and not expect (but be open to) miracles.

Perhaps the most hopeful ones to engage with are the convalescent wounded. These are casualties of their own ill fortune or karma who are recently past the acute stages and are turning their thoughts to their future. They stand at a very exciting crossroads and it is the moments when they hesitate in indecision or are gathering their courage to proceed that the Goddess may easily most touch them in Her own deep and rewarding fashion. Men in this space are very suggestible and vulnerable, and the Aphrodite woman must be very pure in her intentions. Her service is to come to the newly-harrowed field and sow and cultivate the seeds of the man's own Godhead and of his awareness of Divinity imminent in his world.

Just past this stage, when the invigorating winds of his emerging life blow through a man, Aphrodite may appear to reinforce his new changes, to shore up his conviction of rightness, to comfort and assure him that the Goddess-loving man will always get what he needs and often what he wants. This is especially pleasurable for both partners, for the man is feeling his creative strength and is in a space to offer thanks to his gods for the rich feast his life is becoming. The Aphrodite woman may feel challenged to rise to meet the surging yang energy offered by such a man, and she is well-rewarded.

Through Us They Meet

There is a very special kind lover who may call upon the Aphrodite woman, and this is the dear friend. Our clansmen may wish to drink from Her fount for reasons having nothing to do with wounding or healing, but simply to make a true offering at the Yoni altar, or even for the sheer pleasure of celebrating kinship in the worship of our gods. In some ways these are very pure meetings of peers, equally giving and receiving the flow of the holy polarity, free from process, free from a sense of the passing of time. The healing of rifts arising from Pagan politics, the balming of hurts from other affairs, the celebration of the turning of the year, the bonding of tribe to tribe by the sexual liaisons of key members, all these are served well by sexual sharing among friends.

Let us speak now of partnering the God. In some sense, this is what we are doing in all true rites of Aphrodite. In our Aphrodite selves we are constantly drawing forth the God through the man with whom we make love, calling to Him, inviting Him, invoking Him into the mortal man before us. We worship at the altar of the Lingam, drawing forth the God's unique presence by praise of voice and tongue and lips. We ourselves become the great Yoni altar, before which the God may worship the Goddess, currying Her pleasure and making Himself very welcome within. Each is open to inspired poetry of word, sound and motion, calling out to the God and Goddess visualized in Love and Passion:

"She walks the woodland path and in a sunlit meadow, She knows Him there, she scents His musk...."

Like a doe she appears in his wood, fills his senses

With her song of longing, by voice and vulva...."

"She shows herself in the Sun, His rays penetrate her,

She flirts with the God in the trees: "You come, too, Lord!""

We may be pleased and surprised at the

Art by Virgil Finlay—from "Ishtar"

power of the God's response, and we should be prepared to surrender to possession by our Goddess when She meets the God. At such times the veil between ritual and real life becomes thin indeed, and as priestess we become a copper wire, conducting the electromagnetic current of the Lady's love for the Lord to our partner and receiving it from him in the great circular polarity which gives rise to existence itself.

We must not underestimate the potential magnitude of this current compared to the carrying capacity of ourselves as devoted learners and seekers of the Flow. Pure gold and pure copper have a tremendous capacity for current *because they are pure and offer no resistance.* This is an important point to remember, one which priests and priestesses who conduct great rituals for many people know very well. When the energy builds in the *hieros gamos,* the Great Marriage of the Lord and the Lady, any impurities of intent soon heat up and become very uncomfortable to cling to. Call to the Lady and let them go! Surrender selfish gain, reservations, fears to the greater thing that you are doing, for by letting all impurities be swept away we remain one with the Current itself and real-ize the great reward of our Service: Union as One.

We Are Our Own Elders

The initiation of the young in the mysteries of Love is another kind of service we perform. When a young girl has her first moon, we offer her our time and loving counsel with regard to affairs of the heart, the nature of men and the honor, responsibilities and pleasures of being a woman. A maiden must be aware of her own autonomy and be given wards, such as the condom committment, permission to say yes and the firm affirmation of her right and power to say no. We often find young women who were not given these Goddess-rights by their own mothers. It is incumbent upon free folk of all persuasions to transmit these blessings and to any young woman who trusts us.

Blessed is the man who meets Aphrodite early in his sexual life, and blessed are his lovers who come after. The joyous instruction of a young Goddess-man in the arts of

pleasuring a woman is a service to him and to all the women he makes love to for the rest of his life. It is a great pity that our young are forced to learn their loving from partners who do not themselves know what it is about. As Aphrodite women, we are aware of the benefits of expert instruction, of raising the standards of sexual giving and receiving, and of cultivating a visceral devotion to the Goddess in men of the generations which follow us. But of all services, this requires the greatest discretion, not only because of societal prejudice, but most critically because of the sex-role confusion imparted to the young by the media and the great probability of youthful attachment. The Aphrodite woman who sends a Goddess-intoxicated young man forth into his life does all beings a great service.

Afterglow

As with any claiming or reclaiming of any extraordinary paradigm, there is much to be discovered. We owe it to ourselves and the human evolutionary process to proceed with humility, confidence and vigor. A relationship that has a beginning, a middle and an end is not a failure, it is a completion. Dedication to the Goddess of Love takes different forms for each women and changes over the life of one woman. We who choose this path will be much rewarded by clear, honest communication with each other. In fact, half the work we do is with other women, some of whom are sister priestesses, others are threatened by our practice, and many are potential agents of Aphrodite themselves.

Though what I have said above is directed to women having heterosexual relationships, it is probable that much of it applies equally to men and people engaged in homosexual relationships. The time is ripe for men to speak out as priests of Eros, and for similar discussions of same sex erotic sacred service. The effort to draw forth and balance our sexuality is a central component of the great revolution of consciousness that is all around us and in us....

GE Vol. XXVI, No. 100 (Spring 1993) 26–28

In Defense of Polarity

by Deborah Lipp

The Spring 1993 issue of *Green Egg* carried two articles opposing traditional Wiccan polarity as being both confining and homophobic. As a traditional Wiccan, I write to offer a different view.

A polarity system is, in a way, a view of creation. If the universe began as an undifferentiated whole, then differentiation is the beginning of life as *we* know it. The ultimate polarity is that of Is/Is Not. Our reality is made up of boundaries: the window ends at the window sill, the window sill ends at the wall, and so on. If there were nothing but the window, with no beginning or end, we would not be able to define a window. We learn to understand reality by understanding boundaries.

Not all boundaries are paired—a window is not particularly the opposite of any one thing—but paired boundaries, polarities, are not only extremely prevalent, they are an essential part of cognitive processing. Learning opposites is one of the signs of development of a young child's brain. Up/down, in/out, near/far and other such polarities are how we place ourselves in the universe.

Gender is one of the first polarities we learn, and perhaps the most important in all cultures throughout the world. The first question that most people ask about a newborn baby is: what gender? Symbolizing all polarity through the polarity of gender is a way of boiling polarity down to a quintessential statement.

Furthermore, there is present, in the physicality of gender, a particular charge or energy. A man, simply by being male, has an energy about him that is polar to the energy of a woman. That polarity is often accompanied by a sexual charge, but sexual desire does not define, nor is it necessary to, the spark generated by a man and woman bringing their polar energies to bear in a magical working. Ivo Dominguez, Jr., in his article on this subject, cited a working between a gay man (himself) and a straight woman. He suggested that the power raised by this indicated the existence of other kinds of gender polarities than those used in traditional Craft. I suggest, instead, that the orientation of the pair involved does nothing to mitigate their physical gender, and that the power raised was that same male/female power that traditionalists have been criticized for using.

As I understand it, the very essence of homophobia is the assumption that physical gender is the proper determinant of sexual orientation. To say that homosexuality makes working within a gender-based polarity system difficult or impossible is to say that gay men aren't really men and can't raise male energy, or that lesbians aren't really women and can't raise female energy. This is patently false. A gay man is still a man. He has a penis, he has testosterone, he has male pheromones. Failure to function within the strictures of cultural gender roles is not confined to gayness, nor does it alter gender-energy. Wiccan ritual expresses cosmic reality, not Western sexism. Of course, there are other ways of expressing cosmic reality. Many people who are taught traditional Craft are taught that sexual excitement is one result of polarity working. It is, in fact, one way of knowing that the working is going well. I teach people to expect this more as a warning than as a requirement. Sometimes, two people who are not normally attracted to each other, consecrating wine (for example) together, might find themselves shocked by desirous feelings. It is important that they know in advance that those feelings are part of the magic and not a determinant of the future of their relationship.

Excitement, though, is a by-product of polar working, not its source. I (a primarily heterosexual woman) have worked with many heterosexual men with whom I shared no sexual spark whatsoever. My feelings toward a particular man might be too sisterly to generate horny energy. But gender energy was present, and effective ritual was the result.

Mongo BearWolf's article quotes the Farrars as follows: "We have even had one or two homosexual members during our coven's history, when they have been prepared to assume the role of their actual gender while in a Wiccan context...." BearWolf interprets this to mean that "being gay is all right as long as it is not brought into the circle." I find both of these statements objectionable, and for the same reason. Both assume that being gay is somehow the equivalent of being a different gender. Why shouldn't gays and lesbians be their actual gender, both in and out of a Wiccan circle? And why should being male or female inside a circle mean leaving one's gayness outside?

BearWolf has a good point when he mentions that gender polarity metaphors are basically heterosexual. However, I don't feel that it is the place of straight priests and priestesses to provide new metaphors. To me, there is something offensive, something marginalizing, about the members of a majority making decisions about what does and does not work for the members of a minority. Gays and lesbians need to develop their own metaphors, based upon their own understanding of who they are and what their relationships to the Gods and nature are like.

It may be that some uniquely gay metaphors would not work well in a coven that is using gender-polarity metaphors. I do not find a problem with this. No one in our community has an exclusive hold on truth, or exclusive access to the Gods. Nonetheless, there are many exclusive covens and other groups. Musical covens exclude the tone-deaf. Celtic covens exclude those not interested in Celtic mythology. Female covens exclude men. None of these exclusivities is based in morality—they do not say that it is wrong to be tone-deaf, or to prefer Greek mythology, or to be male. Just so, if gays and lesbians choose to form their own groups, where they can explore metaphors that may exclude straights, it is not because it is wrong to be either gay or straight.

As far as fertility magic goes, I confess to believing that heterosexual metaphors are necessary. No matter what our orientation may be, we were all born of heterosexual union. The miraculous spark of life is created when sperm meets ovum. Metaphors about the fertility of creativity and so on spin off from the basic fertility of new life, new birth. If we symbolize that, we should symbolize it in the manner of creating life. Sex magic works

on a number of levels, horny energy is juicy, useful energy with or without fertility as a component. However, if I were working a fertility ritual through the use of sex magic, I would not consider oral sex, anal sex, or any other non-fertile form of sex to be the proper culmination of that ritual.

There are other metaphors besides fertility that can be used to promote creative energy, productive work, or a good crop. Joyous excitement is one. To bring joyous excitement to creativity through the use of sex magic would not require any particular type of sex, number of partners, or interesting position. To fulfill a goal through the use of sex magic might require orgasm as the symbol of fulfillment. Fertility is one particular thing, expressed in nature in a particular way; it is not the only thing. But to remove the natural course of fertility (heterosexual union) from our fertility magic denatures it and runs counter to the goals of nature-based religion.

Gender-based polarity works for me, and for many like me. Its particular flavor of energy appeals to me, and I am happy in rituals that follow its flow. I am happy to include gays, lesbians, bisexuals, accountants, programmers, insurance agents and furry animals in my circle, provided we all get along. If we don't get along, then go with the Goddess, there's probably another circle in the next town. One of the joys of our community is its plurality. Many Gods means that no one God must be all things, and many circles means that no one circle must be all things. Plurality gives us permission to be different without necessarily being better or worse. And that permission applies equally to radical changes of customary world views and comfortable complacency with those same world views. May we all find joy with the Gods, however we meet Them.

Deborah Lipp became a Gardnerian Witch in 1982 and a High Priestess in 1986. She's been published in many Pagan publications, including *New Witch*, *The Llewellyn Magical Almanac*, *Pangaia*, and *Green Egg*. She is also a lifetime member of Ár nDraíocht Féin (ADF) and was on its original Board of Directors.

GE Vol. XXVII, No. 104 (Spring 1994) 20–21

The Return of Pan:
An Ecology of Male Sexuality

by *Jesse Wolf Hardin* (art by Nybor)

"I yam what I yam" —Popeye

"It is the difference between men and women, not the sameness, that creates the tension and delight." —Edward Abbey

"If I could tell you what it means, there would be no point in dancing it."
—Isadora Duncan

I AM A MAN. THERE! I'VE SAID IT! No apologies.

What shame can there be in the way coarse-grained muscles sheath these mammalian bones, or the way they swell and brace at the first hint of need? Stretched over their fluid bulk is skin sensitive to the slightest touch, though slashed and abraded countless times in intimate physical interaction with the rest of the living planet-body. This sun-licked envelope has worn well against the pitfalls of play and the wounds of earnest combat, a diary of my life written in blissful memories and flaming scars. I love the sweat and push of every test, whether scaling giant cliffs or extending the intense ballet of primal coitus. I love the way this body slowly and patiently experiences every fold, every aromatic nuance of the wildflowers, yet sets the weighty lodgepole in its place, rages and roars against adversity.

I am a man—no way around it. I could shave off my ample facial hair, conceal my musculature in loose-fitting garments, temper my (at times) arrogant posturing, resist making proud eye contact and still I am incontrovertibly male. I am engaged in my maleness. I rise up from the depths of my male scent as the first creatures rose from the primordial seas. I am buffeted and driven by uniquely male hormones, a mortal sail filled with the masculine instincts of countless generations. Long before both man and woman began their shared journey away from primalcy, long before patriarchal civilization took over the hearts and souls of the *populus,* there existed *male* energy, inseparable from the flesh and will of the Earth. It fueled and colored the lives of my male ancestors, from the first Y chromosome through reptilian and primate courtesans, from my early Celt and Norse predecessors to my known relatives. I am of the Earth. I am animal. I am mammal. I am male. Together these aspects of my identity form the context of my being. These are the "givens," the *corpus mundi,* the terrestrial/contextual/experiential basis and body from which I must work. I make no apologies for my being.

For over sixteen thousand years humankind has moved steadily away from its Earthen, tribal, land-based roots. In pursuit of physical, emotional and psychic safety and comfort, we now live lifestyles that jeopardize not only some distanced and abstracted "Nature," but our personal survival as well. Thanks to the preponderance of white males at the helm of the sinking civilized state, those of us born through no choice of our own into light-skinned, male bodies may find ourselves vilified in a kind of focused racism/sexism. At times we of European decent are made to feel responsible for the genocide committed by others in ages past. If born male as well, we may feel we have to soften, dilute or "tame" our maleness.

In a world where those resisting the industrial paradigm often characterize it as an expression of male energy, it's no wonder I've felt encouraged to cultivate the characteristics of softness, peacefulness, creativity, emotionality and intuition ascribed to the feminine "side." I did indeed benefit from nourishing these aspects of myself, breaking loose from the rigid macho-male model in a spiraling liberational samba...but the very fact that these characteristics can exist as aspects of a male body means they are as much "masculine" as they are "feminine." Is a gay man necessarily *feminine?* I cannot accept that in crying over sad songs, nuzzling small animals, tending to the needs of children, writing poetry or learning to make love real, real slow, I have gotten "in touch with the woman within." Nor do I believe a woman is tapping any latent reservoirs of male energy when she exhibits the strength, aggression, purposefulness or drive regularly attributed to men.

The extent to which I have been affected by gender issues is illustrated by my timid doctoring of flyers promoting my writing. Shortly before his untimely death, friend and caustic author Edward Abbey sent a quote for my use, referring to me as an "artist, poet and man—and good at all three." Recent low esteem for whatever the word "man" has come to mean in this age could be graphed in the reactions to his quote, ranging from sharp scolding to unrestrained laughter.

I am a man!

No more apologies for my masculine build, Viking propensities or male wolfen scent. In service to the living Earth, we have no time to indulge in stereotyping ourselves with predictable behavior, and little energy for defending ourselves from being stereotyped by others. By even the most conservative of both scientific and prophetic estimates, we are likely the last generations with any chance of engineering a return to ecological balance. It is crucial to understand how elements of gender typing and male dominance (or male impotence, for that matter) factor into our empowerment and practice. The danger is in focusing on too narrow a definition of "self," becoming endlessly taken up in "process," unable to escape the cycle of therapy long enough to act in a physical way on the very-physical plane. Separate from a global/ecological context, gender issues, like other personal, social and political issues, can become a tragic distraction from the vital tasks at hand. Embodied within our experience of and defense of the Mother Earth, gender understanding and gender equality serve both the individual "self" and the inclusive, biotic, terrestrial "self."

Reclaiming their innate connection to the Earth, many women have set aside a special place in their home or garden for an altar to the Earth Goddess in all her many forms. Often escaping from the limiting precepts of some male-centered religion, they help return the balance by attending to the energetically female manifestations of the Earth. In response, "men's groups" have brought back the pan-cultural archetype of the Green Man, while seeking to rekindle genetic memories of clanhood and manhood.

Interestingly enough, back when both the human psyche and human ecology were in balance with and interwoven with the rest of wild nature, it was often the men who tended to and served the female icons, while the women invoked and celebrated the male. The man reached out to embrace the energy and lessons of the female spirit, and was in this way made as whole as before the first chromosomal split into two different sexes. By honoring and calling in the spirits represented by the male icons, the woman entered into sacred union, the yin with the yang.

Women have finally gained a degree of acknowledgement as autonomous, responsible, awakened sexual beings. For historically reserved or repressed women, the full expression of their sexuality may be seen as evidence of their liberation. Males, with historical social license to be more sexually outgoing, may now only be considered "liberated" or "evolved" (whether straight or gay) to the degree that they sublimate their sexuality. It is unfortunate when male sexuality, unimposed and often unexpressed, is considered inappropriate and "politically incorrect."

Sexual energy, whether male or female, is the electrical charge that animates life. Sexuality in no way requires "culmination" in a sexual act. It invigorates and enlivens our every waking moment, adds momentum to our every pacing dream. Acted out on the physical plane, sexual energy has the power to free us from our mental control and dialogue, rushing us back to the immediacy of present time, back into our sensitized bodies, back I to the ecstatic state of oneness with the rest of the living world.

Orgasm enforces the dissolution of perceived boundaries and the abandonment of social status, insuring the complete surrender of the ego/self to the borderless, seamless experience of the "all." Men, in spite of their seeming preoccupation with at least the mechanic aspects of sex, share with modern women the fear of ecstasy (from *ekstasis:* standing outside one's self), the fear of lunacy, of not "coming back," of leaving the safety of schedules, careers and co-dependent relationships behind in a mad, abandoned flight. For whatever reasons of destiny I have had no life partners, but my blessed time with lovers has been an initiation to the Goddess, a rite culminating in the abolition of constraint and the animation of magic. [It should be noted that since this writing Wolf has found a beloved mate in Loba who shares his work in the beautiful canyons of the Gila wilderness.] My icons for this gifting are Pan and his North American counterpart, *Kokopelli.*

It takes very little prodding for me to recall the feel of long silky fur covering my spry legs, or of polished horn spiraling from my skull. Pan symbolizes natural male energies the way the early Goddess effigies symbolize the feminine. Pan is the ancient wise one who prefers to be thought a fool, and a perpetual boy-child earnestly engrossed in the fine art of play. Never to be restrained,

he leaps away from convention and sloth, preferring the enticement of adventure to placidity or placation. With his panpipes he charms the birds and entertains his lovers. He is there for them.

On this continent the horned flute player is Kokopelli, loaded down with a heavy burden-basket filled with the sorrows of our confused kind, the agony of the besieged Earth Spirit, and the hopeful seeds of promise and rebirth. Carved into volcanic cliffsides, Kokopelli can still be seen doing a jig as he plays his magic flute. He teaches that no matter how heavy our load we must continue to dance our dance and sing our song....

The actual physical act of climbing up to see him on the rocks is a return to the source, to the context. Phallic projections rise next to vaginal sandstone clefts, at the foot of womb-like caves. Male and female energies touch and mingle without losing their distinctions. In this touching, the male and female expressions of the Earth, and the rock climber as well, become one. There is no longer any question or any answer, only the uninhibited act of *being—and* the empowerment of Gaian union.

"Within and around the Earth, within and around the hills, within and around the mountain, your authority returns to you..." —A Tewa Prayer
...the authority to be yourself.

Jesse Wolf Hardin is founder and teacher of Animá earth-inspired practice, and the author of five books including *Gaia Eros* (New Page 2004). He and his partners offer inspiring online Animá correspondence courses, as well as host students and guests at their enchanted canyon and true ancient place of power. Opportunities include weekend retreats, personal counsel, shamanic vision quests, resident internships, and special Apprenticeships for the most dedicated. Annual events include the Wild Womens Gathering, and the Medicine Woman and Shaman Path intensives. Contact: The Animá Wilderness Learning Center & Medicine Woman Tradition, Box 688, Reserve, NM 87830. *www.animacenter.org mail@animacenter.org*

GE Vol. XXXII, No. 135 (Sept.–Oct. 2000) 4–7

Chapter 11.
Future Visions
Introduction
by Chas S. Clifton

N HIS BOOK *WHAT IF? RELIGIOUS THEMES IN SCIENCE FICTION*, MIKE ALSFORD SUGGESTS that one persistent question for writers of science- and fantasy fiction is "Where are we going and how do we get there?" This question has been asked persistently by contemporary Pagans. *Green Egg* writer Tom Williams once put it this way: "We and all those who sense and long for the new age find ourselves in a search for metaphors, and it is here that a particular genre of literature can be of great use to us." No other religious group has ever so happily embraced sci-fi/fantasy for ideas about how its visions might play out, how magic might work, or how "the new" might become the familiar. Just today on a Pagan email list I read a discussion about how the flashy magical transformations that one sees in books and movies are not really how magic works, but they enable us to visualize in an external way changes that really take place in more subtle and more inner ways. In his essay "Speculative Theurgy" Ramfis S. Firethorn states simply, "It is *imperative* to understand the nature of science fiction in order to understand the nature of Neo-Paganism."

What is that nature? Much of it has to do with what religious-studies scholars call "re-enchantment" and what Firethorn in the same essay calls the Sense of Wonder—the Sense of Wonder that monotheistic religion was losing in the twentieth century. It was in science fiction books, not church, that inquiring young minds could ask, "*What if* there is really something to the spiritual dimension? *What if* there is an invisible reality of such powerful yet subtle substance that our instruments cannot detect it?—and yet which can interact with us?" One of those books, of course, was Robert Heinlein's *Stranger in a Strange Land*, which so powerfully pulled the rug out from under established religion that it helped to inspire the Church of All Worlds. Science fiction and fantasy work, of course, because they appeal to the imagination and the senses, not merely to the intellect—which is not to say that science fiction writers do not solve intellectual puzzles and provide pleasure for their readers in so doing. Science fiction is not about doctrine, it is about experience—and that is what it shares with Paganism.

How Science Fiction/Fantasy Affects Its Readers

*by **Vann Baker** (art by Oberon Zell)*

As with most things, Science Fiction/Fantasy affects different people in different ways. However, among most consistent readers of Science Fiction/Fantasy, there seem to be several traits shared by almost all of them, namely, a broader sense of depth and scope into the world of today, and a desire to be fooled and stimulated with truly imaginative and realistic ideas, concepts, themes, etc. Readers of Science Fiction/Fantasy are usually more acutely aware of the problems of Ecology, Utopia (and Dystopia), and changes in society brought about by technological advancements. Readers of Science Fiction/Fantasy are generally impervious to what some nonreaders would consider shocking or revolting new ideas, and readers of Science Fiction/ Fantasy are usually ready to consider seriously theories and concepts others would scoff at. Science Fiction/Fantasy readers tend to think of things in terms of Mankind as a whole, or sometimes the galaxy as a whole, rather than think of things in a local or national sense.

Because of Science Fiction/ Fantasy's more or less unique nature (since it often deals with Earth in the future and ventures beyond our solar system—often encountering intelligent life), its readers are more than casually acquainted with the virtues and incapacities of Utopia, Ecology, Sociology, etc. Other types of fiction rarely deal with these subjects, and Science Fiction/Fantasy is practically the only fictional literature which speculates into Man's future here on Earth and elsewhere. Science Fiction/Fantasy is, to the author's knowledge, the only literature which approaches current subjects and problems and asks, "What if...?" or "If this is allowed to continue...?" Science Fiction/Fantasy, undoubtedly, uses many common plots and themes repeatedly, but can do so without actually duplicating stories outright because there are so many different possibilities of viewpoint which can be used. Each time a new or different approach is used, the reader is stimulated, since his knowledge and reasoning is expanded by the addition of new concepts.

Readers of Science Fiction/Fantasy are generally impervious to "shocking" or "revolting" new ideas. If a reader of Science Fiction/Fantasy is a serious reader—that is, a constant or compulsive reader—he or she usually accepts as possible or highly probable what he or she is reading. Otherwise, why would they spend so much time reading it? As the reader proceeds along in the realm of Science Fiction/Fantasy, he or she will encounter many strange and unusual ideas and situations, many, many more than if he or she were reading strictly fiction. Fiction, whether it be Mystery, Adventure, Gothic, etc., deals only with the present and sometimes past situations and events here on Earth. Science Fiction/Fantasy, however, takes the reader into both the future and to worlds other than Earth—where many surprises, often completely convincing, await.

If it was suddenly announced that humans had made contact with extraterrestrials, most Science Fiction/Fantasy readers would not be shocked, and probably only mildly disturbed, for they have read about similar encounters many times before. They would know what the possible results of such a meeting could be; whereas the person or persons who do not read Science Fiction/Fantasy would probably be quite surprised and a little upset, since they would not have any idea of what would or could happen after such a meeting. Another example of the above is that one of the author's friends—who reads very little Science Fiction/Fantasy—was very disturbed with much of Robert A. Heinlein's *Stranger In A Strange Land,* but the author, who reads quite a bit of Science Fiction/Fantasy, was not so shocked by the book, and found it to be extremely interesting and witty.

Science Fiction/Fantasy readers tend to think of things as they relate to Mankind as a whole, or the galaxy as a whole. The reader learns that advancements in technology have a profound effect upon practically all of Mankind. As mentioned earlier, Science Fiction/Fantasy takes the reader beyond the present and often into the depths of space—into other solar systems, galaxies or even into parallel universes. The reader's imagination and thinking are expanded to include the possibility that, compared to the rest of the universe, Earth and its countless problems might be like comparing an ant to a man. Books such as *Dune* by Frank Herbert, *The Foundation Trilogy* by Isaac Asimov, and many short stories have conditioned or made the reader aware of the fact that Earth is really quite a tiny place, and perhaps not nearly as complex as Man usually thinks it is.

Science Fiction/Fantasy's effects upon its readers are subtle and varied, but generally speaking, the reader becomes more open-minded and receptive to new ideas and possibilities.

Genesis—
As It Was in the End
*by **Bob Bader**, President,*
St. Louis Herpetological Society

In the end, when the Earth was completed, there were trees, meadows, wildlife and countless waterways. Man dwelt upon the lands of the Earth and he said, "Let us build our homes on this place of beauty." Man built cities of concrete and steel and the meadows were gone. Man saw his cities and said, "It is good."

On the second day man looked upon the waterways of the Earth and said, "Let us use the waters to dispose of our wastes so that they will be washed away." The waters became polluted and the fishes died, but the wastes were washed away. And man said, "It is good."

On the third day man looked upon the forests and said, "Let us use these trees for our homes and our luxuries." And man did. The land was made barren and the forests were gone, but there were new homes to be lived in. And man said, "It is good."

On the fourth day man saw that there were animals everywhere. Man said, "Let us cage these animals for our pleasure and kill them for profit and sport." And it was done. Soon there were no more wild animals left on the land. And man said, "It is good."

On the fifth day man looked to the sky and said, "Let us burn our wastes and put them into the sky, for surely the wind will blow them away." And man did, but the air became filled with smoke and the wind could not blow the fumes away. The air became heavy and it choked and burned, but man's wastes were being put into the sky. And man said, "It is good."

On the sixth day man looked at himself; and seeing the many colors and languages, he began to fear and hate. And man said, "Let us make weapons and destroy us." And man's knowledge devised weapons and great machines of war, and the Earth was fired from great battles. And man said, "It is good."

On the seventh day man rested. And the Earth was still, for Man no longer dwelt upon the land. And the wind whispered, "It is good."

The Trip to Heaven

by *Timothy Leary* & *Robert Anton Wilson*

(from THE PERIODIC TABLE OF ENERGY, a work in progress)

THIS ESSAY IS DEDICATED TO THE Imprisoned, especially to those in the cages of the California Archipelago. Prisoners are constantly searching for books that will help them understand the human situation.

"I want to learn about life. About metaphysics."

"Metaphysics means 'beyond physics.' Do you know a lot about physics?"

"No, I'm not innarested in science. I want to know about spiritual things."

"Well, I don't see how you can go beyond physics until you understand physics."

"Then what should I read?"

"Read science-fiction."

"What? That's not spiritual!"

Yes it is, my friend. Listen:

Within the next ten years humanity will have mastered nuclear fusion for star-flight and decoded DNA to provide for genetic engineering, redesigning humanity for life-extension, higher mentality, better health, longevity and eventual immortality. Within twenty years humanity will graduate from gloom-ridden terrestrial mortals to ecstatic cosmic immortals. Pessimism is the most myopic philosophy around; the only realistic thinking is rapturous Utopianism, revolutionary Futurism, PSI PHY. Philosophy of science. Science-fiction.

Within thirty years, humanity will confront a new evolutionary problem, a new basic philosophical choice: To become planetary colonists or star-rovers; space-squatters or time-travelers. The issue is not new. During much of its history *Homo sapiens* has followed a migratory path; the theme of movement is basic to human seed. All epics are trip-journals, chrono-logs: Odysseus, Quixote, Huck Finn, Leopold Bloom.

The basic myth pattern is life, struggle, death, rebirth and eventual "ascent into heaven." The rebirth pattern is the first half of the DNA code, the sexual Immortality, or Immortality-1, through the undying Seed and its molecular intelligence, chemical memory. The ascent into heaven is the second half of the DNA program: escaping gravity, leaving the womb-planet, joining the Cosmic Immortals.

For evidence of the swiftly-arriving Immortality-2, via genetic re-engineering for endless longevity, see Ettinger's *Prospect of Immortality*, Segerberg's *The Immortality Factor*, or Harrington's *The Immortalist*.

No myth system seems to picture "heaven" anywhere but in the stars. Immortalism on one planet is as impossible as "socialism in one country." We conclude that the "coincidental" arrival of immortality and starflight together is absolutely necessary and part of the life-script coded into the DNA.

In the Seventh Circuit of the nervous system (see *Neurologic,* by Timothy Leary, Level Press, 1973) we turn on and tune in to the actual DNA/RNA dialogue within the nucleus of each nerve-cell. The vision of Pan. Planetary consciousness. Jung's "Collective Unconscious." The Atman. The robot ego becomes jarringly aware of its designer's strategy. *The DNA has been moving to this point ever since it was deliberately planted here 3½ billion years ago.* This is Tarot Slot 19, the Solar Intelligence, Sun-God, Cosmic Christ Consciousness, etc. Crowley's Crowned and Conquering Child.

Slot 20 in the Tarot, the "Last Judgement" card or "Resurrection of the DEAD," transcends the terrestrial mortality imprint. The neuro-genetic brain achieves life-unity intelligence as intuited by Oriental philosophers and tribal shamans. Tielhard de Chardin's Omega Point.

The genetic code will then be conscious of the entire scan of its galactic past and of the sequences to come. There is no "higher" or "lower" consciousness at this point. The entire multi-billion-year DNA spectrum is a timeless network, relativistically simultaneous (as indicated by Einstein's equations) and concretely simultaneous in that the entire evolutionary drama exists, alive and conscious, in the DNA spiral which resides within the nucleus of every cell of every sentient being in the galaxy. The undying Body of Buddha—resurrection of the dead in every sense! It is inaccurate to speak of "past, present and future" beyond this point. The "now" of the first bio-survival brain, the second emotional status brain, the third dexterity-coding brain, the fourth mating-protecting brain, the fifth rapturous Turned On brain, the sixth metaprogramming or serial ego brain are all physiological presents. The "now" of the seventh, genetic brain is the spectrum of all the bodies emerging over the multi-billion-year span.

Neurogenetic linkage involves our hooking up with life forms that are "younger" and "older" than us. Every species plays a part in the linkage. (The teen-age girl in Saigon can be regarded as a mechanism for transporting the syphilis germ to Fort Ord, California.) A tremendous shock of humiliation to the human-superiority illusions is involved in making the neurogenetic linkage. "You are not Awake until, looking at a dog, you see yourself," the Sufi says. Just as the emotional Emperor ego (Slot 4) must be transcended in order to master symbolic-objective programs of the Chariot (self-regulator) Slot 7—and jsut as the social Capricorn ego (Slot 11, Wheel of Karma) must be transcended to achieve neurosemantic bliss ego (Slot 14, Death-Rebirth)—so, too, the genetic ego of Slot 19 must "die" and transform in the neurogenetic fusion of Slot 20.

But Slot 20 (Neurogenetic Fusion) is also the transition from biological life to meta-life intelligence. We face here the probability, long intuited by mystics, that the galactic life-cycle is itself but a momentary phase in the galactic energy-process.

The "higher" (older) DNA intelligences have unquestionably learned how to master gravitational force-fields and genetic fusion. They have understood how the life process is created and by what intelligence, for what purposes.

Neurogenetic linkage with these more advanced life forms will take us to the frontier where life merges with and evolves into meta-life.

Evolution itself is pre-programmed to accelerate, to accumulate higher functions, to bind time. We will experience as much neural evolution in the first hundred years after graduating from terrestrial mortality (i.e., after leaving the womb-planet) as we did in our entire 4-billion year gestation since DNA was seeded on Earth.

The first reaction on transcending life and entering electrogravitational consciousness will undoubtedly be similar to the passive-consumer stages in all previous evolutionary circuits. Rapturous exploration, adolescent self-indulgence. Slot 21 marks the entrance to inter-galactic networks and the final shedding of the biological container, as the snake sheds the skin.

There is no need to create inventive prose to describe the Galactic Intelligence. Most of the great religious teachers have deduced the properties and characteristics. We need simply remind the reader that this radiant mind is meta*physiological,* not meta*physical.* It resides in electro-magnetic-gravitational fields of shimmering galaxy-wide consciousness into which the individual neurogenetic 7th circuit brains can input their total consciousness, thereby forming the 8th "brain" of each evolving species.

The Buddhist vow to redeem all sentient beings is no longer a pointless formalism.

But even here, in the highest slot possible within galactic space-time, intelligence must be presumed to be evolving further, seeking wider fusion. Galactic mind can be assumed to be seeding every available planet with "children" who will evolve far enough to rejoin the metaphysiological highest "brain" and aid it in its growth toward fusion with nearby galactic minds and then more distant galaxies and that which lies beyond space-time entirely.

The way outward appears to be the Black Hole. The entire life-stream of the galaxy may be imagined as sperm-stuff hurtling billions of years into fusion within the meta-gravity of the Black Hole itself. "Come home," She murmurs. We answer, "Hold on, we're coming!"

SCIENCE FICTION AS MYTHOS

*Art & article by **Daniel Blair Stewart**, CAW & Feraferia*

EVERY CULTURE NEEDS A *MY-thos,* a body of stories that explains our human relationship to the Universe. Our mythos embodies our beliefs, the knowledge, vision, ideals, even the purpose of our entire civilization. Additionally, a prerequisite for any myth is that it be entertaining, whether told around a campfire or enacted in a temple-theatre.

During the Renaissance, subversive groups of scientists struck what would turn out to be death-blows to the prevailing creation myth of medieval Europe. The opening chapter of the Bible, the account in Genesis of the Garden of Eden, placed a flat Earth in a Universe created in six days by one God. Instead of confirming this, these early astronomers and physicists demonstrated that the Earth was in fact *round,* it orbited the Sun and was *not* the center of a Universe only six thousand years old.

The *coupe de grace* was ultimately delivered by Charles Darwin with the publication of his books, *The Origin of Species* and *The Descent of Man.* After a furor that lasted a century, the scholars of the world were finally forced to agree: literal interpretation of the Biblical creation myth was dead, and with it died the notion that other Biblical stories were factually true.

This left Western Civilization without a mythos.

Nature hates a vacuum; thus the void was filled almost immediately. More than a century ago an intrepid young Frenchman left his home and journeyed as a cabin boy on ships to remote lands in quest of adventure. He must have found it, for he brought back epic tales of imagination and science which speculated upon the future of science, the place of humankind in the Universe,

as well as the big questions of war, ethics and the morality of emerging 19th century technology. The stories of Jules Verne served the same purpose in his culture as mythologies had in former cultures.

H.G. Wells picked up the ball and ran far with it. He pushed the limits of science even deeper into the realms of speculation and ethics. For example, recall the names of the main characters in *The War of the Worlds:* there are none. The narrator is only "me, myself and I," his wife is "my wife," his brother is "my brother." He encounters "the soldier" and "the curate." None of these characters are ever identified by name. Could Wells have been writing the myth of "Everyman"? Could he have *wanted* his readers to search for symbolism? Did he have a Universal Truth to tell? And, if so, does this make his story a myth?

If it looks, sounds and acts like a myth and serves the social, cultural and psychological function of a myth, can it be a myth?

Mythic themes figure prominently in contemporary science fiction. Both *Dune* by Frank Herbert and *Stranger in a Strange Land* by Robert A. Heinlein are science fiction parables about messiahs. (It is interesting to note that the "saviors" in both of these novels found it morally permissible to kill people.)

The messiah in *Dune* is named Paul Atriedes. Christianity was not founded by Jesus, but by Saul of Tarsus, who changed his name to "Paul." Christianity is a desert religion, as are Judaism and Islam, all fanatically messianistic, so Dune, a desert world, was the right planet for a *jihad*, a messianic holy war.

Stranger in a Strange Land is the futuristic parable about a man named after two saints, Valentine and Michael, with the last name of "Smith," a very common name, a recurring Heinlein character name, and a word that means "one who forges tools or jewelry out of metal" (as blacksmith, silversmith, goldsmith). Heinlein has made it clear that he chooses the names of his characters symbolically, one more quality that places his novels in the realm of myth.

Today there exists a legion of devotees to the television science fiction series *Star Trek,* which first aired over 25 years ago and was created by Gene Roddenberry. The Olympian quality of the characters, the circular mandala of the bridge of the starship *Enterprise,* with its Zodiac of characters (Kirk is an Aries, Mr. Spock an obvious Virgo) and the procession of mythical adventures addressing issues important to a scientific society, all combined to make the show endure from one decade to the next, persisting due to its pure mythological *staying power.*

When George Lucas read Joseph Campbell's *The Hero with a Thousand Faces* and was inspired to film the *Star Wars* trilogy, he knew he was playing for keeps. Lucas needed a sure-fire success to secure his career as a film maker. Campbell showed him what ingredients go into the creation of myths. In filming the movie hit of the century, Lucas also related an enduring myth for our culture and further elevated science fiction into the realm of the mythic.

The mythic power of science fiction has shaped other art forms. When the rock group The Jefferson Airplane changed their name to The Jefferson Starship, they released an album entitled *Blows Against the Empire,* about countercultural "freaks" (i.e., "mutants") who leave an ecologically devastated Earth on a starship. They create a perfect

world on another planet in deep space. For this, guitarist and songsmith Paul Kantner received a Hugo award, traditionally given only to science fiction writers.

Was rock group Yes referring to an ice age in their song "Starship Troopers," wherein they describe "Long winters, longer than time can remember"? Considering the third movement of that science fiction rock composition is entitled "Wurm," it would seem lyricist Jon Anderson was setting forth a science fiction creation myth of the last glacial epoch of the Pleistocene, just before our modern era.

Movies and rock'n'roll music were made for science fiction.

In ages past, entire civilizations collapsed when their mythical cosmologies could not be assimilated by rising civilizations they contacted. This phenomenon is called "culture shock." Today a global culture exists that is rapidly assimilating all existing societies. This phenomenon is called "future shock." It affects everyone on this planet, from the affluent elite to the indigenous peasants, although in vastly different ways.

Science fiction helps us anticipate the future. It addresses the questions posed by simply living in a technological age. It reexamines basic philosophical questions from the scientific view. Most importantly, it fulfills our cultural need for mythical archetypes that satisfy metaphysical problems. Science fiction will continue to be the literature of the future because it is the literature of constant change. No other culture has produced a literature of the future.

"Once upon a time there was a Martian...."
"Long ago, in a galaxy far, far away...."
Enter—the Dream Time.

Daniel Blair Stewart joined Feraferia in the early 1970s, thus beginning a career as a Pagan and shaman-of-the-arts. Since then he has written articles and contributed artwork to *Green Egg,* among other publications. He was resident artist aboard the ERA Mermaid Expedition to New Guinea in 1985 and is the author of the science fiction epic, *Akhunaton: the Extraterrestrial King.*

Rites for Future Myths:
Ritual Technology for Self-Initiation
by Antero Alli

HE EARTH IS A VASTLY INTELLIGENT and compassionate entity that has chosen to incarnate *as this planet.* From a "geomantic," or earth-based perspective, we, as individuals and cultures, do not evolve without the Earth. It is more likely that the Earth evolves us. The reciprocal interaction between geography and genes, the Earth and its people, forms the basis for those rituals responsible for maintaining a culture's traditions, for example, the rarefied, isolated heights of Tibetan culture could have only gestated in Himalayan wombs, just as the Yaqui Indian tradition carries the earthy magic of the Sonora Deserts of Mexico. In this sense, cultures are geologically formed entities determined by the topography of their particular planetary location.

Near the genesis of a culture, "originating rituals" emerge as individual human responses to the planetary entity. As this is shared with others (the collective), a group mind is formed. These originating first rituals temper the bonding responsible for germinating a distinct form within the individual, and then its expression to others as a collective process.

Due to the inherent interaction between the planet and Her people, human beings tend to be a highly ritualistic species, and contain within their cellular memory everything they need to know about how rituals work. We shall now explore how a generic ritual technology is buried alive deep within our instincts, imbedded there until it's unearthed, refined and put to work as a ceremonial skill. It is generic because it belongs to nobody and everybody, and remains unfettered by religious dogma, imposed beliefs and brand-name philosophies. Its purpose is the evocation of our own beliefs, visions and myths to live by.

Instinctual Techniques

Once certain instinctual functions are expressed and refined, they serve as "ceremonial enhancers" for strengthening the integrity of any ritual regardless of cultural or religious bias. One such function originates in the central portion of our brain, which brain researcher David McClean coined the R-Complex (after our Reptilian heritage). It refers to home-site selection as it determines how we locate a certain place to create shelter and/or sink roots in.

Why do we live where we do? Here, in America, there are numerous economic and socio-political "reasons" for moving somewhere and making a home, yet...what if we were "economically non-local" (able to make money anywhere) and socially portable enough to live wherever our instincts guided us?! Perhaps we would stay right where we are, perhaps not....

The home-site instinct offers us a fundamental ritual tool as far as it sensitizes us to the task of locating an appropriate setting for sacred ceremony. Each place and each ritual has its distinct intention...certain rites for certain sites, in other words. By adjusting our ritual intention to the "energetic function" of a certain region, we can effectively serve and/or utilize its resources. Rituals requiring containment may do better in the naturally bordered regions of a ravine, canyon or forest. Ceremonies calling for communion with Spirit, or Void, might do well in vast, boundless spaces like deserts or mountaintops.

Coinciding ritual intentions with geography eventually develops the originating mother ritual of geomancy, or Earth divination...where we learn to let our bodies be the natural "tuning forks" they already are. Every outdoor area also tends to express its innate "centers" where trees, rocks and other natural forms converge as if gathered there. Adjoining these centers are natural peripheries, or boundaries, marked by ridges, trees, rivers and other obvious borders. Sometimes the simple question of, "Where is the best place to set up camp?" is enough to help us start detecting the indigenous placement of an area, i.e., its center and periphery, for establishing a settlement that honors the surrounding land.

After a ceremonial location is selected, our territorial instincts can be put to work intentionally by the way we personally own the space for the ensuing ritual. All animals, including humanimals, have their idiosyncratic ways of stalking and claiming turf. By recognizing the boundaries and the center of the selected ritual area, we learn to *consciously* define and mark its space for the temporary dominion essential to uninterrupted focus. An altar might be constructed in the center and each of the four directions, an additional construct to vivify its natural borders. This tends to support the *containment* for minimizing the dispersion often accompanying ritual-design in the vast, breathtaking wilderness beauty.

Another inherent ritual skill is found inside our domestic talent for *converting a house into a home.* It seems that certain people possess, or are possessed by, this more than others; yet everyone has some way of making themselves *at home wherever they are.* This domestic instinct functions towards cultivating a kind of *Rare Area,* one made safe enough to invite a willingness to "drop one's act" as a preparation for the kind of vulnerability effective rituals are made of. (This is the feeling some of us get when we return home to visit a family that accepts us unconditionally.) When developed into a ritual device, this instinct converts into the holy task of *sanctifying a* space...blessing it with spiritual intention. Everyone has their own way, or style, of expressing these basic instinctual responses, which in turn form the basis for creating our own rituals to evoke our future myths to live by.

Future Myths

Future myths emerge as a response to "future memory"...the premonitory recollection that some part of us has already realized itself and guides the rest of us towards our inevitable destiny. This suggests an alternative timeline running *concurrent with and in reversal to* our local chronometric mode.

Traditionally speaking, time moves from past into the future. *According to aboriginal peoples, time also runs from the future back to the past.* If so, our present moments are but outward expanding ripples from the center of who we already are in the future. We have *already happened.*

Futuristic rituals, in turn, activate future memory by helping each individual unveil, forge and realize their own identity, destiny, and dynamic position in the cosmos. Living our future myths tends to "snap" us back into our "element." (Who doesn't know what it's like to be either "in their element" and/or to know when someone else is?) There's a *self-remembering* and a sense of being "on target" and "in sync"...of feeling rooted in oneself while branching out to others. One way to know we're getting closer to our future myths is through the obvious, repeat appearance of meaningful coincidences or: *synchronicity*...the Earth's own "sense of humor."

As we coincide, or synchronize, ourselves with the innate we call forth the benevolent allegiance of the cosmos: Zen. We are "in the Tao." At these higher levels of functioning, or grace, synchronicity becomes the norm and, a sophisticated decision-making device where no choices are made at all save for the *personal autonomy and style* with which one enters any given situation. Australian aborigines refer to this kind of "higher reality" engagement as "the dreamtime" and have developed certain traditional rituals in response to its effects, namely, the synchronicity affording intentional cross-country telepathy and astral travel. In the Western World, we've chosen to exchange these attributes for AT&T and TWA due to our predilection towards other ways of using our minds (read Descartes' *Meditations* and Newton's *Principia*).

From a Western historical perspective, ritual technology has been coveted by Church and State as, among other things, a form of social control. Ritual knowledge is ritual power and usually, "power over others" rather than the empowerment of others. However-er, as people grow more self-governing, they'll naturally seek out new forms to challenge and express their emergent autonomy. These remain unavailable, and, perhaps, non-existent through traditional religious institutions. With the rate of change quantum leaping into the Twenty-first Century, people will look for psychological and kinetic structures flexible enough to *permit the uncertainty* of the times. This seems to be especially obvious here in the United States of America, where people are literally the most free (in the political sense) and yet are constantly seeking greater liberation.

The ritual of the future puts the power back into the hands of the people and, by doing so, catalyzes the start of major cultural transformation. There's no more need to be spoon-fed religions when we are accessing God, or the Source, directly. We can bypass the imposed hierarchy of "middle men"...popes, priests (yes, even shamans), or any external authority figures in lieu of initiating ceremonies between equals. People are looking for a new religion. We are searching for the Tree of Life that will bear the fruit of our own immortality and godhood...a ritual technology for Self-Initiation. And, as the mystics have always said before us, it's all right there within our very human predicament. In the immortal words of master ritualist and philosopher, Georges I. Gurdjieff, "We are not human beings having a spiritual experience, but spiritual beings having a human one."

Antero Alli (b. 11/11/1952) is a Finnish born, Berkeley-based author, ritualist, astrologer and underground filmmaker, and the founder/director of ParaTheatrical ReSearch. Author of *All Rites Reversed?!: Ritual Technology for Self-Initiation* and *AngelTech: A Modern Shaman's Guide to Reality Selection,* he resides with his wife, the composer/singer Sylvi Alli, in Berkeley CA. More info at: *www.paratheatrical.com.*

Vol. XXVIII, No. 110 (Autumn 1995) 20–21

Let They Who Have Ears to Hear, Listen!
The Tree Spirits Whisper To Us
by *John Beggs, Feraferia*

TREE SPRITES, wandering through the forests and able to understand the sensuous whispers of the leaves, bubble always with information. But most of it concerns the delicate encounters, the charming flirtations of clouds and moths, of eclipse and waving grasses. So sensitive are these patterns that they cannot be rendered in our present human language. Just as the cobweb eludes the most skillful mason. Sometimes a friendly and patient Sprite can, taking a fine feather and half a day, joyfully tickle such a comprehension onto a human's skin. With this we must content ourselves until we regain our birthright, the lost sensual language, known to all the living, by which the worms speak to the stars. But now the Sprites have news that can be trans-lated into our language, for it concerns us. Dreaming, curled in the boughs of trees, they are immersed in the rhythm of arboreal souls. Who, then, can doubt what they tell us? For the trees' roots wind downward into geological time, the bedrock of the continent, the dark sun at the Earth's center. Their leaves extend upward to the heavens, gathering the light of near and distant suns. Their roothairs rustle with the chant of earthworms and raise the mineral offerings of the dead. The prophetic dream of a migrant bird voiced in a single startled croak enters through the leaves into slow conjunction with shadows cast by moonlight to form the dreams of the Sprites. The vision unfolds from the root dream that the trees have held since the Pleistocene Era.

GE Vol. VII, No. 61 (Ostara 1974) 22

Speculative Theurgy

*by **Ramfis S. Firethorn** (Jon DeCles) (art by Oberon Zell)*

FOR TWO THOUSAND YEARS THE physical horizons expanded and the spiritual horizons contracted. It was a graceful dance, discovering the realities beyond the limits of the known and desperately seeking for some security in a reality that kept changing; and the seeds for its choreography had been well planted. The polytheism of the world that gave us Homer and his fantastic voyage receded before a slowly expanding monotheism in which, even if you had maps to show you what was beyond the border of the Dark, there was something mysterious and unknowable to cling to; something "unrational" as an all-powerful Deity Who was both vengeful and compassionate. Who *could* order things better than they were, but Who did not for some mystical reason.

The thesis for today is this: it is *imperative* to understand the nature of science fiction in order to understand the nature of Neo-Paganism. That the thesis may fall flat on its face is OK; it is the questions, not the answers, that are important.

John W. Campbell, Jr., once suggested that science fiction *was* the mainstream of literature, for the following reasons:

Science fiction deals with humanity's attempts to understand what is not understood, and to place in human perspective the effects which the increase in knowledge *must* have on the conduct of our lives. In short, it deals with inevitable change and our reaction to it. *This* is the subject matter of nearly *everything* which has survived as literature for more than a century or so: not the minute examination of character which the self-styled literati of the Twentieth Century have attempted to foist off on us as literature; not the small-minded dissection of smaller-minded people whose lives are bounded by the short times in which they live; but rather, the grander sweep of the human adventure as the species learns and grows, fails, falls back, then regroups and begins the upward climb once again.

The proper scope of the realistic fiction so much beloved of the literati is the here and now. The proper scope of science fiction is all that ever was, is, and can be; and it is *that* scope, not the tiny one lauded by academics fascinated by feces, that has been the subject of most of human literature. (I am here echoing Campbell's thesis, so hold those poison pens and the charges of derisiveness until I am finished, will you?)

In truly ancient times the Wonder Tale was the

stock and trade of the story teller by the camp-fire, as, in a sense, it still is. Nobody wants to hear how you caught a so-so fish or killed a medium sized mammoth; but, sadly, hunting and gathering stories require proof, or something suggesting it at the very least. Adventure stories, on the other hand, are aided by the quality of the unknown and the unprovable. Escaping the jaws of an unknown monster is much better, in producing the Sense of Wonder, than killing the world's biggest saber tooth. And encountering strange peoples with strange customs cannot hold a burning brand to encountering supernatural beings who do things inexplicable to human knowledge.

Killing a giant ground sloth is matter for discussion of hunting technique. Not being killed by an unnamable *Thing* is grounds for *Speculation.* And speculation is the basic technique of science fiction.

What if...

It is also the basic technique of spirituality, and hence religion.

What if...

But during that two thousand year hiatus with which we began, there was far less need for speculation than there had been in the past. New discoveries abounded on every side, and during that time what was known as Reality changed so quickly that, rather than feeling the need for strangeness and wonder, there was an increasing tendency to seek familiarness and security.

You can still feel it. It is still a dominant paradigm, that need to *know,* for *sure,* just what the world is, just what Truth is.

Religious establishments worked hard to supply the answers during that period, and if supplying answers meant eliminating data, well, that was some of the price. As we sit here at the end of the Millennium, smugly contemplating our own superior understanding, I wonder how many people understand how thoroughly the orthodoxy of Science adopted that critical attitude of monotheistic spiritual leaders; how willing is the scientist to dispose of data which do not agree with his or her assumptions?

By the end of the Great Age of Machines (the Nineteenth Century) the Answers were no longer providing the sense of security for which they had been formulated; but Science had established itself in a social role which filled the same niche that monotheistic religion had filled for nearly two millennia. More, the level of discovery of truly new and startling data (and, perhaps more important, data which could be assimilated by people of a rather ordinary sort, as opposed to specialists in sciences that gave arcane appearances) was such as to begin a new cycle of Wonder Tales. The Dark reemerged as a place for stories to happen. The bottom of the sea became auctorially accessible and the space between the stars provided plenty of room on which to ruminate and in which to invent.

Inevitably the embarrassing questions appeared, questions implicit in the discovery of human smallness in universal enormity. Monotheism was no longer logical. (In the author's not so humble opinion, Monotheism is the most primitive form of religion; that in which the tribe discovers a God, and not being much aware of what other tribes think and feel, considers the tribal God the only one.) Levies could be built to hold back the flood of questions, but the best that could be accomplished was an uneasy blend of Monism with a new, more cosmic theology. And that, if we consider the reaction which orthodoxy had to Chardin, was not really acceptable to the goal of emotional security.

We were no longer the center of the universe. It might be—and increasingly, the feeling was that we were probably—not alone in the universe, the very apple of the Creator's Eye. Yet so strong was the dominant religious paradigm that nearly a hundred years went by before the average reader was ready to deal with religious speculation in the context of story-telling. Those who made the attempt were well-respected, mind you. Until the media managed to convince young readers that nothing worth reading had been written before 1965, writers such as Olaf Stapledon were held in wide respect, however slow moving their stories may have been: the Sense of Wonder was sufficient to hold a reader's attention, regardless of the lack of shoot-outs or explosions, or sex.

Allow me to offer a graphic model, just

for a moment, of the move of religious thought on a large scale.

From approximately Two Thousand BCE, to Zero Date, theology, and its concomitant partner, theurgy, moved toward ever more complex systems of perception and practice. Deities proliferated and the worship of those Deities became ever more complex and artistic, with a complexity of thought that mirrored the growth of the civilizations in which it occurred. In the two thousand years following Zero Date, secular knowledge proliferated despite the efforts of an increasingly simplified religious establishment.

Note that, in this second two-thousand year period, although the number of religions continued to increase, the focus, as a constant, remained on simplification of concept. The great Gothic cathedrals of Europe were followed by the protestations of the Protestants that worship should return to a simpler format; a view that directly contradicts the imperatives of the life force, which, by its nature, tends to ever more complex systems.

(As a sidebar, one of the current definitions of Life involves its ability to reverse Entropy, i.e., to move toward ever more complex systems rather than simpler ones. The Rainforest is a much better metaphor for life than are the practices of monasteries of almost any religion, Western or Eastern.)

Now, at the end of a second Millennium, our science has become a matter of minute discoveries which offer remarkably little in the way of story telling possibilities, and we have begun to look at Life in terms of bytes of information rather than exploration of star systems. Chaos Physics is fun, but it doesn't offer much comfort, as Einstein discovered and tried to disprove. In response to the Uncertainty Principle, Art has offered us role playing games in place of novels. Fun, perhaps, but not much in the way of spiritual discovery. (Not that it can't go that way, just that it hasn't so far.)

Anyway, as we were forced think about life other than our own, it was inevitable that we would be forced to exist. Perhaps more important, when confronted with the anger of the serious Fundamentalists, one can always retreat behind "It's only a story." And

many did, and still do.

But the Fundamentalists are *right* in one very important sense. Ideas are *powerful,* and once one has entertained an idea one has it in one's repertoire of considerations: where it may blast holes in one's sense of wholeness.

Much of the early opposition to science fiction and fantasy as a serious literature comes from the fear that the ideas contained in the stories might compromise the security of the locked room which theology had become. 'Trouble is, no organism can survive in a medium of its own creation. A closed universe, a locked room, will eventually suffocate its inhabitants.

Imagine the Sense of Wonder of a boy in the heart of the Bible Belt; a boy who has attended church for his whole life, and is convinced that the worst heretics in existence are the Roman Catholics down the street; who, in the heart of the Great Depression, is suddenly confronted with the glorious vision of the High Priestess of Ishtar in a hook by Abraham Merritt.

It does not take detailed descriptions of sexual acts to give this boy a stiffy. The mere *fact* of a scantily clad beauty is enough for high marks in such a time and place. But more important, this woman in the story is a *religious* figure, and she does not look at *all* like Mrs. Murphy, who plays the tinny piano for Sunday Service at his church.

What kind of epiphany might be experienced at such a moment? Think of the many things coming into conflict with all the hard and fast Truth this boy has learned. Suddenly Babylon and Ninevah are made manifest, and in very different terms than those offered by Biblical prophets.

It was not only the planets which were opened by the writers who emerged at the end of the machine age: it was Time itself, and thus all the cultures which ever had been.

Even those staid and conservative occultists like Bullwer-Lytton, who had been careful to show us good Christian figures in the rot of Roman society, could not disguise the sense of reality which emanated from the Ancient Gods. The Christian polemic of the major plot of *The Last Days of Pompeii* is given the lie by the final intercession of Isis, manifest in exactly the correctly Pagan way, as She takes revenge on Her apostate priest.

The Breaking Point was upon Western Civilization, and the only place where it was *safe* to express radical religious ideas was in a literature which was deliberately taken as *not serious.*

Just how important the matter was can best be judged by the outrage consistently shown by religious leaders against the cowboy movies of Tom Mix, in which religion and sex were almost inevitably linked, if only in terms which today are almost unobservable. The hero seeing a vision of his beloved superimposed over a church was so scandalous that many churches banned the films.

So there we were, Western Civilization in the grip of a brittle serpent, and the visions kept emerging. Alien Deities. Lost Civilizations. Past times when Magic worked, and Future Time when new faces were worn by new Gods. All of this suffused with the Sense of Wonder which the establishment had worked hard to reserve to the moment of Consecration, when Bread Became Flesh and Water Became Wine.

How pale that profound miracle must have seemed next to the largest electric generator ever built, at the Crystal Palace Exhibition. How less than wondrous the healing of the sick, next to the ultimate miracle of powered flight at Kittyhawk.

It was not that the stuff religion had was had; it was just lacking in pizzazz next to everyday reality. And what religion had possessed, locked in a closed system, was the complete option on the Sense of Wonder.

What if the miracles of the newly available Scriptures of Ancient Civilizations were as *true* as those of the Monotheistic dominant culture? *What if* there really were civilizations on other planets? *Surely* they must have religions?

A really hard question was the basic one of Science: *Can you repeat the phenomenon?*

Consider: there are probably more medically attested miraculous cures on the books in the Twentieth Century than there are explosions of nuclear devices. When you say to a Healer, "Show Me!" people may scoff when the Healer responds, "It doesn't work that way." But just ask a nuclear physicist some time to "Show Me!" a thermonuclear explosion. "You can't just do that every time somebody asks!" is taken as a legitimate answer.

There are consequences. Both to physical and religious actions.

What if everybody just *kept on* rising from the dead?

What if everybody just *kept on* exploding nuclear devices?

The Lost Race category of story must inevitably lead to a serious consideration of serious Anthropology. People who read stories which kindle the Sense of Wonder are likely to pursue the subject further. As surely as all the folks who work in the space program were inspired by reading Heinlein's juveniles; inspired by wanting to *make it so;* just as surely those who read of the wonderful lost civilizations in Burroughs were inspired to bring to life the creations which called forth that Sense of Wonder.

I am reminded of a conversation many years ago with a science fiction fan named Bob Pavlat. We were, at the Washington Science Fiction Association, trying to pin down the images called forth by various catch phrases. The term *Pagan Splendor* came up and Bob said that to him, Pagan Splendor was best exemplified by the bronzed Amerindian woman in a white fur bikini that had just graced the cover of *Astounding Science Fiction* to illustrate Murray Leinster's story *Sand Doom.* I thought about it and realized that to *me* the term Pagan Splendor was best illustrated by a scene from the film *The Prodigal,* in which Lana Turner, in pasties, stood atop a huge golden bull's head, high above a pool of fire, with thousands of dancers and thousands of priests and priestesses, and young men in loin cloths diving to their deaths in sacrifice.

While Rome continued to vest itself well, and maintain the complexity of its ritual, the *performance* of the ritual, the artistic quality, had begun to diminish with the Reformation. It was virtually *absent* from the proliferation of Protestant sects, by design. As the origins of religion in the West are identical with the origins of theater and art, the simplification of religion had become a downhill race.

I may admire the ethical motivations of Protestantism, but frankly, the only thing upon which it has improved is the practice of ritualized guilt; at which it has done a marvelous job.

How could a populous starved for wonder and beauty fail to respond to a literature which offered both these things, and without the kind of commitment which might get you hanged or burned at the stake, or at least confined to prison or an insane asylum? You might face a life of poverty or tedium in a factory, but in the safe pages of a book or pulp magazine you could find a doorway to that expansion of consciousness so highly valued by the folks around the Neolithic campfire, thrilling at something scarier or more wonderful than a mammoth dinner (and the leftovers).

It was inevitable that *someone* would eventually take the next step. Bullwer-Lytton and his cohorts, studying occult sciences within the context of a Monotheistic overview, must inevitably lead to the understanding of the power of Myth, and a slow but painful understanding of what Myth actually *is;* as opposed to what we are still taught it is. The invention of new mythic figures, such as Tarzan, must inevitably lead to a comprehension of the possibilities of the manipulation of the Mythic Unconscious. Had there been no Freud, there would still have been need for a Jung to face the power of the collective unconscious.

Freed of the dubious necessity of proving the reality of one's dreams, the writer or poet may create in the divine sense: may imagine (and remember that *imagine* is a verb!), and having imagined bring into existence. I am assuming that most of my readers understand the relationship between the making of an image and the making of the thing imagined; the one does not *have* to lead to the other, but the latter is not possible without the former.

Next to the burgeoning freedom of literary expression brought on by the Romantic revolution in the Arts, there was also an explosion of scholarship in the related fields of archaeology and anthropology. While writers were free to invent, scientists continued to discover and make available information

that served to underscore the ultimate value and truth of the new dreams and visions. We may know now that there are no canals on Mars, but we didn't when Burroughs, and Otis Adelbert Kline, and later, Ray Bradbury, spun their mythic tales.

Had somebody set up a serious church to honor the Gods of any one of the fictional visions of Mars, that church might today be in some trouble. (Or maybe not, given the continued success of those Apocalyptic Christian sects whose "deadline" has come and gone without anybody being overly troubled.) But that was not the current which eventually flowed, at least as far as I know. Rather, as more knowledge about the past appeared, and people wrote more stories set in a past that was half archaeology and half imagination, it became apparent that religion, as a social institution, could take forms other than those prescribed by the dominant social paradigm.

The emotional door, which is always more important in governing human life than is the intellectual door, was flung open.

What if there is really something to the spiritual dimension? *What if* there is an invisible reality of such powerful yet subtle substance that our instruments cannot detect it?—And yet which can interact with us?

The door was not only open: it was an *enormous door!* It was a range of possibilities as expanded as the scope of science itself.

Now, moving right along next to all the stuff about which I have been writing here was another powerful force, and one which had not, so far, joined the torrent.

With the extreme diminishment of women's status and valuation following the various stages of the Industrial Revolution there was a reaction which was to take fully two hundred years to meet up with the currents I have described. Oh, there were exceptional women throughout the period who accomplished things in the areas I have described; but the difficulty which women had in having their needs and ideas taken seriously during this period mitigated against their becoming overly involved in forms of literature and other forms of expression which owed their freedom and safety to the very fact of *not* being taken seriously. Only in recent years has the full impact of Mary Shelly's work been given full consideration. I have yet to see a full examination of the work of Mathilde of Beyreuth!

Yet this concurrent rebellion was to be crucial in its impact on the general religious paradigm. Simply *because* women had been increasingly excluded from the religious establishment, and because the whole of the feminine mystique had been scoured out of the theology of the West, a enormous vacuum had appeared. And, as we all know, *Nature Abhors a Vacuum.* While a healthy theurgy with regard to the Goddess Mary continued in practice, the mythological underpinnings of the practice were continually eroded; leaving a great big *need.*

It is curious to note how very few tales dealt with Witchcraft during the first century of growth of the literature of science fiction and fantasy. There was plenty written about high sorcery and high magic in ancient kingdoms. Magic swords abounded, and towers in which fearful wizards conjured terrible demons, but people who practiced simple magic in a religious context were peculiarly absent. Then two literary events occurred which crystallized the saturated fluid of literary speculation. The publication of Margaret Murray's *The God of the Witches,* and the publication of Robert Graves' *The White Goddess.*

The problems of scholarship in both these works are irrelevant to this discussion. Their significance is that they served to unite the currents of ever-growing Feminist thought with the imaginative literature which had come to be known as Science Fiction and Fantasy. They linked traditional occultism to an anthropological thread which restored the Divine Feminine (to use Goethe's phrase) to a theoretically balanced religious Paganism.

I remember the passionate enthusiasm with which the great writer Judith Merrill recommended to me the reading of *The White Goddess,* and the delight with which Marion Zimmer Bradley discussed *The God of the Witches.* (Mind you, this was a long time ago: those brilliant women may have changed their views on these books by now: we haven't discussed them since the early 60s.) There was but one further link to be forged in the chain of influences which would eventually

bread the dikes and set the flood free, and that, of course, was the publication of Gerald Gardner's work on Wicca.

Keep in mind here that I am moving about in time quite a lot. Social movements do not happen with the straightforward neatness of linear plot construction. Gregor Mendel's work on genetics was not disseminated for a long time after it was done, and therefore its significance to society was delayed. At the same time that Mendel was doing his work, in the same religious establishment, the young Leos Janacek was getting his basic attitudes toward the construction of music established. Mendel's work would eventually prove among the most important of his age. Janacek would eventually compose the first and most incredible science fiction operas, but because his subject matter was so astonishing to his contemporaries it would be nearly a hundred years before it reached popularity outside his native country. Whether these two men ever met is a matter of speculation. That there was a brief period in which they occupied close space is undeniable, as is their much later significance. But none of this seems to have been part of any neat, linear, sequence of events. It is more like a canvas painted according to the laws of Chaos Physics.

One final capstone had to be pulled to bring down the whole edifice of Western religious totalitarianism, and it is significant that this single moment in religious and literary history occurred not in a deep and serious work of philosophy but in a conscientiously popular satire, a work as profound in its reverberations as Voltaire's *Candide.*

Theodore Sturgeon described Robert A. Heinlein's *Stranger in a Strange Land* as a book which "examines every major tenet of Western Civilization, finds them wanting, and offers something better." Indeed, it would be hard for anyone who actually lived through the horrible stultification of the 50s in America to assess how profound was the effect of this book on the civilization which it satirized. For that matter, it would be even harder for anyone who did *not* live through those times to make the assessment, so thorough have been the effects which followed upon its publication. Reaction to it was never lukewarm.

People laughed at the popping of balloons in the shape of sacred cows, or, if they were true devotees of the dominant paradigm, threw it across the room in anger. But a surprisingly large number of people took the speculations it offered on the possibilities of human relationships quite seriously, and set out to experiment with those speculations.

While the status of the highly artificial Nuclear Family continued to reach its half life with the rapidity of chain reaction, the newly recognized Alternative Family continued to grow in strength: not always successfully, mind you, but with at least as much success as the subject of the Nuclear Family experiment. Institutions which had been promoted as ancient and eternal came under the scrutiny of satire and were forced to either evolve or decay rapidly.

It was an important book all around: far more so than its author could ever have imagined.

And most curious of all the social upheavals which followed its publication was that brought about by a very few lines tucked in amidst a large body of broader satire; a section not even very satirical in its content. I refer to the scene in which Michael Valentine Smith does his "magic show" at the church. It is a throw-away scene, but it sets up a background against which the rest of the story can play out. Mike has brought back the ancient worship of the Mother Goddess, we are told; and that is just about *all* we are told about the artistic expression and ceremony of the Church of All Worlds. And that is also just about all there is that touches on the concept of Paganism in a book which is basically a retelling of the story of Jesus!

It is, however, *enough.*

When the Church of All Worlds moved from the pages of a novel to the realm of nonprofit religious corporation, it could have taken any number of structural pathways to its eventual form. The one it chose, however, was closely tied to the model of Feminist Wiccan practice. (It could just as easily have used a Christian model, given the content of the book, and established another sect of primitive Christianity; that *also* happened after the publication of the book, many times.) The result was the unification of a feisty new paradigm and the coining of the term Neo-Pagan.

Once the *word* was there, in print, one could discuss it. One could draw distinctions between Neo-Pagan and Pagan, and then one could *need* to invent other words to describe all the fine lines between the suddenly very public, and very fast growing, new theologies and theurgies.

This lead to the opening of new fields for new writers to till, so that a whole new class of story emerged; a story in which the writer was not merely *imagining* the magic and the religious background, but working with it in the same way that a competent science fiction writer works with physics or chemistry. The publishers had a difficult time with it at first, giving names such as "contemporary urban fantasy" to the new genre; but, for the moment, they have decided to call it Magic Realism. Mind you, most of them have no idea what is going on, but they *can* understand that there are rules and they *can* most of the time, figure out whether or not the rules are being followed.

It makes a difference in the way the plot works.

And that, to quote another source, completes the circle, which is now open and unbroken. Unbroken because the stories are at the beginning and the end of it, and all along the perimeter, containing the stuff within. Open because this article is of the nature of science fiction, not of the nature of religion. It is written to inspire people to talk about ideas, to speculate, not to offer answers. Or, I could call it about Fantasy, in which case it would be an article to cause people to speculate about ethics rather than ideas.

John W. Campbell, Jr., was famous for publishing articles in *Astounding Science Fiction* which were designed, primarily, to make his writers *think.* To force them to consider things they had not considered before. I suspect that *Green Egg Magazine* owes more to that Campbellian philosophy and outlook than to any other single source. I can think of no other publication devoted to such wide-ranging, catch-as-catch-can speculation on theological or theurgical subject matter.

Vol. XXIX, No. 118 (March–April 1997) 4–8, 44

The Rocket Scientist & the Guru: Stargate 1946

by *T. Allen Greenfield*

"At about the same time that Parsons was trying to incarnate an extraterrestrial entity, he also claimed that he had met a Venusian in the desert of New Mexico— an odd foreshadowing of the claims of later 'contactees' such as George Adamski in the early 1950s." —Jay Katz, *Saucers of the Illuminati*[1]

THE SO-CALLED "BABALON WORK-ing" conducted by John Whiteside Parsons and L. Ron Hubbard between January 4 and March 4, 1946, has been the object of much speculation, mythologizing and wonder.

This speculation is due in part to the involvement of two charismatic and brilliant Bohemians of that period. Parsons (1914-1952) was a major force in the early development of solid fuel booster rockets, for which work the International Astronomical Union eventually named a Lunar Crater in his memory. He was an OTO member from 1941, and served for a short period as Master of Agape Lodge OTO in the 1940s. He died under mysterious circumstances in an explosion in 1952.

The other participant, pulp fiction author La Fayette Ron Hubbard (1911–1986), eventually founded the Church of Scientology and has been the center of stormy controversy in the decades since.

Both men were students of magick, especially the sexual magick of Meister Crowley. According to Bent Corydon, Hubbard once confided in his son, Ron Jr., "Secrets, techniques and powers I alone have refined, improved on, applied my engineering principles to. Science and logic. THE keys! My keys to the doorway of the Magick; my magick! THE power! NOT Scientology power! MY power! The real powers of Solomon...." Hubbard Sr. made clear he was talking about the sex magick central to the OTO system, but with a unique twist: "Sex by will, Love by will—no caring and no sharing—no feelings.... Sex is the route to power. Scarlet women! They are the secret to the doorway. Use and consume. Feast. Drink the power through them. Waste and discard them."[2]

The idealist Jack Parsons could hardly have understood what sort of man he was dealing with; he wrote Crowley in February, 1946: "About three months ago I met Ron.... He is a gentleman.... He moved in with me about two months ago, and although Maggy and I are still friendly, she has transferred her sexual affections to Ron."[3]

While Parsons was convinced that Hubbard, as he wrote Crowley, "is in complete accord with our own principles"[4] and proceeded to enter into a joint financial venture with the future Father of Scientology, Crowley was writing his eventual successor as OTO Grand Master, Karl Germer, "From our brother's account he has given away both his girl and his money—apparently it's the ordinary confidence trick."[5] Parson's friend Alva Rogers, who witnessed these events as they unfolded, described Hubbard's role in this way: "Ron was a persuasive and unscrupulous charmer, not only in social groups, but with the ladies. He was so persuasive and charmingly unscrupulous that within a matter of a few weeks he brought the entire house of Parsons down around poor Jack's ears. He did this by the simple expedient of taking over Jack's girl for extended periods of time."[6]

It was against this background that Parsons and Hubbard embarked upon "The Babalon Working"—an elaborate sexual magick experiment designed to bring Babalon into physical manifestation.

The whole concept of the "Magical Child" has several distinct interpretations. In the more orthodox and traditional view, sex magick is employed to Manifest, by an act of Pure Will, a magical being the material bases of which are the sexual fluids themselves. A more literal interpretation holds that magical rituals such as "The Star Sapphire" will produce a "Moon Child"—that is, a living child who serves as host to a superbeing, that is, the child is an "avatar" in Eastern terms, or an Incarnation of the Divine in Western thought. Yet a third interpretation is that sex magick is, simply, the "Yoga of Sex" and the "Magical Child" is the Transformed Sex Magician Himself!

Hubbard and Parsons were ostensibly aiming at the second, literal interpretation; to manifest a Scarlet Woman willing to conceive a child who would embody the transformative goddess-being Babalon.

Crowley wrote Germer: "Apparently Parsons or Hubbard or somebody is producing a moonchild. I get fairly frantic when I contemplate the idiocy of these louts."[7]

The reaction was certainly excessive. Crowley's successor as Grand Master of the OTO in the 1980s, Hymenaeus Beta, noted that an adequate chronicle of Parsons' "now-famous 'Babalon Working' of 1946 EV has yet to be published.... Most published accounts focus on his friendship and falling-out with Church of Scientology founder L. Ron Hubbard without appraising the larger issues of what was actually being attempted, and why."[8] Certainly, Parsons' own description of the Working is based upon fundamentals of Ceremonial and Sexual Magick.

In *The Book of Babalon-January 4-March 4, 1946 EV,* Parsons outlines the entire experiment, including the reasons for it: "The present age is under the influence of the force called, in magical terminology, Horus. This force relates to fire, Mars, and the Sun, that is, to power, violence and energy.... This force is completely blind, depending upon the men and women in whom it manifests and who guide it.... The catastrophic trend is due to our lack of understanding of our own natures. The hidden lusts, fears, and hatreds resulting from the warping of the love urge, which underlie the natures of all Western peoples, have taken a homicidal and suicidal direction. This impasse is broken by the incarnation of another sort of force, called **Babalon.** The nature of this force relates to love, understanding, and Dionysian freedom, and is the necessary counterbalance or correspondence to the

manifestation of Horus."

Thus far, Parsons is reasoning in a sound manner. Keep in mind, however, that he is working with his "friend" Hubbard, then in the very process of making off with Parsons' money and lover; a man who was to tell his son, Ron Jr., a few years later, to use and discard Scarlet Women. In what sense "scarlet?" the younger Hubbard asked? "Scarlet," the Scientology Source replied, "the blood of their bodies; the blood of their souls...bend their bodies; bend their minds; bend their wills; beat back the past."[9]

This is a distortion of Crowley's teaching. The latter observed in the same context, "We do opine that it is better and easier that the other party should be in ignorance of the sacred character of the Office. It is enough if that assistant be formed by Nature signally for the physical task, robust, vigorous, eager, sensible, hot and healthy; flesh, nerve and blood being tense, quick, and lively, easily enflamed, and nigh inextinguishable."[10]

Crowley suggests that a partner in sexual magick should, ideally, in his opinion, be involved for the sake of sensual pleasure, pure and simple. Hubbard, on the other hand, is telling his own son how to enslave minds, bodies and souls. Parsons, who wrote extensively on the subject of freedom, must have had no idea of what type of person he was engaged in High Magick with.

In any case, Parsons goes on to narrate that "in January 1946 I had been engaged in the study and practice of Magick for seven years, and in the supervision and operation of an occult lodge for four years,[11] having been initiated into the Sanctuary of the Gnosis by the Beast 666, Fra. 132, and Fra. Saturnus.[12] At this time I decided upon a Magical operation designed to obtain the assistance of an elemental mate."[13] In a sense, deprived of his former lover, Parsons was "going for broke" in looking for a partner to create a magical child with; "All or nothing—I have no other terms," as he put it to Crowley.[14]

Beginning on January 4, 1946 at 9:00 p.m., Parsons and Hubbard employed the powerful Enochian Air Tablet, using an Air Dagger, parchment talisman, invocations, conjurations, Enochian Calls and invocations, and appropriate banishings.[15] According to Parsons, at various times over subsequent days, wind storms were raised, electrical power was disrupted (January 14), during which Hubbard allegedly had a candle knocked from his hand by Something; several witnesses saw a "brownish yellow light about seven feet high"[16] which Parsons banished.[17]

On January 18 Parsons and Hubbard were out in the Mojave Desert when Parsons suddenly had an epiphany, and realized the experiment was accomplished.[18] "I returned home," he tells us, "and found a young woman answering the requirements[19] waiting for me."

For the next month he invoked Babalon with her as his partner, "as was proper to one of my grade"[20]— in other words, by the sexual Eucharist of the Mass of the Holy Ghost.

While his magical partner visited in New York, on February 28, Parsons returned to the Mojave, and received a "communication" he referred to as *Liber 49, The Book of Babalon,* which identifies its source as Babalon Herself. It should be noted that Hubbard was also away then. *Tiber 49* asserts, among other things, "the working is of nine moons.... And she shall wander in the witchwood under the Night of Pan, and know the mysteries of Goat and the Serpent, and of the children that are hidden away.... I will provide the place and the material basis, thou the tears and blood.... Thy tears, thy sweat, thy blood, thy semen, thy love, thy faith shall provide. Ah, I shall drain thee like the cup that is of me, Babalon[21] ...Let me behold thee naked and lusting after me, calling upon my name.... Let me receive all thy manhood within my Cup, climax upon climax, joy upon joy. Gather together in the covens as of old.... Gather together in secret, be naked and shameless and rejoice in my name"[22]

It is interesting that much of this anticipates the emergence of Wicca, at a time when Gerald Gardner in England was only beginning to formulate his ideas. Parsons spent much of the remainder of his short magical career writing on the subject of "witchcraft." In any event, when Parsons communicated the Good News to Crowley, the old Magus was perplexed, or amused, or, conceivably both. He wrote Parsons, "You have me completely puzzled by your

remarks. I thought I had a morbid imagination, as good as any man's, but it seems I have not. I cannot form the slightest idea what you can possibly mean."

Apparently undaunted, upon Hubbard's return Parsons prepared to impregnate his magical partner, impressed by a vision Hubbard had "of a savage and beautiful woman riding naked on a great cat-like beast."

According to Francis King's account, "Parsons was High Priest and had sexual intercourse with the girl, while Hubbard who was present acted as scryer, seer, or clairvoyant." This occurred on the first three days of March, 1946.

The aftermath is the subject of much rumor, and points out the high significance of sexual magick. "This secret is the true Key to Magick," said Crowley, "that is, by the right use of this secret man may impose his Will on Nature herself...."

Hubbard took off with Parsons' former partner and the funds of their joint enterprise. Parsons caught up with Hubbard in July of 1946 in Miami, having to evoke Bartzabel[23] to raise a storm at sea, forcing Hubbard back to shore. Ron Hubbard nevertheless married Parsons' former lover the following month, and went on to write *Dianetics, The Science of Mental Health* and, eventually, to organize the Church of Scientology, built upon a hidden mythos of a 75 million year old disaster in which the inhabitants of a 76 planet galactic federation were blown up by a dictator named Xenu. This science fiction "space opera" from Hubbard's pulp fiction days forms a bizarre underpinning to an already bizarre story.[24]

The remainder of the tale depends entirely on whom you talk to. Was a "magical child" conceived ritually March 4, 1946, born into this world as Babalon Incarnate on or about "nine moons" later, on or about December 4, 1946? Is such a being, a woman of about 50, alive today?

Or was there a more ethereal "birth"— perhaps, on a spiritual level, the true "birth date" of Gardnerian Wicca and its various descendent bodies, and on a more material level, the birth of modern "second wave" feminism. Surely, the timing of the Babalon Working and the arrival of the Post War Baby Boom is simultaneous in an eerie sort of way.

UFO buffs have of late been touting a theory that Hubbard came to Parsons with a purpose more grandiose than "the ordinary confidence game."

In pulp magazine circles, he had encountered any number of occultists and border occultists (Talbot Mundy, Col. Arthur Burks, Major Donald Keyhoe, Ray Palmer and Richard S. Shaver come to mind[25]), and had already formulated the core of the "inner Scientology teaching" outlined above.

He wished to bring this other world into Manifestation, but lacked the technical knowledge to do so. So, he came to the innocent sex magician Jack Parsons. In this version, the Babalon Working, guided by Hubbard, had little to do with "Babalon" and more to do with the hideous Old Ones of the H.P. Lovecraft Cthulhu Mythos. "A door opened; something came through" is the essence of this thesis, and the appearance of the first "flying saucer" case the following year is considered, in this outré rumor, not coincidental at all.

The Babalon Working permanently alienated Parsons from Crowley, but the work of the ill-fated rocket scientist has more recently been reevaluated in a more favorable light by present day occultists and UFOlogists alike.

Endnotes

1 In point of fact, Adamski had been trying to sell his Venusian story as science fiction several years earlier—that is, at about the same time as Parsons alleged experience in New Mexico.
2 Quoted from *L. Ron Hubbard, Messiah or Madman?* by Bent Corydon and L. Ron Hubbard, Jr. (Lyle Stuart, 1987) p. 307.
3 *Ibid.* pp. 255-56
4 *op. cit.* p. 256
5 *op. cit.* p. 258
6 *op. cit.* p. 259
7 *op. cit.* p. 257, but frequently quoted in various sources; See also Crowley's novel *Moonchild*.
8 *Freedom Is a Two Edged Sword* by John W. Parsons (Falcon Press/OTO 1989) introduction by Hymenaeus Beta, p. 7
9 Corydon & Hubbard, *op. cit.* p. 307.
10 De Arte Magica
11 Agape Lodge OTO
12 This is a significant "crew" of initiators,

indeed. The Sanctuary of the Gnosis refers to the Ninth Degree of the OTO System, the most exalted of the regular initiatory degrees. The Initiators here mentioned are Aleister Crowley, the then Grand Master of the Order, W.T. Smith, the U.S. National Grand Master, and Karl Germer, who served after Crowley's death as Grand Master until the early 1960s.

13 *The Collected Writings of Jack Parsons,* Part One, *The Book of Babalon,* introduction, "Conception."
14 Corydon & Hubbard, *op. cit.* p. 257
15 This is standard ceremonial magical ritual practice.
16 *Book of Babalon,* Parsons, p 6; also quoted by Corydon & Hubbard, *op. cit.* p. 256
17 These are common side effects in serious magical rituals.
18 This is, of course, the same area that the Adamski Orthon contact took place a few years latter, the area in which Dr. Wilhelm Reich, M.D. conducted his experiments with shooting down UFOs with Orgone Energy, and various other UFO-related events.
19 Marjorie Elizabeth Cameron (b. 1922 - d. 1995), or the future Ms. Parsons; *see Freedom Is... op. cit.* Also *The Magical Link,* Spring-Summer, 1995.
20 *Book of Babalon, op. cit,* p. 4
21 After Liber Cheth, a Class A Holy Book of the Thelemic Canon.
22 *Book of Babalon, op. cit.* pp. 5-9
23 A powerful magical being
24 Corydon & Hubbard, *op. cit.* p. 364
25 Except for Mundy, the present author has met with all of the pulp writers mentioned here.

Allen H. Greenfield (b. 1946) is an American occultist, UFOlogist, writer, editor, and Gnostic Bishop of Ecclesia Gnostica Universalis who resides in Atlanta, Georgia. A past (elected) member of the British Society for Psychical Research, and the National Investigations Committee on Aerial Phenomena (from 1960), he has twice been the recipient of the "UFOlogist of the Year Award" of the National UFO Conference (1972 and 1992). A Borderland Science Research Associate, he has personally conducted onsite UFO abduction investigations. Author of *Secret Cipher of the UFOnauts,* he is also a past President of the Atlanta Science Fiction Organization. *http://tausirhasirim.livejournal.com*

Vol. XXIX, No. 118 (March–April 1997) 32–35

A Greeting to Old Friends —The Kali Yuga Song

*by **Diane Darling**, 1987 (illustrated by Oberon Zell)*

I know that we're all wondering why
She called us here together.
Prob'ly not just to speculate
About the local astral weather.
Might as well explore the place,
Might as well team up,
'Cause we need every one of us,
Our magick, love and luck.

Welcome to Kali Yuga, my friend.
Funny how we meet again and again.
How many times have I seen your face
Across time and space?
Welcome to Kali Yuga, my friend.

It's the sovereign state of confusion
When She shows Her darkest Face.
Where's the One who loves us?
Who's this bitch that's in Her place?
The shit flies thick and heavy,
We cry and clutch our breast.
It's only Mamma Kali come
To shake us out of our nest.

So, welcome to Kali Yuga, my friend.

In every age the wise folk tell
Of a coming cleansing time.
We can read their words in our mother
    tongue
A miracle so sublime.
The wisdom of the ages
Is ours to comprehend.
The gods speak through the pages of
Great books and the hearts of friends.

So, welcome to Kali Yuga, my friend...

So we were warned and here we are
The Age of the Great Hag.
With a secret smile and a sense of style
It doesn't have to be a drag.
May as well not piss and moan
It's part of the design.
If I love you and you love me,
We'll get through just fine.

So, welcome to Kali Yuga, my friend...

Merry meet and merry part
Merry meet again.
Well met in Kali Yuga, my friend.
Hail Kali Yuga again!

GE Vol. XXIII, No. 91 (Samhain 1990) inside front

Chapter 12.
Pagan Fiction
Introduction

*by **Chas S. Clifton***

 LONG WITH ALL THE HISTORICAL AND VISIONARY ARTICLES, *GREEN EGG* RAN SOME fiction too. Ed Fitch's "New Dawn" was one of my favorites, and with the advances made in computer-generated imagery since it was written, I think that it would make a good movie too. Or do I just have a soft spot for talking animals—talking Pagan animals?

Meanwhile, Don Wildgrube's "lost" children in the forest evokes the spirit of Rudyard Kipling's *Puck of Pook's Hill*, while SF novelist Marion Zimmer Bradley offers a quick Goddess-feminist parable. Eric Hartlep's "Have You Seen the Goddess Naked?" is another sly parable—anything with the Moon in a tuxedo catches my interest too.

Finally, you may have heard the saying, attributed to the British anthropologist Margaret Murray, that "the gods of the old religion become the devils of the new." Keep this in mind when reading Gareth Bloodwine's re-telling of the famous story of the 1920s bluesman Robert Johnson selling his soul in exchange for musical talent.

A Midsummer's Eve

story and art by **Don Wildgrube**, CAW

 HE EVENING SUN WAS SLOWLY disappearing behind the distant trees, coloring the sky in shades of red and gold. The shadows lengthened and the yard become alive with the flashes of the firefly lights. Off in the distance the tree frogs began to sing, helped by an occasional night bird.

Jimmy and Lisa stopped playing, listened to the chorus and looked at the sky. It was getting too dark to see the toys in the sandbox.

"We'd better get inside, Mom will be calling us to bed soon," Lisa said at length.

"Just a few minutes longer, Lisa," replied Jimmy.

"What's that?" she whispered.

In the shadows a figure darted from tree to rock, to bush, to tree. A small figure, not too small, but small indeed.

"Let's find out what it is!" Jimmy said excitedly.

"We'd better not, we have to go in."

"Oh, come on!"

"Okay," she sighed.

Silently they crept up to the figure, ducking into the shadows. As they approached, it darted ahead of them just barely in sight.

"What is it?" asked Lisa.

"I don't know."

"It looks kind of like a rabbit."

"It's too big for a rabbit."

"But it has ears sticking up."

"No, that's a pointed hat."

"Is it a small person?"

"I think so."

Now they were running as fast as possible, but the small figure was faster and soon it was out of sight. It was then they first stopped and noticed the big trees and the darkness.

"We'd better go back," said Lisa with a note of fear in her voice.

"Yeah, it's getting too dark," said Jimmy equally as fearful.

They turned to go back to their house, but as they looked around them everything was strange. They had played in these woods hundreds of times, but now it seemed so strange.

They began to walk back to where they thought their house was. They could see better now—their eyes were becoming accustomed to the darkness and the big round silver moon was rising in the sky.

They walked on and on. Two scared children in a foreign world of moonlight, trees and shadows.

"Look, there's a light!" exclaimed Lisa.

The children ran towards the glow in the distance. As they got closer they heard strange music.

They finally came to a small clearing in the woods. The glow came from a fire in the center of the clearing. Around the fire small people danced around, holding hands and singing. They were small, but not too small.

"I'm scared, let's go," whispered Jimmy.

"Why are you scared? They're singing and are happy," said Lisa. "Let's get closer."

Lisa moved closer, followed by Jimmy.

It was then they saw a lady, a beautiful lady, dancing with them. She had flowers in her

hair, vines entwined around her arms. She was the most beautiful person they had ever seen.

The dancing stopped. The lady looked up directly at the children.

They were too scared to run. They just stood there.

"May we help you?" the beautiful lady said.

"We're lost," said Lisa.

"And frightened," added Jimmy.

"Come closer, but be careful where you step."

With that they looked down at their feet. Two rabbits were standing beside Jimmy and three partridges were standing by Lisa. All around the edge of the clearing were animals: frogs, toads, birds, rabbits, skunks, raccoons, 'possum, deer, bobcats, and many, many more.

They were careful where they stepped and the creatures moved to let them by. Now a frog would hop aside, now a snake would glide away, insects would scurry to and fro. Soon they were at the circle. The lady took them by the hand and they sat within the circle near the fire.

"Why are you frightened?" inquired the lady.

"We were all alone in the woods."

"And we have to get home."

"You were alone?" asked the lady. "How can you be all alone in the woods? You didn't look; you have brothers and sisters all around you. Do you hear the frogs singing? Do you hear the night birds warbling? Listen to the insects buzzing and chirping. The woods are alive. The trees murmur and rustle their leaves when our friend, the wind, comes to visit. In the smallest bit of the Earth, to the greatest trees, all of them are your friends. Did you see the big silver disk rise in the sky? It lit your way.

"As long as you want them, you are never far from a friend.

"Now you want to go home."

"Yes, we do," Lisa said, "but we wish we could stay with you."

"I can always be with you. Here," said the lady, as she picked up two shimmering dew drops from the grass.

Placing one drop in Jimmy's hand and one in Lisa's, she said, "Now close your hands tightly, and when you open them you will have something to remember me by."

Although the children wanted to return home, they sat quietly by the lady while she and the little people sang sweet songs of flowers, summer skies, and peaceful streams. Soon they began to nod their heads, their eyes closed, and they drifted into dreams of the lady and of all she had told them.

"Jimmy—Lisa!" called their mother. "Now, where can those children be?"

"Here they are," called their father from the corner of the yard. "Look, they're sound asleep."

"Let's not wake them. I'll carry one in, you carry the other."

"Okay," replied the father, I wonder what they're clutching so tightly in their hands?"

"Let's see—Oh, these must be some playthings they found. We'll just set them by their beds. They can have them when they wake up," said the mother as she looked at the small silver disks with the five pointed stars engraved on them.

GE Vol. VII, No. 63 (Litha 1974) 35–36

Can't Hardly Keep From Cryin'

by **Gareth Bloodwine** (art by Daniel Blair Stewart)

ANCE! DANCE, AND THE HUMAN rhythm of the merry pulse twirls way into the pipe of the Lord, His fingers flying over that pipe, His lips in a long sweet exhalation of a kiss, blowing out the melody of madness and delight. But there were no dancers in the hollow echoes. The Lord brushed sweat away with horny hands and wiped it on His furry flanks; He consumed Himself in a gasping wheeze, desperately whistled through the pipe, unheard. The thin sound died in the clamor of countless multitudes, a thousand times as many people as there were when the Dance was all. When had the wilderness become mostly crusted and cleared for growing food? When had strange stinking machines begun to roar over countless hard stripes lashed into the flesh of the world? How had people everywhere become deaf to the Lord's music in their blood, numb for a dozen generations? No Dance, no breath for the pipe. No breath for the pipe, and the Lord lies dead, forgotten to death by the heirs of His joy. But I'm not dead. Calling Me by a thousand names, even the names I loathe, still they crave to celebrate Me, to give Me the breath for the pipe, to return their joy a thousandfold!

How exhausting was the search in the swirling mobs of humanity, most completely ignorant of his precious life and heritage, but the Lord listened, clutching His pipe as He circled the world, His fingers dancing on the silent pipe, His last breath hoarded against the End, listening.

"Robert! Robert, what're you doin' down there?"

The young man could barely hear the harsh voice over the sounds of a hundred feet stamping on the loose floor boards, the crowd of people laughing and drinking to the thud of calloused fingers driven against the steel strings of a guitar, metal and wood singing of defiance and despair. I'm going to Kansas City, sorry but I can't take you, 'cause you got the powder, I got the fuse, now you gone and left me an' I's burning with the blues.

Robert sat outside the dilapidated shack with his ear pressed against the splintery boards, clutching his Sears guitar, trying to coax out that sound, that voice. His sore fingers bled again from squeezing those strings, but the only blues drifting into the Mississippi night were coming from inside the juke joint. He grimaced and beat on the strings again. "Robert! I told you get out from here! Nobody want to hear that thing!" Maybelle looked around the side of the building to where the young man sat crouched as close to the musicians as he could get.

"Miz Maybelle, don't throw me out! I'm not botherin' anybody, just tryin' to get it down. Please, Maybelle!"

"Don't `Miz Maybelle' me! There's always a ruckus when you around, and I just won't put up with it anymore!"

Inside, the voice of a man in an ugly mood got quickly louder and louder, but the guitar player didn't miss a note. The voice of a girl getting angry was punctuated by the sound of breaking glass.

"Robert, you clear out of here! After I throw Big Fred out, I'll give him you to work on if you still back here! Not git!" Without waiting for an answer, the big woman turned to run inside, pushing past a drunk couple who had staggered out to find their jalopy in the moonlight.

The girl recognized the forlorn young man standing there holding the cheap guitar.

"Why, it's little Robert! Hey, baby! Play us a song! Play us a song, honey!" She pulled her dress up to her knees and began a little dance, humming to herself, "Hate to hear that lonesome whistle...Hey, boy, what you waiting for?"

"Lookin' good, Lurleen," her escort muttered. He wheeled unsteadily to Robert, supporting himself with a strong hand around Lurleen's waist. "Beat it."

"Now Otis," she said, looking up with half-lidded eyes and a little smile, "don' go hittin' on little Robert." She pressed up close to him, turning her gaze on the young man standing ten feet away with his guitar and his memories of Lurleen's mocking laugh when he'd made a private suggestion in the darkness a month before. "Let's go get something nice." She kissed Otis, moving prettily as his hands slid up her chest. Eventually she detached her lips and turned back to Robert. "Get you a nickel, boy, you find the car and bring it `round." She winked. Otis distracted her with his hands as she dismissed Robert with the flick of her wrist.

Damn it to hell! Robert ground his teeth and walked away from the lovers, away from the juke, past all the old cars lined up, the guitar weighing ten pounds, and then a hundred, and then a thousand with each step down the dirt road to the gray asphalt that ran parallel to the railroad tracks a few miles into town. The songster's voice and the wailing sound of his jack-knife sliding along the strings faded so slowly with Robert's heavy steps on the gravel: I love that woman, but she don' love me at all, gave her all my money, another mule kickin' in my stall. Ain't got nothing, sat right down and cried, there ain't nothin' but to catch a train and ride.

"Oh, Mister Johnson! Mister Johnson, over here!"

"That you, Shinbone?"

"Why, Robert, you draggin'. If that guitar's that heavy, you ought to get you a case for it." The tall man stepped onto the road, his feathers and beads shining in the moonlight. "You looking poorly, Robert. 'Bout time you tried a little oil on it, got the essence of the Conqueror right here for you." He held an unlabeled vial of a dark fluid. "Ol' John the Conqueror fix what's ailin'. Only a quarter."

Robert's tired stride hesitated for a single step, then went back to the plodding rhythm, shoe leather scraping forward one heavy effort at a time. "Ain't no John the Conqueror gonna give me what I want," he muttered.

"Oh yeah? What's her name?"

Too tired to shake his head, Robert answered in the same tone, "Ain't a chick." Then he stopped a moment and faced Shinbone. The tall man smiled, and the beads and shiny things seemed to move with a mind of their own. Charms for the women, charms for the boss, charms for the jail. Trivial problems in Robert's eyes, making Shinbone small, too. The voodoo man shrank just standing there on the road under the moon. "You ain't got nothin' for me, Shinbone." His fingers curled more tightly around the guitar. Shinbone saw it.

"Ahh," said the magic man. "That box ain't puttin' out, is that it?"

The casual tone unlocked all of Robert's rage. He yelled at the man, "I been beatin' my fingers to the bone, I got all this music in me, I feel it, I feel it, but it just, it just don't—fuck it, Shinbone! and fuck you and your roots and your candles and your Bible, all of it! I tell you, I'd trade my soul for the music in me in this box, and you ain't got nothin' for me, so just get out of my way 'fore I wrap this fuckin' box around your neck! Hear?" He found himself holding the guitar over his head like an axe and breathing heavily, white fog puffing out of his mouth like a train in the cold night silence. In a moment a startled frog relaxed and began to croak again. Shinbone hadn't moved.

"You in bad shape, Robert." the magic man said. "Careful you don't get what you askin' for." He took out a tawdry amulet which caught the pale light from the moon as he swung it gently to and fro. "You need that Lurleen to distract you, Robert, and I got what you need—"

"Get outta my way, Shinbone." He said it again with less menace and more exhaustion. "Get outa my way." He opened his mouth, but there was nothing more to say.

"Go get some sleep, Robert. You put some more work on that box, you get it. Wait and see, you get it real soon."

Robert just turned away and began

trudging down the road. Shinbone called after him, "Go on back to yo' Mama's house and rest up 'fore you do anything foolish, an' stay out of the oak trees, if you gonna talk stupid like you was doing. Hearin' me, Robert?"

One foot after another, like Lurleen with one wink after another, like Big Bob Jackson tuning up his guitar and pounding his huge thumb on the E string, and the locomotive charged out of that guitar, its whistle wailing on the high E string with those thick fingernails snapping the steel against the fingerboard, leaning his head back with his eyes squeezed shut and his left heel thumping on the floor and the blues in his voice and all the people dancing, and "I ain't showin' you nothin' " in between the songs, Big Bob Jackson telling the little squirt what every guitar player had to hear as he was growing up to learn the music. Wasn't that Lurleen squeezing herself against Big Bob Jackson only last Saturday? What did it matter to him, when he had Marys and Mamies and Bessies aplenty to choose from, and a jar full of coins from the juke's customers to spend?

I ain't killin' myself on the fuckin' farm, Robert thought, a fantasy jar of money in front of his face. It dissolved and he saw his Mama instead, looking stern with her hands on her hips. "Robert," she said, "you stop playin' that Devil's music right now! I got Reverend Jones comin' here right now, pray all that Devil music right out of you. Oh Robert! You such a good boy, but that sportin' crowd you with, they gonna take your soul away, make you a hard man if you live long enough, break your Mama's heart! Now lookit this music here, 'I got the Light of Jesus,' come on, now, Robert, you play this for Reverend Jones when he gets here." "But, Mama, it just ain't the music I got in me!" "Oh, help me Jesus! Help me Jesus, my little boy got the Evil in him, Reverend Jones, help me Jesus!" "Mama, stop screeching like that!" "My baby gonna be damned to Hellfire, Jesus, please help me!" "Mama"—one foot in front of the other, pushing down the damp leaves, brushing aside the lowest branches, pale dappled darkness high above until grass moved under his feet and the sharp blue-white light of the full moon looked into the meadow.

The light hit Robert in the face, waking him up. Thick tree trunks crowded shoulder to shoulder in a circle all around him, a single set of footprints leading right to him. Not even the sound of insects disturbed the breath he dragged in and out between parted lips. Catching his breath, knowing he was alone at last, he swung the guitar strap over his left shoulder, grabbed the five chord, and began to play.

Most of the notes were right but too many were wrong, and for every wrong note, he squeezed those strings harder and beat his thumb against them harder until the skin ripped and the dirt darkened at his feet. "Corrina, Corrina," he began, thumping his left heel into the dirt, "where you been so long?" but it didn't swing, and for all the work, he didn't hear the blues, only the sound of his desperation. "Ain't had no lovin' since...since...you...been...." He just couldn't do it. Just bad noise. Far away, the clickety boogie of train wheels on the track came into the forest, and as he listened to the soothing syncopation, the whistle blew a long, a short, another long, half a dozen notes in the steam chord of the locomotive with more real music in it than all the years of Robert's yearning and working. Fuck it, he thought, with a long, low sigh. Just lay down with that track for my pillow and let that train take all my blues away. Clickety snick.

That breathy whistle blew again, a long low note, and then another, different note, far away, back away from the train tracks into the forest. Idly, Robert turned away to search out the lonesome whistle. Four more notes, all different.

Somebody blowin' flute out here, Robert thought. He squinted his eyes and examined the edge of the meadow. More notes. Dude played pretty good.

Like the trick picture of the lady at her night table who flashed into a grinning skull, Robert saw the branches of an old tree turn into two bent elbows and a long straight wooden pipe. A barechested brown man with long brown hair and beard stood in the moonlight, playing the weird music. After only a few more bars he took the pipe from his lips and with a slightly jerky gait, stepped forward into the light. His legs and feet were narrow and his flanks were broad. Robert, with a fear that turned his hands and feet to ice and stopped the breath in his lungs, saw that shaggy fur covered his legs, instead of pants.

The piper smiled like the warm sun and gestured at the guitar with his pipe. Then he began to play again, never taking his eyes off Robert's. The polished wood began to sing and the piper began to move from one foot to another.

Robert stretched out the little crick in his neck and suddenly he was tapping his feet to the music and swaying back and forth on his ice cold legs. Play, the music said, play your guitar, come and join me in the song. He wrapped his sore left hand around the A change and he struck at the strings. The piper nodded and moved some more.

A note or two, then chords all strung together— Robert listened to the harmony in his heart as the piper played and the cheap guitar began to sing for the first time in its life. Robert listened to his guitar as though the wood and steel were possessed, his fingers dancing on the fingerboard and dancing over the sound hole to the shrill sweet twisting music of the piper. The thing with haunches instead of thighs laughed through his pipe and danced and kicked up his hooves in joy, sending the music spinning out of the meadow on its way, and with the pipe held high in triumph, faced the young man who had accompanied him.

Tears poured down Robert's face as he soloed all the life and blues in the rhythm of his heart. The piper had unlocked it; Robert knew it could never be locked up again. One and one is two, two and two is fo', I'm on my way, baby, ain't comin' back no mo'. The sweet melody followed the pipe's haunting into the night, the notes from bended strings

fading away into the frowning trees that circled around them. The two creatures of music stared at each other.

Too late, Robert thought. I'm damned to hell.

The pulse in his neck pounded as he made himself strong enough to stick his hand out and say, "Hello, Devil."

The piper's voice sounded like he had just woken from a century's sleep. "I know who you mean," he said, "but I'm not the Devil."

"No need to fool me, Devil, I seen a picture of you in the Book." Robert looked down at the piper's feet, animal feet, cloven animal feet like the Book said. "You got everything but the horns."

"Sometimes I have them, too." He sat down, leaned one arm on the ground. "Do you think the painter of the picture saw the Devil?"

"Well, of course, he..." Robert stopped short. How did the painter know what to paint? "Why you talkin' like that, Devil? You the Devil, why don't you say so?"

"I'm a lot older than your Devil," the piper said, as friendly as ever. "I'm a lot older than the Book, too."

"Devil, they ain't nobody got feet like that 'cept you, so you gotta be the Devil!" He stamped his feet and shouted, "You heard ma call you when I's with Shinbone, and here you are! And you gave me the music, just like I asked for. So don't mess with me, Mister Devil, just get out that book I gotta sign. If you want my soul, fine! Whatever I got to do to keep those blues!"

"The music is a free gift, Robert Johnson," the piper said. "I don't want to take your soul. I want to give it to you."

"Devil, you a liar! Liar! Everybody say so. I know you want something."

The piper smiled, shaking his head. "What I want, Robert Johnson, is for you to take your music to people so they can dance.

I need people to dance. Share this love and pleasure with them."

Robert smiled. "I sure want to share some lovin' pleasure with Lurleen."

"You share your music with her and she will share her love with you."

"You promisin' me that, Devil?"

The piper smiled. "It never fails."

A wave of lassitude swept over Robert, buckling his knees, forcing him to the ground next to the Piper. He gently cushioned his guitar on the dirt against the moist aroma of new green life and forest floor. "How come I don't smell fire and brimstone?"

"Robert Johnson, I am not the Devil, and your insistence will not turn me into him."

"Sho enough. Then who are you? No, don't tell me. If you got another name, it'd just mean 'Devil' to me."

"But I'm not the Devil!"

"Sho enough." Robert lay back on the dirt with his hands behind his head, staring up at the sky. In the east, the faintest indigo began to stain the starlit blackness.

"Robert Johnson, I've given the gift of music to few men, but every one has had the gratitude to lead the dancers in at least one dance for me—"

Robert sat up suddenly. "What you sayin', Devil? I ain't bringin' you any more souls! You want some more, you gotta go out and find yo' own!"

"I don't want any souls! I want dancing!"

Robert leapt to his feet, snatching at the guitar. "The Devil don't want no souls! I ain't no fool, man! I get people dancin', they be dancin' for themselves, mebbe for me, but nobody gonna dance for the Devil! Nobody!" He began to back up out of the meadow. "You got Robert Johnson, Devil, but I ain't draggin' anyone with me! You hear?"

"I am not the Devil!" the piper screamed, but Robert had already turned to run blasting through the trees, the branches whipping at his face and stinging his fists, still clutching the old Sears guitar, tripping and half falling over roots and stones, panting and jumping until at last he got to the gravel road, a stone's throw from the bullet-riddled stop sign at the intersection where the asphalt began. He had barely stopped when a beat-up jalopy pulled alongside.

"Robert, that you?" Lurleen's voice called out. "Let's give him a ride, Otis."

Otis grunted and let Robert get into the back seat, then slammed the jalopy into gear and started jerking on down the road.

"Where you been, Robert? You look like you been havin' a fight with the woods."

"Yeah, Robert," Otis said, "you stink like a damn goat. You piss in those pants, or what?"

Robert scrunched down in the seat, exhausted. "I met someone in the woods," he said quietly. "We had a fight."

"Well, how about playing us a song? Play a song, Robert," Lurleen asked, as Otis muttered, "Oh, for Chris' sake..."

Robert sat himself up, a huge effort, and pulled the guitar onto his lap as Lurleen rested her chin on her arm looking into the back seat. What a night, Robert thought. What a crazy dream.

Oh, baby. He found that he didn't have to think about the notes. He squeezed his eyes shut against the pain in his fingers, and when he opened them, he saw Lurleen looking into his face. Baby, don't you want to go. Back to that ever-light city, sweet home Chicago. Two and two is four, baby, four and four is eight. Come on, Lurleen, don't you hesitate.

Lurleen started to say something, but thought the better of it, and just laid her head on her arm and smiled at Robert, a soft friendly smile.

Dance! Dance in the crowded jukes and regular dime-admission dance halls when Robert plays, so loud that My pipe is lost in it all! Dance, staring at each other in the oldest, hottest dance of all, forgetting the Lord of the Dance Who needs a moment of remembrance!

The Lord set off on His search again, too proud to beg, with hardly enough wind to sound the pipe. Just enough to try once more, if ever the chance should come, listening.

Gareth Bloodwine has been a Pagan encountering the gods since the late sixties and part of the Pagan community since 1985. An initiate of the Western Occidental Healing Tradition since 1974, he lives in the land of the saguaro cactus and horny toad.

Vol. XXVIII, No. 109 (Summer, 1995) 16–19, 60

Have You Seen the Goddess Naked?

by **Eric C. Hartlep** (art by Daniel Blair Stewart)

GOOD GOD, MOTHER," I SAID. "Can't you at least wait a respectable time before you start bringing lovers to the house?"

"What's a respectable time?" she said. The Moon, standing beside her, dressed in a tuxedo, said nothing. "His own religion said 'till death do us part.' Well, he's dead. Why should I wait—a moment or another eon?"

I was embarrassed. After all, in the fading light I could still see the last of the mourners following Father's casket around the curve in the driveway. Soon it would be totally dark.

Mother took the Moon by the hand and they went behind a curtain of fall-ripened apple trees on the far side of the garden. I saw flashes of my Mother's white gown through the branches and a glimpse of her suitor's pale features when he glanced back at me over his shoulder.

It was a difficult moment for a son. I wanted to follow my Father, but he was dead. At the same time, I didn't want to leave my Mother, though considering her moans coming by way of the apple grove, I clearly wasn't needed.

Should I have gone to the funeral by myself? On the one hand, Mother might lock me out of the house if I left. She and I hadn't been seeing eye to eye lately, and she can be unpredictable. On the other hand, I didn't want to stand around waiting for them to finish. They might have been at it ten thousand years, for all I knew. I could still hear her groans echoing off the trees.

Since I had nowhere else to go, I walked over.

Mother heard me coming (well, I heard her, so we were even). The two of them were having a casual smoke by the time I pushed the last branches aside to get a clear view.

"What do you want, dear?" she asked. I stood staring, my mouth agape. I must have looked for all the world like a fool, not what you might expect from the son of an earthly Mother and a heavenly Father. Mother leaned toward the Moon, murmured something in his ear, then pulled away. In a stage whisper she said, "It's the stifling upbringing his Father insisted on—makes them so curious about sex." They smiled strangely at each other and giggled.

I began to feel very out of place. Her voice had been nonchalant, though Mother was clearly not glad to see me, and who could blame her? With Father dead, what was I to her, but another mouth to feed? I hemmed and hawed for a few moments that dragged on like centuries.

"It's the funeral, isn't it, dear?" she said, winking at the Moon, who smiled, showing a surprisingly broad row of teeth.

I nodded, then hurriedly looked down and scuffed one foot at a pebble lying in the unformed dust, my hands clasped behind my back.

"You've got to understand, dear, that your Father is dead and nothing we can do will change that. He's been dead for years, really, but they kept him on life support, pumping him full of evangelism, begging the spin doctors to raise him up a second time. Millions made donations—it was really touching. You can't say they didn't try."

Well, the tears were coming now, falling

in the dust, giant drops rolling at my feet like fish eyes, refusing to soak in and make room for the next batch already sliding off my nose. Seeing this, Mother tried to cheer me up.

"Honey, you know I'm sad, too. We had a lot of good years, your Father and I. What was it? Six thousand, eight thousand?" She turned to the Moon, who only shrugged.

"I thought it was only two thousand," I said, confused.

"Oh, no, dear. That's what your Father wanted you to believe. Well, who's counting, after all? All I know is, it's thousands more than most couples ever get!

"Before you were born he changed names like a snake sheds its skin, always putting a new face on the same old show and taking it on the road. Then you came along and he felt like settling down. He was tired." For a minute Mother looked at the sky with a wistful expression. "Oh, you should have seen him when he was young: strong and clean and full of promises. He had his mean side, that's true, but he mended his ways after that face lift in Bethlehem. Why, he looked wonderful, ages younger! You'd have sworn he'd been born all over again, the way he acted. But I knew better; you never can fool the wife."

While she spoke, the Moon was beaming at my Mother. His black tuxedo made his face glow as he spun around her in the gathering darkness. First he turned one profile, looking at her with proprietory airs, then he turned his back toward me and I couldn't see him at all in the darkness under the trees. Soon he started to turn back, ever so slightly, just a sliver of white jaw bone catching the light. Gradually his nose and brow came into view, until he stared at Mother full-face from behind, all those teeth protruding in a catty smile. I had the feeling he and Mother had known each other a lot longer than they let on, maybe even before she and my Father met; they just seemed too familiar with each other.

I couldn't stand to watch, and looked down the gravel driveway. The funeral procession had long since departed. Even the wheel tracks left by the wagon, drawn by two white horses, were filling in with leaves falling from the trees that lined the way. Something

in the view struck me as odd, though I couldn't say what. Then I realized that it should be dark—I shouldn't be able to see a thing.

Light was spreading across the drive, cast by some unseen source behind the laurel hedge. I opened my mouth to comment, but stopped when a collection of ghostly shadows appeared, dancing over the ground. Whoever made them were still out of sight, though I heard their raucous laughter getting nearer.

Mother must have heard it too; she squealed like a schoolgirl and said—to the Moon, I assumed—"Get ready! They're coming!"

The shadows grew larger until suddenly a laughing crowd, bathed in golden light, rounded the hedge.

"Do you recognize anyone?" Mother asked.

I looked back. The Moon, nodding and smiling at her, held a plate of hors d'oeuvres in one hand and straightened his tie with the other.

"Mother!" I said. "You're not having a party!"

She didn't seem to hear me. I followed her rapturous gaze to the guests marching toward our house. I recognized a few of them: Mercury, Venus and the other planets. Apollo. Diana. The rest looked like horrors: a feathered serpent, a giant raven, and a collection of gods and beasts I had no desire to meet. I was swept with the sudden urge to run away, and began looking about for a place to hide. But there was no escape, and my feet seemed frozen to the ground.

Out of habit, I clasped my hands and began to pray. I said only two words before it hit me again that my Father was dead. Mother must have seen me twitch, because she put a hand on my shoulder and spoke in a calming tone.

"You don't have to go, dear. Why not stay for the party? Afterward, you can live with us." The Moon nodded and smiled at me. "Just promise to keep your room clean. It can be like old times. Really, sweetheart. A few new rules to follow, but I'm sure you'll catch on."

GE Vol. XXV, No. 99 (Winter 1992–93) 24

ꝐEW ꝒꜲWꝐ

*by **Ed Fitch**, The Pagan Way (art by Gene Day)*

Editor's note: This is my favorite of all the fiction we've published over 40 years of GE. It came out of a "what if?" idea that I had, based on the work being done with teaching sign language to apes. I discuassed it with Ed, who then wrote this wonderful story. —OZ

"Northair 309; Mombuto Center—Radar service is terminated at three two. Contact Nairobi Center one-two-six point three."

"309, roger. Understand, 'Contact Nairobi Center one-two-six point three.' Good day...Nairobi Center, this is Northair 309 over Uhuru at three-two, flight level two-five-zero."

"Northair 309; Nairobi Center, roger squawk ident...Radar contact. Maintain heading and altitude."

"Northair 309; Nairobi Center, you are cleared to descend to one three thousand."

"Nairobi Center; Northair 309, 'Cleared to thirteen thousand feet:' leaving flight level two-five-zero at four-zero."

"Nairobi Center; Northair 309 at thirteen thousand."

"Northair 309; Nairobi Center. Roger, one three thousand. Contact Nairobi Approach Control on one-two-six point three."

"Roger, understand 'contact Nairobi Approach Control at one-two-six point three.' Out...Nairobi Approach Control, this is Northair 309 on one-two-six point three. One three thousand."

"Northair 309; Nairobi Approach Control. You are over Ngala. Turn right to a heading of zero-eight-five. Descend to and maintain five thousand. Weather advisory: runway visual range one mile on runway nine-zero, fog bank moving in from the mountains. Numerous military aircraft in the vicinity of T'bela."

"309 roger. Understand: 'turn right to zero-eight-five, descend to and maintain five thousand.' Leaving thirteen thousand now."

"Northair 309; Nairobi Approach. You are approaching glide path. Turn left to zero-three-five. Cleared for ILS approach runway nine-zero, RVR four thousand feet."

"309 roger, 'turn left to zero-three-five cleared for approach runway ninety.'"

"Northair 309; Nairobi Approach. Traffic at two o'clock: ten kilometers, closing."

"309 roger traffic."

"Northair 309; Nairobi Approach. Traffic now four kilometers; two o'clock. Do you have him in sight? Over."

"Northair 309; Nairobi Approach. Contact Nairobi Tower one-one-three point nine over outer marker. Your traffic is now converging..."

"MAYDAY...MAYDAY...Northair 309 has had a midair...Oh Jesus! Jerry...half the wing's gone...get it up...help me get it up! Christ...we're not gonna make it..."

*   *   *   *   *

Air Crash in Kenya

NAIROBI, Sept. 19 (UPI) - A Boeing 707 jet freighter owned by Northair Atlantic Airways collided with a Kenyan Air Force (KAF) fighter plane while on landing approach to Nairobi International Airport early today. Both aircraft crashed in dense jungle ten miles from the airport. Initial reports state that both officers aboard the small Kenyan Air Force OV-10 fighter plane were killed, but that the three crewmen of the jet cargo craft survived the accident and were rescued by search parties. They are under care at Nairobi General Hospital where their conditions are listed as serious but stable. The names of the injured are being withheld pending notification of their families.

The Northair cargo plane was carrying a load of electronic components plus several laboratory-trained chimpanzees belonging to the Goodall foundation in Johannesburg. The column of smoke from the crash site could be seen from central Nairobi.

(continued on page 26, column 3)

*   *   *   *   *

Apes Freed from Burning Plane

(Related stories on page five.)

NAIROBI, Sept. 20 (AP) - The injured first officer of the cargo jetliner which crashed here yesterday has said that after helping the captain and engineer of the ill-fated jet to safety, he returned to the burning craft to release the chimpanzees...carried as cargo...from their cages. First Officer Grayson Harding, 35, currently in Nairobi General Hospital with internal injuries and burns over thirty percent of his body, told reporters, "I couldn't help it. We'd enjoyed watching them during the flight and...well...they looked and acted so much like people. We couldn't let them die in the fire, and there was no way to get the cages out of the plane."

In Johannesburg Ms. Cecelia Cole, an official of the Goodall Foundation which owned the chimps, said in an interview that the animals were specially trained in the laboratory to use deaf-and-dumb sign language in communicating with one another and with humans. "Chimpanzees are extremely intelligent," said Ms. Cole, "And the ability to communicate clearly and precisely with others makes them very valuable indeed. We had developed this technique back in the early 1970's, and had refined it considerably since then. We were shipping them to our South African preserve to observe just how well they would interact with wild chimps, to examine the theory that only language or the lack of it prevents the anthropoids from developing more complex societies of their own." She said it would be one or two years at least before a new group of animals could be trained.

*   *   *   *   *

Crashed Jetliner Carried Arms

(From the New York Times News Service)

ALGIERS, Sept. 23 - The Ministry of Information for the Kenyan People's Liberation Front (KPLF) charged today that the Northair cargo jet which crashed on approach to Nairobi International Airport of Friday was carrying secret armament and ammunition from the U.S. government to be used by the Kenyan armed forces against KPLF revolutionaries. The Kenyan People's Liberation Front also claimed credit for shooting down the craft. "A special task force of the KPLF, equipped with surface-to-air missiles, destroyed the imperialists' CIA weapons before they reached the hands of the counter-revolutionary lackeys."

At a press conference here the KPLF exhibited a portion of computer circuitry which they said was part of an advanced fire-control system. Liberation Front spokesmen said that at an appropriate future date more of the mass of weaponry found in the wreckage would be exhibited, and that portions would be sent as evidence to the forthcoming People's Tribunal on Genocide meeting in Stockholm next month.

In New York, officials for Northair Atlantic Airway Incorporated denied that any weaponry was being carried on Flight 309. It was claimed that the electronics shown was merely a damaged portion of the core unit for the new general-purpose HAL 1300 computer which was being shipped to Johannesburg. Representatives of the computer manufacturing firm backed this allegation.

Kenyan officials in Nairobi, meanwhile, said that the search of the crash site was being impeded by harassing sniper fire from KPLF guerillas, and that attempts to recapture the escaped chimpanzees of the Goodall Foundation probably would be abandoned.

In Washington, D.C., Senator Frank Church (D-Idaho) demanded a full investigation...

(continued on page 12, column 1)

*   *   *   *   *

Graybeard was hungry. He had not liked that strange traveling cage, nor the moving hut that had contained it. The people were nice, though they didn't really understand Graybeard or the others. Strange, really....

And then something had gone very wrong. Wrong...he was certain of it. The falling, the hurtful sudden stillness, the terrifying smoke and the fire. He covered his brown eyes and shuddered at the memory. And then the one who came in the midst of the flame and smoke to release the others, and finally (after an agonizing, hysterical wait), to unlatch Graybeard's *own* cage. Then a long, terrified run through the thick, strange forest.

Collapsing finally...exhausted in body and in spirit.

Graybeard pulled a long stalk of sweet grass and chewed thoughtfully on it. After resting and pulling himself together he had considered. The forest was strange, but not entirely different from the tree-filled park where he and his friends had been taken for occasional romps. There were tasty grubs and ants there, under logs and in hollow trees...and they were here too, only bigger and tastier!

So he had eaten fairly well, though worried somewhat by the strange smells and noises in this strange, dense wood. And he had begun to wonder... where were his friends? He was the Elder, and they should know about this good food. And anyhow...he didn't like being alone...

Over there... distant, but clear. A call! Definitely a call! He put his hands up to his wrinkled lips and hooted back, as loudly as possible. Then running quickly towards the eager, answering calls.

Not much time had passed before he and Soft-Eye found each other. A delighted greeting dance and relieved, joyous embracing and shouting went on for some time before, finally, they began hand-talk.

("You are safe," she signaled; "We had worried. Some of us are together not far from here. I had gone looking for food of some kind. Called the others and you heard.")

("It is good," he replied. "I want to see the rest of our friends. And maybe there are more still lost that we can find. But...food. Are you hungry?")

("Yes. Long-Arms has made a very good leaf shelter for us in a tree, but we cannot find food.")

("A leaf-shelter. Good idea; wish I had thought of it. But there is food everywhere around. I can show you.")

He did. And after they had eaten they went back to show the others. The first night was frightening, and few of them slept...for the place was much strange. But they adapted quickly, and in the days to follow the little band grew, as others of their friends were found. And they learned from one another, and discussed the usefulness of their ideas in hand-talk.

Limpy had found how to catch little, tasty fish in a stream.

Tiny still hurt from her burns, but she found some good fruits for them to eat...and got sick for awhile on some that, everyone agreed, should not be eaten.

Strong-Toes made a better shelter, more like (so he said) the buildings back home that the human-people had made. No one thought his hut looked that good, but it definitely was better, and all copied it.

Light-Brown found a piece of wood that made a sort of cup when broken properly. Her first crude bamboo container was quickly adopted by the others, and soon every hut had one or more of the water cups.

Silent-One had seen the human-people that occasionally wandered through, and didn't like them. ("They show only hate and blood-lust. I say we stay away from them.") After much discussion they decided to take his advice. Eventually they found a more remote, mountainous region, and moved to it.

After awhile, in a matter of months, the first babies were born.

And almost a year after being stranded in the jungle, the first of the Outsiders had attached themselves to the band, and began picking up the skill of hand-talk. They were awed by the knowledge of the People, and asked to copy the customs of the Band, as well as the magic that the People practiced. ("Nonsense," snapped Graybeard. "This is science, and not magic." But he gave permission.) They attached themselves to the group and eventually were accepted as members, as were the others who joined from time to time.

*　　*　　*　　*　　*

Dion Katella brushed back a strand of her long hair and scanned the lowlands once more from her clifftop camp. The helicopter had deposited her along with her equipment quite rapidly and efficiently. A brief "good luck" from the pilot and the craft moved swiftly off towards the safety of distant Fort Victoria. The chopper seemed to have gotten safely started on its journey without being intercepted by fighters or scout planes from one or another of the constantly warring "Liberation Fronts." Further, her landing seemed not to have been seen by the troops of any such warring group, for in the chaos of revolution, counter-revolution, war, and insurrection which had engulfed Africa these last few decades the civilized status of neutrality was seldom observed.

The Goodall Foundation had heard odd stories of these mountains, tales brought out by refugees from what had once been Nairobi Province of long-collapsed Kenya. People had spoken of a race of intelligent anthropoids someplace in these remote mountains, of apes who had driven off the warring tribespeople and who maintained this place for their own. And someone had remembered...a generation and more ago, a crashed cargo plane with a load of chimps from the Foundation, well trained in hand-language. And she had been the volunteer chosen to attempt the contact.

Dion viewed her encampment with satisfaction. All was well hidden from detection by humans, with the radio working and ready for use when she desired to leave, and food and supplies aplenty. Tomorrow she would begin her search, though it seemed likely that the ones she sought may already have spotted her.

In the meantime, night was coming on, and she had to secure the camp from stray predators. Absently, Dion fingered the silver pentagram which hung about her neck.

For in the years which had passed, the West had been changing also...drawing renaissance and spiritual sustenance from its own distant past. The Paganism of a distant and almost mythological age had returned.

The mundane necessities of security and dinner cared for, Dion relaxed for awhile, watching the full moon rise over the forested mountains. The night was alive with the cries of uncounted small and large creatures and the air soft with scents familiar and strange. But humankind was absent, and Nature was as peaceful as She ever became.

Quietly humming a hymn, Dion cleared the table in her tent and spread it with dark velvet. From a wooden case she brought forth the small statuette of a lovely woman, and set about it the antlers of a deer. Then small and beautifully crafted sculptures which suggested a leaping flame, flowing water, a crystalline jewel, and a delicate, floating mist. Finally, a trio of flickering candles and pungently sweet incense.

She extinguished the other lights about the camp, then exchanged her rugged field jumpsuit for a light and flowing robe of white.

A long and silent pause before the altar for meditation, and she drew forth a carven and engraved dagger. Sweeping it before her so that the blade seemed to strike silvery sparkles in the light of the candles, she intoned the evocation.

Winds of the airy heights
Blow soft and pure
Sweeping about me.
Flames of sun's heat
Burn hot and joyous
Billowing about me.
Waters of the flowing torrents
Flow cool and refreshing
Washing about me.
Hills most dark and mossy
Be peaceful and healing
Encompassing about me.

A pause of silence for a short period, and she continued.

O Lady most knowing,
Of the steady moon and glistening stars
Whose slender fingers encompass the night,
Grant peace, and understanding, and unity...

Three dark, almost manlike figures were standing beyond the altar.

A long moment in the light of the candles, flickering before, but now seeming most bright and steady in the sudden stillness. Perhaps the jungle sounds from outside were muted for some moments...for silence seemed heavy and sudden.

Stillness. Silence. The curling and drifting of incense smoke from the altar. The supple, dark hands of one figure moved in a familiar pattern.

("We give you welcome and greetings to our land. But we do not understand what it is that you are doing. Strange.")

Dion smiled, though carefully so as not to show her teeth, for such an expression might be misunderstood. She gestured back. ("It is good to see you, friends. I had not expected to meet you so soon. It is good, though. But why strange?")

The three large chimps conferred excitedly among themselves for a moment, then one replied. ("You came here alone, but you stand here now surrounded with mist and with cold fire. And we see Others with you who are not really...really") He fumbled for the words, and a companion continued.

("We see you standing with a woman,") she signed. ("She is powerful and good. But we cannot tell if She is of your kind of or ours!")

Dion felt the joy of the triumph for which she had hardly dared hope. After a pause she answered. ("There is much for us to talk about, good people, and much to explain. Shall we begin?")

In the flickering of the three candles began the start of understanding and friendships. And the dawn of a new age.

Vol. VIII, No. 74 (Samhain 1975) 23–26

A Feminist Creation Myth
by *Marion Zimmer Bradley*

Way back when God was inventing the world (as everyone now knows, God is a woman) and was busily engaged in separating the Light from the Darkness, Her small daughter interrupted Her, demanding "Mommy, I'm hungry!"

"Hush, dear," said God, "I'm busy creating the world; run along and play with the left-over cosmic dust, or something."

"But I'm *hungry!*"

And so God summoned up divine patience, stopped in the middle of Creation, and invented a peanut-butter sandwich for Her child, and then attempted to get back Her interrupted flow of thought. But like every female artist before and after this episode, She discovered that it was damn near impossible. Oh, She finished inventing the world, all right, and looked upon it, and found that it was good, but nothing like it would have been if Her first divine creative impulse hadn't been interrupted in its first flow. The only good thing that came of this was that She remembered to give some of Her patience to women, thinking that if She could stop in the middle of creation, so could they.

Well, the years, and the centuries, and the millennia went by, and the original errors increased and multiplied, and the mistakes She'd made in the beginning, when She was interrupted, kept on getting worse; and finally God looked on Her work and discovered that it was not good, and that the only thing to do was to throw it all out and start over.

And just as She was poised to begin the work of destruction that would sweep it all into the vast Uncreated so that She could start over, Her small daughter rushed in and demanded "Mother! What are You doing?"

Interrupted once again in the major work of Her existence, God summoned up eternal patience once more and explained, "I'm housecleaning, dear, I'm going to throw out all this old junk."

And (as has happened to every woman, everywhere, every time) Her small daughter said in outrage "Mother, you can't do that! I *need* all those things!"

And so God held Her hand, which is why this world is still in such an unGodly mess.

GE Vol. VIII, No. 72 (Lughnasad 1975)

In Despair of My Calling

*by **Stephen B. Pearl** (art by Daniel Blair Stewart)*

'LL JUST LAY HERE FOR A WHILE longer. Then it will be over. No point in trying anymore. Everything's turned sour, all the hopes I had: build a world, a new, fresh Earth for my children. Hah!

Dust, blasted red dust, like everything else on this godsforsaken ball of rock. Mars, they were right to give you the warrior's name. Everything about you is a battle.

I can't fight any longer. I've no strength left. Gentle Gaia, Mother, I have failed you. I am sorry.

My dreams lie strewn about me: my precious lichens, taken from the Mother's breast, scattered about at the bottom of my pit, waiting with me for the end. I tried, Goddess knows I tried! The corporations wouldn't, but *me, I* did, *I tried*—and failed.

Even though I grew up during the dead time of space exploration, I remember I was always fascinated by Mars. As a kid I collected books on the Red Planet, the probes, the information they gathered, everything. In my late teens I helped lobby to reopen the manned exploration program, stuffing envelopes, getting petitions signed, so many...but we succeeded! Thanks to our efforts a whole 9% of the military budget was diverted into space exploration. Well, it was done more because with arms reduction they had to find places to spend the money or face economic recession. Even so, *we won!*

After the first manned Martian landing, progress was swift. The multi-nationals, smelling a fast buck, a world they could rape without environmentalists getting in their way, fell in behind the banner of space exploration. They set up strip mines and smelters to take the iron ore that makes up so much of the surface of Mars, turning it into steel.

They shipped coal in from Earth to fire the smelters; the most disgusting, sulphur-ridden brown coal. Mars would have gone the way of Venus, with her sulphurous atmosphere, except for money. It was expensive to haul coal in from Earth, so later, instead of letting waste gases escape into the atmosphere, they recaptured them, separated the carbon dioxide, split the carbon off and reused it in the smelting while the oxygen supplied the bases' needs. Gas leaks over the following ten or so years caused substantial changes in the Martian atmosphere.

Then, when the Supreme Court decision went against the multi-nationals, the doors were suddenly opened to private prospectors. Opened to anyone who could afford to get there, that is. I had taken some geology at the University and was still in fair shape for a man in his late 30s, so I signed aboard the first prospectors' charter. Cost me everything, too, damn it all! Nothing to go back to, even if I could. Don't even have the return fare.

When we landed on Mars, I staked my claim and began to dig out my dwelling unit. Those first nights in a space tent with no room to move, barely enough to doff and don my suit, and the knowledge that all there was between me and cold, dry death was 3mm of plastic—those were the worst. But I kept working. I cut my shelter, digging deep under the rock, then linking in the prefabricated pieces of the living and work rooms. It was such a relief to stand in that chamber and unsuit for the first time, knowing I was encased in rock as well as plastic.

Then I began digging again, mining. I was right about that at least: I found rubies. Not large ones, by Martian standards, but the quality was good and I could get by. That's when I began my *real* work.

In my personal chest I had brought from Earth lichen spores and a few greens. I began growing these in the corner of my hydroponics chamber, trying for hybrids that would adapt to the Martian environment. What better way to serve the Mother than to bring Life to Her brother planet?

But I failed, and now my poor lichens lay scattered about me, sinking into the cold red rock of Mars. Funny how they die off in stripes like that...sad....

But, back then, I dug another pit, a shaft leading to the surface from my mine. At the shaft's base the air pressure was nearly 4 psi and I could go outside wearing only heavy clothes and an O_2 tank, except at noon, when solar radiation was too intense. This was my proving ground, the testing place for my lichens, an area where I could leave them in the climate which will soon be the Martian norm. I could observe them.

I observed them, alright. I watched them die, one after another. Some lived a week, some a month, some only seconds, but every one died. Without exception they all disappeared into the blasted red rock that makes up Mars. Even the Earth rocks I brought turn red after a time in this pernicious, frozen hell.

I even called on Gaia, setting my circle in the deep pit, by the eerie Martian sunlight, invoking Her and the Horned One, pleading for their aid. It never came. I couldn't even feel them here on this barren ball of biting

red dust. Nothing survived in the pit.

The last straw was when the lichens in my shelter began to die, leaving only damned red rocks.

Everything in this purgatorial hell is red. Blood red, spilt blood, warrior world, warrior gods, Ares, Athena, battle something....

Something? A TV special back home a long time ago: aggressive corals attacking passive corals. Warrior corals, warrior world....

Breep! My air alarm. Have to hurry, it's only so...!?!

I rise, snatching up the rock with the yellow lichen and red incursions and run to my shelter. I hardly notice the lights change on the wall of the air lock: I am watching the rock in my hand.

Then I am in. I run through the cluttered mess of my living quarters into the lab and place the rock under the microscope.

There it is! I see war in miniature, as the red lichen, so suited to hide among the iron-stained rock of Mars, drives inroads against the less aggressive yellow lichen. *I have not failed!* Some of my early hybrids must have mutated under the intense radiation of the sun shining directly down the shaft, and become this new warrior strain, unique to Mars!

For a long minute, I sit back and think. Just as a child cannot and should not be an exact duplicate of its parents, why should life on Mars be the same as life on Earth? Mars must take the seeds of Life given it and adapt them.

I take up another O_2 tank and return to my shaft. I set my circle again. Though I know the Moon back home is in its last quarter, I also know that above me shine two full Martian Moons. I prepare my altar, draping it in red and behind it I prop an old print of two medieval swordsmen having it out.

I begin my rite. I call to Ares, Warrior Lord and to Athena, Warrior Goddess, and I am answered! I raise my eyes from my altar and gaze about. Red lichen peek from crevices everywhere in my pit and the Gods and Goddesses of Mars cluster nigh.

The war for Life has won its first victory.

GE Vol. XXV, No. 97 (Summer 1992) 10

Resources: Pagan Publications

In the 40 years since Green Egg *first appeared, many Pagan publications have come and gone. Here are the best available as of July, 2008; I apologize for any omissions.—OZ*

The Accord. E-zine journal of the Council of Magickal Arts. 4/yr. Free. CMA, POB 66100, Houston, TX 77266. *http:// magickal-arts.org/comm-accord.html*

Broomstix. A FREE e-zine for Pagan kids that features crafts, rituals, myth, stories, and poetry. 8/yr. *www.Broomstix.com*

The Cauldron. A hardcopy magazine featuring Traditional Witchcraft, Wicca, Paganism and Folklore. 4/yr; sub. UK£14/US$40 (cheques payable to M.A. Howard) BM Cauldron, London WC1N 3XX, England. *www.the-Cauldron.fsnet.co.uk*

Circle Magazine. A 72-page hardcopy general Pagan magazine with wide distribution. 4/yr. Cover price: $5.95; sub.$19. Circle, POB 9, Barneveld, WI 53507 *www.circlesanctuary.org/circle*

Circle Guide to Pagan Groups. A comprehensive hardcopy spiral-bound directory, updated every few years. $18. Circle, POB 9, Barneveld, WI 53507 *www.circlesanctuary.org/guide/*

Circle Times. Occasional e-bulletin serving Circle Network with news of events & projects sponsored or co-sponsored by Circle Sanctuary. 24/yr. FREE. *www.circlesanctuary.org/network*

Crossroads. An international academic e-zine journal featuring well-researched articles on history, religion, philosophy and classics. *www.uq.edu.au/Crossroads/ current.html*

Eolas A FREE online magazine of modern and ancient Celtic and Druidic spirituality and lore. 4/yr. www.WhiteOakDruids.org

He Epistole. A hardcopy magazine and ezine specifically geared towards Hellenic (Greek) Paganism, reconstructionist and syncretic. 4/yr; FREE. *http://neokoroi.org/newsletter.htm*

Faerie Nation. A hardcopy magazine founded by author Francesca de Grandis; deals with all aspects of being fey-touched and magical. 3/yr; sub. $12. Make checks to Francesca De Grandis, POB 145, Meadville, PA 16335. *www.Outlaw-Bunny.com/faerienation.html*

Full Moon Rising. A hardcopy magazine/ partial ezine of general Pagan interests. 4/yr; sub. $15. 1900 Empire Blvd., #102, Webster, NY 14580. *www.FullMoonRisingMagazine.com*

Green Egg: Legendary Journal of the Awakening Earth. The classic Pagan journal, reborn in e-zine form. 6/yr; sub. $20. Ariel Monserrat, Editor; Oberon Zell, Founder. 257 Simplicity Lane, Sneedville, TN 37869 *www.GreenEggZine.com*

The Hedgewytch, BM Hedgewytch, London WC1N 3XX, England

Idunna. Journal of the Troth, dedicated to old Norse/Germanic religion and practice. 4/yr. Sub. $20. POB 1369, Oldsmar, FL 34677. *www.theTroth.org/ publications/Idunna.html*

NewWitch, an 80-page hardcopy magazine of cutting-edge Pagan lifestyle, people, and ideas. 4/yr. Cover price $6; sub. $22. BBI Media, PO Box 687, Forest Grove, OR 97116. *www.NewWitch.com*

The Oak Leaf. Hard copy Pagan magazine from the Church of Spiral Oak. Has a center pull-out kids' magazine called *The Acorn.* 4/yr. Sub. $10. Church of Spiral Oak, POB 13681, Akron, OH 44334. *www.SpiralOak.com*

Oak Leaves. Journal of Ár nDraíocht Féin: A Druid Fellowship (ADF). Articles, songs, rituals of Druidry and Neo-Paganism. 4/ yr. Sub. $25. ADF, POB 17874, Tucson, AZ 85731. *www.ADF.org*

Open Ways. A hardcopy magazine of general Paganism and magic; primarily for readers in the Pacific Northwest. 8/yr; cover price $1; sub. $8. POB 17604, Portland, OR 97217. *www.9houses.org/OpenWays*

The Pagan Activist. An ezine devoted to Pagan activism, both locally and globally. www.thePaganActivist.com

Pagan Dawn. Journal of the Pagan Federation; formerly *The Wiccan,* founded 1968. 4/yr. Sub. UK£14. BM Box 7097, London WC1N 3XX, UK. *www.PaganFed.org*

Pagan Moonbeams: A FREE electronic Pagan homeschool newsletter for both parents and kids packed full of ideas and information to aid in walking the Pagan path. 8/yr. *http://PaganMoonbeams.com*

PanGaia. A superb 80-page hardcopy magazine of in-depth Paganism for thinking people. 4/yr. Cover price: $5.95; sub.$22. BBI Media, PO Box 687, Forest Grove, OR 97116. *www.PanGaia.com*

Parabola. A hardcopy multireligious journal dedicated to exploring common themes. 4/yr. Cover price: $9.50; sub. $29.95. Parabola, 20 W. 20th St. 2nd flr, New York, NY 10011. *www.parabola.org*

Pentacle. A spectacular hardcopy magazine covering all aspects of green Paganism, from the UK. 4/yr; sub. £20 (USA). Pentacle Magazine, 78 Hamlet Rd., Southend on Sea, Essex SS1 1HH UK. *www.PentacleMagazine.org*

Pomegranate: The Journal of Pagan Studies. A hardcopy international, peer-reviewed journal of academic Pagan studies. 2/yr. Sub. $65. Chas S. Clifton, Dept. of English, Colorado State University-Pueblo, 2200 Bonforte Blvd., Pueblo, CO 81001. *www.EquinoxJournals.com/ojs/index.php/POM*

Quest. Devoted to the Western magickal heritage since 1970. Witchcraft, Mysteries, occultism. Editor: Marian Green. 4/yr. Sample $5; sub. $20 (USA). BMC-SCL QUEST, London WCIN 3XX, UK.

Reclaiming Quarterly. Hardcopy magazine of grassroots Pagan activism from Reclaiming. 4/yr. POB 14404, San Francisco, CA 94114. *www.ReclaimingQuarterly.org*

Rending the Veil: Occult Resources for Magicians. An e-zine focusing on Ceremonial, Hermetic, Alchemical and other less common forms of magick, with some Pagan and Shamanic, too. 8/year. www.RendingTheVeil.com

SageWoman. A hardcopy magazine celebrating the Goddess in every woman. 4/year. Cover price: $7.50; sub. $22. BBI Media, PO Box 687, Forest Grove, OR 97116. www.SageWoman.com

Silverstar Magazine. An e-zine focusing on a wide variety of occult and Paganism-related topics. 2/yr. *www.HorusMaat.com/silverstar*

The Simple Witch Hardcopy spiral-bound magazine of general Witchcraft, fiction and nonfiction. 4/yr. Sub. $15. *www.theSimpleWitch.com*

The Spirit Guide to Spellcraft. A gorgeous full-color hardcopy magazine of Witchcraft, magick and Paganism in the Southern hemisphere. Editor She' D'Montford. 4/yr. Cover price AU$6.95. Metier Media Pty Ltd, POB 6019, Mitchelton, QLD 4053, Australia. *www.Spellcraft.com.au*

Tapestry. Hardcopy newsletter of the Tucson Area Wiccan-Pagan Network (TAWN). 4/yr. Sample $5; sub. $15. POB 482, Tucson, AZ 85702. *www.TAWN.org*

Traditions Magazine. Hardcopy magazine centered on Paganism, magick, and the occult. Scholarly articles on archaeology, cosmology, customs, folklore, hagiography, herbalism, history, and mythology. *www.TraditionsMagazine.com*

Touchwood. E-zine of Clan Cornovii, a hereditary Pagan Tradition in the UK. Provides a forum for all Druids, Heathens, Pagans, Witches, and Wizards. Free. www.Touchwood-magazine.co.uk

The Unicorn. Wiccan newsletter published continuously since 1976, by the Rowan Tree Church. Editor: Paul Beyerl. 8/yr. Sub. $13 US. POB 0691, Kirkland, WA 98083. www.theRowanTreeChurch.org

Weavings. E-zine published by Iowa Pagan Access Network (IPAN). 8/yr. FREE. *www.IPAN.org*

White Dragon. Hardcopy UK-focused Pagan magazine, since Samhain 1993. 4/yr. White Dragon, 103 Abbotswood Close, Winyates Green, Redditch, Worcestershire B98 0QF England. *http://WhiteDragon.org.uk/index.htm*

The Wiccan/Pagan Times. Pagan e-zine published since 1999 by Imajicka and Boudica. FREE. *www.TWPT.com*

Wiccan Rede. A hardcopy English/Dutch Craft magazine published in the Netherlands by Gardnerian Witches since 1979. Editors: Merlin & Morgana. 4/yr; 80 pp. POB 473, 3705 AL, Zeist, The Netherlands. *www.SilverCircle.org/WiccanRede.htm*

The Witches' Almanac. Annual collection of various almanac-type information of interest to magical practitioners, as well as recipes, spells, etc. Founded in 1971 by Elizabeth Pepper (d. 2005). $8.95. *www.TheWitchesAlmanac.com*

Yggdrasil. A small hardcopy journal of Heathen religion and Norse mythology, published continuously since 1981. Editrix: Prudence Priest. 4/yr; 16 pp. Sample $3; sub. $10. Freya's Folk, PMB 165, 537 Jones St., San Francisco, CA 94102. *www.FreyasFolk.org*

OTHER TITLES FROM NEW PAGE BOOKS

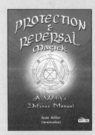

About the Editor

Oberon Zell-Ravenheart (b. 1942) is a respected leader and Elder in the worldwide magickal community. An initiate in several different Traditions, he has created and participated in many Pagan and interfaith groups and projects, playing a major role in reclaiming the spiritual heritage of pre-Christian Europe. In 1962, Oberon co-founded the Church of All Worlds, a Pagan church with a futuristic vision, which became the first legally established church to ordain women as Priestesses. In 1970, he had a profound Vision of the Living Earth which he published as the earliest version of what has become known as "The Gaia Thesis."

First to apply the terms "Pagan" and "Neo-Pagan" to the newly emerging Nature Religions of the 1960s, and through his publication of the award-winning *Green Egg* magazine (1968-), Oberon was instrumental in the coalescence of the modern Pagan community, and is so acknowledged in numerous histories.

Oberon is the primary artist of The Mythic Images Collection, producing beautiful altar figurines and jewelry designs of Gods, Goddesses, and mythological creatures. He is the author of *Grimoire for the Apprentice Wizard* (2004), *Companion for the Apprentice Wizard* (2006), *Creating Circles & Ceremonies* (with Morning Glory—2006), and *A Wizard's Bestiary* (with Ash DeKirk—2007). He is also Founder and Headmaster of the online Grey School of Wizardry. Oberon lives in Sonoma County, NorCalifia, with Morning Glory, his beloved wife of 35 years. *www.OberonZell.com*

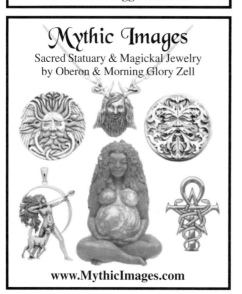